VHDL
Analysis and Modeling of Digital Systems

McGraw-Hill Series in Electrical and Computer Engineering

Senior Consulting Editor

Stephen W. Director, Carnegie Mellon University

Circuits and Systems
Communications and Signal Processing
Computer Engineering
Control Theory
Electromagnetics
Electronics and VLSI Circuits
Introductory
Power and Energy
Radar and Antennas

Previous Consulting Editors

Ronald N. Bracewell, Colin Cherry, James F. Gibbons, Willis W. Harman, Hubert Heffner, Edward W. Herold, John G. Linvill, Simon Ramo, Ronald A. Rohrer, Anthony E. Siegman, Charles Susskind, Frederick E. Terman, John G. Truxal, Ernest Weber, and John R. Whinnery

Computer Engineering

Senior Consulting Editors

Stephen W. Director, Carnegie Mellon University
C. L. Liu, University of Illinois at Urbana-Champaign

Bartee: *Computer Architecture and Logic Design*
Bell and Newell: *Computer Structures: Readings and Examples*
Garland: *Introduction to Microprocessor System Design*
Gault and Pimmel: *Introduction to Microcomputer-Based Digital Systems*
Givone: *Introduction to Switching Circuit Theory*
Givone and Roesser: *Microprocessors/Microcomputers: Introduction*
Hamacher, Vranesic, and Zaky: *Computer Organization*
Hayes: *Computer Organization and Architecture*
Horvath: *Introduction to Microprocessors using the MC 6809 or the MC 68000*
Kohavi: *Switching and Finite Automata Theory*
Lawrence-Mauch: *Real-Time Microcomputer System Design: An Introduction*
Levine: *Vision in Man and Machine*
Navabi: *VHDL: Analysis and Modeling of Digital Systems*
Peatman: *Design of Digital Systems*
Peatman: *Design with Microcontrollers*
Peatman: *Digital Hardware Design*
Ritterman: *Computer Circuit Concepts*
Rosen: *Discrete Mathematics and Its Applications*
Sandige: *Modern Digital Design*
Sze: *VLSI Technology*
Taub: *Digital Circuits and Microprocessors*
Wear, Pinkert, Wear, and Lane: *Computers: An Introduction to Hardware and Software Design*
Wiatrowski and House: *Logic Circuits and Microcomputer Systems*

Also Available from McGraw-Hill

Schaum's Outline Series in Electronics & Electrical Engineering

Most outlines include basic theory, definitions, and hundreds of solved problems and supplementary problems with answers.

Titles on the Current List Include:

Acoustics
Basic Circuit Analysis, 2d edition
Basic Electrical Engineering
Basic Electricity
Basic Equations of Engineering
*Basic Mathematics for Electricity and
   Electronics*
Digital Principles, 2d edition
Electric Circuits, 2d edition
Electric Machines and Electromechanics

Electric Power Systems
Electronic Circuits
Electronic Communication
Electronic Devices and Circuits
Electronics Technology
Feedback and Control Systems, 2d edition
Microprocessor Fundamentals, 2d edition
State Space and Linear Systems
Transmission Lines

Schaum's Solved Problems Books

Each title in this series is a complete and expert source of solved problems containing thousands of problems with worked out solutions.

Related Titles on the Current List Include:

3000 Solved Problems in Calculus
*2500 Solved Problems in Differential
   Equations*
3000 Solved Problems in Electric Circuits
2000 Solved Problems in Electromagnetics

2000 Solved Problems in Electronics
3000 Solved Problems in Linear Algebra
2000 Solved Problems in Numerical Analysis
3000 Solved Problems in Physics

Available at your College Bookstore. A complete list of Schaum titles may be obtained by writing to: Schaum Division

McGraw-Hill, Inc.
Princeton Road, S-1
Hightstown, NJ 08520

VHDL
Analysis and Modeling of Digital Systems

Zainalabedin Navabi

Northeastern University

McGraw-Hill, Inc.

New York   St. Louis   San Francisco   Auckland   Bogotá   Caracas
Lisbon   London   Madrid   Mexico   Milan   Montreal
New Delhi   Paris   San Juan   Singapore   Sydney   Tokyo   Toronto

This book was set in Times Roman by Electronic Technical Publishing Services.
The editors were Anne T. Brown and John M. Morriss;
the production supervisor was Denise L. Puryear.
The cover was designed by Joseph Gillians.
Project supervision was done by Electronic Technical Publishing Services.
R. R. Donnelley & Sons Company was printer and binder.

VHDL
Analysis and Modeling of Digital Systems

2 3 4 5 6 7 8 9 0   DOC   DOC   9 0 9 8 7 6 5 4 3 2

ISBN 0-07-046472-3

Library of Congress Cataloging-in-Publication Data

VHDL: analysis and modeling of digital systems / Zainalabedin Navabi
   p.   cm. — (McGraw-Hill series in electrical and computer engineering)
Includes bibliographical references and index.
ISBN 0-07-046472-3
1. VHDL (Computere hardware description language)   2. Digital integrated
circuits—Design and construction—Data processing.
I. Title.   II. Series.
TK7874.N36   1993
621.39'2—dc20   92-24858

ABOUT THE AUTHOR

Zainalabedin Navabi is Associate Professor of Electrical and Computer Engineering at Northeastern University in Boston. Dr. Navabi is a senior member of IEEE, IEEE Computer Society, ACM, and Euromicro societies. He holds a BS degree in Electrical Engineering from the University of Texas at Austin, and MSEE and PhD from the University of Arizona. He has published many papers in the area of VLSI and CAD tools and environments, in journals and proceedings. Dr. Navabi has been involved in the design and definition of hardware description languages and tools since 1977, and has developed several HDL based simulators and hardware synthesis tools. He has held teaching and research positions at the University of Arizona in Tucson, Sharif University of Technology in Tehran, and Northeastern University in Boston. At the present time he teaches courses related to CAD, VLSI, and Digital System Design and Organization at Northeastern University. Dr. Navabi is involved in research focusing on utilization of hardware languages in digital system design environments. This research includes simulation, synthesis, modeling, and testing of hardware.

In the memory of my father,
Mohammad-Hussein Navabi,
who devoted his life to his family.

CONTENTS

PREFACE

This textbook introduces the Standard IEEE 1076 VHDL hardware description language. The intended audience includes students who have a basic knowledge of digital system design and engineers involved in various aspects of digital systems design and manufacturing. The emphasis in this book is on using VHDL for the design and modeling of digital systems and the material presented is suitable for an upper division undergraduate or a first year graduate course. For a one semester course on VHDL alone, the book can be used in its entirety. For a course on modeling or CPU design with VHDL, this book should be complemented by additional material in a related area.

Starting with introductory material on design automation and hardware description languages, this book presents a brief history of VHDL and its evolution into a standard hardware description language. Following this background material, the text presents a minimum set of VHDL elements necessary for generating basic designs, as well as timing concepts and concurrency related issues. This is followed by a presentation of the VHDL language from a low-level to a high-level fashion. The first concepts presented are more closely related to hardware which are easier for hardware designers to comprehend. Structural and gate list representations of hardware are described immediately after the basic concepts have been covered. This material is followed by descriptions of more advanced concepts for higher level hardware representations. Dataflow and behavioral level of hardware descriptions are the next topics. In the sections on dataflow description, clocking schemes and sequential circuit modeling are covered, while other sections describe behavioral descriptions and high level design representation. The book ends with a top-down design example that takes advantage of various levels of abstractions in VHDL.

VHDL examples are presented beginning in Chapter 3. The examples in Chapter 3 consist of partial code shown to illustrate certain language issues. These examples are not complete and cannot be simulated as presented in the book. The examples in the rest of the chapters, however, are complete and have been carefully chosen so that their execution and simulation depend on the content of the material covered prior to the presentation of the example. These examples therefore, can be executed without having to refer to the later parts of the book.

Each chapter includes problems related to the chapter material. Although the book can be used on its own to learn concepts of VHDL, it benefits the reader most if used with a simulation program. There are presently several low cost VHDL simulation software programs available and many vendors of more expensive software programs offer substantial discounts for educational use of their software.

OVERVIEW OF THE CHAPTERS

An outline of the contents in this text is given here. Chapters 1 and 2 are introductory and contain material with which many readers may already be familiar. It is, however, recommended that these chapters not be completely omitted, even by experienced readers. The language syntax and semantics are described in Chapters 3 through 8. The last chapter contains an example, but does not present any new language concepts or constructs. The chapters progressively develop the utility package which is included in its final form in Appendix A.

Chapter 1 gives an overview of the digital design process and the use of hardware description languages in this process. Levels of abstractions are defined here and then referred to in the rest of the text.

Chapter 2 describes the initiation and evolution of VHDL. It is important to become familiar with the terms and vocabulary used in this chapter.

Chapter 3 is a key chapter. The first part of this chapter shows the overall structure of VHDL. In the second part, important timing and concurrency issues are discussed. This chapter should be understood completely before continuing with the rest of the text.

Chapter 4 discusses wiring and component interconnections. Examples illustrate how components are instantiated, bound, and tested.

Chapter 5 presents design organization and parameterization. It discusses the use of subprograms and packages and shows how generic designs can be described and configured.

Chapter 6 offers a description of type declaration and usage in VHDL and discusses operations and operand types. The last part of the chapter contains information about attributes.

Chapter 7 discusses various signal assignments and dataflow descriptions. State machines, tri-state gates, and bussing structures are explained in detail. It also shows how complete designs can be described at the dataflow level of abstraction.

Chapter 8 covers the behavioral description of hardware. It discusses high level timing issues, handshaking, and behavioral representation for state machines. Text I/O is also discussed in this chapter. The last part of the chapter presents the VHDL description of several standard MSI parts and uses them in a complete design.

Chapter 9 ties it all together. All modeling techniques learned in the previous chapters are used to describe a CPU. The CPU is partitioned into registers, buses and logic units with each unit separately designed and described. The data section wires these components and a control section generates signals for control of data. The method used for partitioning and describing this CPU is also used to generate its VLSI layout.

Appendix A contains a package of utility functions and definitions. Appendix B provides sample sessions on four VHDL simulation environments software programs.

Appendix C offers VHDL descriptions for several standard MSI packages, while Appendix D presents complete behavioral and dataflow descriptions of the processor covered in Chapter 9. Appendix E contains VHDL language grammar syntax and Appendix F details the STANDARD and TEXT I/O packages.

INSTRUCTION MATERIAL

Instruction material to assist the educators teaching VHDL with this text is available from the publisher. This material includes a solutions manual, examples diskette, and a solutions diskette. The solutions manual contains solutions to the end-of-chapter problems along with a description and a simulation run for each. The examples diskette contains VHDL code, a test bench, simulation command file, and simulation report of all the examples presented in Chapters 4 to 9. The second diskette contains VHDL descriptions and simulation report files for the end-of-chapter problems of Chapters 3 to 9. Other teaching material for use in Digital Design or VLSI related courses is also available, and can be obtained by contacting McGraw-Hill or the author.

ACKNOWLEDGMENTS

Comments, reviews, and support of many people helped in the development of this book and the author wishes to thank them.

The idea for this book started from a set of course notes the author prepared for ECE 3401, a graduate course at Northeastern University. As this material evolved into a book, students in this course and my graduate students helped with reviewing the book and made useful suggestions.

Professor John G. Proakis, chairman of Electrical and Computer Engineering at Northeastern University, was very supportive and encouraged the development of this book. His leadership in the ECE Department has helped to create an ideal environment for research, teaching, and development of research and teaching material.

The following reviewers read many versions of this book and made suggestions that were very helpful in improving its contents: James H. Aylor, University of Virginia; Dong S. Ha, Virginia Polytechnic Institute and State University; Fred Hill, University of Arizona; John W. Hines, Wright-Patterson Air Force Base; and William Hudson, Kansas State University. The comments of Mr. Tedd Corman of View*logic* Systems Incorporated, who reviewed many chapters of the book, provided a helpful industrial perspective.

The editors and staff of McGraw-Hill, Inc. also were very helpful in providing timely feedback on reviewers' comments. For the selection of good reviewers, compilation of review responses, and making useful suggestions for improving the manuscript, I am particularly indebted to the ECE editor, Ms. Anne T. Brown.

Lastly, I want to express appreciation to my wife, Irma Navabi, and my sons Arash and Arvand, who have put up with my working habits for many years. This writing project was particularly intensive and they tolerated many late hours, missed vacations, and irregular eating and sleeping hours.

Zainalabedin Navabi

VHDL
Analysis and Modeling of Digital Systems

# CHAPTER 1

HARDWARE
DESIGN
ENVIRONMENTS

As the size and complexity of digital systems increase, more computer aided design tools are introduced into the hardware design process. The early paper-and-pencil design methods have given way to sophisticated design entry, verification, and automatic hardware generation tools. The newest addition to this design methodology is the introduction of Hardware Description Languages (HDL). Although the concept of HDLs is not new, their widespread use in digital system design is no more than a decade old. Based on HDLs, new digital system CAD (Computer Aided Design) tools have been developed and are now being utilized by hardware designers. At the same time researchers are finding more ways in which HDLs can improve the process of digital system design.

This chapter discusses the concept of Hardware Description Languages and their use in a design environment. We will describe a design process, indicate where HDLs fit in this process, and describe simulation and synthesis, the two most frequent applications of HDLs.

1.1 DIGITAL SYSTEM DESIGN PROCESS

Figure 1.1 shows a typical process for the design of digital systems. An initial design idea goes through several transformations before its hardware implementation is obtained. At each step of transformation, the designer checks the result of the last transformation, adds more information to it and passes it through to the next step of transformation.

Initially, a hardware designer starts with a design idea. A more complete definition of the intended hardware must then be developed from the initial design idea.

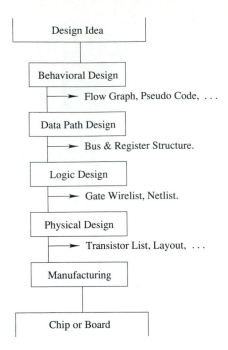

FIGURE 1.1
A digital system design process.

Therefore, it is necessary for the designer to generate a behavioral definition of the system under design. The product of this design stage may be a flow chart, a flow graph, or pseudo code.

The next phase in the design process is the design of the system data path. In this phase, the designer specifies the registers and logic units necessary for implementation of the system. These components may be interconnected using either bidirectional or unidirectional buses. Based on the intended behavior of the system, the procedure for controlling the movement of data between registers and logic units through buses is then developed. Figure 1.2 shows a possible result of the data path design phase. Data components in the data part of a circuit, communicate via system buses, and the control procedure controls flow of data between these components.

Logic design is the next step in the design process, and involves the use of primitive gates and flip-flops for the implementation of data registers, buses, logic units, and their controlling hardware. The result of this design stage is a netlist of gates and flip-flops.

The next design stage transforms the netlist of the previous stage into a transistor list or layout. This involves the replacement of gates and flip-flops with their transistor equivalents or library cells. This stage considers loading and timing requirements in its cell or transistor selection process.

The final step in the design is manufacturing, which uses the transistor list or layout specification to burn fuses of a field programmable device or to generate masks for IC fabrication.

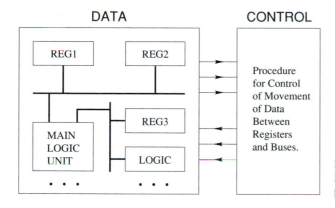

FIGURE 1.2
Result of the data path design phase.

1.1.1 Design Automation

In the design process, much of the work of transforming a design from one form to another is tedious and repetitive. These activities, as well as activities for verification of a design stage output, can be done at least in part by computers. This process is referred to as Design Automation (DA).

Design automation tools can help the designer with design entry, hardware generation, test sequence generation, documentation, verification, and design management. Such tools perform their specific tasks on the output of each of the design stages of Figure 1.1. For example, to verify the outcome of the data path design stage, the bussing and register structure is fed into a simulation program. Other DA tools include a synthesizer that can automatically generate a netlist from the register and bus structure of the system under design.

Hardware description languages provide formats for representing the outputs of various design stages. An HDL-based DA tool for the analysis of a circuit uses this format for its input description, and a synthesis tool transforms its HDL input into an HDL which contains more hardware information. In the sections that follow, we discuss hardware description languages, digital system simulation, and hardware synthesis.

1.2 HARDWARE DESCRIPTION LANGUAGES

Hardware description languages are used to describe hardware for the purpose of simulation, modeling, testing, design, and documentation of digital systems. These languages provide a convenient and compact format for the hierarchical representation of functional and wiring details of digital systems. Some HDLs consist of a simple set of symbols and notations which replace schematic diagrams of digital circuits, while others are more formally defined and may present the hardware at one or more levels of abstraction. Available software for HDLs include simulators and hardware synthesis programs. A simulation program can be used for design verification, while a synthesizer is used for automatic hardware generation.

In this section, examples of three hardware description languages are presented and discussed. The languages chosen represent the outputs of the first three design stages of Figure 1.1. In the code examples that follow, upper case letters are used for keywords and reserved words of the language.

1.2.1   A Language for Behavioral Descriptions

Instruction Set Processor Specification (ISPS) is a hardware description language for describing the behavior of digital systems. This language was developed at Carnegie-Mellon University and is based on the ISP notation which was first introduced by C. G. Bell in 1971. ISPS was designed for hardware simulation, design automation, and automatic generation of machine relative software (compiler-compilers). This language is a software-like programming language, but it includes constructs for specifying movement of data between registers and buses. CPU-like architectures can easily and efficiently be described in ISPS. The description of the Manchester University Mark-1 computer as it appeared in the ISPS reference manual is given in Figure 1.3.

The declarative part of this description indicates that the machine has an 8K, 32-bit memory (*m*), a 16-bit instruction register (*pi*), a 13-bit control register (*cr*), and

```
mark1  :=
  BEGIN
  **  memory.state  **
  m[0:8191]<31:0>,
  **  processor.state  **
  pi\present.instruction<15:0>'
      f\function<0:2>  := pi<15:13>,
      s<0:12>  := pi<12:0>,
  cr\control.register<12:0>,
  acc\accumulator<31:0>,
  **  instruction.execution  **  {tc}
MAIN  i.cycle  :=
  BEGIN
  pi = m[cr]<15:0> NEXT
  DECODE f =>
    BEGIN
  0\jmp    := cr = m[s],
  1\jrp    := cr = cr + m[s],
  2\ldn    := acc = - m[s],
  3\sto    := m[s] = acc,
  4:5\sub  := acc = acc - m[s],
  6\cmp    := IF acc LSS 0 => cr = cr + 1,
  7\stp    := STOP(),
      END  NEXT
  cr = cr + 1 NEXT
  RESTART i.cycle
  END
```

FIGURE 1.3
An ISPS example, a simple processor.
(Source: M. R. Barbacci, The ISPS Computer Description Language, Carnegie-Mellon University, 1981, p. 70.)

a 32-bit accumulator (*ac*). Also shown in this declarative part is the renaming of bits 15 to 13 of *pi* to *f*, and its bits 12:0 to *s*. The instruction execution of this machine begins by moving a word from the memory into the *pi* register. Following this fetch, a decode language construct decodes function bits of *pi* (*f* is equivalent to *pi*⟨15:13⟩). Based on these bits, one of the seven instructions of *mark1* is executed. For example, if *f* is 3, a store (*sto*) instruction will be executed which causes the accumulator to be stored at address *s* (bits 12 to 0 of *pi*) of the memory. When an instruction execution is complete, *cr* is incremented by 1, and the next instruction cycle begins.

This example shows that ISPS is easy to read and is close to the way a designer first thinks about the behavior of a hardware component. Referring to Figure 1.1, ISPS is most appropriate for representing the output of the behavior design stage of a design process. An ISPS simulator, therefore, can validate the initial plans of a designer for the design of a CPU-like architecture.

1.2.2 A Language for Describing Flow of Data

AHPL (A Hardware Programming Language) was developed at the University of Arizona, and has been used as a tool for teaching computer organization for over two decades. In fact, this language started as a set of notations for representation of hardware in an academic environment. These notations were used instead of spatially inefficient schematic diagrams. The evolution of the initial set of notations led to the development of the AHPL hardware language. The development of a compiler and a simulator established a place for this language in the family of hardware description languages.

Figure 1.4 shows an AHPL example description. This is a 4-bit sequential multiplier that uses the add-and-shift multiplication method. The circuit receives two operands from its *inputbus*, and produces the result on its 8-bit *result* output.

The description begins with the declaration of registers and buses. The circuit requires three 4-bit registers for the two operands and the intermediate results, a single flip-flop for the *done* indicator, and a 2-bit counter (*count*) for the number of bits shifted out of the first operand register. The external *dataready* and *inputbus* signals are declared as EXINPUTS and EXBUSES, respectively. The last of the declarations, CLUNITS, indicates the presence of combinational logic networks implementing a 2-bit incrementer and a 4-bit adder.

The circuit sequence part follows the declarations. Step 1 receives the operands and stores them in *ac1* and *ac2* registers. If there is a 1 on the *dataready* line, control proceeds to Step 2, otherwise Step 1 remains active. Step 2 sets the *busy* flip-flop to 1 and causes Step 3 to be skipped if *ac1[3]*, which is the least significant bit of the *ac1* register, is zero. In Step 3 the addition of the partial products is accomplished. Step 4 right shifts the catenation of the *extra* and *ac1* registers, increments the counter, and activates Step 2 if *count* has not reached (1,1). If the *count* register contains (1,1), control will proceed to Step 5 where the catenation of the *extra* and *ac1* registers is placed on the 8 *result* lines, a 1 is placed on line *done*, and the *busy* flip-flop is reset to zero. Step 5 returns control to step 1, waiting for another set of operands.

```
AHPLMODULE: multiplier.
   MEMORY: ac1[4]; ac2[4]; count[2]; extra[4]; busy.
   EXINPUTS: dataready.
   EXBUSES: inputbus[8].
   OUTPUTS: result[8]; done.
   CLUNITS: INC[2](count); ADD[5](extra; ac2);
1  ac1 <= inputbus[0:3];   ac2 <= inputbus[4:7];
   extra <= 4$0;
   => (~^dataready)/(1).
2  busy <= \1\;
   => (^ac1[3])/(4).
3  extra <= ADD[1:4](extra; ac2).
4  extra, ac1 <= \0\, extra, ac1[0:2];
   count <= INC(count);
   => (^(&/count))/(2).
5  result = extra, ac1;   done = \1\;   busy <= \0\;
   => (1).
   ENDSEQUENCE
   CONTROLRESET(1).
END.
```

FIGURE 1.4
An AHPL example, showing a
sequential multiplier.

1.2.3 A Language for Describing Netlists

Another way to describe a digital system is by its netlist, which specifies the interconnections of its components. A subset of the Genrad Hardware Description Language
(GHDL) can be used for this purpose. Figure 1.5 shows a logic diagram of a full-adder,
and its corresponding GHDL structural description.

   The description specifies primitive gate types and their rise and fall delays.
Following a primitive specification, its instantiations that correspond to the gates of
the full-adder are listed. The description also shows inputs, outputs, and internal nodes
of the circuit.

   The examples in this section present three very different ways of describing
hardware. The information contained in these descriptions varies in the detail of the
hardware that they present. Each description is suited for a Computer Aided Design
(CAD) tool at a different design stage. The ISPS description contains high level
behavioral information and can serve as a modeling tool for a hardware designer
as well as a CAD system user interface. The AHPL description, however, contains
more architectural information and is more appropriate for describing a circuit for
design and construction. The third description, GHDL, differs from both the ISPS and
AHPL descriptions in that it contains information that a CAD tool can use for detailed
analysis or manufacturing of a circuit.

1.3 HARDWARE SIMULATION

In a design automation environment, HDL descriptions of systems can be used for the
input of simulation programs. Simulators may be used to verify the results of any of the
design stages in Figure 1.1. In addition to the circuit description, a simulator needs a

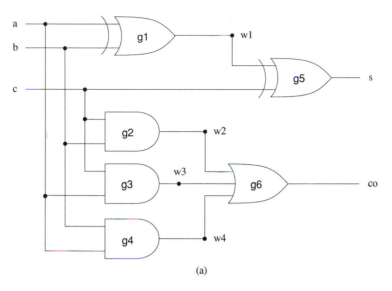

(a)

```
CCT full_adder (a, b, c, s, co)
XOR (RISE = 16, FALL = 12)
     g1 (w1, a, b),
     g5 (s, w1, c);
AND (RISE = 12, FALL = 10)
     g2 (w2, c , b),
     g3 (w3, c, a),
     g4 (w4, b, a);
OR (RISE = 12, FALL = 10)
     g6 (co, w2, w3, w4);
INPUT a, b, c;
WIRE w1, w2, w3, w4;
OUTPUT s, co;
ENDCIRCUIT full_adder
```

(b)

FIGURE 1.5
A Full-Adder, (a) logic diagram, (b) GHDL description.

set of simulation data or stimuli. The simulation program applies this data to the input description at the specified times and generates responses of the circuit. The results of a simulation program may be illustrated by waveforms, timing diagrams, or time-value tabular listings. These results are interpreted by the designer who determines whether to repeat a design stage if simulation results are not satisfactory.

As shown in Figure 1.6, simulators can be used at any design stage. At the upper levels of the design process, simulation provides information regarding the functionality of the system under design. Simulators for this purpose normally undergo a very quick run on their host computers. Simulation at a lower level of design process, for example, gate level or device simulation, runs much more slowly, but provides more detailed information about the timing and functionality of the circuit. To avoid

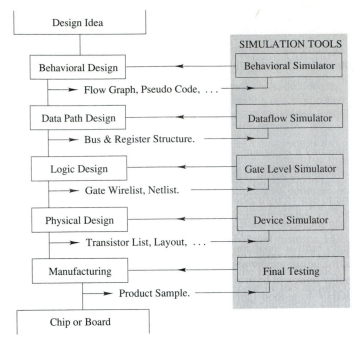

FIGURE 1.6
Verifying each design stage by simulating its output.

the high cost of low level simulation runs, simulators should be used to detect design flaws as early in the design process as possible.

Regardless of the level of design to which a simulation program is applied, digital system simulators have generally been classified into *oblivious* and *event driven* simulators. In oblivious simulation, each circuit component is evaluated at fixed time points, while in event driven simulation, a component is evaluated only when one of its inputs changes.

1.3.1   Oblivious Simulation

As an illustration of the oblivious simulation method, consider the gate network of Figure 1.7a. This is an exclusive-OR circuit that uses AND, OR, and NOT primitive gates, and is to be simulated with the data provided in Figure 1.7b.

The first phase of an oblivious simulation program converts the input circuit description to a machine readable tabular form. A simple example of such a table is shown in Figure 1.8. This table contains information regarding the circuit components and their interconnections, as well as the initial values for all nodes of the circuit.

After the initialization of the circuit, the simulation phase of an oblivious simulation method reads input values at fixed time intervals, applying them to the internal tabular representation of the circuit. At time t_i, input value of a and b are read from an input file. These values replace the old values of a and b in the value column

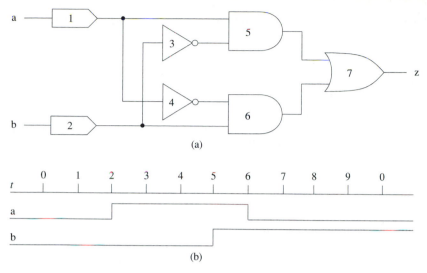

(a)

(b)

FIGURE 1.7
An exclusive-OR function in terms of AND, OR, and NOT gates, (a) logic diagram, (b) test data.

GATE	FUNCTION	INPUT 1	INPUT 2	VALUE
1	Input	a	—	0
2	Input	b	—	0
3	NOT	2	—	1
4	NOT	1	—	1
5	AND	1	3	0
6	AND	4	2	0
7	OR	5	6	0

FIGURE 1.8
Tabular representation of exclusive-OR circuit for oblivious simulation.

of the table of Figure 1.8. Using these new values, the output values of *all* circuit components will be reevaluated, and changes will be made to the value column of the affected components. A change in any value column indicates that the circuit has not stabilized, and more reevaluation of the table may be necessary. Sequential computation of all output values continues until a single pass through the table necessitates no new changes. At this time, all node values for time t_i will be reported, the time indicator will be incremented to t_{i+1}, and new data values will be read from the data file.

1.3.2 Event Driven Simulation

Event driven simulation, while more complex than oblivious simulation, is a more efficient method of digital system simulation. In event driven simulation, when an input is changed only those nodes that are affected are reevaluated. A data structure suitable for implementing event driven simulation of our simple gate level example of Figure 1.7 is shown in Figure 1.9.

The first phase of an event driven simulation program converts the circuit description to a linked list data structure like that in Figure 1.9. In the second phase of the simulation, a change on an input triggers only those nodes of the linked list for which an input changes. For example, at time t_2 ($t = 2$) in Figure 1.7b, transition of a from '0' logic level to '1' causes node 1 of the linked list to change its output from '0' to '1'. Since this node feeds nodes 3 and 6, these nodes will also be evaluated which causes their outputs to change to '0' and '1', respectively. These changes then propagate to nodes 5 and 7 until the output value is evaluated. No further computations will be done until t_5 when input b changes.

As shown above, event driven simulation does not evaluate circuit nodes until there is a change on an input. When an event occurs on an input, only nodes that are affected are evaluated and all other node values will be unchanged. Since activities occur only on relatively small portions of digital circuits, evaluation of all nodes at all times, as done in oblivious simulation, is unnecessary. Because of parallelism in hardware structures, event driven simulation is a more suitable simulation method for digital systems. The speed of this method justifies its more complex data structure and algorithm.

1.4   HARDWARE SYNTHESIS

A design aid that automatically transforms a design description from one form to another is called a synthesis tool. Hardware description languages are useful media for input and output of hardware synthesizers. Present synthesis tools replace the designer or provide design guidelines for performing one or more of the design stages in Figure 1.1. Application of various synthesis tools to the design stages of this figure is shown in Figure 1.10.

Many commercially available synthesis tools use the output of the data path design stage as input and produce a netlist for the circuit (tool category 2 in Figure 1.10). Tools that generate layout from netlists (tools 3 above) have been available and in use for over a decade. At the present time, development of synthesis programs is being concentrated on ways of producing efficient hardware from general behavioral descriptions of systems (tool categories 1, 4 or 6).

1.5   LEVELS OF ABSTRACTION

The design stages in Figure 1.1 use hardware descriptions at various levels of abstraction. The difference in the levels of abstraction becomes clear when we compare the three hardware description examples in Section 1.2.

The ISPS example presented a readable descriptionof the behavior of the Mark-1 computer. This description does not contain information on the bussing structure of the Mark-1 and does not provide any timing or delay information. The AHPL description of the multiplier described this system based on the flow of data through its registers and buses. This description provides clock level timing, but does not

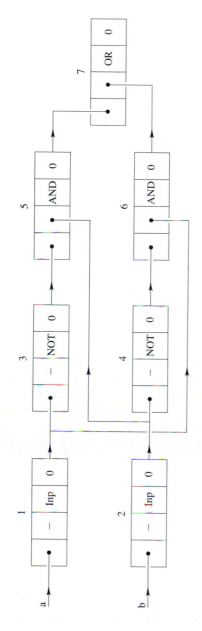

Legend:

In1	In2	Fnc	Out

In1: Input 1; In2: Input 2; Fnc: Function; Out: Output Value.

FIGURE 1.9
Linked list representation of exclusive-OR circuit for event driven simulation.

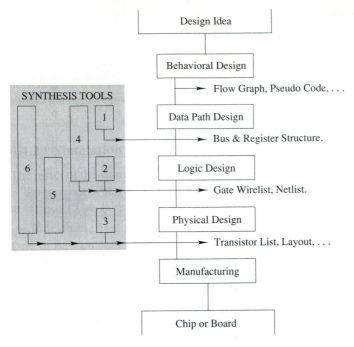

FIGURE 1.10
Categories of synthesis tools in a design process.

contain gate delay information. The third description in Section 1.2 is the structural description of a full-adder in GHDL. This description style provides detailed timing information, but becomes very lengthy and unreadable when used for large circuits.

Classifying descriptions of hardware based on the information they contain can be found in the literature. In this book, we take a simple view of this matter and consider abstraction levels of hardware at *behavioral*, *dataflow* or *structural* levels. The ISPS description of Mark-1, the AHPL description on the sequential multiplier, and the GHDL description of the full-adder are examples of these levels of abstraction. The following paragraphs define these abstraction levels.

A behavioral description is the most abstract. It describes the function of the design in a software-like procedural form, and provides no detail as to how the design is to be implemented. The behavioral level of abstraction is most appropriate for fast simulation of complex hardware units, verification and functional simulation of design ideas, modeling standard components, and documentation. For simulation and functional analysis, a behavioral model is useful since the details of the hardware, which may not be known to the user of the components, are not required. Such descriptions present an input-to-output mapping according to the data sheet specification provided by the component manufacturer. Descriptions at this level can be accessible to non-engineers as well as the end users of a hardware component, and can also serve as a good documentation media. The operation of large systems can also be modeled at this level for end users and manual writers.

A dataflow description is a concurrent representation of the flow of control and movement of data. Concurrent data components and carriers communicate through buses and interconnections, and a control hardware issues signals for the control of this communication. The level of hardware detail involved in dataflow descriptions is great enough that such descriptions cannot serve as an end user or nontechnical documentation media. This level of description, however, is abstract enough for a technically oriented designer to describe the components to be synthesized. Dataflow descriptions imply an architecture and a unique hardware. Simulation of these descriptions involves the movement of the data through registers and busses, and therefore is slower than the input-to-output mapping of behavioral descriptions. The function of the hardware is evident from dataflow descriptions.

A structural description is the lowest and most detailed level of description considered, and is the simplest to synthesize into hardware. Structural descriptions include a list of concurrently active components and their interconnections. The corresponding function of the hardware is not evident from such descriptions unless the components used are known. On the other hand, the hardware is clearly implied by these descriptions, and a simple wire router or printed circuit board layout generator can easily produce the described hardware. A structural description that describes wiring of logic gates is said to be the hardware description at gate-level. A gate level description provides input for detailed timing simulation.

1.6 SUMMARY

This chapter presented introductory material that relates to design of digital systems with hardware description languages. The intention was to give the reader an overall understanding of hardware description languages, the design process based on HDLs, design tools, and simulation and synthesis. The last part of the chapter discussed levels of abstraction that we will reference throughout the book.

REFERENCES

1. Wakerly, J. F., "Digital Design Principles and Practices," Prentice-Hall Inc., Englewood Cliffs, N.J., 1990.
2. Miczo, A., "Digital Logic Testing and Simulation," Harper & Row Publishers, New York, 1986.
3. Barbacci, M. R., et. al., "The ISPS Computer Description Language," Carnegie-Mellon University, 1981.
4. Hill, F. J., and G. R. Peterson, "Digital Systems: Hardware Organization and Design," 3rd ed., John Wiley, New York, 1987.
5. "System HILO GHDL Tutorial," Genrad Limited, Fareham, England, 1988.
6. Navabi, Z., and J. Spillane, "Templates For Synthesis From VHDL," *Proc. of the 1990 ASIC Seminar and Exposition*, September 1990.
7. Walker, R. A., and D. E. Thomas, "A Model of Design Representation and Synthesis," *Proc. of 22nd Design Automation Conference*, 1985.

PROBLEMS

1.1. Suggest a data path for the Mark-1 computer of Section 1.2.1.

1.2. Show the graphical representation of the data path of the four bit multiplier of Section 1.2.2.

1.3. Show a state diagram for the control part of the Multiplier circuit of Section 1.2.2.

1.4. Redesign the full-adder circuit of Section 1.2.3 using only two-input NAND gates. Show the GHDL description for this design.

1.5. Write pseudo code for implementing the oblivious simulation method of Section 1.3.1.

1.6. Write pseudo code for implementing the event driven simulation method of Section 1.3.2.

CHAPTER
2

VHDL
BACKGROUND

For the design of large digital systems, much engineering time is spent in changing formats for using various design aids and simulators. An integrated design environment is useful for better design efficiency in these systems. In an ideal design environment, the high level description of the system is understandable to the managers and to the designers, and it uniquely and unambiguously defines the hardware. This high level description can serve as the documentation for the part as well as an entry point into the design process. As the design process advances, additional details are added to the initial description of the part. These details enable the simulation and testing of the system at various levels of abstraction. By the last stage of design, the initial description has evolved into a detailed description which can be used by a program controlled machine for generation of final hardware in the form of layout, printed circuit board, or gate arrays.

This ideal design process can exist only if a language exists to describe hardware at various levels so that it can be understood by the managers, users, designers, testers, simulators, and machines. The IEEE standard VHDL hardware description language is such a language. VHDL was defined because a need existed for an integrated design and documentation language to communicate design data between various levels of abstractions. At the time, none of the existing hardware description languages fully satisfied these requirements, and the lack of precision in English made it too ambiguous for this purpose.

2.1   VHDL INITIATION

In the search for a standard design and documentation tool for the VHSIC (Very High Speed Integrated Circuits) program, the United States Department of Defense (DoD) in the summer of 1981 sponsored a workshop on hardware description languages at Woods Hole, Massachusetts. This workshop was arranged by the Institute for Defense Analysis (IDA) to study various hardware description methods, the need for a standard language, and the features that might be required by such a standard. Because the VHSIC program was under the restrictions of the United States International Traffic and Arms Regulations (ITAR), the VHDL component of this program was also initially subject to such restrictions.

In 1983, the DoD established requirements for a standard VHSIC Hardware Description Language (VHDL), based on the recommendations of the "Woods Hole" workshop. A contract for the development of the VHDL language, its environment, and its software was awarded to IBM, Texas Instruments, and Intermetrics corporations. Work on VHDL started in the summer of 1983. At that time language specifications were no longer under ITAR restrictions, but these restrictions still applied to government developed software.

VHDL 2.0 was released only 6 months after the project began. This version, however, allowed only concurrent statements, and lacked the capability to describe hardware in a sequential software-like fashion, a shortcoming that would seriously jeopardize the applicability of the language for high level behavioral descriptions. The language was significantly improved, as this and other shortcomings were corrected when VHDL 6.0 was released in December of 1984. Development of VHDL-based tools also began in 1984.

In 1985, ITAR restrictions were lifted from VHDL and its related software, and the VHDL 7.2 Language Reference Manual (LRM) copyright was transferred to IEEE for further development and standardization. This led to the development of the IEEE 1076/A VHDL Language Reference Manual (LRM), which was released in May of 1987. Later that year version B of the LRM was developed and approved by REVCOM (a committee of the IEEE Standards Board). VHDL 1076-1987 formally became the IEEE standard hardware description language in December of 1987.

2.2   EXISTING LANGUAGES

Early in the VHSIC program it was found that none of the existing hardware description languages could be used as a standard tool for the design, manufacturing, and documentation of digital circuits ranging from integrated circuits to complete systems. Part of the study for the development of the requirements of a VHSIC language, however, concentrated on the capabilities, shortcomings, and other characteristics of eight hardware description languages that were available at that time. These languages were AHPL, CDL, CONLAN, IDL, ISPS, TEGAS, TI-HDL, and ZEUS. We briefly describe the important features of these languages in order to provide a framework for understanding the VHDL requirements that are discussed in the next section.

2.2.1 AHPL

AHPL (A Hardware Programming Language) is an HDL for describing hardware at the dataflow level of abstraction. This language uses an implicit clock for synchronizing assignments of data to registers and flip-flops, but does not provide support for describing asynchronous circuits. The language descriptions consist of interacting concurrent modules, and hierarchy of modules is not supported. Data types in AHPL are fixed and restricted to bits, vectors of bits, and arrays of bits. Procedures or functions are only allowed in the context of combinational logic units. Delay and constraint specifications are not allowed in AHPL and assignment of values to buses and registers all occur at the same time without delay, since they are synchronized with an implicit clock.

2.2.2 CDL

CDL (Computer Design Language) is a hardware description language developed in an academic environment mainly for instruction in digital systems. This language is strictly a dataflow language, and does not support design hierarchy. In CDL, micro-statements are used for transfer of data into registers. Conditional micro-statements use if-then-else constructs and can be nested.

2.2.3 CONLAN

The CONLAN (CONsensus LANguage) project began as an attempt to establish a standard hardware description language. This platform consists of a family of languages for describing hardware at various levels of abstraction. Base CONLAN (*bcl*), for example, is the base language for all member languages. All operations in CONLAN are executed concurrently. CONLAN allows hierarchical description of hardware but has limited external use.

2.2.4 IDL

IDL (Interactive Design Language) is an internal IBM language with limited outside use. IDL was originally designed for automatic generation of PLA structures, but it was later extended to cover more general circuit descriptions. Hardware in IDL can be described in a hierarchy of structures. This language is primarily a concurrent hardware description language.

2.2.5 ISPS

ISPS (Instruction Set Processor Specification) is a very high level behavioral language and was mainly designed to create an environment for designing software based on a given hardware. Although the language is primarily targeted for CPU-like architectures, other digital systems can easily be described in it. Timing control in ISPS is limited. The "NEXT" construct allows timing control between statements of behavioral descriptions, but it is not possible to specify gate level timing and structural details.

2.2.6   TEGAS

TEGAS (TEst Generation And Simulation) is a system for test generation and simulation of digital circuits. Although several extended versions of this language have behavioral features, the main language (TEGAS Description Language or TDL) is only structural. Digital hardware can be described hierarchically in this language. Detailed timing specification can be specified in TDL.

2.2.7   TI-HDL

TI-HDL (Texas Instruments Hardware Description Language) is a multi-level language for the design and description of hardware. It allows hierarchical specification of hardware and supports description of synchronous, asynchronous, and combinatorial logic circuits. Behavioral descriptions in TI-HDL are sequential and software-like, and use if-then-else, case, for, and while constructs for program flow control. This language has fixed data types with no provision for adding user defined types.

2.2.8   ZEUS

The ZEUS hardware description language is a nonprocedural language that was created at General Electric Corporation. This language supports design hierarchy and allows definition of systems by their functionality or their structural arrangements. Timing in ZEUS is at the clock level and there are no provisions for gate delay specification or detailed timing constraints. Because of this timing arrangement, asynchronous circuits cannot be described in ZEUS. This language provides a close link to physical layout.

2.3   VHDL REQUIREMENTS

A DoD document entitled "Department of Defense Requirements for Hardware Description Languages," released in January of 1983, clearly stated the requirements for the VHSIC hardware description language. The present VHDL satisfies the requirements set forth in this detailed document. This section briefly describes the main features of VHDL requirements.

2.3.1   General Features

The DoD requirement document specifies that the VHSIC hardware description language should be a language for design and description of hardware. It indicates that VHDL should be usable for design documentation, high-level design, simulation, synthesis, and testing of hardware, as well as a driver for a physical design tool.

It emphasizes that VHDL is for the description of hardware from system to gate, and it clearly specifies that system software is not an issue and that physical design does not need to be addressed. Since in an actual digital system, all small or large elements of the system are active simultaneously and perform their tasks concurrently, the concurrency aspect of VHDL is heavily emphasized. In a hardware description language, concurrency means that transfer statements, descriptions of components, and instantiations of gates or logical units are all executed such that in the end they appear to have been executed simultaneously.

2.3.2   Support for Design Hierarchy

The DoD requirement document specified the need for hierarchical specification of hardware in VHDL. This feature is essential for a multi-level hardware language. A design consists of an interface description and a separate part for describing its operation. Several descriptions may exist for describing the operation of a design, all corresponding to the same interface description. The operation of a system can be specified based on its functionality, or it can be specified structurally in terms of its smaller subcomponents. Structural description of a component can be accomplished at all design levels. At the lowest levels, components are described by their functionality and use no subcomponents.

As an example of hierarchy in a digital system, consider the description for a processor shown in Figure 2.1. At the top level, the CPU may be described by the structural interconnection of registers, multiplexers, logic units such as the *alu* (Arithmetic Logic Unit), and perhaps sections of behavioral descriptions (shown by an array of small rectangles). The CPU can be simulated only when the operation of each of these components is specified. Components can either be specified behaviorally or they can be specified in terms of smaller subcomponents. For example, the *counter* may be specified by its behavior and the *alu* by interconnection of its individual components. Each of the *alu* components may be partitioned and described by interconnection of a multiplexer, an adder, and random logic. Figure 2.1 shows *logic* described by its behavior, while the *mux* component is described in terms of primitive gates. At the lowest level, the primitive gates should either be described by their behavior or exist in a design library which is accessible to the simulator.

2.3.3   Library Support

For design management, the need for libraries is specified for VHDL. User defined and system defined primitives and descriptions reside in the library system. The language should provide a mechanism for accessing various libraries. A library can contain only an interface description of a design, but several specifications of the operation of a system can reside in the same library.

Descriptions and models that are correct should be placed in the library after they have been compiled by the language compiler. In addition, libraries should be accessible to different designers.

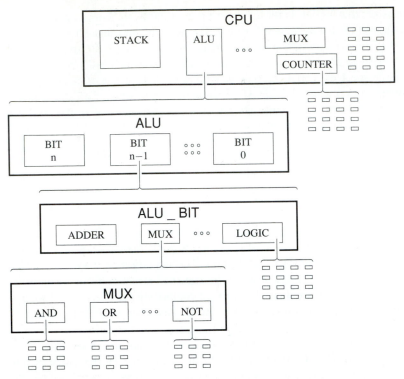

FIGURE 2.1
Example for hierarchical partitioning.

2.3.4 Sequential Statement

Although the strong features of a hardware description language should be its support for concurrent execution of processes and statements, the VHDL language requirements also specify the need for software-like sequential control. When a hardware designer partitions a system into concurrent components or subsections, the designer should then be able to describe the internal operational details by sequential programming language constructs such as case, if-then-else, and loop statements.

An example for the use of this feature is in the top-down design of a digital system such as the CPU shown in Figure 2.1. After an initial partitioning of the system into subcomponents, the designer concentrates on the hardware design of one of the subcomponents, for example, the *alu*. While this component is being designed, high level models for other components of this system will provide a simulation environment in which the component under design can be tested and simulated.

Sequential statements provide an easy method for modeling hardware components based on their functionality. Sequential or procedural capability is only for convenience—and the overall structure of the VHDL language remains highly concurrent.

2.3.5   Generic Design

In addition to inputs and outputs of a hardware component, other conditions may influence the way it operates. These include the environment where the hardware component is used, and the physical characteristics of the hardware component itself. It should not be necessary to generate a new hardware description for every specific condition. Furthermore, many hardware components in various logic families, for example, the *LS*, *F*, and *ALS* series of the 7400 logic family, are functionally equivalent, and differ only in their timing and loading characteristics.

A good hardware description language should allow the designer to configure the generic description of a component when it is used in a design. Generic descriptions should be configurable for size, physical characteristics, timing, loading, and environmental conditions. The ability to describe generic models of hardware was a DoD requirement for the VHDL language.

2.3.6   Type Declaration and Usage

A language for the description of hardware at various levels of abstractions should not be limited to Bit or Boolean types. VHDL requirements specify that the language ought to allow integer, floating point, and enumerate types, as well as user defined types. Types defined by the system or by the user should be placed in the library of the language environment and their use should be transparent to the user.

The language should provide the capability to redefine language operators for types that are defined by the user. For example, the language provides Boolean operators such as AND, OR, and NOT for the predefined logic values. A user needing a multi-level logic should be able to redefine these operators for the newly defined multi-level logic type.

In addition, a hardware description language should allow array type declarations and composite type definitions, such as statements or records in programming languages. The DoD document also specifies a strongly typed language and strong type checking.

2.3.7   Use of Subprograms

The ability to define and use functions and procedure was another VHDL requirement. Subprograms can be used for explicit type conversions, logic unit definitions, operator redefinitions, new operation definitions, and other applications commonly used in programming languages.

2.3.8   Timing Control

The ability to specify timing at all levels is another requirement for the VHDL language. VHDL should allow the designer to schedule values to signals and delay the actual assignment of values until a later time. For handshaking and gate or line delay modeling in the sequential descriptions, it should be possible to wait for the occurrence of an event or for a specific time duration.

The language should be general and it should allow any number of explicitly defined clock signals. The clocking scheme should be completely up to the user, since the language does not have an implicit clocking scheme or signal.

Constructs for edge detection, delay specification, setup and hold time specification, pulse width checking, and setting various time constraints should be provided.

2.3.9 Structural Specification

The DoD requirements for a standard hardware description language specified that the language should have constructs for specifying structural decomposition of hardware at all levels. It also should be possible to describe a generic one-bit design and use it when describing multi-bit regular structures in one or more dimensions. This requires constructs for iteration in the description of structures.

2.4 THE VHDL LANGUAGE

In its present form, VHDL satisfies all requirements of the 1983 DoD requirements document. The experience, researchers, software developers, and other users with VHDL since it became the IEEE standard in 1987 indicates this language is sufficiently rich for designing and describing today's digital systems.

As originally required, VHDL is a hardware description language with strong emphasis on concurrency. The language supports hierarchical description of hardware from system to gate or even switch level. VHDL has strong support at all levels for timing specification and violation detection. As expected, VHDL provides constructs for generic design specification and configuration.

A VHDL design entity is defined as an *entity declaration* and as an associated *architecture body*. The entity declaration specifies its interface and is used by architecture bodies of design entities at upper levels of hierarchy. The architecture body describes the operation of a design entity by specifying its interconnection with other design entities, by its behavior, or by a mixture of both. The VHDL language groups subprograms or design entities by use of *packages*. For customizing generic descriptions of design entities, *configurations* are used. VHDL also supports libraries and contains constructs for accessing packages, design entities, or configurations from various libraries.

A typical VHDL design environment is depicted in Figure 2.2. This figure shows that an analyzer program translates a VHDL description into an intermediate form and places it in a design library. The analyzer is responsible for lexical analysis and syntax check. Operations on the design library, such as creating new libraries, deleting the old, or deletion of packages or design entities from a library are done through the design environment. VHDL-based tools use the intermediate format from the design library. One well developed tool is the VHDL simulator, which simulates a design entity from the design library and produces a simulation report. A hardware synthesizer, test vector generator, or a physical design tool are examples of other VHDL-based tools.

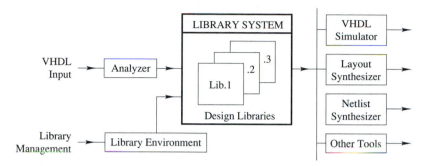

FIGURE 2.2
An example VHDL environment.

VHDL-based tools are widely available on platforms ranging from personal computers to multi-user Unix or Ultrix machines. Simulators for full VHDL IEEE 1076 are also available for a variety of platforms. In addition, several synthesis programs that take a subset of VHDL as input and generate a netlist are commercially available.

2.5 A VHDL-BASED DESIGN PROCESS

This section illustrates a way VHDL can facilitate the process of digital system design. For this purpose, we use a small sequence detector example and perform the design steps presented in Figure 1.1. At each step, we discuss how VHDL can be used to verify the result of that design stage.

In the field of digital system design, sequence detectors are representative of a large class of controller circuits. A CPU controller, for example, can be regarded as a generalization of such circuits. We will now consider the *sequence_detector* example shown in Figure 2.3. This circuit has *enable*, *x_in*, and *y_in* inputs. Once it has been enabled, it searches for a sequence of 110 on the *x_in* input. When the 110 sequence is found, it generates an output equal to the complement of the *y_in* input. The output of this system is on the *z_out* line.

As shown in Figure 1.1, the first step in the design of a digital system is to reproduce the system's behavioral design specification. Our system consists of a clocking circuit and a finite state machine (FSM) that detects the 110 sequence. The state machine shown in Figure 2.4 is the outcome of the "behavioral design" stage for the design of the FSM part.

FIGURE 2.3
Sequence detector.

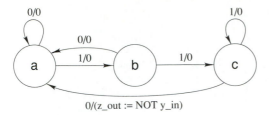

FIGURE 2.4
Mealy State Machine for the FSM part of the
110 sequence detector.

To verify this design stage, a VHDL description that corresponds to the FSM of Figure 2.4 should be developed and simulated. Such a description uses high level software-like language constructs and is at the behavioral level of abstraction, which is discussed in Chapter 8 of this book. The designer should perform the simulation with test data on the inputs of the circuit and verify the results. Errors at this level are mostly due to an incorrect interpretation of the problem and should be corrected before performing lower level design stages.

After satisfactory simulation of the behavioral description, the designer performs the next design stage, which is the data path design. For the FSM part of the circuit, the data path design involves the generation of next-state tables for the flip-flops of the circuit. Figure 2.5a shows the state assignment and transition tables for the FSM. These tables lead to the next-value equations for $V0$ and $V1$ state variables, and the output equation for z_out, as shown in Figure 2.5b.

The result of the data path design stage can be verified by developing a VHDL description based on the equations in Figure 2.5b. Such a description, at the dataflow level of abstraction, uses language constructs for specifying Boolean expressions and clock level timing which are covered in Chapter 7 of this book. Test data developed for verifying the behavioral design stage can also be used to test the dataflow description. Incorrect test results indicate errors in the development of the next-value and output equations. Since a dataflow simulation is faster than gate or transistor simulation and since a dataflow description is easier to debug than a description at a lower level,

STATE	V0	V1	x_in 0	1
a	0	0	00, 0	01, 0
b	0	1	00, 0	10, 0
c	1	0	00, y'	10, 0
-	1	1	-- -	-- -

V0+, V1+, z_out

(a)

$V0+ = x\_in \cdot V1 + x\_in \cdot V0$
$V1+ = x\_in \cdot V1' \cdot V0'$
$z\_out = x\_in' \cdot V0 \cdot y\_in'$

(b)

FIGURE 2.5
Data path design of FSM, (a) next-state tables,
(b) next-value and output equations.

design errors should be found and corrected at this stage before performing the next design stage.

The last stage of the design process is performed after successful simulation of the dataflow VHDL model of the FSM. In this last stage, the designer uses logic gates and flip-flops to implement the equations of Figure 2.5b. Before actual implementation of the circuit, one more VHDL simulation should take place. For this phase, the simulation model is a structural description of the circuit which uses gates and flip-flops from a user design library. This simulation phase can be used for functional verification of the system, as well as for detailed timing analysis. An undesired response at this level is either due to timing problems or a structural design error. To correct this type of error, the designer needs to revise only the gate level implementation; upper level design stages need not be repeated.

The above discussion illustrates incremental design of a sequence detector, where every step of the design is checked by simulation. Synthesis tools ease this step-by-step design process by automatic translation of descriptions at higher levels of abstractions into lower levels. For example, several commercially available VHDL-based synthesis tools can use a FSM description as input and generate a netlist of gates and flip-flops.

2.6   SUMMARY

This chapter provided the reader with the history of the development of VHDL and some of the ideas behind this work. With this standard HDL, the efforts of tool developers, researchers, and software vendors have become more focused, resulting in better tools and more uniform environments. In the last part of the chapter we discussed some of the features of VHDL and its use in a design process. In addition to being an instrument for illustrating design process in VHDL, the example serves as a review of basic logic design techniques.

REFERENCES

1. Dewey, A., and A. Gadient, "VHDL Motivation," IEEE Design and Test of Computers, Vol. 3, April 1986.
2. Aylor, J. H., R. Waxman, and C. Scarratt, "VHDL—Feature Description and Analysis," IEEE Design and Test of Computers, Vol. 3, April 1986.
3. Nash, J. D., and L. F. Saunders, "VHDL Critique," IEEE Design and Test of Computers, Vol. 3, April 1986.
4. "IEEE Standard VHDL Language Reference Manual," IEEE Std. 1076-1987, The Institute of Electrical and Electronic Engineers, Inc., 1988.

PROBLEMS

2.1. Write pseudo code for the behavioral description of the state machine in Figure 2.4.

2.2. Complete the design of the Mealy machine in Figure 2.4.

CHAPTER
3

BASIC
CONCEPTS
IN VHDL

Various concepts of a language, be it a software or hardware language, are interdependent. A general knowledge of all of the language is therefore needed before advanced concepts are described in detail. The intent of this chapter is to give the reader this overall view of the VHDL language. For those who are interested only in gaining a basic knowledge of this language, this chapter can be useful and self-contained. In the first part of this chapter, a complete VHDL description is developed for the sequence detector of Chapter 2 to give the reader a general understanding of the structure of the language. The second part of this chapter is devoted to timing issues in VHDL. The examples presented in this chapter focus on specific areas of the language. In Chapters 4 through 8, further details of the language are described and presented with complete examples.

3.1 BASIC CONCEPTS

The VHDL language is used to describe hardware components and systems. Many language features in VHDL, therefore, are designed to facilitate this usage. In its simplest form, the description of a component in VHDL consists of an interface specification and an architectural specification. As shown in Figure 3.1, the interface description begins with the ENTITY keyword and contains the input-output ports of the component. Other external characteristics of a component, such as time and temperature dependencies, can also be included in the interface description of the component. The name of the component comes after the ENTITY keyword and is followed by IS, which is

```
ENTITY  component_name  IS
    input  and  output  ports.
    physical  and  other  parameters.
END  component_name;
```

```
ARCHITECTURE   identifier   OF   component_name   IS
    declarations.
BEGIN
    specification  of  the  functionality  of  the
    component  in  terms  of  its  input  lines  and  as
    influenced  by  physical  and  other  parameters.
END    identifier;
```

FIGURE 3.1
Interface and architectural specifications.

also a VHDL keyword. An architectural specification begins with the ARCHITEC-TURE keyword, which describes the functionality of a component. This functionality depends on input-output signals and other parameters that are specified in the interface description. As shown in Figure 3.1, the heading of an architectural specification includes an identifier and the name of the component. A functional description of the component starts after the BEGIN keyword. Although VHDL is not case sensitive, for clarity we use uppercase letters here for its keywords and standard definitions.

Several architectural specifications with different identifiers can exist for one component with a given interface description. For example, a component can have one architectural specification at the behavioral level and another at the structural or gate interconnections level. For simulations in which the functionality of a system is under test, the behavioral architectural specification is used. In other simulations where the exact timing response of the component is to be verified, the architectural specification at the structural level is used. This situation is shown in Figure 3.2, where *component_i* has several architectural specifications, three of which are identified by their levels of abstractions as described in Chapter 1. These three descriptions of

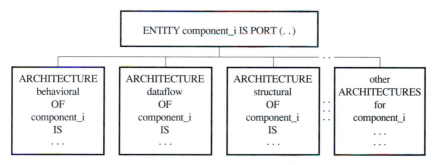

FIGURE 3.2
Multiple architectural specifications.

component_i are distinguished by referring to them as *component_i (behavioral)*, *component_i (dataflow)*, and *component_i (structural)*. Although the *behavioral*, *dataflow*, and *structural* identifiers are not part of the language, we use them to specify levels of abstraction in VHDL descriptions.

In addition to multiple architectural specifications, VHDL allows an architecture to be configured for a specific technology or environment. For example, the *structural* description of *component_i* of Figure 3.2 can be designed such that it can be configured for CMOS or NMOS technology without a change in its functional description. This is a parametrization issue that is discussed in Chapter 5.

3.1.1   An Illustrative Example

An example in this section uses the *sequence_detector* of the previous chapter to illustrate interface and architectural specifications and various levels of abstraction in VHDL. We take a different point of view from that in Chapter 2 in developing a VHDL description for this example. This VHDL description is done in a top-down fashion. In this design strategy, the circuit is repeatedly partitioned into smaller components until the entire design is decomposed into low level components that exist in a certain design library. For our example, we also decompose parts of the circuit into primitive logic gates and flip-flops.

As shown in Figure 3.3, the example circuit is partitioned into a *clock_component* and an *fsm_component*. We assume that the *clock_component* is an off-the-shelf part and need not be described in detail. The *fsm_component*, on the other hand, is to be designed in terms of smaller components and is described in detail. The gate level implementation of the *fsm_component*, as shown in Figure 3.4, consists of AND gates, OR gates, Inverters, and rising edge flip-flops.

The following sections present descriptions corresponding to this design. Uppercase letters for the VHDL language keywords are used in all descriptions.

3.1.2   Interface Description

At the top level, a system can be described by its interface description. At this level, the input and output ports of the system are specified. The interface description for

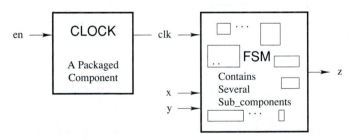

FIGURE 3.3
Sequence detector block diagram.

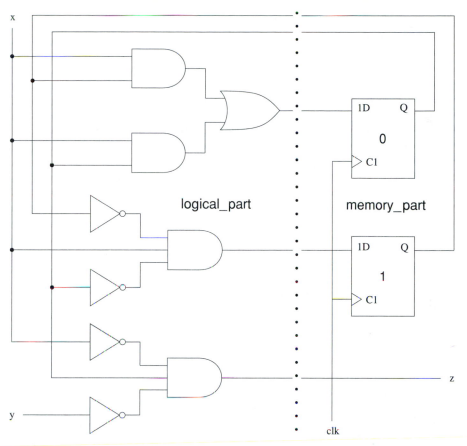

FIGURE 3.4
Gate level implementation of the FSM component.

the *sequence_detector* in VHDL is shown in Figure 3.5a. The first line of this figure specifies the name of the component. This is followed by the PORT keyword with the name of the ports in parentheses ( ). The three inputs of the *sequence_detector* are named *x_in, y_in,* and *enable* and the single output of this circuit is named *z_out.* The keywords IN and OUT specify the mode of the port signals. A signal that is declared as mode IN cannot be assigned a value from within the component. Likewise, an OUT signal cannot be used on the right hand side of a signal assignment. The interface list of the *sequence_detector* also includes the types of the input-output signals. We are using type BIT which is part of the standard package in VHDL. Other types, for multi-value logic, can be defined and added to user libraries. This is discussed in Chapter 6.

As shown in Figure 3.3, the *sequence_detector* consists of a *clock_component* and an *fsm_component.* Figure 3.5b illustrates the interface descriptions of these components. The syntax used is similar to that of Figure 3.5a. The names of the input and output ports of these components are independent of those of the enclosing component.

```
ENTITY sequence_detector IS
    PORT (x_in, y_in, enable : IN BIT; z_out : OUT BIT);
END sequence_detector;
```
                              (a)

```
ENTITY fsm_component IS
    PORT (x, y, clk : IN BIT; z : OUT BIT);
END fsm_component;
ENTITY clock_component IS
    PORT (en : IN BIT; ck : OUT BIT);
END clock_component;
```
                              (b)

```
ENTITY logical_part IS
    PORT (in0, in1, q0, q1 : IN BIT; d0, d1, out1 : OUT BIT);
END logical_part;
ENTITY memory_part IS
    PORT (d_in0, d_in1, clocking: IN BIT; d_out0, d_out1: OUT BIT);
END memory_part;
```
                              (c)

FIGURE 3.5
Interface descriptions, (a) for the *sequence_detector*, (b) for the components of *sequence_detector* after the first partitioning, (c) For the components of *fsm_component* after its first partitioning.

Although it may be clear to the reader that the *x_in* input of the *sequence_detector* is the same as the *x* input of the *fsm_component,* this is not evident from the signal names. This correspondence will be defined later in the architectural specification of the *sequence_detector*.

Figure 3.4 demonstrates how the gate level implementation of the *fsm_component* partitions it into smaller components. A natural partitioning would be to separate the logic and the memory parts, as shown by the dotted line in Figure 3.4. The two flip-flops constitute what will be referred to as the *memory_part*, and the section of the circuit that consists of AND, OR and NOT gates constitutes the *logical_part*. Figure 3.5c shows the interface description for the *memory_part* and the *logical_part*. A block diagram corresponding to this partitioning is shown in Figure 3.6. This block diagram corresponds to the ENTITIES in Figure 3.5c. As noted before, various components can have their own independent port names. Naming conventions should depend on the component's function rather than on the environment in which it is used.

The interface description of all the major components are now complete. The following section addresses the architectural specifications of these components and the formation of a VHDL description for the *sequence_detector*.

3.1.3   Architectural Description

The functionality of a component is described in VHDL architectural bodies. This description can be in terms of other components, or in the form of a definition that

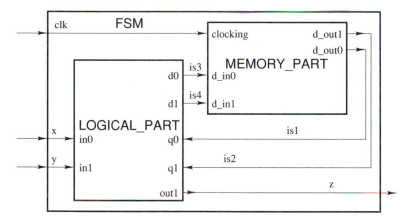

FIGURE 3.6
FSM internal block diagram. This unit is partitioned into a *memory_part* and a *logical_part*.

specifies the values of output signals in terms of the inputs (input/output mapping). It is also possible to mix these two forms of descriptions.

The description of the *sequence_detector* is done according to the tree structure shown in Figure 3.7. The description of the terminal nodes of this tree is self-contained, and that of the nonterminal nodes is in terms of the other components. For a complete description of the *sequence_detector*, all five components should be described in VHDL.

At the highest level, the *sequence_detector* is partitioned into the *clock_component* and the *fsm_component*. The VHDL description for this component, shown in Figure 3.8, specifies the wiring shown in Figure 3.3.

The VHDL description begins with the ARCHITECTURE keyword. Components that are needed within this architecture are then declared. A component declaration includes the name of the component and its ports. In the simple form we are using in this chapter, the port names in the component declarations are the same as those of the actual component. An *internal_line* for carrying the output of the *clock_component* into the clock input of the *fsm_component* has also been declared in the declarative part of the description in Figure 3.8.

The BEGIN keyword starts the body of the description in which the two components of the *sequence_detector* are instantiated. Instantiation refers to naming a

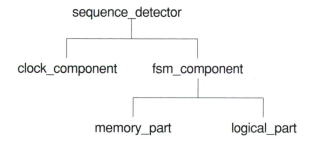

FIGURE 3.7
Tree structure of the *sequence_detector*. VHDL descriptions will correspond to branches shown here.

```
ARCHITECTURE structural OF sequence_detector IS
    COMPONENT
        clock_component PORT(en: IN BIT; ck: OUT BIT);
    END COMPONENT;
    COMPONENT
        fsm_component PORT(x,y,clk:IN BIT; z:OUT BIT);
    END COMPONENT;
    SIGNAL internal_line : BIT;
BEGIN
    c1 : clock_component PORT MAP (enable, internal_line);
    c2 : fsm_component PORT MAP (x_in, y_in, internal_line, z_out);
END structural;
```

FIGURE 3.8
Wiring major components of the *sequence_detector*.

component within another component for use as a subcomponent. Every instantiation begins with an arbitrary label, specifies the component name, and lists a mapping between the port names in the instantiation and the actual component. The signals that are the inputs or outputs of the *sequence_detector* or signals that have been declared in the declaration part can be used in the port map. The description specifies that the *clock_component* uses the *enable* input of the *sequence_detector* as its first input line, and it connects its output to the signal declared as *internal_line*. The *fsm_component* uses the *x_in* and *y_in* inputs of the *sequence_detector* as data inputs. It also uses the *internal_line* signal as the clock input, and it places its output in the *z_out* output of the *sequence_detector*.

Signals in the instantiations will be mapped to the ports of the instantiated component according to their ordering in the port map list. This is known as positional association of formal to actual elements. For example, ports of the *fsm_component* are mapped as shown in Figure 3.9.

Referring back to the tree structure in Figure 3.7, the description of the top node of this tree is now completed. Next, we move down one level and describe the *fsm_component* and the *clock_component*. The *fsm_component* is described at the structural level, and the *clock_component* at the behavioral level. Figure 3.10 shows the structural description of the *fsm_component*, specifying the wiring between the *logical_part* and the *memory_part* in accordance with the block diagram in Figure 3.6. In the declarative part, the *logical_part* and the *memory_part* components as well as

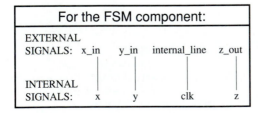

FIGURE 3.9
Mapping of internal and external signals of the *structural* architecture of *sequence_detector*.

four intermediate signals of type BIT are declared. In the body of the architecture of the *fsm_component*, component instantiations and port mappings take place. The signals *is1, is2, is3*, and *is4*, also shown in Figure 3.6, are used as carriers for connecting the input/output ports of the *logical_part* and the *memory_part*.

Figure 3.11 shows the behavioral description of the *clock_component*. The only input of this component is the *en* line and its output is *ck*. The description begins with the ARCHITECTURE keyword followed by an identifier that is in turn followed by the name of the component.

The PROCESS keyword begins the behavioral description of the *clock_compo-nent*. The process statement in VHDL is used for all behavioral descriptions. The syntax of language constructs in a VHDL process is similar to that of most high level software languages in that variables can be declared and used in processes. High level looping and branching constructs such as for-loop and if-then-else can also be used in a process. The process statement in Figure 3.11 declares the *periodic* local variable and initializes it to '1'. When the execution of the description of Figure 3.11 begins, if

```
ARCHITECTURE structural OF fsm_component IS
    COMPONENT logical_part
        PORT (in0, in1, q0, q1 : IN BIT; d0, d1, out1 : OUT BIT);
    END COMPONENT;
    COMPONENT memory_part
        PORT (d_in0, d_in1, clocking:IN BIT; d_out0, d_out1:OUT BIT);
    END COMPONENT;
    SIGNAL is1, is2, is3, is4 : BIT; -- intermediate signals
BEGIN
    c1 : logical_part PORT MAP (x, y, is1, is2, is3, is4, z);
    c2 : memory_part PORT MAP (is3, is4, clk, is1, is2);
END structural;
```

FIGURE 3.10
Structural architecture of FSM component.

```
ARCHITECTURE behavioral OF clock_component IS
BEGIN
    PROCESS
        VARIABLE periodic: BIT := '1';
    BEGIN
        IF en = '1' THEN
            periodic := NOT periodic;
        END IF;
        ck <= periodic;
        WAIT FOR 1 US;
    END PROCESS;
END behavioral;
```

FIGURE 3.11
Behavioral description of clock component.

the clock is enabled, i.e., *en* is '1', *periodic* will be complemented and assigned to the *ck* output signal of the *clock_component*. Following this assignment, a wait statement causes the execution of the process to be suspended for 1 microsecond. When this time expires, the process executes again, and complements *periodic* if *en* is '1', or holds the old value of *periodic* if *en* is '0'. Variables can be declared and used inside processes but they cannot be declared globally. Information can be transferred only between processes via signals. To use the value of a variable outside an architecture, it must be assigned to a declared signal. The := symbol is used for variable assignments, while <= is used for assignments into signals. Unlike signals, variables have no direct hardware significance and they do not have timing associated with them. These issues are discussed in the section on timing in this chapter, and also in Chapter 8. When execution of a process completes, it returns to the beginning and repeats the entire process. This causes the *ck* signal to be complemented every one microsecond, thus generating a periodic clock.

Moving down one more level to the lowest level of the tree in Figure 3.7, we now describe the *memory_part* and the *logical_part* in VHDL. The *logical_part* is described at the dataflow level of abstraction and is identified as such. Dataflow descriptions use various forms of VHDL signal assignment construct for describing the operation of hardware. The description, illustrated in Figure 3.12, consists of three Boolean equations that are assigned to the three outputs of the *logical_part*. A signal assignment can have an AFTER clause which specifies the delay associated with the assignment. We use this delay to account for the gate delays. The three signal assignments in this description are concurrent and are always active. When a signal on the right hand side of any of the three assignments changes in value, the right hand side expression is evaluated and a value scheduled to be placed in the destination signal after the specified time. This behavior is similar to the way actual hardware components work. All components of a digital circuit are always active. As soon as a change occurs on an input of a gate, the gate starts propagating the effect of the new input value to its output.

At the dataflow level of abstraction, clocking schemes and register transfers can be precisely and conveniently specified. We have, therefore, used this level of abstraction for description of the *memory_part* also. The interface description of Figure 3.5c indicates the inputs and outputs of the *memory_part,* and Figure 3.13 shows the architectural specification of this part. As shown in this figure, the description of *memory_part (dataflow)* begins with the ARCHITECTURE keyword and includes a

```
ARCHITECTURE dataflow OF logical_part IS
BEGIN
    d0 <= ( in0 AND q0 ) OR ( in0 AND q1)    AFTER 12 NS;
    d1 <= ( NOT q0 ) AND ( NOT q1 ) AND in0    AFTER 14 NS;
    out1 <= ( NOT in0 ) AND ( NOT in1 ) AND q0    AFTER 14 NS;
END dataflow;
```

FIGURE 3.12
Dataflow description of the *logical_part*.

```
ARCHITECTURE dataflow OF memory_part IS
BEGIN
    BLOCK (clocking = '1' AND clocking' EVENT)
    BEGIN
        d_out0 <= GUARDED d_in0 AFTER 11 NS;
        d_out1 <= GUARDED d_in1 AFTER 11 NS;
    END BLOCK;
END dataflow;
```

FIGURE 3.13
Dataflow description of *memory_part*.

single block statement. This statement is used here to specify the clocking scheme. The expression in parentheses after the BLOCK keyword is the guard of the block. When the clock input (*clocking*) to the *memory_part* is '1', and there has been a change on this signal (an EVENT), then the guard expression of the block is TRUE. This situation arises when the *clocking* signal makes a low-to-high transition. The guard, therefore, represents the rising edge of the *clocking* signal. The keyword GUARDED on the right hand side of a signal assignment, enables the assignment only if the corresponding guard signal is true. In the body of the block, signal assignments to the two outputs of the *memory_part* are guarded by the rising edge of the *clocking* signal. The *d_in0* and *d_in1* inputs are assigned only to the *d_out0* and *d_out1* outputs on the rising edge of *clocking*. At all other times, these outputs hold their old values, regardless of the events on the *d_in* inputs.

Signal assignments in Figure 3.13 take place 11 nanoseconds after the rising edge of the *clocking*. This delay is to account for the internal delay of the flip-flops. Having defined all five components of the tree in Figure 3.7, the VHDL description of our *sequence_detector* is now complete. To run the descriptions and simulate the functionality of the circuit, component bindings have to be completed, and a test bench must be developed for the circuit. Chapters 4 and 5 deal with various forms of binding components of a design to actual components. Chapter 4 shows simple test benches, and the behavioral language constructs described in Chapters 6 and 8 provide more convenient methods of testing circuits.

3.1.4 Subprograms

As in most high level languages, VHDL allows the definition and use of functions and procedures generally referred to as subprograms. Most of the high level behavioral constructs in VHDL can be used in the body of functions and procedures. Subprograms can be declared, defined, and invoked much the same way as in software languages. Values returned or altered by subprograms may or may not have a direct hardware significance. For example, we can use functions to represent Boolean equations, for type conversions, or for delay value calculations. While Boolean expressions may correspond to actual logic circuits, the other two applications do not represent hardware structures.

A procedure can be useful for type conversions, for description of counters, for analog to digital converters, or simply for outputting internal binary data in integer form. The *byte_to_integer* procedure for converting 8-bit binary data to integer is illustrated in Figure 3.14. A type declaration declares *byte* as an array of eight bits. Description of the *byte_to_integer* procedure uses this type (*byte*) to define its input vector. The procedure begins with the PROCEDURE keyword, followed by the identifier of the procedure and by its interface list. In the declarative part of this procedure, the *result* variable is declared as an integer and initialized to zero. In the body of the *byte_to_integer* procedure, a loop of eight iterations adds the weight of the bit positions, for the bits of the input that are '1', to the *result*. At the end of the loop the value in the *result* variable is assigned to the *oi* output.

As an example function, we replace part of the Boolean expressions in Figure 3.12 with a function. As shown in this figure, as well as in Figure 3.4, the logic at the *d* input of flip-flop 1 is the same as the logic for the *z* output. Instead of repeating the same expression for *d1* and *out1*, a function can be used for this purpose as shown in Figure 3.15.

In the declarative part of function *f* variable *x* is declared and in the body of *f* it is assigned to the appropriate Boolean expression. This expression is the return value of the function. The new description of the *logical_part* that takes advantage of function *f* is shown in Figure 3.16.

```
TYPE byte IS ARRAY ( 7 DOWNTO 0 ) OF BIT;
   ...
PROCEDURE byte_to_integer (ib : IN byte; oi : OUT INTEGER) IS
   VARIABLE result : INTEGER := 0;
BEGIN
   FOR i IN 0 TO 7 LOOP
      IF ib(i) = '1' THEN
         result := result + 2**i;
      END IF;
   END LOOP;
   oi := result;
END byte_to_integer;
```

FIGURE 3.14
Type conversion procedure: converting bytes to integers.

```
FUNCTION f (a, b, c : BIT) RETURN BIT IS
   VARIABLE x : BIT;
BEGIN
   x := ( (NOT a) AND (NOT b) AND c );
   RETURN x;
END f;
```

FIGURE 3.15
A simple Boolean function in a VHDL function definition.

```
┌ARCHITECTURE functional_dataflow OF logical_part IS
├BEGIN
│    d0 <= ( in0 AND q0 ) OR ( in0 AND q1)    AFTER 12 NS;
│    d1 <= f (q0, q1, in0)    AFTER 14 NS;
│    out1 <= f ( in0, in1, q0)    AFTER 14 NS;
└END functional_dataflow;
```

FIGURE 3.16
Description of *logical_part* of the *fsm_component* using functions.

3.1.5   VHDL Operators

Behavioral descriptions in VHDL can include most of the operations found in software languages. The text of behavioral descriptions resembles that of software programs except that constructs for control and time modeling are also included. Figure 3.17 shows the operations that can be used in VHDL.

Logical operators can be used for operands of the predefined BIT and BOOLEAN types and the result of the operation will be the same type as the operands. Relational operators always generate a Boolean result regardless of the type of operands. Operands of arithmetic operators must be of the same type and the result reflects the type of the operands. The concatenation operator is used for concatenating arrays of elements. For example, assuming *x_byte* and *y_byte* are two 8-bit arrays of BITs, the following concatenation forms a 16-bit array of BITs.

x_byte & y_byte

The type of the elements in concatenated arrays must be the same. This operator is particularly useful for merging buses or registers. In the chapters that follow, these operators are used and their application and usage becomes clear. In Chapter 6, types and issues related to types, such as type conversion and qualification, are discussed.

3.2   TIMING AND CONCURRENCY

In an electronic circuit, all components are always active and there is a timing associated with every event in the circuit. VHDL, being a language for describing such circuits, has constructs for accurate modeling of timing and concurrency in digital circuits. Concurrent constructs of the language are used in concurrent bodies and sequential statements are used in sequential bodies. An architecture is a concurrent body, while the body of a process statement is a sequential body. A sequential body within a concurrent body executes concurrently with concurrent constructs within the same body. Timing relationships between signals and various bodies in VHDL are complex and important. To illustrate these concepts, we start with the example in Figure 3.18.

Each gate in this circuit is assumed to have a delay of 12 nanoseconds. While all three inputs are high, the output at a stable '1' level, and nodes w, x, and y are at '0', '1', and '0', respectively. As illustrated in Figure 3.19, if input a switches from

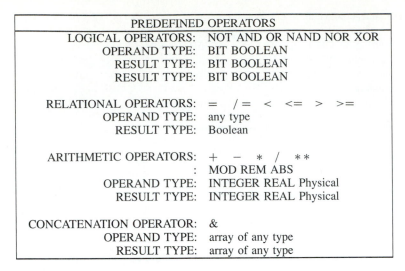

PREDEFINED OPERATORS	
LOGICAL OPERATORS:	NOT AND OR NAND NOR XOR
OPERAND TYPE:	BIT BOOLEAN
RESULT TYPE:	BIT BOOLEAN
RESULT TYPE:	BIT BOOLEAN
RELATIONAL OPERATORS:	= /= < <= > >=
OPERAND TYPE:	any type
RESULT TYPE:	Boolean
ARITHMETIC OPERATORS:	+ − * / **
:	MOD REM ABS
OPERAND TYPE:	INTEGER REAL Physical
RESULT TYPE:	INTEGER REAL Physical
CONCATENATION OPERATOR:	&
OPERAND TYPE:	array of any type
RESULT TYPE:	array of any type

FIGURE 3.17
Basic VHDL predefined operators.

'1' to '0', gates *g1* and *g2* concurrently react to this change. As shown in the timing diagram in Figure 3.20, the *g1* gate causes node *w* to go to '1' after 12 ns, and *g2* causes node *x* to go to '0' after the same amount of time. At this time, gates *g3* and *g4* see a change at their inputs and they start reacting to their new input conditions. The change at the *x* input of *g4* turns the output off after 12 ns. At this same time, the change on *w* has caused node *y* to become '1'. The OR gate (*g4*) now has a '1'at its *y* input, which causes it to go back to '1' only 12 ns after it has gone to zero. As shown in Figure 3.20, this causes a 12 ns wide zero glitch on the output of the circuit which must be properly represented in a simulation model of this circuit.

   This analysis would be more complex if the gates had unequal delay values, or if other inputs change when the circuit has not stabilized. From this   analysis of

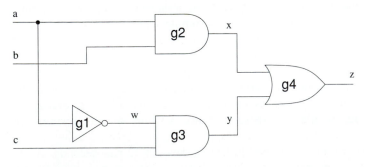

FIGURE 3.18
A gate circuit to illustrate timing and concurrency.

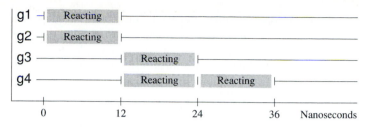

FIGURE 3.19

Gates of Figure 3.18 reacting to changes originated by *a* changing from '1' to '0'.

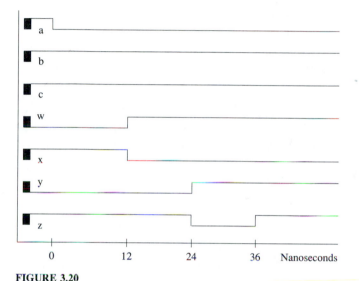

FIGURE 3.20

Timing diagram resulting from input *a* of circuit of Figure 3.18 changing from '1' to '0' at time zero.

a small example it is clear that treatment of timing and concurrency is especially important in a hardware language. For this reason, the VHDL language has a timing component associated with the signals and it provides constructs for concurrent signal assignments. Programming in VHDL requires a good understanding of these concepts, which are discussed here.

3.2.1   Objects and Classes

In a software language, a variable contains a value and can accept new values through assignment statements. Constants, on the other hand, have fixed values throughout a program run. Because it is necessary to model timing in a hardware language, VHDL, in addition to variables and constants, also supports signals. In the VHDL terminology, a signal, a variable, or a constant is called an object, and "signal," "variable," or "constant" are considered classes of objects. For example, a variable is an object whose class is variable.

As with variables, signals can receive values during a simulation run. We often use the term "carrier" to refer to objects that receive values and to objects that can be used for carrying values from one point in the program to another. Global carriers are carriers that can be used across architectural specifications. Only signals can be global carriers in VHDL.

3.2.2   Signals and Variables

A carrier in VHDL can be declared as a signal or as a variable. Signals have hardware significance and have a time component associated with them. The assignment symbol for signals is <= which has a nonzero time component. The scheduling for assignment of the right hand side to the signal can be specified by use of an AFTER clause. Signals can be used in sequential as well as concurrent bodies of VHDL, but they can only be declared in concurrent bodies of VHDL.

Variables, on the other hand, do not have a time component associated with them, and are mainly used for intermediate values in the software sense in behavioral descriptions. The standard := assignment is used to assign values to variables. Variables can only be declared and used in sequential bodies of VHDL, and they are local to the body in which they are declared. Sequential bodies in VHDL include *processes, functions*, and *procedures*. The syntax and the sequentiality of these bodies is similar to that found in most software languages.

Variables are discussed in conjunction with functions and procedures in Chapter 5 and again in conjunction with process statements in Chapter 8. Basic concepts of signal assignments are emphasized in the remainder of this chapter. Some complex issues related to signal assignments are covered more fully in Chapter 7 to complete our discussion of this important VHDL concept.

3.2.3   Signal Assignments

In its simplest form, a signal assignment consists of a target signal on the left hand side of a left arrow and an expression for defining a waveform on the right hand side (with no AFTER clause). Such an assignment specifies that the right hand side be assigned to the left hand side *delta* time later. Physically this time is zero seconds, but it has nonzero scheduling significance. For example, an assignment that is scheduled to occur two *delta* times later will be done after an assignment that is scheduled to occur after one *delta*, and the result of the later assignment will not be available for the earlier assignment. Both assignments, however, occur before the smallest physical time unit. This will become clearer when we discuss concurrency later in this section.

Optionally, a signal assignment can include an AFTER clause specifying that a physical time delay is to occur before the assignment to the left hand side takes place. If this time delay is zero, the simple form described above will apply.

Signal assignments can have *inertial* or *transport* delays. The *delay* architecture of the *example* entity in Figure 3.21 includes an assignment with inertial delay and an assignment with transport delay. Unless the TRANSPORT keyword is used in a signal assignment, the delay is considered to be the inertial type.

Inertial delays can be used to model delays through capacitive networks, such as the one shown in Figure 3.22 which corresponds to the first assignment of Figure 3.21. If a pulse whose width is less than five nanoseconds occurs on *waveform*, it will not appear on *target1*. On the other hand, the same pulse on *waveform* appears on *target2* exactly five nanoseconds later.

Figure 3.23 shows timing diagrams of *target1* and *target2* of Figure 3.21, when the same waveform (*waveform*) is used on the right hand side of both assignments. Also shown in this figure is the Exclusive-Or of *target1* and *target2* to illustrate their differences. Note that differences occur only when positive or negative pulses shorter than five nanoseconds appear on *waveform*.

Gate delays are caused by the internal resistance and capacitance of the gates and, therefore, are inertial. Carrier delays in electronic circuits that are caused by wire capacitance are also inertial. Since most hardware constructs can be represented by inertial delays, this is the default in signal assignments.

3.2.4 Concurrent and Sequential Assignments

In a software language, all assignments are sequential. This means that the order in which the statements appear is significant because they are executed from the top to the bottom. Sequential descriptions are the simplest to program and understand. As described earlier, events in hardware components are concurrent, and they need to be represented as such. Concurrent and sequential bodies of VHDL are discussed here.

```
ARCHITECTURE delay OF example IS
    SIGNAL target1, target2, waveform : BIT;
    -- this is a comment
BEGIN
    -- the following illustrates inertial delay
    target1 <= waveform AFTER 5 NS;
    -- the following illustrates transport delay
    target2 <= TRANSPORT waveform AFTER 5 NS;
    -- this architecture continues
END delay;
```

FIGURE 3.21
VHDL description for the demonstration of transport and inertial delays.

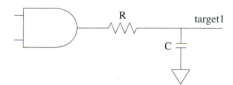

FIGURE 3.22
The RC delay is best represented by an inertial delay.

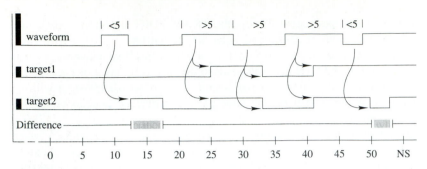

FIGURE 3.23
Illustrating the difference between inertial and transport delays.

3.2.4.1 CONCURRENCY. In an architectural body, all signal assignments are concurrent. When the value of a signal on the right hand side of an assignment changes, the entire right hand side waveform is evaluated and the result is assigned to the left hand side target. In Figure 3.21, for example, if the value of *waveform* changes, the new value will be scheduled for assignment to *target1* after five nanoseconds. Multiple assignments in the body of an architecture are simultaneously active, and the order in which they appear is not significant. Using concurrent assignments, an exact VHDL representation of the circuit in Figure 3.18 is shown in Figure 3.24.

This description consists of four concurrent assignments representing the four gates of Figure 3.18. When an input changes, the events in this description follow those of the actual circuit exactly. Since all the delays are caused by the gates, inertial delays are used for all of the assignments in Figure 3.24.

Multiple concurrent assignments can only be done to the same signal if a resolution function is provided to calculate a single value from several simultaneously driving values. Such signals are said to be resolved, and are be discussed in Chapter 7.

```
ENTITY figure_18_example IS
    PORT (a, b, c : IN BIT; z : OUT BIT);
END figure_18_example;

ARCHITECTURE   concurrent OF figure_18_example IS
    SIGNAL w, x, y : BIT;
BEGIN
    w <= NOT a AFTER 12 NS;
    x <= a AND b AFTER 12 NS;
    y <= c AND w AFTER 12 NS;
    z <= x OR y AFTER 12 NS;
END concurrent;
```

FIGURE 3.24
VHDL description for the gate level circuit in Figure 3.18 for the demonstration of timing and concurrency.

3.2.4.2 EVENTS AND TRANSACTIONS. Events and transactions are often referenced when discussing signal assignments. When a waveform causes the value of the target signal to change, an *event* is said to have occurred on the target signal. When a value is scheduled to be assigned to a target signal after a given time, a *transaction* is said to have been placed on the *driver* of the target signal. A transaction that does not change the value of a signal is still a transaction, but it does not cause an event on the signal. A transaction is represented by a value-time pair in parentheses. The value is the current value if the time element is zero; otherwise, the value is the future value for the driver of the signal.

As an example, consider the description in Figure 3.25. The declaration of signals *a*, *b*, and *c* causes the creation of these signals with '0' initial values. The initial value of each of these signals appears as though it has been the value of the signal for an infinitely long time prior to the start of simulation. Creation of the signals is referred to as *elaboration*, and assigning their initial values to them is called *initialization*.

After the initialization phase, values of *a*, *b*, and *c* signals are all zero. At the start of the simulation, at time 0 (this and other time values in the discussion of this example are in nanoseconds), the value of '0' on *a* causes a ('1',5NS) transaction to be scheduled for *b*, and a ('0',10NS) transaction for *c*. Also at this time, a '1' is scheduled for the *a* signal after 15 nanoseconds, causing a ('1',15NS) transaction on the driver of this signal. At time 5, the time element of the scheduled transaction for *b* becomes zero, and its value becomes current, which causes the value of this signal to change from '0' to '1'. This change of value is an event on *b*. Five nanoseconds later, at time 10, the scheduled transaction on *c* becomes current (its time element becomes zero), causing a driving value of '0' on this signal. Since at this time the value of *c* is already '0', this transaction does not cause an event on *c*.

Figure 3.26 shows events and transactions on signals in the description in Figure 3.25. Shaded areas signify transactions, and reverse modes signify initial values. Figure 3.26a shows the resulting timing diagram, with shaded areas indicating the transactions when they become current. Figure 3.26b shows the transactions that are placed on the *a*, *b* and *c* signals at the time this placement takes place. Figure 3.26c shows the transactions that exist on the signals before they become current. When a transaction is placed on the driver of a signal, it stays there and its time value decreases linearly with time until it becomes current. Figure 3.26c only shows transactions at five nanosecond intervals. A transaction is represented by a vertical box; the height of the box signifies the value of the time element in the transaction.

```
ARCHITECTURE demo OF example IS
   SIGNAL a, b, c : BIT := '0';
BEGIN
   a <= '1' AFTER 15 NS;
   b <= NOT a AFTER 5 NS;
   c <= a AFTER 10 NS;
END demo;
```

FIGURE 3.25
A simple description for illustrating events and transactions.

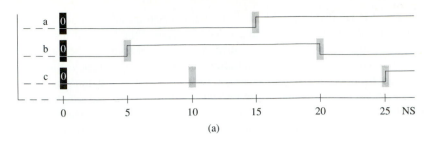

(a)

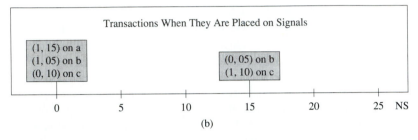

(b)

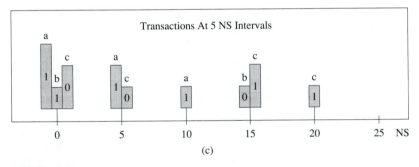

(c)

FIGURE 3.26
Events and transaction that occur on signals in Figure 3.25, (a) The resulting timing diagram showing transactions when they become current, (b) Transactions when they are placed on signals, (c) Transactions as their time values approach zero to become current.

No new transactions are placed on the signals in Figure 3.25 until time 15. At this time the transaction that was placed on the drive of *a* at time 0 becomes current, and changes the value of this signal to '1'. This event causes a ('0',5NS) transaction on *b* and a ('1',10NS) transaction on *c*. When these transactions become current; i.e., their time elements become 0 at time 15+5 NS and 15+10 NS, respectively, the values of *b* and *c* are the opposite of the values of their corresponding transaction. Therefore, both transactions cause events on these signals, at time 20 on *b*, and at time 25 on *c*.

3.2.4.3 DELTA DELAY. In the example presented in Figure 3.24, nonzero delays were used. For the purpose of demonstrating the concept of *delta* time delay, we consider another version of the circuit description shown in Figure 3.18. This description, shown in Figure 3.27, uses zero delay assignments for the internal nodes of the circuit

```
ARCHITECTURE  not_properly_timed  OF  figure_18_example  IS
    SIGNAL  w, x, y  :  BIT  :=  '0';
BEGIN
    y  <=  c  AND  w;
    w  <=  NOT  a;
    x  <=  a  AND  b;
    z  <=  x  OR  y  AFTER  36  NS;
END  not_properly_timed;
```

FIGURE 3.27
VHDL description for demonstrating the *delta* delay.

and a delayed assignment, with cumulative worst case delay of 36 nanoseconds for the z output.

    In our analysis of this description we use the same input values used in the analysis that led to the timing diagram in Figure 3.20. The new timing diagram, showing the events and transactions (shaded areas), is shown in Figure 3.28. As before, we assume that a, b, and c external signals are initialized to '1'; that is, their values prior to time zero and at time zero are '1'. We also assume that, external to this description, a '0' is assigned to the a signal at time zero. Since a is a signal, this new value appears on it a *delta* time later at time 1δ. One *delta* time after input a changes, nodes w and x receive their new values; that is, w becomes '1' (value of NOT a) and x becomes '0' (value of a AND b) at time 2δ. The event on x causes a zero value to be scheduled for output z after 36 nanoseconds, causing a ('0',36NS) transaction of driver of z. The event on w causes the expression for y to be evaluated, and as a

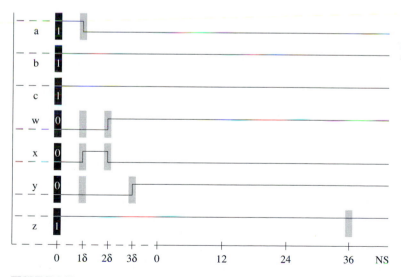

FIGURE 3.28
Timing diagram for the description of Figure 3.27, showing delta delays.

results the value at node *y* changes one *delta* time after *w* changes; it changes from '0' to '1' at time 3δ. The event on *y* then causes the output expression to be evaluated which again results in scheduling a new value on the output 36 nanoseconds after this event, placing a ('1',36NS) transaction on the driver of *z*.

The second transaction on the driver of the *z* output ('1',36NS) overwrites the first ('0',36NS), and since the value of *z* is already '1' the dominant transaction causes no event on this line. Although the steady state value on *z* is correct, the intermediate values on *z* are not modeled according to the actual circuit. Note that transactions on *x* and *y* at time zero do not translate to transactions on the *z* output 36 nanoseconds later. This is because the physical time delay absorbs all delta delays. Notice a glitch on *x* at zero time. Explanation of this glitch is left as an exercise.

Another example for illustrating *delta* time, transactions, and concurrency is shown in Figure 3.29. This description is for a chain of two zero-delay inverters, with *a* being the first input, *c* the output, and *b* the midpoint. Signals *a*, *b*, and *c* are initialized to '0'. A '1' is assigned to *a* causing a transaction on *b*, which in turn causes transaction on *c*.

The timing diagram in Figure 3.30 indicates that all transactions occur at zero time between $0 + 1\delta$ and $0 + 3\delta$. Every transaction in this analysis causes an event to occur. At time zero, *a*, *b*, and *c* signals have values that are specified in the declarations of the signals. At this time, a '1' is scheduled for *a*, and the comple-

```
ARCHITECTURE concurrent OF timing_demo IS
    SIGNAL   a, b, c : BIT := '0';
BEGIN
    a <= '1';
    b <= NOT a;
    c <= NOT b;
END concurrent;
```

FIGURE 3.29
Description for a chain of two inverters, demonstrating *delta*, transactions and concurrency.

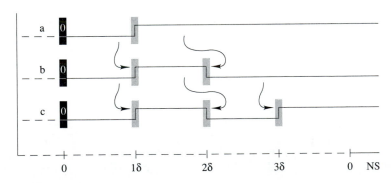

FIGURE 3.30
Timing diagram for *timing_demo* description of Figure 3.29.

ment of *a*, whose value is still '0' at time zero, is scheduled for *b*; therefore, both *a* and *b* will have ('1',0NS) transactions on their drivers. Also at time zero, the complement of signal *b*, whose value is '0' at this time, is scheduled for the *c* signal, causing the placement of a ('1',0NS) transaction on the driver of *c*. One *delta* time later at *1δ*, signals *a*, *b*, and *c* receive their new values which are all '1's. The new value on *a* causes a transaction on *b* one *delta* time later at *2δ*, which results in an event that changes *b* to '0'. Similarly, the value of *b* at *1δ* causes an event on *c* at *2δ*. The event on *b* at time *2δ* causes the right hand side of the assignment to *c* to be evaluated which causes another event on *c* one *delta* time later at *3δ*.

3.2.4.4 SEQUENTIAL ASSIGNMENTS.

Assignments to signals in the sequential bodies of VHDL, for example, in the body of process statements, are done sequentially. This means that the order in which signal assignments appear is important, and it is legal to make multiple assignments to simple nonresolved signals. When a new transaction is to be placed on the driver of a signal, the transactions that are already scheduled for that signal will then be considered. The new transaction will either overwrite the previous transactions or be appended to them, depending on the timing of the new transaction and the type of the assignment.

A new transaction on the driver of a signal scheduled *before* an already existing transaction always overwrites the existing transaction. A new transaction on the driver of a signal scheduled *after* the already existing transaction is appended to the existing transaction if the delay is of transport type. For inertial delays, the new transaction scheduled after the existing transaction overwrites the existing transaction if it has a different value. Figure 3.31 summarizes this discussion on effective transactions on the driver of a signal. These issues will become clearer in the following examples.

When a sequential signal assignment statement is executed, a *(v1,t1)* transaction will be placed on the driver of the target signal. If an inertial assignment causes a second transaction *(v2,t2)* to be placed on the driver of the same signal, the first transaction will be overwritten by the second transaction if *t2* is less than *t1*. For example, in the description of Figure 3.32, the ('1',5NS) transaction is completely discarded, resulting in the timing diagram of Figure 3.33.

	TRANSPORT	INERTIAL
New Transaction is BEFORE Already Existing	Overwrite existing transaction.	Overwrite existing transaction.
New Transaction is AFTER Already Existing	Append the new transaction to the driver.	Overwrite existing if different values otherwise keep both.

FIGURE 3.31
Effective transactions on the driver of a signal when multiple sequential assignments are made to the signal.

```
 ARCHITECTURE  sequential   OF  overwriting_old  IS
    SIGNAL   x : tit := 'Z';
 BEGIN
    PROCESS
    BEGIN
       x <= '1'  AFTER  5  NS;
       x <= '0'  AFTER  3  NS;
    WAIT;
    END PROCESS;
 END sequential;
```

FIGURE 3.32
Overwriting an old transaction. The new transaction is scheduled *before* the existing.

FIGURE 3.33
Timing of
overwriting_old(sequential)
description of Figure 3.32.

On the other hand, if $t2$ of the most recent transaction $(v2,t2)$ is greater than $t1$ of the previous transaction $(v1,t1)$, the first transaction will be discarded if $v1$ is not equal to $v2$, and both transactions will affect the target signal if $v1$ is equal to $v2$. Figure 3.34 demonstrates the different value case, while Figure 3.35 demonstrates the case in which the values of the transactions are equal.

In the description of Figure 3.32, and the following descriptions that are used for illustration of the current topic (3.32, 3.34, 3.35, 3.36, and 3.37), signal x is declared as *tit*, which stands for trinary digit. We are assuming that this is a user defined type that takes on 'Z', '0', and '1' values, where 'Z' represents high impedance. Type definitions will be illustrated in Chapter 6. Another new feature used in this description which has not been discussed is the use of the wait statement without a time expression.

```
 ARCHITECTURE sequential OF discarding_old IS
    SIGNAL x : tit := 'Z';
 BEGIN
    PROCESS
    BEGIN
       x <= '1' AFTER 5 NS;
       x <= '0' AFTER 8 NS;
    WAIT;
    END PROCESS;
 END sequential;
```

FIGURE 3.34
Discarding previous transactions of different value. The new transaction is scheduled *after* the existing, and has a different value.

This statement suspends the process forever, causing it to be executed only once. The wait statement will be discussed in detail in Chapter 8.

In Figure 3.34, a ('1',5NS) transaction is placed on the driver of the *x* signal by the first assignment. The second assignment generates the ('0',8NS) transaction which causes the ('1',5NS) transaction to be removed. Therefore, the only transaction on the driver of *x* is ('0',8NS). This transaction causes the 'Z' value on *x* to go to '0' at 8 ns.

In Figure 3.35, a ('0',5NS) transaction is placed on the driver of the *x* signal by the first assignment. The second assignment generates the ('0',8NS) transaction. Since the value of both transactions are '0', they will both remain on the driver of *x*. The *x* signal will, therefore, go to '0' at 5 ns and remain at this level.

Let us again assume that a *(v1,t1)* transaction is placed on the driver of the target signal. If a transport assignment causes a second transaction *(v2,t2)* to be placed on the driver of the same signal, the first transaction will be overwritten by the second transaction if *t2* is less than *t1*, just like an inertial assignment. If, however, *t2* is greater than *t1*, the second transaction will be appended to the first transaction. Figure 3.36 shows the case where a transport assignment causes a previous transaction to be overwritten, and Figure 3.37 includes an example in which the new transport assignment appends a new transaction to the existing transaction.

In Figure 3.36, a ('1',5NS) transaction is placed on the driver of the *x* signal by the first transport assignment. The second transport assignment generates the ('0',3NS) transaction which causes the ('1',5NS) transaction to be removed. As a result of the only remaining transaction on the driver of *x*, this signal will change value from 'Z' to '0' at 3 ns.

In Figure 3.37, a ('1',5NS) transaction is placed on the driver of the *x* signal by the first transport assignment. The second transport assignment generates the ('0',8NS) transaction which is appended to ('1',5NS). The two transactions cause *x* to go to '1' at 5 ns, and to '0' at 8 ns.

Figure 3.23 illustrates that glitches shorter than the inertial delay of a signal assignment do not appear on the output of the signal, while glitches of any size are delayed simply by the transport delay of a signal assignment. The difference in the

```
ARCHITECTURE sequential OF saving_all IS
  SIGNAL x : tit := 'Z';
BEGIN
  PROCESS
  BEGIN
    x <= '0' AFTER 5 NS;
    x <= '0' AFTER 8 NS;
    WAIT;
  END PROCESS;
END sequential;
```

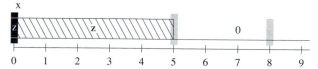

FIGURE 3.35
Saving previous transactions of same value. Transactions with the same value are both kept on the driver of *x*.

```
ARCHITECTURE sequential OF discarding_old IS
   SIGNAL x : tit := 'Z';
BEGIN
   PROCESS
   BEGIN
      x <= TRANSPORT '1' AFTER 5 NS;
      x <= TRANSPORT '0' AFTER 3 NS;
      WAIT;
   END PROCESS;
END sequential;
```

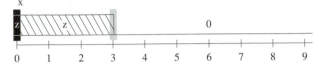

FIGURE 3.36
Discarding previous transactions. The new transaction is scheduled *before* the existing one.

```
ARCHITECTURE sequential OF saving_all IS
   SIGNAL x : tit := 'Z';
BEGIN
   PROCESS
   BEGIN
      x <= TRANSPORT '1' AFTER 5 NS;
      x <= TRANSPORT '0' AFTER 8 NS;
      WAIT;
   END PROCESS;
END sequential;
```

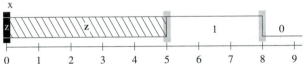

FIGURE 3.37
Appending transactions. Delay type is transport, and the new transaction is *after* the existing one.

way glitches are handled by inertial and transport delays can be explained by the sequential placement of transactions on the driver of a signal. Consider, for example, the assignment of signal a_glitch to i_target and t_target signals in Figure 3.38.

Signals a_glitch, i_target, and t_target are initially zero. At time 10 NS, a_glitch changes from '0' to '1', which causes the placement of a ('1',5NS) transaction on i_target, and an equivalent transaction on the driver of the t_target signal. Two nanoseconds later, at 12 ns, the time element of these transactions is reduced by 2 ns, and the transactions become ('1',3NS). Also at time 12 ns, another event occurs on a_glitch which changes its value from '1' to '0'. This event causes placement of new ('0',5NS) transactions on the drivers of the two target signals. On the i_target, because of the inertial delay, the already existing ('1',3NS) transaction is overwritten by the new ('0',5NS) transaction as shown in the lower right box in Figure 3.31. This transaction becomes current five nanoseconds later, and appears just as a transaction on i_target. On the other hand, because of the transport delay of the t_target, at time 12 the already existing ('1',3NS) transaction on this signal is appended by the new ('0',5NS) transaction (see the middle box in the last row of Figure 3.31). Three nanoseconds later, at 15 ns, the first transaction becomes current causing a

```
 ┌─ARCHITECTURE glitch OF inertial_transport_demo IS
 │    SIGNAL i_target, t_target, a_glitch : BIT := '0';
 ├─BEGIN
 │    a_glitch <= '1' AFTER 10 NS, '0' AFTER 12 NS;
 │    i_target <= a_glitch AFTER 5 NS;
 │    t_target <= TRANSPORT a_glitch AFTER 5 NS;
 └─END glitch;
```

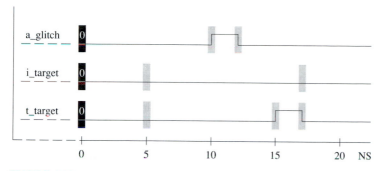

FIGURE 3.38
Glitches in inertial and transport delays.

'0' to '1' event on *t_target*. The other transaction on the driver of this signal becomes current at 17 ns which causes it to return to '0' at this time. The overall effect is that the 2 ns glitch on *a_glitch* appears just as a single transaction on *i_target*, but it fully appears on the *t_target* after the specified delay.

The two nanosecond pulse on the *a_glitch* signal can also be explained in terms of the sequential placement of transactions on the driver of the signal. The assignment to this signal in Figure 3.38 consists of two waveform elements, '1' after 10 ns and '0' after 12 ns. In an inertial assignment, the very first waveform element causes an inertial assignment, and all subsequent elements are treated as transport. In a transport assignment, all waveform elements are placed on the driver of a signal with transport delay. Because inertial delay is used in the assignment of values to *a_glitch*, this statement appears as a sequential assignment with inertial delay followed by a second sequential assignment with transport delay. The first assignment causes the (1,10NS) transaction to be placed on the driver of *a_glitch*, and the second assignment, being transport, appends the (0,12NS) transaction to the driver of this signal.

3.3   CONVENTIONS AND SYNTAX

In all the VHDL code in this book, we use vertical lines on the left hand side of the code to illustrate nesting levels. Indentation is also used, but the vertical bars make it easier to follow the beginning and end of a section of the code. In all VHDL code, we use uppercase letters for VHDL keywords, predefined entities, and standards. All other code, including names and labels, is in lowercase. When a VHDL keyword or predefined name is used in the text, it is also in uppercase. All other parts of code used in the text are in *italics*.

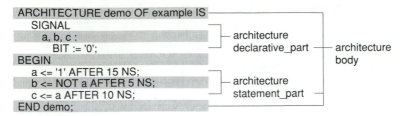

FIGURE 3.39
Syntax details of the architecture body of the *demo* architecture of *example* entity.

The syntax of VHDL is shown in illustrations such as Figure 3.39. This format is extracted from a VHDL program, with individual elements isolated to make labeling easy. These "syntax details" are only for the example code that is being discussed when the illustration is presented, and do not necessarily present the general syntax of the language. However, they are designed to cover as much of the general case as possible. For example, Figure 3.39 indicates that the main parts of an architecture body are the declarative part and the statement part but it obviously does not show all the variations of these language constructs. Where variations are important, we highlight them by showing syntax details in other examples. Appendix E shows the complete syntax of VHDL, from which all the "syntax details" illustrations of this book are drawn.

As stated earlier, VHDL is not case sensitive and has a is free format. In VHDL, long statements can continue over several lines. For comments, a pair of dashes (– –) is used. This pair, anywhere in a line, makes the rest of the line a comment. VHDL keywords are reserved words, and cannot be used for identifiers or as any other name. The complex syntax of the language can be overcome by developing templates of VHDL code for various applications.

3.4 SUMMARY

The first part of this chapter introduced the concept of design entity, and showed examples of VHDL descriptions at the three levels of abstractions that were introduced in Chapter 1. This introductory part is intended to provide the reader with a sample of the VDHL constructs and the general organization of the language. The second part of the chapter presented important issues regarding signals, delay types, transactions, delta delay, and other timing issues. We described signal assignments in concurrent and sequential bodies of VHDL, and showed how transactions appear on a signal in these bodies. An understanding of the timing issues presented in the second part of this chapter is essential to understanding VHDL.

REFERENCES

1. "IEEE Standard VHDL Language Reference Manual," IEEE Std. 1076-1987, The Institute of Electrical and Electronic Engineers, Inc., 1988.

2. Lipsett, L., C. Schaefer, and C. Ussery, "VHDL: Hardware Description and Design," Klewer Academic Publishing, Boston, 1988.

PROBLEMS

3.1. Write a dataflow description for an Exclusive OR gate.

3.2. Write a dataflow description for a Full Adder.

3.3. Wire four Full Adders to build a Nibble Adder.

3.4. Modify the Description of the Sequence Detector to detect the 101 sequence. Your circuit should detect overlapping sequences.

3.5. Write a behavioral description for a clock generator generating two nonoverlapping clock phases.

3.6. Write a procedure for converting integers between 0 and 255 to a byte.

3.7. List all the transactions in the following description:

```
ARCHITECTURE concurrent OF timing_demo IS
   SIGNAL   a, b, c : BIT := '0';
BEGIN
   b <= NOT a;
   c <= NOT b;
END concurrent;
```

3.8. List all the transactions in the following description:

```
ARCHITECTURE concurrent OF timing_demo IS
   SIGNAL   a, b, c : BIT := '0';
BEGIN
   a <= '1' AFTER 2 NS;
   b <= NOT a AFTER 3 NS;
   c <= NOT b AFTER 4 NS;
END concurrent;
```

3.9. List all the transactions in the following description:

```
ARCHITECTURE sequential OF timing_demo IS
   SIGNAL   a, b, c : BIT := '0';
BEGIN
   PROCESS
   BEGIN
      a <= '1';
      b <= NOT a;
      c <= NOT b;
   WAIT;
   END PROCESS;
END sequential;
```

3.10. Show the waveform on x:

```
ARCHITECTURE  sequential    OF  saving_all  IS
    SIGNAL   x : tit := 'Z';
BEGIN
    PROCESS
    BEGIN
        x <=   TRANSPORT  '1'  AFTER  5  NS;
        x <=   TRANSPORT  '0'  AFTER  8  NS;
        x <=   TRANSPORT  '1'  AFTER  6  NS;
        WAIT;
    END PROCESS;
END sequential;
```

3.11. Show the waveform on x:

```
ARCHITECTURE  sequential    OF  saving_all  IS
    SIGNAL   x : tit := 'Z';
BEGIN
    PROCESS
    BEGIN
        x <=  TRANSPORT  '0'  AFTER  5  NS;
        x <=  '0'  AFTER  3  NS;
        x <=  '1'  AFTER  11  NS;
        WAIT;
    END PROCESS;
END sequential;
```

3.12. For the architecture description shown below, show the list of all transactions on the signals. Include all initial transactions, final transactions, and those that are discarded. Each transaction should be specified as a parenthesized list of value and time (v,t). Show the resulting waveforms on all the signals. The WAIT UNTIL statement suspends the process until the condition becomes true. See Fig. P3.12.

3.13. Explain the glitch on signal x in Figure 3.28. *Hint*: the initial value of all signals are zero.

3.14. Explain the transactions on the w and y signals in Figure 3.28 at time 1δ.

3.15. The VHDL code shown below places a two nanosecond positive pulse on a. Assume that *toggle_when_transaction* returns the complemented value of its first argument when a transaction occurs on its second argument; otherwise, it returns the value of its first argument. Likewise, the *toggle_when_event* function returns the complemented value of its first argument when an event occurs on its second argument; otherwise, it returns the value of its first argument. Considering the assignments in this VHDL code, show all the transactions and events that occur on the t and e signals in a timing diagram. See Fig. P3.15.

3.16. Describe transactions on i_target and t_target signals in Figure 3.38, if the width of the glitch on a_glitch is seven nanoseconds.

3.17. We can use a signal assignment with inertial delay to remove pulses that are smaller than a certain width. Using only signal assignments, write a code fragment for removing positive pulses that are greater than a certain width.

```
┌ARCHITECTURE examining OF problem IS
│   TYPE qit IS ('Z', '1', '0', 'X');
│   SIGNAL w : qit := '0';
│   SIGNAL x : qit;
│   SIGNAL y : qit := 'Z';
│   SIGNAL z : qit := '1';
│   SIGNAL a, b : BIT;
├BEGIN
│   a <= '0', '1' AFTER 20 NS;
│   b <= '0', '1' AFTER 40 NS;
│  ┌p1: PROCESS
│  ├BEGIN
│  │   w <= '1' AFTER 8 NS;
│  │   w <= '1' AFTER 10 NS;
│  │   WAIT UNTIL a = '1';
│  │   w <= '0';
│  │   y <= TRANSPORT '1' AFTER 5 NS;
│  │   WAIT UNTIL b = '1';
│  │   w <= '1' AFTER 10 NS;
│  │   w <= '0' AFTER 13 NS;
│  │   w <= 'Z' AFTER 08 NS;
│  │   x <= '1';
│  │   y <= TRANSPORT '0' AFTER 12 NS;
│  │   y <= TRANSPORT 'Z' AFTER 15 NS;
│  │   WAIT;
│  └END PROCESS p1;
│   z <= x;
└END examining;
```

FIGURE P3.12

```
┌ARCHITECTURE challenging   OF transaction_vs_event IS
│   SIGNAL  a : BIT := '1';
│   SIGNAL  t, e : BIT := '0';
├BEGIN
│   a <= '0', '1' AFTER 10 NS, '0' AFTER 12 NS, '0' AFTER 14 NS;
│   t <= toggle_when_transaction (t, a);
│   e <= toggle_when_event (e, a);
└END challenging;
```

FIGURE P3.15

3.18. Using a single signal assignment, and using signal y as the source, generate signal x such that this new signal is a copy of y, except if there are pulses on y that are greater than width w. Pulses longer than w are trimmed when they appear on x.

CHAPTER
4

STRUCTURAL SPECIFICATION OF HARDWARE

To describe a system at the structural level, the components of that system are listed and the interconnections between them are specified. Because this level of abstraction closely corresponds to the actual hardware, it is easiest for hardware designers to understand and use. Software oriented readers, on the other hand, should pay attention to concurrency features in the language that is introduced in this chapter.

VHDL provides language constructs for concurrent instantiation of components, the primary constructs for structural specification of hardware. Other language constructs that support this level of abstraction include those for 1) the selection of a component from a certain package or parts library, 2) binding or associating the usage of a component to an available library, 3) wiring mechanisms, and 4) constructs for specification of repetitive hardware. This chapter describes all the constructs that are needed for the structural specification of digital systems.

The first part of this chapter presents a hierarchical description of a circuit and describes it in VHDL. This example illustrates the main language constructs for structural descriptions. A test bench in this part demonstrates a simple method for testing circuits. The second part of the chapter illustrates more advanced features of the language that can be used to associate components of a structural description with existing designs. An example in this part illustrates alternatives to using such language constructs.

Throughout the chapter, a set of notations and vocabulary is introduced for presenting and referencing VHDL descriptions. The vocabulary is consistent with that

56

used in the IEEE VHDL 1076 Language Reference Manual (LRM). The development and enhancement of these notations continues throughout the book as new language constructs are introduced.

4.1   PARTS LIBRARY

This section presents VHDL descriptions for an inverter, a two-input NAND gate, and a three-input NAND gate. These primitive gates are used to form larger circuits in the later parts of this chapter and are regarded as off-the-shelf components or predefined cells of a library. The gate models are kept simple and use only VHDL simple signal assignments for the description of their operations.

4.1.1   Inverter Model

Figure 4.1 shows the logical symbol for an inverter, the VHDL description, and a graphical representation. The entity declaration of the inverter, shown in Figure 4.1b and further detailed in Figure 4.2, describes the inverter interface.

Figure 4.2 indicates that a port clause is bracketed between the beginning and end indications of an entity declaration. The port clause gives the declaration of all input and output ports of the entity. Two interface signal declarations are used to declare the *i1* input and the *o1* output ports of the inverter. The type of *i1* port is BIT and its mode is IN. The *o1* port is also of type BIT and its mode is OUT. The IN and OUT modes for *i1* and *o1* specify that these signals are the input and the output of the inverter. Ports can also have an INOUT mode which is mainly used for bidirectional lines. Type BIT is a predefined VHDL type. In addition to standard types, user defined types are also allowed. Type definition and usage are discussed in

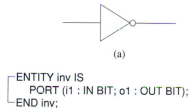

(a)

```
ENTITY inv IS
    PORT (i1 : IN BIT; o1 : OUT BIT);
END inv;
```
(b)

```
ARCHITECTURE single_delay OF inv IS
BEGIN
    o1 <= NOT i1 AFTER 4 NS;
END single_delay;
```
(c)

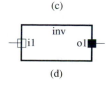

(d)

FIGURE 4.1
Inverter (a) symbol, (b) entity declaration, (c) architecture body, (d) notation.

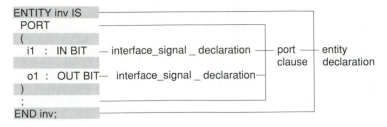

FIGURE 4.2
Details of the entity declaration of inverter.

Chapter 6. However, only predefined types are used in the design examples presented in this chapter and in Chapter 5.

Figure 4.1c shows the architecture body of *inv*, identified as *single_delay*. This architecture describes the internal operation of the inverter. A single signal assignment bracketed between the BEGIN and END keywords constitutes what is referred to as the statement part of the *single_delay* architecture of *inv*. This statement sets the complement of *i1* input to *o1* output, with a 4 nanosecond delay. The <= symbol specifies the direction of assignment. When an event occurs on *i1* (i.e., *i1* changes value), the complement of the new value of *i1* is scheduled for the *o1* signal 4 ns later. TIME is a predefined type in VHDL and its units range from femtoseconds to hours. Other time units can also be defined.

Figure 4.1d shows a graphical representation for the interface description of the inverter. This symbol corresponds to the inverter entity declaration and is referred to as its *interface aspect*. A rectangular box represents the interface aspect of a hardware unit and includes its input/output ports as well as the entity name of its VHDL description. Input ports are shown by hollow boxes and output ports by black boxes. A half-filled box signifies the bidirectional port. The entity name is shown inside the rectangular box. Figure 4.3 shows the elements of aspect notation that we have introduced thus far.

Later in this chapter, *composition aspect*, which corresponds to an interconnection specification of smaller hardware units in order to form larger ones, will be presented. Presentation of aspect notation will be completed in Chapter 5. This notation provides a graphical correspondence to VHDL descriptions and is not part of the LRM.

4.1.2   NAND Gate Models

Logical symbols, entity declarations, architecture bodies, and interface aspects for a two-input and a three-input NAND gate are shown in Figures 4.4 and 4.6, respectively.

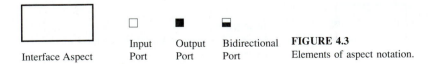

Interface Aspect

Input Port   Output Port   Bidirectional Port

FIGURE 4.3
Elements of aspect notation.

(a)

```
ENTITY nand2 IS
    PORT (i1, i2 : IN BIT; o1 : OUT BIT);
END nand2;
```

(b)

```
ARCHITECTURE single_delay OF nand2 IS
BEGIN
    o1 <= i1 NAND i2 AFTER 5 NS;
END single_delay;
```

(c)

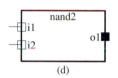

(d)

FIGURE 4.4
Two-input NAND (a) symbol, (b) entity declaration,
(c) architecture body, (d) notation.

As in the case of the inverter, the entity declaration of *nand2* has two interface signal declarations. The first interface declaration includes two signals, namely *i1* and *i2*. Since the type and mode of these two port signals are the same, they may be declared together by a single interface signal declaration so that mode and type need to be specified only once. Figure 4.5 shows the details of the *nand2* port clause. It indicates that *i1* and *i2* constitute an identifier list which, together with mode and type, form one of the interface signal declarations of the port clause of the two-input NAND gate. Declaration of all the interface signals forms the port interface list.

For the three-input NAND description in Figure 4.6b, the statement part consists of a single statement that assigns the NAND result of the *i1*, *i2* and *i3* signals to the output *o1* signal. An event on any of these input signals causes evaluation of the right hand side expression, and the new value will be assigned to *o1* after a delay of six nanoseconds. The part of the right hand side of a signal assignment, where values to be assigned to the left hand side target are specified, is referred to as the *waveform* in the VHDL syntax.

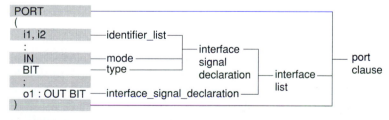

FIGURE 4.5
Port clause details for *nand2*.

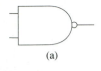

(a)

```
ENTITY nand3 IS
    PORT (i1, i2, i3 : IN BIT; o1 : OUT BIT);
END nand3;
```
(b)

```
ARCHITECTURE single_delay OF nand3 IS
BEGIN
    o1 <= NOT (i1 AND i2 AND i3) AFTER 6 NS;
END single_delay;
```
(c)

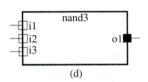

(d)

FIGURE 4.6
Three-input NAND (a) symbol, (b) entity
declaration, (c) architecture body, (d) notation.

The primitive gates described in this section provide a sufficient set of parts for the description of larger components. Because of the few language tools that have been discussed and are available to us at this point in the book, the models that have been presented were limited in their capability to model timing and other physical characteristics of actual gates. More accurate gate models with better handling of timing and loading characteristics are developed in later chapters.

4.2 WIRING OF PRIMITIVES

Wiring of the primitive gates for generation of larger designs is demonstrated in this section. In VHDL, the operation of a design entity can be described in terms of its subcomponents. To completely specify this operation, we must indicate the component interconnections and link them to a set of available library cells. The main language constructs that support this style of hardware description are signal declarations, component declarations, configuration specifications, and component instantiations. These constructs are discussed here. For this purpose, a single bit comparator is designed and described in terms of the inverter and the NAND gates of the previous section.

4.2.1 Logic Design of Comparator

A single bit comparator circuit (*bit_comparator*) has two data inputs, three control inputs, and three compare outputs. The logical symbol for this circuit is shown in Figure 4.7. The three control inputs provide a mechanism for generation of multi-bit comparators by cascading several *bit_comparators*.

The *A>B* output is 1 if the *A* input is greater than the *B* input (*AB* is 10) or if *A* is equal to *B* and the > input is 1. The *A=B* output is 1 if *A* is equal to *B* and the

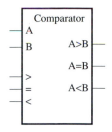

FIGURE 4.7
Logical symbol of a single bit comparator.

= input is 1. The $A<B$ output is the opposite of the $A>B$ output. This line becomes 1 if A input is less than B output (AB is 01) or if A is equal to B and the $<$ input is 1. Based on this functional description of the *bit_comparator*, Karnaugh maps for its three outputs are extracted as shown in Figure 4.8.

Boolean expressions for the three outputs of the *bit_comparator* resulting from applying minimization methods to the Karnaugh maps in Figure 4.8 are shown below. To avoid confusion, these expressions use *gt*, *eq* and *lt* instead of the $>$, $=$, and $<$ symbols used in the logical symbol in Figure 4.7. Other notational changes have been made for readability purposes.

Equation 4.1a   a_gt_b = a . gt + b'. gt + a . b'

Equation 4.1b   a_eq_b = a . b . eq + a'. b'. eq

Equation 4.1c   a_lt_b = a'. lt + b . lt + a'. b

Using DeMorgan's theorem, equations 4.1a to 4.1c can be transformed into equations 4.2a to 4.2c respectively. These equations have an appropriate form for all NAND and inverter implementations, which is of course what is available in our library of parts. The gate-level circuit diagram of the *bit_comparator*, resulting from these equations, is shown in Figure 4.9.

Equation 4.2a   a_gt_b = ((a . gt)'. (b'. gt)'. (a . b')')'

Equation 4.2b   a_eq_b = ((a . b . eq)'. (a'. b'. eq)')'

Equation 4.2c   a_lt_b = ((a'. lt)'. (b . lt)'. (a'. b)')'

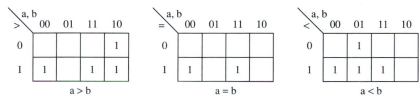

FIGURE 4.8
Karnaugh maps for the outputs of the single bit comparator.

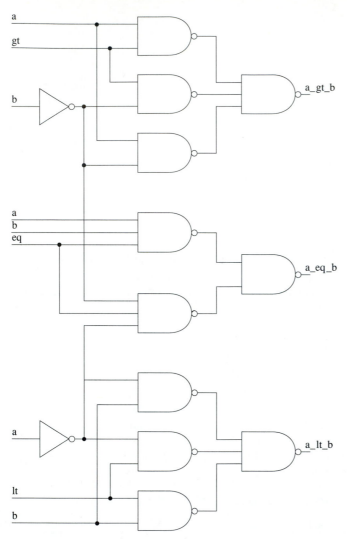

FIGURE 4.9
Logical diagram of *bit_comparator*.

4.2.2   VHDL Description of *bit_comparator*

At this point, we have completed the design of the single bit comparator and its definition in terms of our available primitive gates. Next, the VHDL description of this unit consisting of an interface and an architectural description will be developed.

The interface description of the *bit_comparator* corresponds to its logical symbol as shown in Figure 4.7. For this circuit, the interface aspect and its VHDL entity declaration (which is based on this aspect) are shown in Figure 4.10. Notations depicted in Figure 4.3 are used in the interface aspect of the *bit_comparator*. The entity

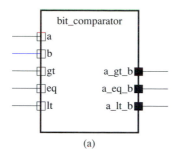

(a)

```
ENTITY bit_comparator IS
    PORT (a, b,                    -- data inputs
    gt,                            -- previous greater than
    eq,                            -- previous equal
    lt : IN BIT;                   -- previous less than
    a_gt_b,                        -- greater
    a_eq_b,                        -- equal
    a_lt_b : OUT BIT);             -- less than
END bit_comparator;
```

(b)

FIGURE 4.10
Interface description of *bit_comparator*, (a) interface aspect, (b) entity declaration.

declaration follows the same syntax used for the interface descriptions in Section 4.1 of this chapter. The two identifier lists in the port clause of this entity declaration contain five input ports and three output ports.

At the structural level the operation of the *bit_comparator* can be described in terms of its subcomponents and according to the gate level implementation in Figure 4.9. The description of this operation will be contained in a VHDL architecture body. The composition aspect of the *bit_comparator*, which corresponds to this body, is shown in Figure 4.11. This has been achieved by replacing the gates in Figure 4.9 with their interface aspects, as presented in Section 4.1. It consists of a graphical representation of interconnection specifications for the interface aspects of all its subcomponents. Names of input and output ports for components that constitute the *bit_comparator* are shown in their respective interface aspects. These names are local to the units they are used in and must not be confused with the same names used in other interface aspects. For example, several components in Figure 4.11 use *i2* for their port name, but *i2* is a different signal in each component. Signals immediately contained in the composition aspect of the *bit_comparator* are also unique. These signals are named either by the port names of the *bit_comparator*, such as *a*, *b*, *eq*, etc., or they are given arbitrary, but meaningful, names. Naming intermediate signals is necessary for the identification of each interconnection segment. Their names will be used in the VHDL description of the *bit_comparator*.

The architecture body that corresponds to the composition aspect in Figure 4.11 is shown in Figure 4.12. This body is the structural level description of the operation of the *bit_comparator* whose entity declaration is shown in Figure 4.10b. The first

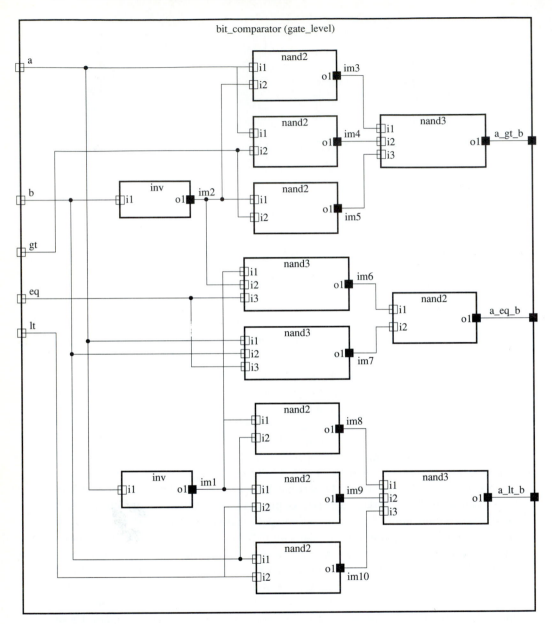

FIGURE 4.11
Composition Aspect of *bit_comparator*.

line of this VHDL description identifies the description as *gate_level* architecture for
the *bit_comparator* entity. The rest of the description, which consists of a declarative
part and a statement part, specifies the components and the way they are used in this
architecture.

```
ARCHITECTURE gate_level OF bit_comparator IS
   COMPONENT n1 PORT (i1: IN BIT; o1: OUT BIT); END COMPONENT;
   COMPONENT n2 PORT (i1, i2: IN BIT; o1: OUT BIT); END COMPONENT;
   COMPONENT n3 PORT (i1, i2, i3: IN BIT; o1: OUT BIT);
   END COMPONENT;
   FOR ALL : n1 USE ENTITY WORK.inv (single_delay);
   FOR ALL : n2 USE ENTITY WORK.nand2 (single_delay);
   FOR ALL : n3 USE ENTITY WORK.nand3 (single_delay);
   -- Intermediate signals
   SIGNAL im1,im2, im3, im4, im5, im6, im7, im8, im9, im10 : BIT;
BEGIN
   -- a_gt_b output
   g0 : n1 PORT MAP (a, im1);
   g1 : n1 PORT MAP (b, im2);
   g2 : n2 PORT MAP (a, im2, im3);
   g3 : n2 PORT MAP (a, gt, im4);
   g4 : n2 PORT MAP (im2, gt, im5);
   g5 : n3 PORT MAP (im3, im4, im5, a_gt_b);
   -- a_eq_b output
   g6 : n3 PORT MAP (im1, im2, eq, im6);
   g7 : n3 PORT MAP (a, b, eq, im7);
   g8 : n2 PORT MAP (im6, im7, a_eq_b);
   -- a_lt_b output
   g9 : n2 PORT MAP (im1, b, im8);
   g10 : n2 PORT MAP (im1, lt, im9);
   g11 : n2 PORT MAP (b, lt, im10);
   g12 : n3 PORT MAP (im8, im9, im10, a_lt_b);
END gate_level;
```

FIGURE 4.12
Architecture body of *bit_comparator* identified as *gate_level*.

Figure 4.13 shows the syntax details of the architecture body in Figure 4.12. Subcomponents in the *gate_level* description of the *bit_comparator* are *inv*, *nand2*, and *nand3*. The declarative part includes a component declaration and a configuration specification for each of these components. Component declarations define the interface to the component in an instantiation statement in the statement part of an architecture, and configuration specifications associate such an instance with an existing entity. For example, in the case of the *n3* component, a component declaration defines the ports of instantiations of *n3* (referred to as local ports) to be the same as those of the *nand3* entity, that is, (i1, i2, i3 : IN BIT; o1 : OUT BIT). The configuration of *n3* specifies that for all instantiations of this component (ALL : *n3*) the *single_delay* architecture of the *nand3* entity which exists in the WORK library should be used. In the configuration specification following the keyword FOR, the keyword ALL specifies that the association with the specified existing entity applies to *all* instances of that component. If different bindings are to be used for different instances of a component, the list of labels that binding applies to must be used instead of this keyword.

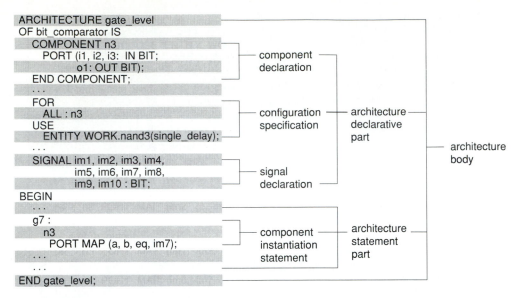

FIGURE 4.13
Syntax details of the architecture body of *bit_comparator*

Alternatives in the use of component declarations and configuration specifications are discussed later in this chapter. The word WORK in the configuration specification specifies the library where the *single_delay* architecture of the *nand3* entity resides. This is the default library and it refers to the current *work*ing library. Definition of new libraries are discussed in the section on design organization in Chapter 5. The default library is used in all the examples in this chapter.

In addition to the above constructs for defining components, the description in Figure 4.12 and the partial description in Figure 4.13 also include a signal declaration declaring several signals of type BIT. The keyword SIGNAL begins the declaration and is followed by a list of identifiers. BIT, the type indication for the signals, ends the declaration. Signals declared here are used as intermediate signals in the statement part of the *gate_level* architecture of *bit_comparator*, and are the same as those used in the composition aspect of the *bit_comparator*. Figure 4.13 indicates that the signal declarations are part of the architecture declarative part.

The architecture statement part describes what is shown graphically in the composition aspect of Figure 4.11. It consists of several instantiations of components that are declared and configured in the architecture declarative part. The wiring between these components is specified here. All component instantiations are concurrent and the order in which they appear is not important. An analogy exists between this ordering and the place of interface aspects of subcomponents of the *bit_comparator* within its composition aspect. It is clear that the operation of the *bit_comparator* does not depend on where interface aspects of its components are placed, it only depends on how they are interconnected.

Component instantiation statements include a label, component name, and association between the actual signals that are visible in the architecture body of the *bit_comparator* and the ports of the component being instantiated. Syntax details of the instantiation statement shown in Figure 4.13 are given in Figure 4.14. For this statement, *g7* is a label for instantiation of *n3* which is bound to the *nand3* entity. The mapping of ports specifies that the first three ports of this component are connected to the *a*, *b*, and *eq* inputs of the *bit_comparator*. These signal names are the primary ports of the *bit_comparator* entity and therefore are visible within its *gate_level* architecture body. The last port of *nand3*, which is its output, is connected to the *im7* intermediate signal. The next instantiation statement in the statement part of the architecture body of the *bit_comparator* (Figure 4.12) uses *im7* for the second input of a *nand2* component.

The last statement in Figure 4.12 ends the *gate_level* structural description of the single bit comparator. After a successful analysis of the gate_level architecture of the *bit_comparator* and all its subcomponents by a VHDL simulation system, this design entity becomes available in a design library and can be used in other designs. Designs that can use this unit include a test bench for it or a multi-bit comparator. The next section illustrates the latter.

4.3 WIRING ITERATIVE NETWORKS

In addition to language constructs for declaration, configuration, and instantiation of components, VHDL includes higher level constructs that can be used for definition of repetitive hardware at the structural level. Such constructs are discussed in this section. The example used is a 4-bit comparator and is referred to as a *nibble_comparator*. This circuit uses the *bit_comparator* circuit.

4.3.1 Design of a 4-Bit Comparator

A 4-bit comparator with two 4-bit data inputs, three control inputs, and three compare outputs is shown in Figure 4.15. The functionality of this circuit is similar to that of the *bit_comparator*. For the *nibble_comparator*, the discussion in Section 4.2.1 applies to 4-bit positive numbers instead of single bits of data. The *A>B* output is 1 when data on the *A* input, treated as a 4-bit positive number, is greater than the 4-bit positive number on *B*, or when data on *A* and *B* are equal and the > input is

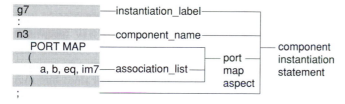

FIGURE 4.14
Component instantiation statement syntax details.

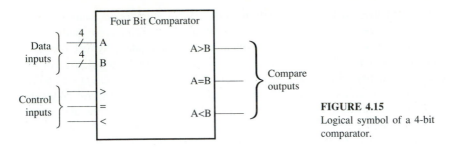

FIGURE 4.15
Logical symbol of a 4-bit comparator.

1. This arrangement makes it possible to wire together several *bit_comparator*s, or *nibble_comparator*s, or both for building comparators of any size.

The *nibble_comparator* can easily be built by cascading four *bit_comparator*s as shown in Figure 4.16. In this circuit, compare outputs of each of the *bit_comparator*s, for example, *A>B*, *A=B*, and *A<B* of Bit 1, are connected to similarly named control inputs of a more significant bit, for example, >, =, and < of Bit 2. The control inputs of the least significant bit, that is, >, =, and < of Bit 0, are considered as the control inputs of the *nibble_comparator*, and the compare outputs of the most significant bit, that is, *A>B*, *A=B*, and *A<B* of Bit 3, are the compare outputs of the 4-bit comparator circuit. When comparing two positive numbers with this arrangement, more significant comparator bits generate appropriate outputs if they can be determined by their corresponding data bits. A comparator bit only uses the outputs of a less significant bit if its own data bits are equal. With this scheme, the compare outputs of the *nibble_comparator* are generated faster by not having to depend on all *bit_comparator*s if the result can be determined by a few most significant bits. For example, when

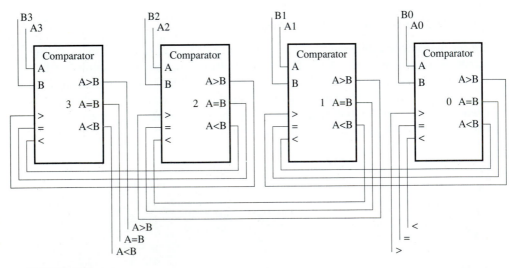

FIGURE 4.16
A 4-bit comparator using four single bit comparators.

comparing 0100 and 0011, the result is determined by bits 2 and 3 and there is no need for propagation of data through all four *bit_comparator*s.

4.3.2   VHDL Description of a 4-Bit Comparator

The interface aspect of the *nibble_comparator* and its entity declaration in accordance to this aspect are shown in Figures 4.17a and 4.17b respectively. The input and output ports of the interface aspect are the same as those of the logical symbol in Figure 4.15, which has a different naming convention. The entity declaration uses *nibble_comparator* as the entity name. The port clause of this declaration has three interface declarations for declaring data inputs, control inputs, and compare outputs. The *a* and *b* data inputs are 4-bit arrays of bits, and for their declaration the BIT_VECTOR type has been used. As with type BIT, BIT_VECTOR is a predefined type in VHDL and is available in the default standard package. Definition and usage of new packages and types are discussed in the section on design organization in Chapter 5.

The composition aspect of the *nibble_comparator*, shown in Figure 4.18, is derived from the schematic diagram in Figure 4.16. All signals in this aspect of the 4-bit comparator have names assigned to them. For those signals that are not primary ports of the *nibble_comparator*, intermediate names, *im(0)* through *im(8)*, are used. This figure indicates that four copies of the *gate_level* architecture of *bit_comparator*, shown in figure 4.12, are used for structural level implementation of the *nibble_comparator*.

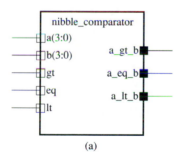

(a)

```
ENTITY nibble_comparator IS
    PORT (a, b, : IN BIT_VECTOR (3 DOWNTO );    -- a and b data
          gt,                                    -- previous greater than
          eq,                                    -- previous equal
          lt : IN BIT;                           -- previous less than
          a_gt_b,                                -- a > b
          a_eq_b,                                -- a = b
          a_lt_b : OUT BIT);                     -- a < b
END nibble_comparator;
```

(b)

FIGURE 4.17
Interface description of *nibble_comparator*, (a) interface aspect, (b) entity declaration.

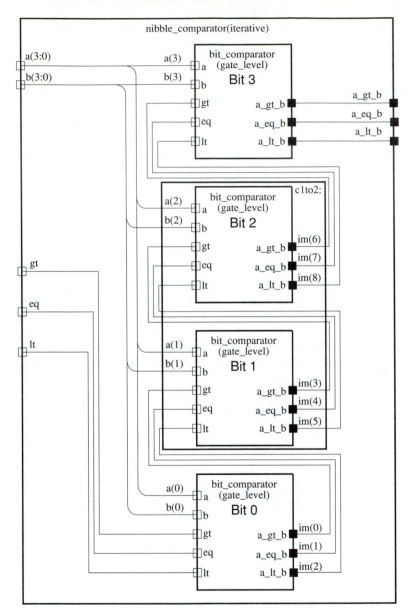

FIGURE 4.18
Composition aspect of *nibble_comparator*.

The VHDL description for the operation of this circuit directly corresponds to its composition aspect and is shown in Figure 4.19.

The name chosen for identifying this architecture is *iterative* and the reason for this selection will become evident shortly. In the declarative part, *comp1* is declared

```
┌ARCHITECTURE  iterative  OF  nibble_comparator  IS
│    COMPONENT  comp1
│        PORT  (a,  b,  gt,  eq,  lt  :  IN  BIT;  a_gt_b,  a_eq_b,  a_lt_b  :  OUT  BIT);
│    END  COMPONENT;
│    FOR  ALL  :  comp1  USE  ENTITY  WORK.bit_comparator  (gate_level);
│    SIGNAL  im  :  BIT_VECTOR  (  0  TO  8);
├BEGIN
│    c0:  comp1  PORT  MAP  (a(0),  b(0),  gt,  eq,  lt,  im(0),  im(1),  im(2));
│    c1to2:  FOR  i  IN  1  TO  2  GENERATE
│        c:  comp1  PORT  MAP  (a(i),  b(i),  im(i*3-3),  im(i*3-2),  im(i*3-1),
│                      im(i*3+0),  im(i*3+1),  im(i*3+2)  );
│    END  GENERATE;
│    c3:  comp1
│    PORT  MAP  (a(3),  b(3),  im(6),  im(7),  im(8),  a_gt_b,  a_eq_b,  a_lt_b);
└END  iterative;
```

FIGURE 4.19
Iterative architecture of *nibble_comparator.*

as a component with a port clause that is the same as that of the *bit_comparator* entity. Also in this part, by using a configuration specification, it is further specified that all instantiations of the *comp1* component are to be bound to the *gate_level* architecture of *bit_comparator*. In the statement part, four individual instances of *comp1* would complete the description of the *nibble_comparator*. In order to illustrate the use of higher level VHDL constructs, however, we have used two instances of *comp1* for the first and the last bits of the comparator, and the rest of the bits are instantiated in an iterative fashion, taking advantage of the VHDL generate statement.

In Figure 4.19, an instance of *comp1* that is labeled *c0* specifies wiring of a *bit_comparator* according to Bit 0 in Figure 4.18. Within the body of the *nibble_comparator*, the outputs of this bit are named *im(0)*, *im(1)*, and *im(2)*. Following the statement labeled *c0*, a generate statement labeled *c1to2* is used for wiring two *bit_comparators* for bits 1 and 2 of the 4-bit comparator. This statement uses a FOR loop with index *i* changing from 1 to 2. In the first iteration through the loop, the value of *i* is 1. Replacing *i* with this value in the port map of *comp1* results in the association list shown in Figure 4.20 for this instance of *comp1*. Therefore, it can be seen that the control inputs of the first instance of *comp1* generated by the generate statement are connected to *im(0)*, *im(1)*, and *im(2)* which are the output signals of the *c0* instance of *comp1*. The next and the final iteration through the FOR loop wires another *bit_comparator* according to Bit 2 of Figure 4.18. In Figure 4.19, the last instance of *comp1* is labeled *c3* and produces compare outputs of the most significant comparator bit. The outputs are named *a_gt_b*, *a_eq_b* and *a_lt_b* which are the same as the primary outputs of the *nibble_comparator*. This implies that the outputs of the last *bit_comparator* (Bit 3 in Figure 4.19) are directly connected to the outputs of the *nibble_comparator*.

If it were only for a 4-bit comparator, in which the first and last bits need to be treated individually, the use of generate statement would not be justified. For

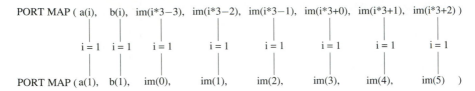

FIGURE 4.20
Association list of *c* instance of *comp1* within generate statement.

description of larger comparators, however, this method can substantially reduce the number of lines of code. Also, due to the use of generate statement, the description in Figure 4.19 can easily be changed to a description for any size comparator.

The syntax details of the generate statement in Figure 4.19 are shown in Figure 4.21. The statement begins with a label and, using a FOR loop for the generation scheme, it generates two instances of *comp1*. The *c1to2* label can optionally be placed at the end of the generate statement after the END GENERATE. A generate statement is considered to be like any other statement in the architecture statement part. It is a concurrent statement and several generate statements can be nested. Another form of the generate statement uses IF followed by a condition for the generation scheme instead of the FOR loop. Taking advantage of this form and using nested generate statements, a more flexible version of the architecture body of the *nibble_comparator* is developed and shown in Figure 4.22.

In the declarative part of this new description, a constant declaration is used for declaring the constant *n* as a predefined INTEGER type with a value of 4. This constant is used for declaring the size of *im* and for the range specification of the FOR loop generation scheme. The architecture body of Figure 4.22 can be used to describe the operation of any size comparator by declaring an appropriate value for constant *n*. VHDL also provides language constructs that allow declarations to be made based on the size of input vectors. To avoid presenting too many language issues at the same time, we have chosen not to take advantage of such constructs in this example. Such issues are addressed in Chapter 6.

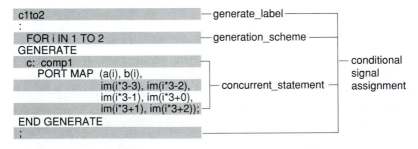

FIGURE 4.21
Component instantiation statement syntax details.

```
ARCHITECTURE iterative OF nibble-comparator IS
   COMPONENT comp1
      PORT (a, b, gt, eq, lt : IN BIT; a_gt_b, a_eq_b, a_lt_b : OUT BIT);
   END COMPONENT;
   FOR ALL : comp1 USE ENTITY WORK.bit-comparator (gate_level);
   CONSTANT n : INTEGER := 4;
   SIGNAL im : BIT_VECTOR ( 0 TO (n-1)*3-1);
BEGIN
   c_all: FOR i IN 0 TO n-1 GENERATE
      l: IF i = 0 GENERATE
         least: comp1 PORT MAP (a(i), b(i), gt, eq, lt, im(0), im(1), im(2) );
      END GENERATE;
      m: IF i = n-1 GENERATE
         most: comp1 PORT MAP (a(i), b(i),
                        im(i*3-3), im(i*3-2), im(i*3-1), a_gt_b, a_eq_b, a_lt_b);
      END GENERATE;
      r: IF i > 0 AND i < n-1 GENERATE
         rest: comp1 PORT MAP (a(i), b(i), im(i*3-3), im(i*3-2), im(i*3-1),
                        im(i*3+0), im(i*3+1), im(i*3+2) );
      END GENERATE;
   END GENERATE;
END iterative;
```

FIGURE 4.22
A more flexible *iterative* architecture of *nibble_comparator*.

The architecture statement part in Figure 4.22 contains a generate statement which is labeled *c_all*, and which encloses three more generate statements labeled *l*, *m*, and *r*. Respectively, these three statements are used for port map specification of the *least* significant, *most* significant, and the *rest* of the bits of a comparator of size *n*. Since generate statements are concurrent statements, the order in which they appear inside the outer generate statement is unimportant. The comparator in this figure specifies the same wiring as that shown in Figure 4.19. Simulation results of these two versions of the *nibble_comparator* are identical.

4.4 MODELING A TEST BENCH

Testing the *nibble comparator* involves generating a test bench description and using it to provide stimuli to the input ports of the 4-bit comparator. A test bench must contain the circuit under test and should have sources for providing data to its inputs. Containment of the *nibble_comparator* as well as application of waveforms to its inputs can be modeled in VHDL. Development of a test bench for the comparator circuit requires the use of language constructs that are generally not considered to be at the structural level. In order to stay within the scope of this chapter, we develop only a simple test bench that only requires the use of signal assignments and component instantiations.

4.4.1 VHDL Description of A Simple Test Bench

The composition aspect of a test bench for the *nibble_comparator* is shown in Figure 4.23. The test bench does not have external ports. It provides waveforms for the *a* and *b* inputs, and connects the *gt*, *eq*, and *lt* control inputs to *gnd*, *vdd*, and *gnd*, respectively. This programs the comparator such that the *a_gt_b* (or *a_lt_b*) output becomes 1 only when *a* is greater than *b* (or *a* is less than *b*). Had the *gt* control input been connected to *vdd*, its corresponding output would become 1 when *a* is greater than or equal to *b*.

 The VHDL description of the test bench is shown in Figure 4.24. The entity declaration specifies the entity name as *test_bench*. The absence of a port clause in this declaration indicates that there are no input or output ports for the test bench. The architecture of *test_bench* is identified as *input_output*, and the *comp4* component is declared in its declarative part. The local ports of this component are the same as the ports of the *nibble_comparator* entity. The configuration specification that follows the component declaration associates the *a1* instance of *comp4* to the *iterative* architecture of the *nibble_comparator*. Since only one instance of *comp4* is used, using *a1* or the ALL keyword in the configuration specification, are equivalent. Local signals *a*, *b*, *eql*, *lss*, *gtr*, *vdd*, and *gnd* are also declared in the declarative part. The *vdd* and *gnd* signals are initialized to '1' and '0', respectively. In VHDL, the := symbol is used for initialization of all objects and the default initial value for the standard BIT type is '0'. The statement part of Figure 4.24 contains three concurrent statements. The statement labeled *a1* is an instantiation of *comp4* and it specifies wiring to the ports of the *nibble_comparator* according to the composition aspect of Figure 4.23. The other two statements are signal assignments specifying waveforms to be applied to the *a* and *b* local signals. Each waveform consists of several elements each specifying a value and a time. After time 0, the four bits of signal *a* will have the "0000" value. The "1111" value is scheduled for these four bits at 500 nanoseconds, and other values follow at 500 ns or 1000 ns intervals. For readability of the test vectors on *a* and *b*, values are assigned to both inputs at each time interval. If the newly assigned values are the same as the values that an input already has, the new values do not cause

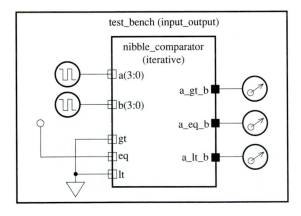

FIGURE 4.23
A test bench for *nibble_comparator*, the composition aspect.

```
ENTITY nibble_comparator_test_bench IS
END nibble_comparator_test_bench ;
--
ARCHITECTURE input_output OF nibble_comparator_test_bench IS
   COMPONENT comp4 PORT (a, b : IN bit_vector (3 DOWNTO 0);
                          gt, eq, lt : IN BIT;   a_gt_b, a_eq_b, a_lt_b : OUT BIT);
   END COMPONENT;
   FOR a1 : comp4 USE ENTITY WORK.nibble_comparator(iterative);
   SIGNAL a, b : BIT_VECTOR (3 DOWNTO 0);
   SIGNAL eql, lss, gtr : BIT;
   SIGNAL vdd : BIT := '1';
   SIGNAL gnd : BIT := '0';
BEGIN
   a1: comp4 PORT MAP (a, b, gnd, vdd, gnd, gtr, eql, lss);
   a2:   a <= "0000",                ---- a = b (steady state)
            "1111" AFTER 0500 NS, -- a > b (worst case)
            "1110" AFTER 1500 NS, -- a < b (worst case)
            "1110" AFTER 2500 NS, -- a > b (need bit 1 info)
            "1010" AFTER 3500 NS, -- a < b (need bit 2 info)
            "0000" AFTER 4000 NS, -- a < b (steady state, prepare for next)
            "1111" AFTER 4500 NS, -- a = b (worst case)
            "0000" AFTER 5000 NS, -- a < b (need bit 3 only, best case)
            "0000" AFTER 5500 NS, -- a = b (worst case)
            "1111" AFTER 6000 NS; -- a > b (need bit 3 only, best case)
   a3 : b <= "0000",               ---- a = b (steady state)
            "1110" AFTER 0500 NS, -- a > b (worst case)
            "1111" AFTER 1500 NS, -- a < b (worst case)
            "1100" AFTER 2500 NS, -- a > b (need bit 1 info)
            "1100" AFTER 3500 NS, -- a < b (need bit 2 info)
            "1111" AFTER 4000 NS, -- a < b (steady state, prepare for next)
            "1111" AFTER 4500 NS, -- a = b (worst case)
            "1111" AFTER 5000 NS, -- a < b (need bit 3 only, best case)
            "0000" AFTER 5500 NS, -- a = b (worst case)
            "0000" AFTER 6000 NS; -- a > b (need bit 3 only, best case)
END input_output;
```

FIGURE 4.24

Test bench for *iterative* architecture of *nibble_comparator*.

events on this input. Values on *a* and *b* test the 4-bit comparator for most of its key operations.

The test bench used here is a simple one and we will continue using this style until more convenient data application methods are described in the later chapters. Chapter 6 describes several procedures that simplify development of test benches. Reading data from external files is discussed in Chapters 6 and 8.

Before analyzing simulation results, two points are worth mentioning. First, names used for local signals are *a* and *b* which are the same as those of the *nibble_comparator* input ports. This is done only for clarity, and any other name could be used for the local signals of the test bench. The port map determines the association between *a* of the *nibble_comparator* and the local *a* of the test bench. The second point has to do with the statement labels. While instantiation or generate statements require a label, labeling signal assignments is optional. The *a2* and *a3* labels, therefore, can be removed without violating the VHDL syntax. Where options exist, descriptions should generally be written for better readability.

4.4.2 Simulation

The result of the simulation run in which the *input_output* architecture of the *test_bench* is the top unit is shown in Figure 4.25. Simulation begins at 0 nanoseconds and ends at 6015 ns. This table shows only the times that an event occurs on one of the signals

TIME (NS)	SIGNALS				
	a(3:0)	b(3:0)	gtr	eql	lss
0000	"0000"	"0000"	'0'	'0'	'0'
0005	......	......	...	'1'	...
0500	"1111"	"1110"	...	...	...
0544	......	......	'1'	...	...
0548	......	......	...	'0'	...
1500	"1110"	"1111"	...	...	...
1544	......	......	'0'	...	...
0548	......	......	...	'0'	...
1500	"1110"	"1111"	...	...	...
1544	......	......	'0'	...	...
1548	......	......	...	...	'1'
2500		"1100"	...	...	...
2533	......	......	...	...	'0'
2537	......	......	'1'	...	...
3500	"1010"	......	...	...	...
3522	......	......	'0'	...	...
3526	......	......	...	...	'1'
4000	"0000"	"1111"	...	...	...
4500	"1111"	......	...	...	...
4544	......	......	...	'1'	...
4548	......	......	...	...	'0'
5000	"0000"	......	...	...	...
5011	......	......	...	'0'	...
5015	......	......	...	...	'1'
5500	......	"0000"	...	...	...
5544	......	......	...	...	'0'
5548	......	......	...	'1'	...
6000	"1111"	......	...	...	...
6011	......	......	'1'	...	...
6015	......	......	...	'0'	...

FIGURE 4.25
Simulation report for simulating the test bench in Figure 4.24. All events are observed.

being observed. New values of signals are shown when their values change. Dots indicate that the signals hold their previous value.

Five nanoseconds after the start of the simulation the "0000" values on a and b cause the eql output to become 1. For generating a 1 on the a_gt_b or a_lt_b outputs, the longest delay occurs when all but the least significant bits of a and b are the same. This situation occurs at times 500 ns and 1500 ns for the greater-than and less-than cases, respectively. For both cases, it takes 48 ns for the circuit to reach steady state. As seen from the simulation run at times 4500 and 5500 ns, the worst case delay for the a_eq_b output is also 48 ns. The fastest that this circuit can produce results is when its two operands are different only in their most significant bits. This occurs at times 5000 ns and 6000 ns, where the circuit produces appropriate outputs and reaches steady state only 15 ns later. Between the worst case of 48 ns and the best case of 15 ns, other delay values occur when bits 1 or 2 of the two operands are different. The event on the b input at 2500 ns, for example, causes the two operands to differ only in bit 1. The propagation of values, therefore, must occur through bits 1, 2, and 3 of the comparator, causing a 37 ns delay before the circuit reaches steady state at 2537 ns time. At 3500 ns, the event on the a input causes bits 2 of the two operands to be different. The result of this comparison becomes available at 3526 ns after propagating through bits 2 and 3.

The circuit we are simulating has several levels of hierarchical nesting. The *test_bench* contains the *nibble_comparator* which contains four instances of the *bit_-comparator*, each of which contains several instances of inverters and NAND gates. Events that occur on the ports of the outermost components pass through the intermediate components, and reach the signal assignments that describe the operation of the innermost components. Evaluation of these assignments may result in generation of events on the output ports of the components that they are enclosed in. Such events will cause other components to evaluate their outputs or pass the events down to subcomponents within them. For an event in the architecture body of *test_bench*, evaluation of statements continues until the circuit reaches steady state. Outputs of a component are evaluated only if an event occurs on at least one of its inputs. Consider for example, the situation at 3500 ns, when bit 2 of a changes. This event causes events on input ports of *bit_comparator* number 2 (see Figure 4.18) which travel downward to eventually cause events on the right hand side of the signal assignments forming the Boolean expressions of the gates (see Figure 4.11) of this comparator bit. After these Boolean expressions are evaluated, they cause events upward to reach the output ports of comparator bit number 2. Since the outputs of this bit are connected to the input ports of bit 3, a similar downward and then upward propagation of events occurs inside this comparator bit. In the simulation of a VHDL description, such events occur, and at each stage only the affected statements are evaluated.

4.5   BINDING ALTERNATIVES

Configuration specifications in the architecture declarative part of a VHDL description associate an instance of a component with a design entity. So far in this chapter, we have used the combinations of *component declarations*, *configuration specifications*, and *component instantiation* in their simplest forms. VHDL, however, allows other forms of configuration specificationsthat make component instantiations significantly more flexible than previously presented.

For the purpose of illustration, consider the clocked, level-sensitive, set-reset latch of Figure 4.26. The structural level VHDL description of this circuit, using the *single_delay* architecture of the *nand2* entity in Section 4.1 for all its NAND gates, is depicted in Figure 4.27. This description uses four instances of *nand2* and generates the output of the latch on the *im3* signal. Since port signal *q* is an output (its mode is OUT), its value cannot be read. This implies that signal *q* cannot be used as input to any component, nor can it be used on the right hand side of a signal assignment. Therefore, we have used the *im3* intermediate signal for connecting the output of the *g3* instance of *nand2* to the input of the *g4* instance of this entity. A signal assignment statement is used to assign values of *im3* to *q*. The output of the latch, therefore, follows the output of the *g3* NAND gate. Because of the signal assignment,

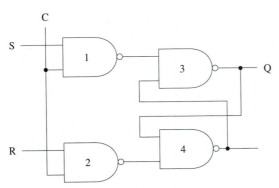

FIGURE 4.26
Logical diagram of a simple latch.

```
ENTITY sr_latch IS PORT (s, r, c : IN BIT; q : OUT BIT);
END sr_latch;
--
ARCHITECTURE gate_level OF sr_latch IS
   COMPONENT n2 PORT (i1, i2: IN BIT; o1: OUT BIT);
   END COMPONENT;
   FOR ALL : n2 USE ENTITY WORK.nand2 (single_delay);
   SIGNAL im1, im2, im3, im4 : BIT;
BEGIN
   g1 : n2 PORT MAP (s, c, im1);
   g2 : n2 PORT MAP (r, c, im2);
   g3 : n2 PORT MAP (im1, im4, im3);
   g4 : n2 PORT MAP (im3, im2, im4);
   q <= im3;
END gate_level;
```

FIGURE 4.27
VHDL description of set-reset latch.

q lags behind *im3* by one *delta*. Since the *delta* time is not real time, this does not add any additional delay to the output of the circuit.

The above implementation of the latch uses four identical gates with the same exact delays. Besides not representing a realistic design in which no two gates in the same package have exactly the same delay, the simulation of this circuit presents stability problems. Specifically, on initialization or for any other reason, if nodes *im3* and *im4* end up with the same value while the clock is zero, the circuit oscillates. However, this problem can be remedied easily by using a NAND gate with a different delay for the *g3* gate.

For the two-input NAND gate, a different architecture which has a smaller delay than the *single_delay* architecture of Figure 4.4c, is shown in Figure 4.28. The *single_delay* and *fast_single_delay* architectures of *nand2* have the same interface and are two different architecture bodies for the same entity declaration in Figure 4.4b.

The composition aspect and the architecture body of another version of *sr_latch* are shown in Figure 4.29. This design uses the *fast_single_delay* architecture of *nand2* for two of its NAND gates. All but the configuration specifications in the new *gate_level* architecture body of *sr_latch* are the same as the structural description of Figure 4.27. In the architecture body of Figure 4.29b, two configuration specifications are used. The first one binds instances of *n2* that are labeled *g1* and *g3* to the *fast_single_delay* architecture of the *nand2* entity, and the second configuration specification binds *g2* and *g4* instances of *n2* component to the *single_delay* architecture.

Since the *single_delay* architecture in *nand3* of Section 4.1 has a different delay than that of *nand2*, the problem of latch stability can also be solved by using *nand3* instead of the new fast two-input NAND gate. This usage demonstrates still another configuration mechanism in VHDL. A new composition aspect and architecture body for the *sr_latch* are shown in Figure 4.30. This version of the *gate_level* architecture of *sr_latch* uses the *single_delay* architecture of *nand3* for *g2* and *g4* instances of *n2*. The statement part of the architecture body of Figure 4.30b is the same as the original *gate_level* architecture of *sr_latch*. In the declarative part, however, component declarations and configuration specifications are done differently.

A component declaration is used to declare *n2* with *x*, *y*, and *z* local ports. This declaration presents a virtual design entity interface that is used in the component instantiation statements of the statement part. In their port maps, component instantiations specify an association between actual signals, for example, *s*, *c*, and *im2* for *g1*, and *x*, *y*, and *z* local ports.

The first configuration specification in Figure 4.30 binds the *single_delay* architecture of *nand2* to instances of *n2* that are labeled *g1* and *g3*. The port map aspect

```
ARCHITECTURE fast_single_delay OF nand2 IS
BEGIN
    o1 <= i1 NAND i2 AFTER 3 NS;
END fast_single_delay;
```

FIGURE 4.28
A faster NAND gate.

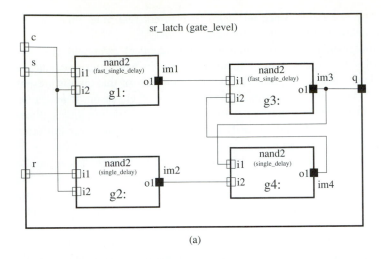

(a)

```
ARCHITECTURE gate_level OF sr_latch IS
    COMPONENT n2 PORT (i1, i2: IN BIT; o1: OUTBIT); END COMPONENT
    FOR g1, g3 : n2 USE ENTITY WORK.nand2 (fast_single_delay);
    FOR g2, g4: n2 USE ENTITY WORK.nand2 (single _delay);
    SIGNAL im1, im2, im3, im4 : BIT;
BEGIN
    g1 : n2 PORT MAP (s, c, im1);
    g2 : n2 PORT MAP (r, c, im2);
    g3 : n2 PORT MAP (im1, im4, im3);
    g4 : n2 PORT MAP (im3, im2, im4);
    q <= im3;
END gate_level;
```

(b)

FIGURE 4.29
SR-latch, using gates with different delays, (a) composition aspect, (b) architecture body.

associates x, y, and z local ports with the formals of the *nand2* entity, namely with *i1*, *i2*, and *o1*. The second configuration specification is used for configuring *g2* and *g4* instances of *n2*. These instances are associated with the *single_delay* architecture of *nand3*, which exists in the WORK library (the current working library). The optional port map associates local ports x, x, y, and z with *i1*, *i2*, *i3*, and *o1* of the *nand3* entity. Together, component instantiations, component declarations, and configuration specifications form a two-step association between signals of the statement part and the ports of *nand3*. For the *g2* instance of *n2*, this two-step association is illustrated in Figure 4.31. In the first step, actuals r, c, and *im2* are associated with x, y, and z local ports. In the second step, x, y, and z local ports are associated with formal ports of *nand3*. The net result is association of r, r, c, and *im2* with *in1*, *in2*, *in3*, and *o1*, respectively.

Configuration specification constructs in the previous section did not include port map specifications. With this language construct, specifying port maps is optional, and if missing, the association defaults to local port names declared within component

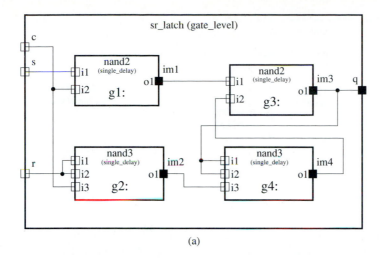

(a)

```
ARCHITECTURE gate_level OF sr_latch IS
   COMPONENT n2 PORT (x, y: IN BIT; z: OUT BIT); END COMPONENT;
   FOR g1, g3 : n2 USE
      ENTITY WORK.nand2 (single_delay) PORT MAP (x, y, z);
   FOR g2, g4: n2 USE
      ENTITY WORK.nand3 (single _delay) PORT MAP (x, x, y, z);
   SIGNAL im1, im2, im3, im4 : BIT;
BEGIN
   g1 : n2 PORT MAP (s, c, im1);
   g2 : n2 PORT MAP (r, c, im2);
   g3 : n2 PORT MAP (im1, im4, im3);
   g4 : n2 PORT MAP (im3, im2, im4);
   q <= im3;
END gate_level;
```

(b)

FIGURE 4.30
SR-latch, using *nand2* and *nand3* gates, (a) composition aspect, (b) architecture body.

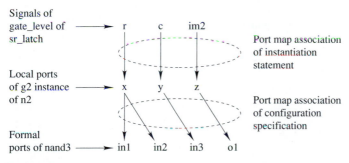

FIGURE 4.31
Two-step association.

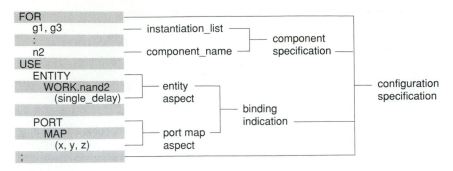

FIGURE 4.32
Configuration specification syntax details.

declarations. In such cases, local port names and formals of the design entity must be the same. In Sections 4.2 to 4.4, we have taken advantage of this default and where components are used, they are declared with the same port clause as that of their corresponding entity declarations.

To study other alternatives in configuration specifications, consider the syntax details of the construct for configuration in the *g1* and *g3* instances in *n2* of Figure 4.30, as shown in Figure 4.32. The instantiation list consists of the *g1* and *g3* labels. Other possibilities for this list are the keywords ALL or OTHERS. Configuration specifications that use OTHERS instead of a list of labels specify that the binding that follows applies to those labels of the component for which a binding has not been specified in the previous configuration specifications. For example, *g2, g4* in the instantiation list of the second configuration specification in Figure 4.30 can be replaced with OTHERS. The binding indication in Figure 4.32 has an entity aspect and a port map aspect. As previously discussed, when the port map aspect is absent, local port associations default to formal ports of the entity in the entity aspect that has the same name.

4.6 SUMMARY

A structural description for a design consists of a wiring specification of its subcomponents. In this chapter, the definition and usage of components in larger designs was illustrated. Generate statements also were introduced as a convenient way to describe repetitive hardware structures and a notation was defined for graphical representation of structural descriptions. In addition, various forms and options in component declarations and configuration specifications were discussed. Using simple gates, the reader should now be able to design larger digital circuits with many levels of component nesting.

REFERENCES

1. Wakerly, J. F., "Digital Design Principles and Practices," Prentice-Hall Inc., Englewood Cliffs, N.J., 1990.

2. "IEEE Standard VHDL Language Reference Manual," IEEE Std. 1076-1987, The Institute of Electrical and Electronic Engineers, Inc., 1988.
3. Lipsett, L., C. Schaefer, and C. Ussery, "VHDL: Hardware Description and Design," Klewer Academic Publishing, Boston, 1988.
4. Armstrong, J. R., "Chip-Level Modeling with VHDL," Prentice-Hall Inc., Englewood Cliffs, N.J., 1988.

PROBLEMS

4.1. Write VHDL descriptions for a two-input NOR gate and an XOR gate. Use single delay models similar to the ones used in Section 4.1. Use 4 ns and 7 ns delays for the NOR and XOR respectively. Use inertial delays.

4.2. The following description uses gates presented in Section 4.1 and the XOR gate in Problem 4.1. At time t_0 the values on the a and b inputs are '1', and the circuit is in steady state. At t_1 the value of a changes to '0'. Draw a detailed timing diagram and analyze the timing behavior of this circuit due to the event on a. Does a glitch appear on the output of the circuit? In any case, keeping the delay at 7 ns, how can you modify the XOR model of the previous problem to reverse the situation? The solution to this problem depends on code developed in Problem 4.1.

```
 ┌ENTITY problem_2 IS PORT (a, b : IN BIT; z : OUT BIT);
 └END problem_2;
    --
 ┌ARCHITECTURE glitch OF problem_2 IS
 │   COMPONENT n2 PORT (i1, i2: IN BIT; o1: OUT BIT); END COMPONENT;
 │   FOR ALL : n2 USE ENTITY WORK.nand2 (single_delay);
 │   COMPONENT n3 PORT (i1, i2, i3: IN BIT; o1: OUT BIT);
 │   END COMPONENT;
 │   FOR ALL : n3 USE ENTITY WORK.nand3 (single_delay);
 │   COMPONENT x2 PORT (i1, i2: IN BIT; o1: OUT BIT); END COMPONENT;
 │   FOR ALL : x2 USE ENTITY WORK.xor2 (single_delay);
 │   SIGNAL i1, i2 : BIT;
 ├BEGIN
 │   g1 : n2 PORT MAP (a, b, i1);
 │   g2 : n3 PORT MAP (a, b, b, i2);
 │   g3 : x2 PORT MAP (i1, i2, z);
 └END glitch;
```

4.3. The following description uses gates presented in Section 4.1 and the XOR gate in Problem 4.1. If the a and b inputs are both '1' and a changes to '0', a glitch will appear on the z output of this circuit. Analyze the timing of this circuit showing all events that lead to the glitch on the output. Change the delay of the XOR model to transport delay. Does the behavior of the circuit change when a changes to '0'? After the '1' to '0' transition on input a, find when input b has to change so that the transport delay in the XOR model makes a glitch appear on the z output that would otherwise not be present. The solution to this problem depends on code developed in Problem 4.1.

```
ENTITY problem_3 IS PORT (a, b : IN BIT; z : OUT BIT);
END problem_3;

ARCHITECTURE glitch OF problem_3 IS
    COMPONENT n2 PORT (i1, i2: IN BIT; o1: OUT BIT); END COMPONENT;
    FOR ALL : n2 USE ENTITY WORK.nand2 (single_delay);
    COMPONENT n3 PORT (i1, i2, i3: IN BIT; o1: OUT BIT);
    END COMPONENT;
    FOR ALL : n3 USE ENTITY WORK.nand3 (single_delay);
    COMPONENT x2 PORT (i1, i2: IN BIT; o1: OUT BIT); END COMPONENT;
    FOR ALL : x2 USE ENTITY WORK.xor2 (single_delay);
    SIGNAL i1, i2 : BIT;
BEGIN
    g1 : n2 PORT MAP (a, b, i1);
    g2 : n3 PORT MAP (i1, b, b, i2);
    g3 : x2 PORT MAP (a, i2, z);
END glitch;
```

4.4. Write a test bench for the *bit_comparator* of Section 4.2. Find the worst case delay for this circuit. Why is this delay not equal to one-fourth of the worst case delay of the *nibble_comparator*? Analyze the timings of both circuits and answer this question.

4.5. Write a description of a Full Adder using the gates of Section 4.1 and XOR gate of Problem 4.1. What is the worst case delay for this circuit? The solution to this problem depends on code developed in Problem 4.1.

4.6. Write a VHDL description for a package of four NAND gates, using the *single_delay* model for each of the gates. Use the following entity declaration.

```
ENTITY four_nand2
    IS PORT (
                i1_a, i2_a, i1_b, i2_b,
                i1_c, i2_c, i1_d, i2_d : IN BIT;
                o1_a, o1_b, o1_c, o1_d : OUT BIT);
END four_nand2;
```

4.7. Use the *four_nand2* package of Problem 4.6 to describe a clocked SR latch. The solution to this problem depends on code developed in Problem 4.6.

4.8. The following description (Fig. P4.8) uses the *four_nand2* package of Problem 4.6. What Boolean function is this description implementing? The solution to this problem depends on code developed in Problem 4.6.

4.9. Use only two *four_nand2* packages of Problem 4.6 to describe a BCD prime number detector. The output is to be 1 when the input BCD number is a prime number. The number 1 is prime a number. The solution to this problem depends on code developed in Problem 4.6.

4.10. Using only XOR gate models of Problem 4.1, write a VHDL description for an 8-bit even/odd parity checker. The circuit has an 8-bit input vector and two outputs. The *odd* output is to become 1 when the number of 1s on the input in odd. The *even* output is the opposite of the *odd* output. Use generate statement(s). The solution to this problem depends on code developed in Problem 4.1.

```
ENTITY unknown IS PORT (a, b, c, d : IN BIT; z : OUT BIT);
END unknown;

--

ARCHITECTURE mystry OF unknown IS
    COMPONENT chip PORT (
            i1_a, i2_a, i1_b, i2_b,
            i1_c, i2_c, i1_d, i2_d : IN BIT;
            o1_a, o1_b, o1_c, o1_d : OUT BIT);
    END COMPONENT;
    FOR ALL : chip USE ENTITY WORK.four_nand2 (packing);
    SIGNAL i1, i2, i3 : BIT;
BEGIN
    g1 : chip PORT MAP (a, b, c, d, i1, i2, i3, i3, i1, i2, i3, z);
END mystry;
```

FIGURE P4.8

4.11. Describe an 8-bit adder using the Full Adder description in Problem 4.5. Take advantage of the generate statement. Write a test bench for this adder, and find the worst case delay. The solution to this problem depends on code developed in Problems 4.1 and 4.5.

4.12. If the inputs to the adder in Problem 4.11 are 2's complement numbers, an overflow may occur when adding two positive or two negative numbers. Use this adder in a design of an 8-bit adder with an overflow indication output. Do not modify the description of the original adder; rather, use it in a top level design that instantiates the adder of Problem 4.11 as well as gates of the overflow detection hardware. The solution to this problem depends on code developed in Problem 4.1, 4.5 and 4.11.

4.13. Using only *nand2* and *nand3* descriptions, write the VHDL description for a D-latch. Start with the description in Figure 4.30. Arrange the gates such that the circuit does not oscillate.

4.14. Use the generate statement to describe an 8-bit latch using the D-latch in Problem 4.13. Your *eight_latch* circuit should have a single clock, an 8-bit *d* input and an 8-bit *q* output. The solution to this problem depends on code developed in Problem 4.13.

4.15. Write VHDL description for a master-slave JK flip-flop. Use the *fast_single_delay* model of *nand2* to avoid oscillation. In addition to this gate, you can use all gates in Section 4.1.

4.16. Use the JK flip-flop in Problem 4.15 to design a 1-bit modular binary counter. Based on this module, build a 4-bit binary ripple up-counter. Design this counter such that it can easily be cascaded for building larger counters. The solution to this problem depends on code developed in Problem 4.15.

4.17. In the following description, the configuration specification is missing. Assume that the only component that you have available is the *nand3 (single_delay)* model. Write appropriate configurations such that this description implements function $f(a,b,c,d,e)$. See Fig. P4.17.

$$f (a, b, c, d, e) = a . b + c . d' + e$$

```
ENTITY function_f IS PORT (a, b, c, d, e : IN BIT; f : OUT BIT);
END function_f;
ARCHITECTURE configurable OF function_f IS
    COMPONENT n1 PORT (w: IN BIT; z: OUT BIT); END COMPONENT;
    COMPONENT n2 PORT (w, x: IN BIT; z: OUT BIT); END COMPONENT;
    COMPONENT n3 PORT (w, x, y: IN BIT; z: OUT BIT); END COMPONENT;

    ...
    SIGNAL i1, i2, i3, i4 : BIT;
BEGIN
    g0 : n1 PORT MAP (d, i1);
    g1 : n1 PORT MAP (e, i2);
    g2 : n2 PORT MAP (i1, c, i3);
    g3 : n2 PORT MAP (a, b, i4);
    g4 : n3 PORT MAP (i2, i3, i4, f);
END configurable;
```

FIGURE P4.17

CHAPTER
5

DESIGN ORGANIZATION AND PARAMETERIZATION

In a digital system design environment, functional design of a digital system is often done independently of the physical characteristics or the technology in which the design is being implemented. Hardware designers who use 74xx00 series components and designers who use pretested layouts of CMOS cells share many top level design stages. There is still more sharing when hardware designers use various series in the same logic family. Based on technology, power consumption, speed, and temperature range, components are categorized into various libraries from which designers choose specific components.

For supporting such design environments, VHDL provides language constructs for parametrizing and customizing designs, and for definition and usage of design libraries. These constructs enable a designer to generate a functional design independent of the specific technology and customize this generic design at a later stage. Specifically, *library*, *use clause*, *package*, and *configuration declarations* of VHDL are used for grouping or categorizing various components into design libraries and for customizing designs to use components in these libraries. By use of *generic* parameters, VHDL also allows a design to be parametrized such that the specific timing, number of bits, or even the wiring is determined when the design is configured.

Another language issue that can influence the organization of a design is the use of subprograms. As in any high level language, VHDL allows the definition and usage of *functions* and *procedures*. In addition to the important hardware implications of subprograms (which will be discussed in Chapters 6 and 7) these language constructs greatly improve readability and organization of a hardware description.

This chapter discusses subprograms, library packages, design paramterization, and design configuration. We demonstrate how utility functions, procedures, type definitions, or predesigned components can be grouped through utilization of the VHDL package construct. In addition, we will discuss the use of such packages in a design and the use of generic parameters. We also will explain post design specifications of physical characteristics, such as timing, and describe various methods that can be used to configure a design for a specific library of component or physical parameters.

5.1 DEFINITION AND USAGE OF SUBPROGRAMS

In many programming languages, subprograms are used to simplify coding, modularity, and readability of descriptions. VHDL uses subprograms for these applications as well as for those that are more specific to hardware descriptions. Regardless of the application, behavioral software-like constructs are allowed in subprograms. As stated earlier, VHDL allows two forms of subprograms, *functions* and *procedures*. Functions return value and cannot alter the values of their parameters. A procedure, on the other hand, is used as a statement, and can alter the values of its parameters.

5.1.1 A Functional Single Bit Comparator

The *bit_comparator* in Chapter 4 was designed at the gate level, to specify the interconnection of all its gates using component instantiations. A simpler description can be developed by using the Boolean equations (Equations 4.1a to 4.1c) of the three outputs of this circuit.

Equation 5.1a $\quad\quad\quad$ a_gt_b = a . gt + b' . gt + a . b'

Equation 5.1b $\quad\quad\quad$ a_eq_b = a . b . eq + a' . b' . eq

Equation 5.1c $\quad\quad\quad$ a_lt_b = b . lt + a' . lt + b . a'

As evident from the equations of *a_gt_b* and *a_lt_b*, rearranged and repeated here for reference (and also from the schematic diagrams in Figure 4.9), one expression used with different signal names can be made to express both of these outputs. The *a_eq_b* output, however, requires a separate expression. Figure 5.1 shows a VHDL description that is based on these equations and one that takes advantage of the similarities between the *a_gt_b* and the *a_lt_b* outputs.

For the *bit_comparator* entity declaration in Figure 4.10b, the architecture body of Figure 5.1 is an alternative to the *gate_level* architecture in Figure 4.12. The declarative part of the *functional* architecture of the *bit_comparator* contains the body of two function subprograms. The first function returns a BIT value which is a function of w, x, and gl (greater or less). The *a_gt_b* and *a_lt_b* outputs use this function. The other function in the declarative part of the architecture of Figure 5.1 returns

```
ARCHITECTURE  functional  OF  bit_comparator  IS
    FUNCTION  fgl  (w,  x,  gl  :  BIT)  RETURN  BIT  IS
    BEGIN
        RETURN   (w  AND  gl)  OR  (NOT  x   AND   gl)  OR  (w   AND   NOT  x);
    END  fgl;
    FUNCTION  feq  (w,  x,  eq  :  BIT)  RETURN  BIT  IS
    BEGIN
        RETURN   (w  AND  x  AND  eq)  OR  (NOT  w   AND   NOT  x   AND   eq);
    END  feq;
BEGIN
    a_gt_b  <=  fgl  (a,  b,  gt)  AFTER  12  NS;
    a_eq_b  <=  feq  (a,  b,  eq)  AFTER  12  NS;
    a_lt_b  <=  fgl  (b,  a,  lt)  AFTER  12  NS;
END  functional;
```

FIGURE 5.1
A functional *bit_comparator*, using the same function for two outputs.

the BIT value for the expression for the *a_eq_b* output. In the statement part of this architecture, three function calls are used for the three outputs of the *bit_comparator*. When a function is called, it returns its calculated value in zero time. Because of this, and in order for this description to better represent the actual circuit, the values returned by the functions are delayed 12 nanoseconds before they are assigned to the appropriate outputs of the circuit. This delay value is a rough estimate of the worst case propagation delay of each *bit_comparator*, and is based on the 48 ns worst case delay of the *nibble_comparator* discussed in Chapter 4.

The syntax details of the *fgl* function are shown in Figure 5.2. The subprogram specification includes the name of the function, its formal parameters, and the type of the value returned by the function. The subprogram statement part of this description contains a single sequential statement, namely, the return statement. This statement causes the value evaluated by the expression that follows it to be used as the return value of the *fgl* function.

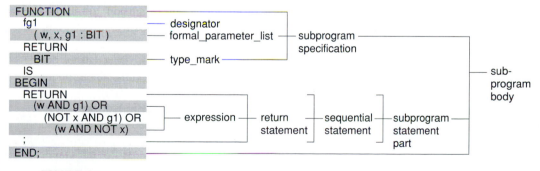

FIGURE 5.2
Syntax details of a subprogram body, a general view.

5.1.2   Using Procedures in a Test Bench

The main purpose of the test bench developed for the 4-bit comparator in Chapter 4 was to apply data to the 4-bit input of the *nibble_comparator*. We will discuss a procedure that can significantly simplify this process, and use another version of the *nibble_comparator* of Chapter 4 to demonstrate it. An architecture for a *nibble_comparator* that uses the *functional* architecture of the *bit_comparator* in Figure 5.1 is shown in Figure 5.3. This architecture is identified as *structural* and is an alternative to the *iterative* architecture of the *nibble_comparator* for the entity declaration of Figure 4.17. The configuration specification in the declarative part of this architecture associates all instances of the *bit_comparator* to the *functional* architecture of this unit.

The *procedural* version of the architecture of the *nibble_comparator_test_bench* shown in Figure 5.4 uses the *apply_data* procedure defined in the declarative part of this architecture to apply 4-bit data to the *a* and *b* inputs of the *structural* architecture in the *nibble_comparator*. The declarative part of this architectur begins with a type declaration declaring *integers* as a thirteen element array of INTEGER. This is a simple form of an array declaration which we use in our examples until the topic of type declaration is described in Chapter 6. The body of the *apply_data* subprogram follows the *integers* type declaration. The rest of the declarative part of the *procedural* architecture of the *nibble_comparator* contains a component declaration, configuration specification, and declaration of intermediate signals.

```
ARCHITECTURE structural OF nibble_comparator IS
   COMPONENT comp1
      PORT (a, b, gt, eq, lt : IN BIT; a_gt_b, a_eq_b, a_lt_b : OUT BIT);
   END COMPONENT;
   FOR ALL : comp1 USE ENTITY WORK.bit_comparator (functional);
   CONSTANT n : INTEGER := 4;
   SIGNAL im : BIT_VECTOR ( 0 TO (n-1)*3-1);
BEGIN
   c_all: FOR i IN 0 TO n-1 GENERATE
      l: IF i = 0 GENERATE
         least: comp1 PORT MAP (a(i), b(i), gt, eq, lt, im(0), im(1), im(2) );
      END GENERATE;
      m: IF i = n-1 GENERATE
         most: comp1 PORT MAP (a(i), b(i), im(i*3-3), im(i*3-2), im(i*3-1),
                                a_gt_b, a_eq_b, a_lt_b);
      END GENERATE;
      r: IF i > 0 AND i < n-1 GENERATE
         rest: comp1 PORT MAP (a(i), b(i), im(i*3-3), im(i*3-2), im(i*3-1),
                                im(i*3+0), im(i*3+1), im(i*3+2) );
      END GENERATE;
   END GENERATE;
END structural;
```

FIGURE 5.3
Structural architecture of a *nibble_comparator*.

```
ARCHITECTURE procedural OF nibble_comparator_test_bench IS
    TYPE integers IS ARRAY (0 TO 12) OF INTEGER;
    PROCEDURE apply_data
        (SIGNAL target : OUT BIT_VECTOR (3 DOWNTO 0);
            CONSTANT values : IN integers;
                CONSTANT period : IN TIME)
        IS
        VARIABLE j : INTEGER;
        VARIABLE tmp : INTEGER := 0;
        VARIABLE buf : BIT_VECTOR (3 DOWNTO 0);
    BEGIN
        FOR i IN 0 TO 12 LOOP
            tmp := values (i);
            j := 0;
            WHILE j <= 3 LOOP
                IF (tmp MOD 2  =  1) THEN
                    buf (j) := '1';
                ELSE buf (j) := '0';
                END IF;
                tmp := tmp / 2;
                j := j + 1;
            END LOOP;
            target <= TRANSPORT buf AFTER i * period;
        END LOOP;
    END apply_data;
    COMPONENT comp4 PORT
        (a, b : IN BIT_VECTOR (3 DOWNTO 0);  gt, eq, lt : IN BIT;
        a_gt_b, a_eq_b, a_lt_b : OUT BIT);
    END COMPONENT;
    FOR a1 : comp4 USE ENTITY WORK.nibble_comparator(structural);
    SIGNAL a, b : BIT_VECTOR (3 DOWNTO 0);
    SIGNAL eql, lss, gtr : BIT;
    SIGNAL vdd : BIT := '1';
    SIGNAL gnd : BIT := '0';
BEGIN
    a1: comp4 PORT MAP (a, b, gnd, vdd, gnd, gtr, eql, lss);
    apply_data (a, 0&15&15&14&14&14&14&10&00&15&00&00&15, 500 NS);
    apply_data (b, 0&14&14&15&15&12&12&12&15&15&15&00&00, 500 NS);
END procedural;
```

FIGURE 5.4
Procedural architecture of *nibble_comparator*.

The *apply_data* procedure uses thirteen integers passed to it via an array of integers (*values*). After converting these integers to 4-bit binary numbers, they are assigned to the *target* signal. The values are applied at the time intervals passed to this procedure via the *period* parameter. The body of *apply_data* uses two loops; the outer loop reads one of the thirteen input integers and the inner loop converts that integer to a 4-bit binary number. This binary number is then assigned to the *target* output of the procedure. Transport delay is used for this assignment so that new transactions are appended to the existing ones. Each time through the loop a new transaction with a time value that is 500 ns more than the time value of the previous transaction is placed on the driver of *target*. The only way to insure that new transactions do not cause the removal of the older transactions when they have different values is to use transport delay. As shown in the table in Figure 3.31, new transactions with different values override the old ones if the delay is inertial.

In the procedural architecture of the *nibble_comparator_test_bench* the statement part consists of a component instantiation statement and two procedure calls to the *apply_data* subprogram. These two calls generate 4-bit data on the *a* and *b* signals every 500 ns. The formal parameters of the subprogram are the *target* signal, thirteen concatenated integers, and a time *period*. Concatenation of integers forms a thirteen element array of integers which is passed to the second formal parameter of the *apply_data* procedure (*values*). As demonstrated in this example, types and classes of formal and actual parameters must match. For example, the class and type of *target* are SIGNAL and BIT_VECTOR, respectively, which match with class and type declared for *a* or *b*. CONSTANT is the default class for a subprogram input and VARIABLE is the default for a subprogram output. A procedure call in the statement part of an architecture is a concurrent statement, and if it does not have any input signals, it is called only once at the beginning of the simulation run.

The simulation report of the *procedural* architecture of the *nibble_comparator_test_bench* (Figure 5.5) indicates that the data applied to the 4-bit inputs of the *nibble_comparator* by the use of the *apply_data* procedure are identical to the data assigned to the inputs of the comparator in the *input_output* architecture of the test bench in Figure 4.24, whose simulation report is shown in Figure 4.25.

Comparing the two simulation reports (Figures 5.5 and 4.25) indicates a difference in the timing of events occurring on the *grt*, *eql*, and *lss* outputs of the two versions of the *nibble_comparator*s. This is due to the cumulative rough delay estimate used with the Boolean functions in the *functional* architecture of the *bit_comparator* in contrast to the gate instantiations used in the *gate_level* architecture of this unit. It must be noted that in terms of the timing of events that occur in the actual hardware, the simulation report in Figure 4.25 is a more precise representation than that in Figure 5.5. The price paid for the convenient description of the *bit_comparator* in Figure 5.1 is the loss of precision in the simulation results.

5.1.3 Language Aspects of Subprograms

The general structure of subprograms was discussed in relation to the *fgl* function in Figure 5.2. The *apply_data* procedure is a larger example, and it contains other language features of subprograms. As shown in Figure 5.6, the procedure begins with a subprogram specification. This part specifies the formal parameter list, which is syntactically similar to an interface list. The first parameter in this list indicates that *target* is a 4-bit signal which can only be written into (its mode is OUT). The mode of the next two parameters is IN, and they are constants of *integers* and TIME types,

TIME (ns)	a(3:0)	b(3:0)	gtr	eql	lss
0000	"0000"	"0000"	'0'	'0'	'0'
0048	......	......	...	'1'	...
0500	"1111"	"1110"	...	...	...
0548	......	......	'1'	'0'	...
1500	"1110"	"1111"	...	...	...
1548	......	......	'0'	...	'1'
2500	......	"1100"	...	...	...
2536	......	......	'1'	...	'1'
3500	"1010"	......	...	...	...
3524	......	......	'0'	...	'1'
4000	"0000"	"1111"	...	...	...
4500	"1111"	......	...	...	...
4548	......	......	...	'1'	'0'
5000	"0000"	......	...	...	...
5012	......	......	...	'0'	'1'
5500	......	"0000"	...	...	...
5548	......	......	...	'1'	'0'
6000	"1111"	......	...	...	...
6012	......	......	'1'	'0'	...

FIGURE 5.5
Simulation report resulting from the *procedural* test bench. All events are observed.

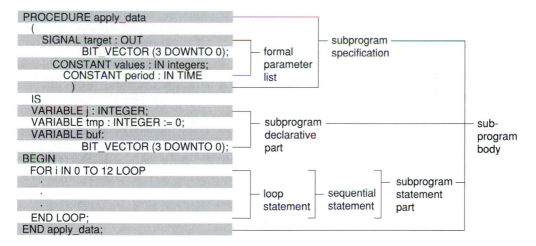

FIGURE 5.6
Details of a subprogram body.

respectively. If the class of an object, for example, SIGNAL or CONSTANT, for the parameters of *apply_data* is not specified, CONSTANT is assumed for the IN mode parameters and VARIABLE is assumed for the OUT mode parameters.

In the subprogram declaration in Figure 5.6, two INTEGER type variables and one BIT_VECTOR type are declared. Variables are initialized to their initial values each time a subprogram is called. If initial values are not specified, default initial values which depend on the type of an object are used. In this case *tmp* is initialized to 0, *j* is initialized to the smallest integer, and *buf* is initialized to the "0000" default. The body of the *apply_data* subprogram consists of a single loop statement. Details of this statement are shown in Figure 5.7.

The iteration scheme used with this loop statement causes the statements within the loop to be executed thirteen times, while *i* changes from 0 to 12. The value of this identifier can be used within the loop and it need not be declared. Referring to Figure 5.4, two variable assignments, a loop statement, and a signal assignment constitute the statement section of the outer loop statement. The inner loop statement uses the WHILE keyword and a condition for its iteration scheme. Within this loop, an if statement, which is detailed in Figure 5.8, assigns '0' or '1' to bits of *buf* according to the divisibility of *tmp* by 2. Each time through the loop, *tmp* is divided by 2 and *j* is incremented to keep the count of the evaluated bits of *buf*. As specified in the condition of the loop, the inner loop terminates when the variable *j* becomes greater than 3. At this time, the *buf* 4-bit vector contains the correct binary representation of the *i*th integer of the *values* array. This 4-bit binary is assigned to the *target* signal after a delay of *i* * *period* (*i* times the *period*). The end of the *apply_data* procedure is indicated by the end statement which is followed by the procedure designator. Using this designator at the end of the procedure is optional.

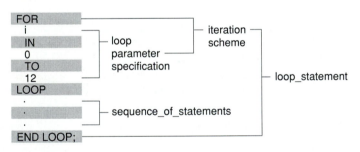

FIGURE 5.7
Loop statement with FOR iteration scheme.

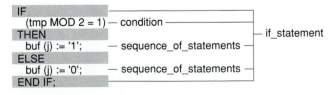

FIGURE 5.8
Details of the if statement of *apply_data* procedure.

The if statement in Figure 5.8, which is contained in the inner loop of *apply_data*, is itself a sequential statement. Sequential statements contained in this statement are simple assignment statements.

5.1.4   Utility Procedures

The *apply_data* procedure is a useful procedure for assigning binary data to multi-bit signals. Other useful procedures include those for converting binary data to integer data, and vice versa. Figure 5.9 shows one such procedure.

The *bin2int* procedure converts a binary vector of any length to its integer equivalent. The procedure assumes that the least significant bit of the input vector is bit number 0. Parameters *bin* and *int* contain the input binary and output integer, respectively. The iteration scheme in the main loop of this procedure indicates that the range of identifier *i* is in *bin*'RANGE. RANGE is an attribute and the value of *bin*'RANGE (read as *bin* **tick** RANGE) is the range of the actual array parameter that is passed to the *bin* formal parameter in the *bin2int* procedure. If this procedure is called to convert an 8-bit binary number whose right hand side least significant bit is bit 0, the range of *i* becomes 7 DOWNTO 0. Attributes and their applications are discussed in Chapter 6. For now, in addition to RANGE, the LENGTH attribute will also be used in this chapter. The result of the LENGTH attribute is the length of the array to which it is applied. For example, the range of *i* in the above procedure could alternatively be specified as (*bin*'LENGTH − 1) DOWNTO 0.

Another utility procedure, this one for converting integers to binary, is shown in Figure 5.10. This subprogram performs the same function as that of the inner loop of the *apply_data* procedure, except that the *int2bin* procedure can be used for data of any size. The *int2bin* procedure places the least significant bit of the resulting binary number in position 0 of the *bin* output and it assumes that the actual parameter associated with *bin* contains bit 0. Since *int* is input, it cannot be written into. The *tmp* variable, therefore, is declared to save the input integer as it is successively divided by two.

```
PROCEDURE bin2int (bin : IN BIT_VECTOR; int : OUT INTEGER) IS
    VARIABLE result: INTEGER;
BEGIN
    result := 0;
    FOR i IN bin'RANGE LOOP
        IF bin(i) = '1' THEN
            result := result + 2**i;
        END IF;
    END LOOP;
    int := result;
END bin2int;
```

FIGURE 5.9
Procedure for binary to integer conversion.

```
PROCEDURE int2bin (int : IN INTEGER;   bin : OUT BIT_VECTOR) IS
   VARIABLE tmp : INTEGER;
BEGIN
   tmp := int;
   FOR i IN 0 TO (bin'LENGTH − 1) LOOP
      IF (tmp MOD 2  =  1) THEN
         bin (i) := '1';
      ELSE bin (i) := '0';
      END IF;
      tmp := tmp / 2;
   END LOOP;
END int2bin;
```

FIGURE 5.10
Procedure for integer to binary conversion.

```
PROCEDURE  apply_data (
   SIGNAL target : OUT BIT_VECTOR (3 DOWNTO 0);
   CONSTANT values : IN integers;   CONSTANT period : IN TIME)
      IS
   VARIABLE buf : BIT_VECTOR (3 DOWNTO 0);
BEGIN
   FOR i IN 0 TO 12 LOOP
      int2bin (values(i), buf);
      target <= TRANSPORT buf AFTER i * period;
   END LOOP;
END apply_data;
```

FIGURE 5.11
Another version of *apply_data* procedure. This version takes advantage of the *int2bin* procedure.

Figure 5.11 shows another example for subprograms and their calling procedure. This is a version for the *apply_data* procedure which takes advantage of the *int2bin* utility procedure of Figure 5.10. This procedure could be written to take any number of integer inputs instead of the fixed thirteen. We defer adding this flexibility until type definitions and attributes are discussed in detail in Chapter 6.

5.2 PACKAGING PARTS AND UTILITIES

In the parts library of a hardware designer, gates or components are grouped according to their technology, physical characteristics, cost, complexity, or simply according to their availability. A designer chooses a certain group of components based on specific design requirements. In VHDL, packages can be used for this grouping of components. VHDL package constructs can also be used for packaging commonly used user defined types and subprograms.

5.2.1 Packaging Components

Gate level architectures of the *bit_comparator* and *sr_latch* in Chapter 4 (Figures 4.12 and 4.27, respectively) include declaration of the individual components that are used for their implementation. Alternatively, component declarations can be packaged and made available to all the architectures that use them. A package declaration containing declarations of *n1*, *n2*, and *n3* is shown in Figure 5.12. Bracketed between the heading of this statement and the END keyword, a package declaration includes components and other declarations as they would appear in the declarative part of an architecture.

Figure 5.13 shows a new version of the *gate_level* architecture of *bit_comparator* that takes advantage of the *simple_gates* package in Figure 5.12. This package has been made visible to the architecture of the *bit_comparator* by placing a use clause before its body.

The use clause specifies the name of the library, the name of the package, and the declarations that are to become visible. The ALL keyword makes all of the declarations in this package visible to the *gate_level* architecture of the *bit_comparator*. Instead of using this keyword, individual declarations can be listed, as depicted in the statement in Figure 5.14.

5.2.2 Packaging Subprograms

In order for various designs to share several subprograms, a package declaration must contain a declaration of the subprograms and the body of the subprograms must reside in a corresponding package body. A package declaration defines the interface of a package and includes the declarations that are to be visible from outside the package. A package body contains declarations that are local to it as well as bodies of locally or externally used subprograms. In the heading of a package body, the keyword BODY follows the PACKAGE keyword. Figures 5.15a and 5.15b show a package declaration and a package body (both named *basic_utilities*) in which the declaration and body of functions *fgl* and *feq* and the procedures *bin2int*, *int2bin*, and *apply_data* presented in Section 5.1, are included.

As discussed in the previous section, the *functional* architecture of the *bit_comparator* and the *procedural* architecture of the *nibble_comparator_test_bench* use these

```
PACKAGE simple_gates IS
    COMPONENT n1 PORT (i1: IN BIT; o1: OUT BIT); END COMPONENT;
    COMPONENT n2 PORT (i1, i2: IN BIT; o1: OUT BIT); END COMPONENT;
    COMPONENT
        n3 PORT (i1, i2, i3: IN BIT; o1: OUT BIT);
    END COMPONENT;
END simple_gates;
```

FIGURE 5.12
A package declaration containing component declarations of simple gates.

```
USE  WORK.simple_gates.ALL;
ARCHITECTURE  gate_level  OF  bit_comparator  IS
    FOR  ALL : n1  USE  ENTITY  WORK.inv  (single_delay);
    FOR  ALL : n2  USE  ENTITY  WORK.nand2  (single_delay);
    FOR  ALL : n3  USE  ENTITY  WORK.nand3  (single_delay);
    -- Intermediate  signals
    SIGNAL  im1,im2,  im3,  im4,  im5,  im6,  im7,  im8,  im9,  im10 : BIT;
BEGIN
    -- a_gt_b  output
    g0 : n1  PORT  MAP  (a,  im1);
    g1 : n1  PORT  MAP  (b,  im2);
    g2 : n2  PORT  MAP  (a,  im2,  im3);
    g3 : n2  PORT  MAP  (a,  gt,  im4);
    g4 : n2  PORT  MAP  (im2,  gt,  im5);
    g5 : n3  PORT  MAP  (im3,  im4,  im5,  a_gt_b);
    -- a_eq_b  output
    g6 : n3  PORT  MAP  (im1,  im2,  eq,  im6);
    g7 : n3  PORT  MAP  (a,  b,  eq,  im7);
    g8 : n2  PORT  MAP  (im6,  im7,  a_eq_b);
    -- a_lt_b  output
    g9 : n2  PORT  MAP  (im1,  b,  im8);
    g10 : n2  PORT  MAP  (im1,  lt,  im9);
    g11 : n2  PORT  MAP  (b,  lt,  im10);
    g12 : n3  PORT  MAP  (im8,  im9,  im10,  a_lt_b);
END  gate_level;
```

FIGURE 5.13
Using package of simple gates in *gate_level* of *bit_comparator*.

```
USE
  WORK.simple_gates.n1,
  WORK.simple_gates.n2,
  WORK.simple_gates.n3;
.
-- n1, n2 and n3 component declarations are  visible
.
```

FIGURE 5.14
An alternative application of the use clause.

subprograms. New versions of these architectures, which take advantage of the *basic_utilities* package, are shown in Figures 5.16 and 5.17, respectively.

   All declarations in the *basic_utilities* package declaration (Figure 5.15a) become visible to the architectures in Figures 5.16 and 5.17 through application of the use clause. Since the necessary subprogram bodies are included in the *basic_utilities* package body (Figure 5.15b), they need not be included in the declarative parts of the architectures where they are used.

```
PACKAGE basic_utilities IS
    TYPE integers IS ARRAY (0 TO 12) OF INTEGER;
    FUNCTION fgl (w, x, gl : BIT) RETURN BIT;
    FUNCTION feq (w, x, eq : BIT) RETURN BIT;
    PROCEDURE bin2int (bin : IN BIT_VECTOR; int : OUT INTEGER);
    PROCEDURE int2bin (int : IN INTEGER;  bin : OUT BIT_VECTOR);
    PROCEDURE apply_data (
        SIGNAL target : OUT BIT_VECTOR (3 DOWNTO 0);
        CONSTANT values : IN integers;  CONSTANT period : IN TIME);
END basic_utilities;
```

FIGURE 5.15a
The *basic_utilities* package declaration.

   A subprogram declaration only needs to be included in a package declaration if the subprogram, whose body is contained in the package body, is to be used from outside of the package. Functions and procedures that are used solely within the package containing their bodies do not have to be declared. This also applies to type declarations in that a type declared in the package declaration becomes visible to all descriptions that use that package, while a type declaration in a package body is only visible to that body.

5.3 DESIGN PARAMETRIZATION

Component models can be parametrized to better utilize gate or component models and to make general models usable in different design environments. The specific behavior of these models is dependent on the parameters that are determined by the design entities that use them. VHDL generic parameters can be used for this purpose. For example, a generic parameter can be used for timing and delay of a generic gate model. When this gate is used in a specific design environment, its generic parameters are determined. Usage of generic parameters and passing of values to these parameters is done in much the same way as it is with ports. The syntax of constructs related to ports and generics are similar, except that the generic clause and generic map aspect constructs use the keyword GENERIC instead of PORT. In general, generics are a means of communicating nonhardware and nonsignal information between designs.

   In order to illustrate the usage of generics, we will revise the comparator example presented in the previous chapter, this time using gate models that have generic timing parameters, as shown in Figure 5.18.

   An inverter, a two-input NAND gate, and a three-input NAND gate are shown in this figure. The entity declarations for these gates include a generic clause and a port clause, as shown in Figure 5.19. The generic clause in each of the gates in Figure 5.18 consists of a generic interface list which contains interface constant declarations for *tplh* and *tphl*. For the inverter, these generic parameters have default values of 5 ns and 3 ns, respectively.

   Default values will be used for *tplh* and *tphl* if these generics are not specified by any other method. The port clause in Figure 5.19 contains an interface list which

```
PACKAGE BODY basic_utilities IS
    FUNCTION fgl (w, x, gl : BIT) RETURN BIT IS
    BEGIN
        RETURN  (w AND gl) OR (NOT x  AND  gl) OR (w  AND  NOT x);
    END fgl;
    FUNCTION feq (w, x, eq : BIT) RETURN BIT IS
    BEGIN
        RETURN  (w AND x AND eq) OR (NOT w  AND  NOT x  AND  eq);
    END feq;
    PROCEDURE bin2int (bin : IN BIT_VECTOR; int : OUT INTEGER) IS
        VARIABLE result: INTEGER;
    BEGIN
        result := 0;
        FOR i IN bin'RANGE LOOP
            IF bin(i) = '1' THEN
                result := result + 2**i;
            END IF;
        END LOOP;
        int := result;
    END bin2int;
    PROCEDURE int2bin (int : IN INTEGER;  bin : OUT BIT_VECTOR) IS
        VARIABLE tmp : INTEGER;
        VARIABLE buf : BIT_VECTOR (bin'RANGE);
    BEGIN
        tmp := int;
        FOR i IN 0 TO (bin'LENGTH - 1) LOOP
            IF (tmp MOD 2  =  1) THEN
                bin (i) := '1';
            ELSE bin (i) := '0';
            END IF;
            tmp := tmp / 2;
        END LOOP;
    END int2bin;
    PROCEDURE apply_data (
        SIGNAL target : OUT BIT_VECTOR (3 DOWNTO 0);
        CONSTANT values : IN integers;  CONSTANT period : IN TIME)
            IS
        VARIABLE buf : BIT_VECTOR (3 DOWNTO 0);
    BEGIN
        FOR i IN 0 TO 12 LOOP
            int2bin (values(i), buf);
            target <= TRANSPORT buf AFTER i * period;
        END LOOP;
    END apply_data;
END basic_utilities;
```

FIGURE 5.15b
The *basic_utilities* package body.

```
USE  WORK.basic_utilities.ALL;
ARCHITECTURE  functional  OF  bit_comparator  IS
BEGIN
      a_gt_b  <=  fgl  (a,  b,  gt)  AFTER  12  NS;
      a_eq_b  <=  feq  (a,  b,  eq)  AFTER  12  NS;
      a_lt_b  <=  fgl  (b,  a,  lt)  AFTER  12  NS;
END  functional;
```

FIGURE 5.16
Using functions of the *basic_utilities* package.

```
USE  WORK.basic_utilities.ALL;
ARCHITECTURE  procedural  OF  nibble_comparator_test_bench  IS
      COMPONENT  comp4  PORT  (
          a,  b  :  IN  bit_vector  (3  DOWNTO  0);  gt,  eq,  lt  :  IN  BIT;
          a_gt_b,  a_eq_b,  a_lt_b  :  OUT  BIT);
      END  COMPONENT;
      FOR  a1  :  comp4  USE  ENTITY  WORK.nibble_comparator(structural);
      SIGNAL  a,  b  :  BIT_VECTOR  (3  DOWNTO  0);
      SIGNAL  eql,  lss,  gtr  :  BIT;
      SIGNAL  vdd  :  BIT  :=  '1';
      SIGNAL  gnd  :  BIT  :=  '0';
BEGIN
      a1:  comp4  PORT  MAP  (a,  b,  gnd,  vdd,  gnd,  gtr,  eql,  lss);
      apply_data  (a,  0&15&15&14&14&14&14&10&00&15&00&00&15,  500  NS);
      apply_data  (b,  0&14&14&15&15&12&12&12&15&15&15&00&00,  500  NS);
END  procedural;
```

FIGURE 5.17
Using procedures of the *basic_utilities* package.

consists of declarations for the input and the output of the inverter. Figures 4.2 and 4.5 illustrate the syntax structure of the port clause construct. Note that the port interface lists for *int_t*, *nand2_t*, and *nand3_t* in Figure 5.18 are identical to those for *inv*, *nand2*, and *nand3* in Chapter 4.

In the architecture bodies in Figure 5.18, appropriate logical expressions are assigned to the outputs of the gates after a delay value that is the average of low-to-high and high-to-low propagation delays. Note that for the default case, for example, *tplh* = 5 ns and *tphl* = 3 ns for the inverter, the time expression of the signal assignments evaluate delay values that are equal to those of similar gates in Chapter 4 (*inv* in Chapter 4 has a 4 ns delay).

Figure 5.20 shows interface aspects for the gates in Figure 5.18. As shown here, line arrows signify generics. This notation becomes part of the aspect notation that we introduced in Chapter 4. The composition aspects of the units using these gates must show how values are associated with these generics.

```
ENTITY inv_t IS
    GENERIC (tplh : TIME := 5 NS; tphl : TIME := 3 NS);
    PORT (i1 : IN BIT; o1 : OUT BIT);
END inv_t;
--
ARCHITECTURE average_delay OF inv_t IS
BEGIN
    o1 <= NOT i1 AFTER   (tplh + tphl) / 2;
END average_delay;

ENTITY nand2_t IS
    GENERIC (tplh : TIME := 6 NS; tphl : TIME := 4 NS);
    PORT (i1, i2 : IN BIT; o1 : OUT BIT);
END nand2_t;
--
ARCHITECTURE average_delay OF nand2_t IS
BEGIN
    o1 <= i1 NAND i2 AFTER   (tplh + tphl) / 2;
END average_delay;

ENTITY nand3_t IS
    GENERIC (tplh : TIME := 7 NS; tphl : TIME := 5 NS);
    PORT (i1, i2, i3 : IN BIT; o1 : OUT BIT);
END nand3_t;
--
ARCHITECTURE average_delay OF nand3_t IS
BEGIN
    o1 <= NOT ( i1 AND i2 AND i3 ) AFTER   (tplh + tphl) / 2;
END average_delay;
```

FIGURE 5.18
Parametrized gate models.

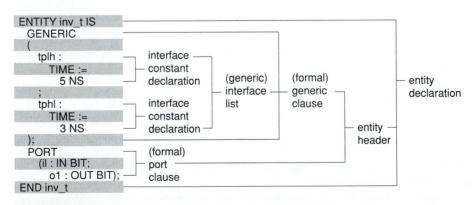

FIGURE 5.19
Details of the entity declaration of inverter with generics.

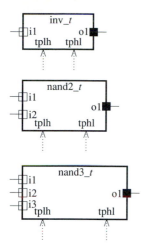

FIGURE 5.20

Interface aspects of *inv_t*, *nand2_t*, and *nand3_t*.

5.3.1   Using Default Values

Figure 5.21 shows an architecture for a *bit_comparator* that is identified as the *default_delay* and uses the gates shown in Figure 5.18. Except for the configuration specifications, this description is the same as the *gate_level* architecture of the *bit_comparator* in Chapter 4 (see Figure 4.12). Configuration specifications in Figure 5.21 associate instances of *n1*, *n2*, and *n3* components with the *average_delay* architectures for *inv_t*, *nand2_t*, and *nand3_t*.

  Since no reference is made in the *default_delay* architecture of the *bit_comparator* to the generics of its components and no association is specified for the formal generic parameters of these components, the default values of generics determine the timing behavior of *average_delay* architecture for *inv_t*, *nand2_t*, and *nand3_t*. This can only be done because the entity declaration in these units includes default values for their generic parameters.

5.3.2   Using Fixed Values

Constants or other generics may be associated with the formal generic parameters of a component. This is done in much the same way that signals are associated with the formal ports of components. Figure 5.22 shows another architecture for the *bit_comparator*. In the declarative part of this architecture, declaration of *n1*, *n2*, and *n3* components includes local generic clauses as well as local port clauses. Each instantiation of any of these components in the statement part of the *fixed_delay* architecture of the *bit_comparator* contains a generic map aspect and a port map aspect.

  The values used in the association list of the generic map aspects shown in Figure 5.23 are associated with the formal generics of *inv_t*, *nand2_t*, and *nand3_t*. These values are used in place of the default values in the generic interface list in the entity declaration for these entities. Since the component declarations do not include

```
ARCHITECTURE default_delay OF bit_comparator IS
    COMPONENT n1 PORT (i1: IN BIT; o1: OUT BIT); END COMPONENT;
    COMPONENT n2 PORT (i1, i2: IN BIT; o1: OUT BIT); END COMPONENT;
    COMPONENT n3 PORT (i1, i2, i3: IN BIT; o1: OUT BIT);
    END COMPONENT;
    FOR ALL : n1 USE ENTITY WORK.inv_t (average_delay);
    FOR ALL : n2 USE ENTITY WORK.nand2_t (average_delay);
    FOR ALL : n3 USE ENTITY WORK.nand3_t (average_delay);
-- Intermediate signals
    SIGNAL im1,im2, im3, im4, im5, im6, im7, im8, im9, im10 : BIT;
BEGIN
-- a_gt_b output
    g0 : n1 PORT MAP (a, im1);
    g1 : n1 PORT MAP (b, im2);
    g2 : n2 PORT MAP (a, im2, im3);
    g3 : n2 PORT MAP (a, gt, im4);
    g4 : n2 PORT MAP (im2, gt, im5);
    g5 : n3 PORT MAP (im3, im4, im5, a_gt_b);
-- a_eq_b output
    g6 : n3 PORT MAP (im1, im2, eq, im6);
    g7 : n3 PORT MAP (a, b, eq, im7);
    g8 : n2 PORT MAP (im6, im7, a_eq_b);
-- a_lt_b output
    g9 : n2 PORT MAP (im1, b, im8);
    g10 : n2 PORT MAP (im1, lt, im9);
    g11 : n2 PORT MAP (b, lt, im10);
    g12 : n3 PORT MAP (im8, im9, im10, a_lt_b);
END default_delay;
```

FIGURE 5.21
Using default values for the generics of logic gates.

default values to be associated with the formal generics of these components, inclusion of generic map aspects with instantiations of these components is required.

5.3.3   Passing Generic Parameters

Still another way to specify generic parameters is to pass values to them through other generics. In the more formal VHDL terminology, this can be stated: associating generics of components with the generic parameters of the architectures that instantiate those components. A version of the single bit comparator (*bit_comparator_t*) with generic parameters, whose entity declaration is shown in Figure 5.24a, illustrates this method.

   This declaration contains a generic interface list that has six formal parameters of type TIME. As shown in Figure 5.24b, the *passed_delay* architecture of *bit_comparator_t*, uses generic map clauses to associate generic parameters in this entity with those in *inv_t*, *nand2_t*, and *nand3_t*. Six generics of the *bit_comparator_t*

```
ARCHITECTURE fixed_delay OF bit_comparator IS
    COMPONENT n1
        GENERIC (tplh, tphl : TIME);   PORT (i1: IN BIT; o1: OUT BIT);
    END COMPONENT;
    COMPONENT n2
        GENERIC (tplh, tphl : TIME);   PORT (i1, i2: IN BIT; o1: OUT BIT);
    END COMPONENT;
    COMPONENT n3
        GENERIC (tplh, tphl : TIME);   PORT (i1, i2, i3: IN BIT; o1: OUT BIT);
    END COMPONENT;
    FOR ALL : n1 USE ENTITY WORK.inv_t (average_delay);
    FOR ALL : n2 USE ENTITY WORK.nand2_t (average_delay);
    FOR ALL : n3 USE ENTITY WORK.nand3_t (average_delay);
-- Intermediate signals
    SIGNAL im1,im2, im3, im4, im5, im6, im7, im8, im9, im10 : BIT;
BEGIN
-- a_gt_b output
    g0 : n1 GENERIC MAP (2 NS, 4 NS) PORT MAP (a, im1);
    g1 : n1 GENERIC MAP (2 NS, 4 NS) PORT MAP (b, im2);
    g2 : n2 GENERIC MAP (3 NS, 5 NS) PORT MAP (a, im2, im3);
    g3 : n2 GENERIC MAP (3 NS, 5 NS) PORT MAP (a, gt, im4);
    g4 : n2 GENERIC MAP (3 NS, 5 NS) PORT MAP (im2, gt, im5);
    g5 : n3 GENERIC MAP (4 NS, 6 NS) PORT MAP (im3, im4, im5, a_gt_b);
-- a_eq_b output
    g6 : n3 GENERIC MAP (4 NS, 6 NS) PORT MAP (im1, im2, eq, im6);
    g7 : n3 GENERIC MAP (4 NS, 6 NS) PORT MAP (a, b, eq, im7);
    g8 : n2 GENERIC MAP (3 NS, 5 NS) PORT MAP (im6, im7, a_eq_b);
-- a_lt_b output
    g9 : n2 GENERIC MAP (3 NS, 5 NS) PORT MAP (im1, b, im8);
    g10 : n2 GENERIC MAP (3 NS, 5 NS) PORT MAP (im1, lt, im9);
    g11 : n2 GENERIC MAP (3 NS, 5 NS) PORT MAP (b, lt, im10);
    g12 : n3 GENERIC MAP (4 NS, 6 NS) PORT MAP (im8, im9, im10, a_lt_b);
END fixed_delay;
```

FIGURE 5.22
Associating fixed values with the generics of logic gates.

constitute three pairs of low-to-high and high-to-low propagation delay values that are used for calculating timing parameters of the three components in this entity. Unlike ports that can be read or written into, depending on their mode, generics can only be read.

To clarify the architectural description presented in Figure 5.24 and in order to keep up with our interface and composition aspect notations, we have shown the composition aspect of the *passed_delay* architecture of the *bit_comparator_t* in Figure 5.25. This figure shows graphically the passing of timing parameters for the *bit_comparator_t* to those of its individual components.

The entity declaration of the *bit_comparator* (Figure 5.24a) does not specify default values for its six generic parameters. This implies that the body using this entity

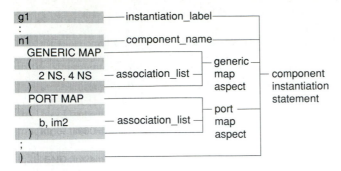

FIGURE 5.23
Component instantiation statement with generic map aspect.

must specify these parameters by declaration or by mapping. The *iterative* architecture of the *nibble_comparator* in Figure 4.19 is rewritten as shown in Figure 5.26 to use the latter version of the single bit comparator.

The *comp1* component is declared with default values for its timing parameters. Because of the absence of generic map aspects from the instantiations of *comp1* in the statement part of the *iterative* architecture of the *nibble_comparator*, the default generic values will be used by the *bit_comparator_t*. The *passed_delay* architecture of the *bit_comparator_t*, in turn, passes these values to *inv_t*, *nand2_t*, and *nand3_t*, which then overwrite the default values in the entity declaration of these units.

For a component whose declaration contains local generics (for example, declaration of *comp1* in the *iterative* architecture of the *nibble_comparator* in Figure 5.26), the absence of a generic map aspect from its instantiation (see, for example, *c0*, *c*, or *c3* instantiations of *comp1*) implies that all such generics are *open*. Instead of complete exclusion of the generic map aspect, it is possible to use it with component instantiations, using the OPEN keyword for the generics whose default values are to be used. For example, the *c0* instantiation of *comp1* can be written as shown in Figure 5.27.

Here, default values, as specified in the declaration of *comp1*, are associated with *tplh1*, *tplh2*, *tphl1*, and *tphl2*. For the *tplh3* and *tphl3* parameters, however, 8 ns and 10 ns will be used, respectively. Another method for associating OPEN with certain generics or ports is to use named association instead of positional association. In this case, values are specified only for the generics whose default values are not to be used. Figure 5.28 shows another possibility for *c0* instantiation of *comp1*. This instantiation, which is equivalent to that shown in Figure 5.27, uses named association for the *tplh3* and *tphl3* parameters. All other generic parameters are assumed OPEN.

As noted, OPEN and named association can be used in generic map aspects as well as port maps. Using OPEN in the association list of a port map aspect implies an open wire (signal) rather than a default value.

This section presented several alternatives for associating constants with generic parameters. The omission of both declaring and mapping of generics, as in the *default_delay* architecture of the *bit_comparator*, is best suited for cases where all in

```
ENTITY bit_comparator_t IS
    GENERIC (tplh1, tplh2, tplh3, tphl1, tphl2, tphl3 : TIME);
    PORT (a, b,                              -- data inputs
          gt,                                -- previous greater than
          eq,                                -- previous equal
          lt : IN BIT;                       -- previous less than
          a_gt_b,                            -- greater
          a_eq_b,                            -- equal
          a_lt_b : OUT BIT);                 -- less than
END bit_comparator_t;
```

(a)

```
ARCHITECTURE passed_delay OF bit_comparator_t IS
    COMPONENT n1
        GENERIC (tplh, tphl : TIME);   PORT (i1: IN BIT; o1: OUT BIT);
    END COMPONENT;
    COMPONENT n2
        GENERIC (tplh, tphl : TIME);   PORT (i1, i2: IN BIT; o1: OUT BIT);
    END COMPONENT;
    COMPONENT n3
        GENERIC (tplh, tphl : TIME);   PORT (i1, i2, i3: IN BIT; o1: OUT BIT);
    END COMPONENT;
    FOR ALL : n1 USE ENTITY WORK.inv_t (average_delay);
    FOR ALL : n2 USE ENTITY WORK.nand2_t (average_delay);
    FOR ALL : n3 USE ENTITY WORK.nand3_t (average_delay);
-- Intermediate signals
    SIGNAL im1,im2, im3, im4, im5, im6, im7, im8, im9, im10 : BIT;
BEGIN
-- a_gt_b output
    g0 : n1 GENERIC MAP (tplh1, tphl1) PORT MAP (a, im1);
    g1 : n1 GENERIC MAP (tplh1, tphl1) PORT MAP (b, im2);
    g2 : n2 GENERIC MAP (tplh2, tphl2) PORT MAP (a, im2, im3);
    g3 : n2 GENERIC MAP (tplh2, tphl2) PORT MAP (a, gt, im4);
    g4 : n2 GENERIC MAP (tplh2, tphl2) PORT MAP (im2, gt, im5);
    g5 : n3 GENERIC MAP (tplh3, tphl3) PORT MAP (im3, im4, im5, a_gt_b);
-- a_eq_b output
    g6 : n3 GENERIC MAP (tplh3, tphl3) PORT MAP (im1, im2, eq, im6);
    g7 : n3 GENERIC MAP (tplh3, tphl3) PORT MAP (a, b, eq, im7);
    g8 : n2 GENERIC MAP (tplh2, tphl2) PORT MAP (im6, im7, a_eq_b);
-- a_lt_b output
    g9 : n2 GENERIC MAP (tplh2, tphl2) PORT MAP (im1, b, im8);
    g10 : n2 GENERIC MAP (tplh2, tphl2) PORT MAP (im1, lt, im9);
    g11 : n2 GENERIC MAP (tplh2, tphl2) PORT MAP (b, lt, im10);
    g12 : n3 GENERIC MAP (tplh3, tphl3) PORT MAP (im8, im9, im10, a_lt_b);
END passed_delay;
```

(b)

FIGURE 5.24
A bit comparator with timing parameters (a) entity declaration, (b) passing generics of bit comparator to its components.

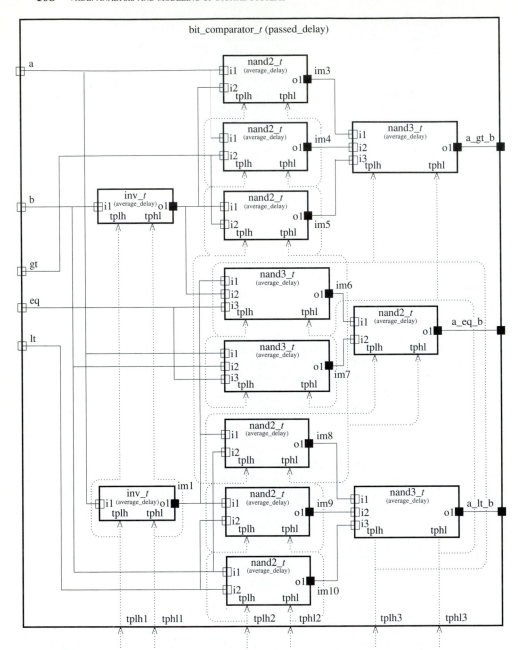

FIGURE 5.25

Composition aspect of *bit_comparator_t*. Dotted lines with arrows indicate generics.

```
ARCHITECTURE  iterative  OF  nibble_comparator  IS
    COMPONENT  comp1
       GENERIC(tplh1  :  TIME  :=  2  NS;  tplh2  :  TIME  :=  3  NS;  tplh3  :  TIME  :=  4  NS;
               tphl1  :  TIME  :=  4  NS;  tphl2  :  TIME  :=  5  NS;  tphl3  :  TIME  :=  6  NS);
       PORT  (a,  b,  gt,  eq,  lt  :  IN  BIT;  a_gt_b,  a_eq_b,  a_lt_b  :  OUT  BIT);
    END  COMPONENT;
    FOR  ALL  :  comp1  USE  ENTITY  WORK.bit_comparator_t  (passed_delay);
    SIGNAL  im  :  BIT_VECTOR  (  0  TO  8);
BEGIN
    c0:  comp1  PORT  MAP  (a(0),  b(0),  gt,  eq,  lt,  im(0),  im(1),  im(2));
    c1to2:  FOR  i  IN  1  TO  2  GENERATE
       c:  comp1  PORT  MAP  (a(i),  b(i),  im(i*3-3),  im(i*3-2),  im(i*3-1),
                             im(i*3+0),  im(i*3+1),  im(i*3+2)  );
    END  GENERATE;
    c3:  comp1  PORT  MAP  (a(3),  b(3),  im(6),  im(7),  im(8),
                          a_gt_b,  a_eq_b,  a_lt_b);
END  iterative;
```

FIGURE 5.26
Passing default values of local generics to the generics of *bit_comparator_t*.

```
ARCHITECTURE  iterative  OF  nibble_comparator  IS
    ...
BEGIN
    c0:  comp1
            GENERIC  MAP  (OPEN,  OPEN,  8  NS,  OPEN,  OPEN,  10  NS)
            PORT  MAP  (a(0),  b(0),  gt,  eq,  lt,  im(0),  im(1),  im(2));
    ...
END  iterative;
```

FIGURE 5.27
Associating constants with some of generics of *bit_comparator_t*, and using defaults for others.

```
ARCHITECTURE  iterative  OF  nibble_comparator  IS
    ...
BEGIN
    c0:  comp1
            GENERIC  MAP  (tplh3  =>  8  NS,  tphl3  =>  10  NS)
            PORT  MAP  (a(0),  b(0),  gt,  eq,  lt,  im(0),  im(1),  im(2));
    ...
END  iterative;
```

FIGURE 5.28
Using named association in the generic association list of *comp1*.

stantiations of a component use the same delay values. The ability to associate values with individual instances of a component, as in the *fixed_delay* architecture of the *bit_comparator*, enables the modeler to account for loading and environmental effects. For example, if an inverter has a fan-out of 2, the values associated with its timing generics can be specified as twice that of an inverter that drives only one gate. In general, using default values in entity declarations or in component declarations is helpful and it alleviates the need to specify the same values for all instances of a component. If needed, these default values can easily be overwritten in the generic map aspects of component instantiations.

We have presented examples for specifying gate delay values in order to demonstrate the use of generics. Other uses of these parameters include passing fan-in and fan-outs, load resistance or capacitance, and even number of bits or size of a hardware structure. For example, size of a general model for a shift register or a memory array can be customized by using appropriate values for their generic parameters.

5.4   DESIGN CONFIGURATION

Binding a component instantiation to an actual component, as described in Section 5 of Chapter 4, does not have to be done in the architecture that uses this component. This binding can be deferred until later and accomplished by a configuration declaration. Therefore, it is possible to generate a generic design and specify the details of timing or a specific component library at a later stage. This way, a generic design can be tested for various logic families or a single test bench can be used to test various versions of the same component. By use of configurations, trying different descriptions of a component in an upper level design can easily be done even at the deepest level of nesting.

5.4.1   A General Purpose Test Bench

Several versions of the *bit_comparator* and *nibble_comparator* have been developed in this and the previous chapter. The *structural* architecture of the *nibble_comparator* in Figure 5.3 and the *iterative* architecture of the *nibble_comparator* in Figure 5.26 are two units that are very different in their underlaying structures. The former wires four *bit_comparator*s that are described by Boolean equations (shown in Figure 5.1), while the latter uses the *bit_comparator*s in Figure 5.24 that are made of gate level components. In spite of their differences, the *procedural* test bench in Figure 5.17 can be made to serve as a test bench for both units. This test bench takes advantage of the *basic_utilities* in Figure 5.15 for the generation of test vectors, and in its architecture body, the association of the *a1* instance of *comp4* with the *structural* architecture of the *nibble_comparator* is done by a configuration specification. Removing this specification converts our test bench to a fairly general purpose tester for different *nibble_comparator*s.

As shown in Figure 5.29, this general purpose test bench is identified as *customizable*. For testing different designs, modifying the test bench and replacing the old test bench with the modified version in the design library can be avoided by developing multiple configuration declarations for the same test bench.

The configuration declaration in Figure 5.30 configures the test bench in Figure 5.29 for testing the *structural* architecture of the *nibble_comparator*. This configuration declaration is identified as *functional*, and it associates the *a1* instance of

```
USE  WORK.basic_utilities.ALL;
ARCHITECTURE  customizable  OF  nibble_comparator_test_bench  IS
    COMPONENT  comp4  PORT  (
        a,  b  :  IN  bit_vector  (3  DOWNTO  0);  gt,  eq,  lt  :  IN  BIT;
        a_gt_b,  a_eq_b,  a_lt_b  :  OUT  BIT);
    END  COMPONENT;
    SIGNAL  a,  b  :  BIT_VECTOR  (3  DOWNTO  0);
    SIGNAL  eql,  lss,  gtr  :  BIT;
    SIGNAL  vdd  :  BIT  :=  '1';
    SIGNAL  gnd  :  BIT  :=  '0';
BEGIN
    a1:  comp4  PORT  MAP  (a,  b,  gnd,  vdd,  gnd,  gtr,  eql,  lss);
    apply_data  (a,  0&15&15&14&14&14&14&10&00&15&00&00&15,  500  NS);
    apply_data  (b,  0&14&14&15&15&12&12&12&15&15&15&00&00,  500  NS);
END  customizable;
```

FIGURE 5.29
A customizable test bench.

```
USE  WORK.ALL;
CONFIGURATION  functional  OF  nibble_comparator_test_bench  IS
    FOR  customizable
        FOR  a1  :  comp4
1   2   3       USE  ENTITY  WORK.nibble_comparator(structural);
        END  FOR;
    END  FOR;
END  functional;
```

FIGURE 5.30
Configuring *customizable* for testing *structural* architecture of *nibble_comparator*.

comp4 with the *structural* architecture of the *nibble_comparator*. There are three levels of nestings in this description, and they are numbered accordingly. Note that these numbers are for illustration only and are not part of the code. The first level is the bracketing of the configuration declaration. The second level is for obtaining visibility into the *customizable* architecture of the *nibble_comparator_test_bench*, and the third level constitutes the binding of *a1* to an actual component. As indicated in the composition aspect of the *functional* configuration of *nibble_comparator_test_bench*, shown in Figure 5.31, a configuration declaration is placed on top of the entity for which component bindings need to be specified. As shown in our aspect notations, we use rounded rectangles to signify configuration declarations and the configuration name is placed in this rectangle. In Figure 5.31 the arrow with a triangular head that points to the *comp4* component illustrates that the binding for this component is specified by the configuration declaration from which the arrow originates.

  In order to test the *iterative* architecture in Figure 5.26, the configuration declaration in Figure 5.32 must be used to configure our general purpose test bench

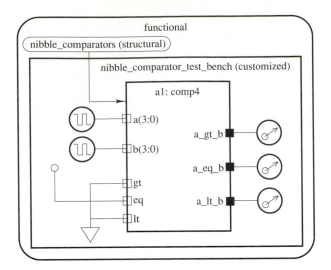

FIGURE 5.31
Composition aspect for *functional* configuration declaration, configuring *customizable* test bench.

```
USE  WORK.ALL;
CONFIGURATION average_delay OF nibble_comparator_test_bench IS
    FOR customizable
        FOR a1 : comp4
            USE  ENTITY  WORK.nibble_comparator(iterative);
        END  FOR;
    END  FOR;
END  average_delay;
```

FIGURE 5.32
Configuring *customizable* for testing *iterative* architecture of *nibble_comparator*.

(*customizable*) to use this unit. This declaration is identified as *average_delay* and it binds the *a1* label of *comp4* to the *iterative* architecture of the *nibble_comparator*.

As in Figure 5.30, the configuration declaration in Figure 5.32 is preceded by a use statement, which makes the entity to be configured visible. The details in the rest of this figure are shown in Figure 5.33.

The heading in this statement specifies an identifier for the configuration declaration and the entity to be configured. This is followed by a block configuration within which the scope is limited to the statement part of the *customizable* architecture of the *nibble_comparator_test_bench*. In this block configuration, binding for all visible components can be specified by individual component configurations. Since our test bench contains only one component, namely the *nibble_comparator*, a single component configuration is needed. Component configurations begin with the FOR keyword followed by component specifications which were discussed in Chapter 4, and shown in Figure 4.32. Following the USE keyword, a binding indication is used to associate the *a1* instance of *comp4* to the *iterative* architecture of the *nibble_comparator*. As shown in this figure, there is only a minor difference between the syntax of component configurations and the configuration specifications discussed in Chapter 4. The former

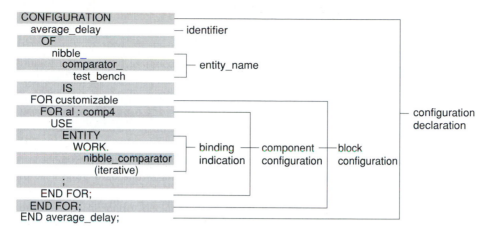

FIGURE 5.33
Details of configuration declaration.

requires END FOR, while the latter, which is used in declarative part of architectures, does not. Component configurations, however, offer more flexibility and many levels of component nestings can be specified within these constructs.

5.4.2   Configuring Nested Components

Initially, a designer may use components based on their functionality rather than timings or specific technology. These designs may be used in upper level designs, which may cause them to be buried under several levels of design hierarchy. Configuration declarations can be extended beyond configuring components of the immediate architectures and be used to configure several levels of component nestings.

Consider, for example, the three *bit_comparator*s that were developed in Section 5.3. These *bit_comparator*s (*default_delay*, *fixed_delay*, and *passed_delay* in Figures 5.21, 5.22, and 5.24, respectively) can be wired into a 4-bit comparator and tested using a single *nibble_comparator* description and a test bench.

The *flexible* architecture of the *nibble_comparator*, shown in Figure 5.34, wires four single bit comparators. Because of the absence of the configuration specification in the declarative part of this architecture, instances of *comp1* are not associated with actual components. Using this *nibble_comparator* and the *customizable* architecture of *nibble_comparator_test_bench* (Figure 5.29), three *bit_comparator*s presented in previous sections can be wired and tested. For this purpose, a configuration declaration must be placed on top of the customizable test bench to 1) associate instances of *comp4* with the *flexible* architecture of *nibble_comparator*, and 2) associate all *comp1* instances of the *flexible nibble_comparator* with the specific *bit_comparator* we are using to construct the 4-bit comparator.

Figure 5.35 shows the composition aspect for a configuration declaration for wiring and testing the *default_delay* architecture of the *bit_comparator*. As shown by the triangular arrows, binding for the *nibble_comparator* and for the instances of the

```
ARCHITECTURE flexible OF nibble_comparator IS
    COMPONENT comp1
        PORT (a, b, gt, eq, lt : IN BIT; a_gt_b, a_eq_b, a_lt_b : OUT BIT);
    END COMPONENT;
    SIGNAL im : BIT_VECTOR ( 0 TO 8);
BEGIN
    c0: comp1 PORT MAP (a(0), b(0), gt, eq, lt, im(0), im(1), im(2));
    c1to2: FOR i IN 1 TO 2 GENERATE
        c: comp1 PORT MAP (a(i), b(i), im(i*3-3), im(i*3-2), im(i*3-1),
                           im(i*3+0), im(i*3+1), im(i*3+2) );
    END GENERATE;
    c3: comp1 PORT MAP (a(3), b(3), im(6), im(7), im(8),
                        a_gt_b, a_eq_b, a_lt_b);
END flexible;
```

FIGURE 5.34
A general purpose *nibble_comparator*.

bit_comparator are specified by this configuration. The VHDL code in Figure 5.36 corresponds to this composition aspect. This description is the *default_bit_level* configuration for the *nibble_comparator_test_bench* and it can be read as follows:

> The *default_bit_level* configuration declaration is for the *customizable* architecture of the *nibble_comparator_test_bench*. Inside this architecture, the *a1* instance of *comp4* is associated with the *flexible* architecture of the *nibble_comparator*. Within the *flexible* architecture of the *nibble_comparator*, the *c0* and *c3* instances of *comp1* are associated with the *default_delay* architecture of the *bit_comparator*. Also within this *flexible* block, inside the *c1to2* generate statement, *c* instances of *comp1* are associated with the *default_delay* architecture of the *bit_comparator*.

At each level of nesting, block configurations are needed to obtain the visibility of a component, and component configurations are needed to associate instances of components with actual components.

Figure 5.37 shows the configuration of the test bench for associating instances of *comp1* with the *fixed_delay* architecture of the *bit_comparator*. Except for the identifiers, this description is identical to that in Figure 5.36.

The third configuration declaration we will discuss is one for wiring and testing the *passed_delay* architecture of the *bit_comparator_t* entity. Since this entity includes generic parameters and the *flexible* architecture of the *nibble_comparator* does not provide default generic values in its declaration of *comp1*, any binding to this entity must include specification of its generic parameters. Figure 5.38 shows the composition aspect of a test bench for testing a *nibble_comparator* consisting of four such bit comparators.

This figure illustrates bindings of *comp4* and *comp1* to appropriate components, as well as association of values with the generics of the single bit comparators. The bit comparators used here use six generic parameters and are represented by the composition aspect in Figure 5.25. The VHDL description corresponding to the composition

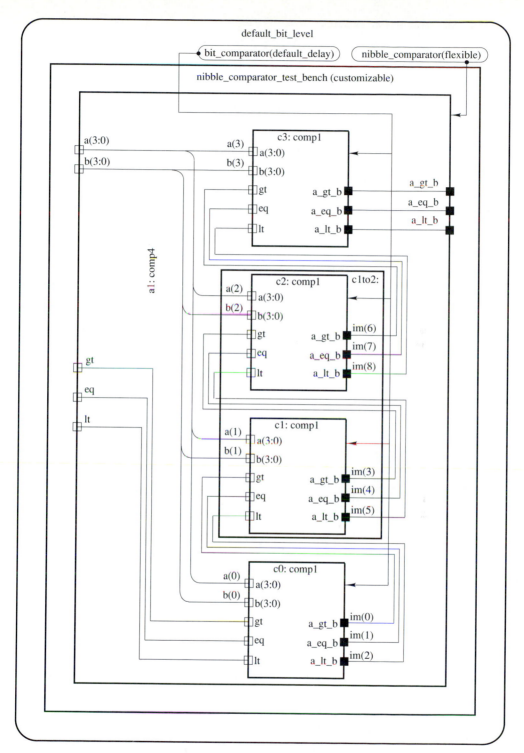

FIGURE 5.35
Composition aspect for configuring *customizable* test bench for testing *default_delay bit_comparator*.

115

```
USE WORK.ALL;
CONFIGURATION default_bit_level OF nibble_comparator_test_bench IS
    FOR customizable
        FOR a1 : comp4
            USE ENTITY WORK.nibble_comparator(flexible);
            FOR flexible
                FOR c0, c3: comp1
                    USE ENTITY WORK.bit_comparator (default_delay);
                END FOR;
                FOR c1to2
                    FOR c: comp1
                        USE ENTITY WORK.bit_comparator (default_delay);
                    END FOR;
                END FOR;
            END FOR;
        END FOR;
    END FOR;
END default_bit_level;
```

FIGURE 5.36
Configuration declaration for configuring *customizable* test bench for testing *default_delay bit_comparator*.

```
USE WORK.ALL;
CONFIGURATION fixed_bit_level OF nibble_comparator_test_bench IS
    FOR customizable
        FOR a1 : comp4
            USE ENTITY WORK.nibble_comparator(flexible);
            FOR flexible
                FOR c0, c3: comp1
                    USE ENTITY WORK.bit_comparator (fixed_delay);
                END FOR;
                FOR c1to2
                    FOR c: comp1
                        USE ENTITY WORK.bit_comparator (fixed_delay);
                    END FOR;
                END FOR;
            END FOR;
        END FOR;
    END FOR;
END fixed_bit_level;
```

FIGURE 5.37
Configuring *customizable* test bench for testing the *fixed_delay* architecture of *bit_comparator*.

aspect in Figure 5.38 is shown in Figure 5.39. Like the *default_bit_level* and the *fixed_bit_level*, the *passed_bit_level* configuration uses nested block configurations and component configurations to the point that instances of *comp1* become visible and the binding for them can be specified. The binding indications of the latter configuration,

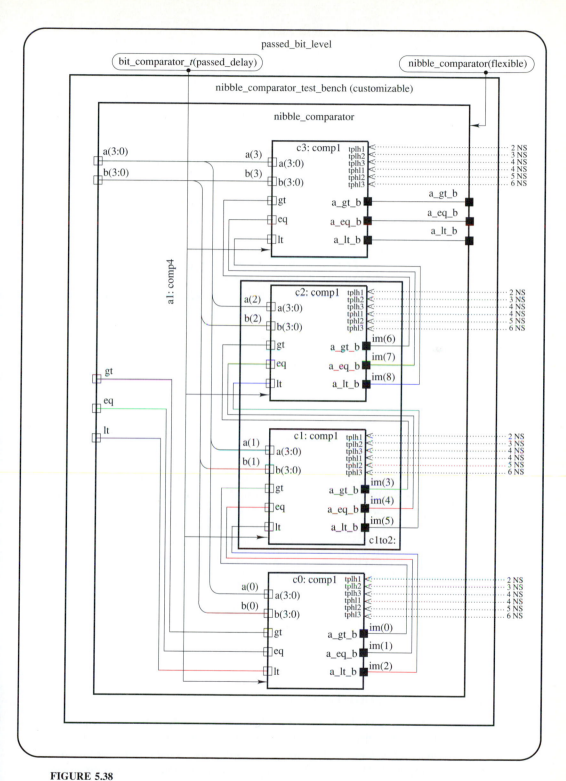

FIGURE 5.38

Composition aspect of the *passed_bit_level* configuration of the test bench for testing *passed_delay* architecture of *bit_comparator_t*.

```
USE WORK.ALL;
CONFIGURATION passed_bit_level OF nibble_comparator_test_benchIS
  FOR customizable
    FOR a1 : comp4
      USE ENTITY WORK.nibble_comparator(flexible);
      FOR flexible
        FOR c0, c3: comp1
          USE ENTITY WORK.bit_comparator_t (passed_delay)
          GENERIC MAP (tplh1 => 2 NS, tplh2 => 3 NS,
                                  tplh3 => 4 NS, tphl1 => 4 NS,
                                  tphl2 => 5 NS, tphl3 => 6 NS);
        END FOR;
        FOR c1to2
          FOR c: comp1
            USE ENTITY WORK.bit_comparator_t (passed_delay)
            GENERIC MAP (tplh1 => 2 NS, tplh2 => 3 NS,
                                    tplh3 => 4 NS, tphl1 => 4 NS,
                                    tphl2 => 5 NS, tphl3 => 6 NS);
          END FOR;
        END FOR;
      END FOR;
    END FOR;
  END FOR;
END passed_bit_level;
```

FIGURE 5.39
Using configuration declarations for component bindings, and specification of generic parameters.

however, contain a generic map aspect in addition to the entity aspect. Generic map aspects specify six delay values for the *bit_comparator*. This unit passes these delay values to the generic parameters of its underlying gates.

Figure 5.40 shows the syntax details of the *flexible* block configuration indicated in Figure 5.39 by the double vertical lines. Enclosed in this block configuration are a component configuration and another block configuration. The component configuration is used for associating *c0* and *c3* instances of *comp1* and for associating constants with the generic parameters of this component. The *c1to2* block configuration is for gaining visibility into the *c1to2* generate statement of the *flexible* architecture of the *nibble_comparator*. A component configuration, enclosed in this block configuration, specifies the binding and generic parameters for the *c* instance of the *comp1* component.

5.4.3   An n-bit Register Example

Thus far, we have presented syntax and applications of configuration declaration. At this point, we close the discussion of this topic with a comprehensive example.

The *single_delay* gate models for *inv*, *nand2*, and *nand3* were discussed in Section 1 of Chapter 4. The more advanced *average_delay* gate models with generic

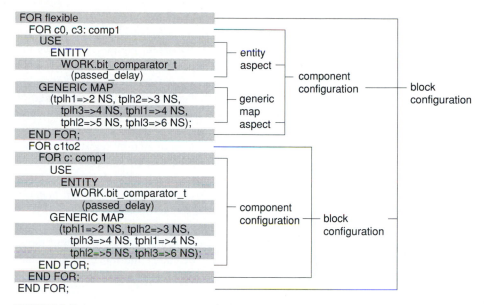

FIGURE 5.40
Details of a block configuration enclosing component configurations and other block configurations.

timing parameters were presented in Section 5.3. This section presents an n-bit register, using unspecified inverters and NAND gates. We will show how this unbound register can be configured to use specific gate models (*single_delay* or *average_delay*) for its underlying logical gates.

Figure 5.41 shows the *gate_level* architecture of a clocked SR-latch. This latch uses four instances of an *n2* component which are not bound to any specific structure.

```
ENTITY sr_latch IS PORT (s, r, c : IN BIT; q : OUT BIT);
END sr_latch;
--
ARCHITECTURE gate_level OF sr_latch IS
    COMPONENT n2 PORT (i1, i2: IN BIT; o1: OUT BIT); END COMPONENT;
    SIGNAL im1, im2, im3, im4 : BIT;
BEGIN
    g1 : n2 PORT MAP (s, c, im1);
    g2 : n2 PORT MAP (r, c, im2);
    g3 : n2 PORT MAP (im1, im4, im3);
    g4 : n2 PORT MAP (im3, im2, im4);
    q <= im3;
END gate_level;
```

FIGURE 5.41
Unbound VHDL description of set-reset latch.

Except for the binding of its components, this description is the same as that in Figure 4.27.

A D-type latch consists of an inverter and an SR-latch. Figure 5.42 shows the VHDL description for such a component. The D input is connected to the Set input of the SR-latch and the complement of the D input (*dbar*) drives its Reset input. As with the SR-latch, in order to keep the description flexible in terms of the usage of components, the *sr_based* architecture of *d_latch* does not specify bindings for the instances of *sr* and *n1*.

Our next level in the design process is the formation of an n-bit register by wiring n D-type latches. This is done in the *latch_based* architecture of *d_register*, shown in Figure 5.43. Note that this figure does not specify binding for the *di* instance of the declared *dl* component. Again, this is for the purpose of keeping the design generic. At a later stage, we bind instances of *dl* to the *sr_based* architecture of *d_latch*.

To generate multiple instances of *dl*, a generate statement with a range equal to that of the input is used. Equating the range of this statement to the *d* input range is achieved by using the RANGE attribute. If, for example, the range of the actual

```
ENTITY d_latch IS PORT (d, c : IN BIT; q : OUT BIT);
END d_latch;
--
ARCHITECTURE sr_based OF d_latch IS
    COMPONENT sr PORT (s, r, c : IN BIT; q : OUT BIT); END COMPONENT;
    COMPONENT n1 PORT (i1: IN BIT; o1: OUT BIT); END COMPONENT;
    SIGNAL dbar : BIT;
BEGIN
    c1 : sr PORT MAP (d, dbar, c, q);
    c2 : n1 PORT MAP (d, dbar);
END sr_based;
```

FIGURE 5.42
Unbound VHDL description of a D-latch.

```
ENTITY d_register IS
    PORT (d : IN BIT_VECTOR; c : IN BIT;   q : OUT BIT_VECTOR);
END d_register;
--
ARCHITECTURE latch_based OF d_register IS
    COMPONENT dl PORT (d, c : IN BIT; q : OUT BIT); END COMPONENT;
BEGIN
    dr : FOR i IN d'RANGE GENERATE
        di : dl PORT MAP (d(i), c, q(i));
    END GENERATE;
END latch_based;
```

FIGURE 5.43
Unbound VHDL description for an n-bit latch.

signal associated with *d* is 7 DOWNTO 0, then the generate statement generates eight instances of *dl*. This description completes the wiring of an n-bit register using basic gate level components.

In order to relate instances of the components used in the *latch_based* architecture of *d_register* to actual entities, a configuration declaration is needed. Figure 5.44 shows the composition aspect for such a configuration. The *average_gate_delay* configuration is placed on top of this architecture and is used to specify the bindings and generic parameters of its components at various nesting levels. All instances of *n1* and *n2* components are associated with the *average_delay* architectures of inverters and NAND gates presented in Figure 5.18.

Figure 5.45 shows the VHDL code that corresponds to this composition aspect. For visibility into an architecture or a block, block configurations are used. For binding a component label to an actual component, component configurations are used. A component configuration is possible only when an instance of that component has been made visible by the use of nested block configurations.

The numbers on the vertical lines in the *average_gate_delay* configuration of the *d_register* identify configuration constructs. The table in Figure 5.46 uses these numerical identifiers to describe the type and purpose of each construct. Column 2 shows whether a construct is block or component configuration. The next two columns indicate the purpose of the configuration, visibility into a block or binding to an entity. The last column shows other configurations that were used to gain visibility into a configuration.

Another configuration for the *d_register* is shown in Figure 5.47. Using this configuration declaration, the *n1* and *n2* components of the latch structures are bound to the *single_delay* architectures of *inv* and *nand2*, respectively. This description does not specify port map aspects for the *g1* and *g3* instances of *n2* or the *c2* instance of *n1*. Therefore, their local ports, from component declarations in the respective architectures (the architecture in Figure 5.41 for *g1* and *g3*, and the architecture in Figure 5.42 for *c2*) will be used for association with the formal ports of *n2* or *n1* components. For instance, the declaration of *n1* in the *sr_based* architecture of *d_latch* (shown in Figure 5.42) declares *i1* as the input and *o1* as output of this component. These local ports are associated with the formal ports of the *single_delay* architecture of *inv*. For the *g2* and *g4* instances of *n2*, however, the configuration declaration in Figure 5.47 specifies a port map aspect. Because of this, the local ports of the *n2* component are associated with *i1*, *i1*, *i2*, and *o1* before they are associated with the formal ports of the *single_delay* architecture of *nand3*. This causes the first two inputs of the three input NAND gate to be tied together and tied to the signal associated with *i1*. Referring to Figure 5.41, *r* is associated with *i1* in the *g2* instance of *n2*, and *im3* is associated with *i1* in the *g4* instance of this component. A similar association was described in Chapter 4. The description in Figure 4.30 uses a configuration specification to achieve what is done by the component configuration of Figure 5.47.

No design is considered complete until it is tested. We close the description of configuration declarations by presenting a test bench for the *single_gate_delay* config-

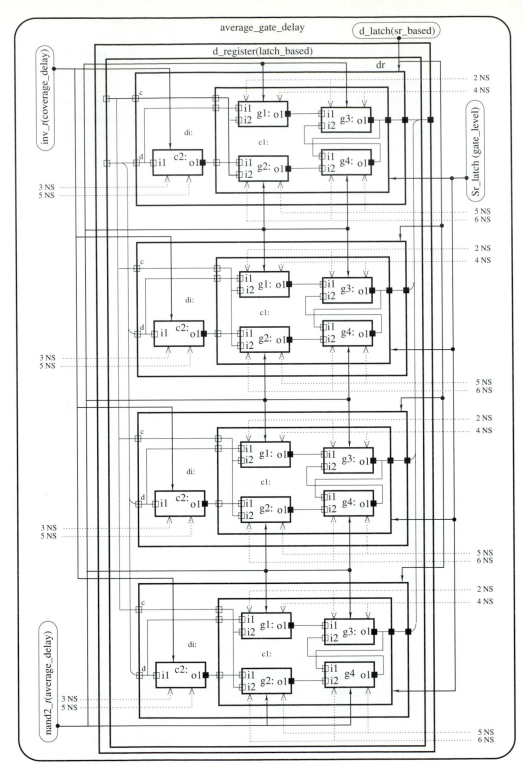

FIGURE 5.44

Composition aspect for configuring the *latch_based* architecture of *d_register*.

122

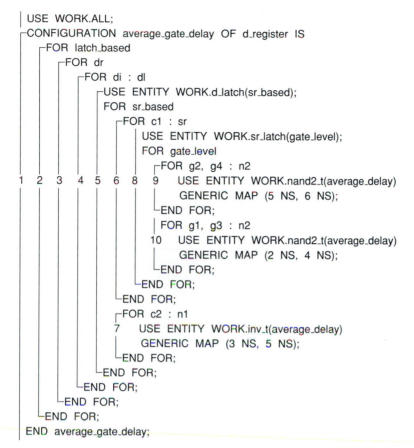

```
 USE  WORK.ALL;
CONFIGURATION  average_gate_delay  OF  d_register  IS
   FOR  latch_based
      FOR  dr
         FOR  di : dl
            USE  ENTITY  WORK.d_latch(sr_based);
            FOR  sr_based
               FOR  c1 : sr
                  USE  ENTITY  WORK.sr_latch(gate_level);
                  FOR  gate_level
                     FOR  g2, g4 : n2
1  2  3  4  5  6  8  9    USE  ENTITY  WORK.nand2_t(average_delay)
                        GENERIC  MAP  (5 NS, 6 NS);
                     END  FOR;
                     FOR  g1, g3 : n2
                    10    USE  ENTITY  WORK.nand2_t(average_delay)
                        GENERIC  MAP  (2 NS, 4 NS);
                     END  FOR;
                  END  FOR;
               END  FOR;
               FOR  c2 : n1
              7    USE  ENTITY  WORK.inv_t(average_delay)
                  GENERIC  MAP  (3 NS, 5 NS);
               END  FOR;
            END  FOR;
         END  FOR;
      END  FOR;
   END  FOR;
END  average_gate_delay;
```

FIGURE 5.45
Configuring *d_register* for using *average_delay* gates.

uration of *d_register*, in Figure 5.48. In the statement part of the architecture shown in this figure, the *reg* component is instantiated. Using a configuration specification in the declarative part of this architecture, the *r8* instance of *reg* is associated with the *single_gate_delay* configuration which resides in the WORK library. 8-bit data is applied to the inputs of *reg*, and 100 ns wide pulses are applied to its clock input. Associating the 8-bit *data* signal with the n-bit *d* input of *d_register* causes this register to be used as an n-bit register.

The letter X preceding the string of values that are assigned to *data* is called a base specifier, and it specifies the base of the values that follow. This construct generates a binary bit string. Letter X is used for hexadecimal, letter O for octal, and letter B for binary base specification. For each base, in addition to the valid values of that base, an underline character can also be used. This character does not contribute to the value of the equivalent bit string and it is used merely for readability purposes.

CONFIG-URATION	BLOCK OR COMPONENT	PURPOSE VISIBILITY OR BINDING TO:		BECOMES VISIBLE BY
1	Config. Declaration	Main	–	–
2	Block	Visibility	latch_based ARCHITECTURE Figure 5.43	1
3	Block	Visibility	dr GENERATE STATEMENT Figure 5.43	1,2
4	Component	Binding	di instance of dl Figure 5.43	1,2,3
5	Block	Visibility	sr_based ARCHITECTURE Figure 5.42	1,2,3,4
6	Component	Binding	c1 instance of sr Figure 5.42	1,2,3,4,5
7	Component	Binding	c2 instance of n1 Figure 5.42	1,2,3,4,5
8	Block	Visibility	gate_level ARCHITECTURE Figure 5.41	1,2,3,4,5, 6
9	Component	Binding	instances g2, g4 of n2 Figure 5.41	1,2,3,4,5 6,8
10	Component	Binding	instances g1, g3 of n2 Figure 5.41	1,2,3,4,5 6,8

FIGURE 5.46
Analyzing configuration constructs of the *average_gate_delay* configuration of d_register.

5.5 DESIGN LIBRARIES

As stated previously, logic families or groups of components can be categorized according to their physical characteristics, price, complexity, usage, or other properties. The VHDL language supports the use of design libraries for categorizing components or utilities. In general, libraries are used for design organization. Specific applications of libraries include sharing of components between designers, grouping components of

```
USE  WORK.ALL;
CONFIGURATION  single_gate_delay  OF  d_register  IS
  FOR  latch_based
    FOR  dr
      FOR  di  :  dl
        USE  ENTITY  WORK.d_latch(sr_based);
        FOR  sr_based
          FOR  c1  :  sr
            USE  ENTITY  WORK.sr_latch(gate_level);
            FOR  gate_level
              FOR  g2, g4  :  n2
                USE  ENTITY  WORK.nand3(single_delay)
                PORT  MAP  (i1, i1, i2, o1);
              END  FOR;
              FOR  g1, g3  :  n2
                USE  ENTITY  WORK.nand2(single_delay);
              END  FOR;
            END  FOR;
          END  FOR;
          FOR  c2  :  n1
            USE  ENTITY  WORK.inv(single_delay);
          END  FOR;
        END  FOR;
      END  FOR;
    END  FOR;
  END  FOR;
END  single_gate_delay;
```

FIGURE 5.47
Configuring *d_register* for using *single_delay* architectures of *inv* and *nand2*.

```
ARCHITECTURE  single  OF  d_register_test_bench  IS
  COMPONENT  reg  PORT  (d  :  IN  BIT_VECTOR  (7  DOWNTO  0);  c  :  IN  BIT;
                         q  :  OUT  BIT_VECTOR  (7  DOWNTO  0) );
  END  COMPONENT;
  FOR  r8  :  reg  USE  CONFIGURATION  WORK.single_gate_delay;
  SIGNAL  data, outdata  :  BIT_VECTOR  (7  DOWNTO  0);
  SIGNAL  clk  :  BIT;
BEGIN
  r8: reg  PORT  MAP  (data, clk, outdata);
  data <= X"00", X"AA"  AFTER  0500  NS, X"55"  AFTER  1500  NS;
  clk <= '0', '1'  AFTER  0200  NS, '0'  AFTER  0300  NS,
                   '1'  AFTER  0700  NS, '0'  AFTER  0800  NS,
                   '1'  AFTER  1700  NS, '0'  AFTER  1800  NS;
END  single;
```

FIGURE 5.48
Test bench for the *single_delay* architecture of *d_register*.

standard logic families, and categorizing special purpose utilities such as subprograms or types.

Predefined libraries in VHDL are the STD library and the WORK library. The STD library contains all the standard types and utilities. BIT, BIT_VECTOR, TIME and all other types that have been used up to this point in this book are defined in this library. Also included in this library are utility functions and procedures for reading and writing external ASCII files. The STD library is visible to all designs. The WORK library is simply a name that refers to the current working library. When a VHDL environment is created for a user, the keyword WORK refers to the root library of the user. As new libraries are created, the user can designate a new default library by equating one of the libraries to the WORK library.

Library management tasks, such as the creation or deletion of a library or aliasing it to WORK, are not part of the VHDL language. These tasks are done outside of VHDL and depend on the specific tool. Using a library, however, is supported by VHDL. The LIBRARY keyword followed by the name of a library makes it visible to a design. The following statement is assumed by all designs:

```
LIBRARY WORK;
```

To illustrate how to use and access libraries, we assume that a VHDL user has defined a library named *ls7400* as part of his design environment. We further assume that the *simple_gates* package declaration in Figure 5.12, the *inv*, *nand2*, and *nand3* entity declarations, and the *single_delay* architectures of these components have been compiled into the *ls7400* library. Figure 5.49 shows how a directory of this library might look.

In order to make the library visible and to make the component declarations in the *simple_gates* package declaration visible to a design, the statements shown in Figure 5.50 must appear in the description of the design.

The description that is shown in Figure 5.51 is another version of the *gate_level* architecture of *sr_latch* that uses the *simple_gates* package declaration in the *ls7400* library. In this description, the use clause is applied to make all component declarations of this package available.

LIBRARY "ls7400"	User:...	Date:...
simple_gates	PACKAGE DECLARATION	date
inv	ENTITY	...
inv(single_delay)	ARCHITECTURE	...
nand2	ENTITY	...
nand2(single_delay)	ARCHITECTURE	...
nand3	ENTITY	...
nand3(single_delay)	ARCHITECTURE	...

FIGURE 5.49
Directory of *ls7400* library containing package declarations, entities and architectures that have been compiled into it.

```
LIBRARY ls7400;
USE ls7400.simple_gates.ALL;
```

FIGURE 5.50
Making all declarations of *simple_gates* package of *ls7400* library available.

For associating g_1, g_2, g_3, and g_4 instances of *n2* in Figure 5.51 with components of the *ls7400* library, this library and its components must become visible to the VHDL description that makes this association. This requires the use of the statements in Figure 5.52 in the VHDL description that includes the corresponding binding indication construct(s).

A binding indication construct can appear in the declarative part of the architecture of Figure 5.51 as part of a configuration specification or it may appear in a configuration declaration as it did in Figure 5.47. In either case, the name of the library must be used before the entity name. Figure 5.53 shows a component config-

```
LIBRARY ls7400;
USE ls7400.simple_gates.ALL;
ARCHITECTURE gate_level OF sr_latch IS
  SIGNAL im1, im2, im3, im4 : BIT;
BEGIN
  g1 : n2 PORT MAP (s, c, im1);
  g2 : n2 PORT MAP (r, c, im2);
  g3 : n2 PORT MAP (lm1, im4, im3);
  g4 : n2 PORT MAP (im3, im2, im4);
  q <= im3;
END gate_level;
```

FIGURE 5.51
Using component declarations of *simple_gates* package of *ls7400* library for description of set-reset latch.

```
LIBRARY ls7400;
USE ls7400.ALL;
```

FIGURE 5.52
Making all entities and architectures of the *ls7400* library available.

```
LIBRARY ls7400;
USE ls7400.ALL;
.
.
.
. . .  _FOR g1, g3 : n2
. . .  _  USE ENTITY ls7400.nand2(single_delay);
. . .  _END FOR;
```

FIGURE 5.53
Using a component configuration for associating *g1* and *g3* instances of *n2* of Figure 5.51 with *nand2* of *ls7400*.

uration that associates *g1* and *g3* instances of *n2* in Figure 5.51 with the *single_delay* architecture of the *nand2* entity in the *ls7400* library.

5.6   SUMMARY

This chapter provides tools for better hardware descriptions and design organization. This chapter began with the definition of subprograms and it emphasized the use of functions and procedures for simplifying descriptions. Two main issues were discussed: 1) using functions to describe Boolean expressions, and 2) using procedures to write better test bench models. Next, the subject of packaging utilities and components was addressed. As stated earlier, this topic is used mainly for the organization of a design. Design parametrization and configuration of designs were also discussed in great detail. Although simple examples and college level exercises can avoid some of these language issues, a large design environment with many logic families and technologies to choose from requires a great deal of library management and parameter specification. We believe VHDL is very strong in this area and that serious designers should learn to take advantage of such capabilities of the language. For small circuits and experimental models, design parametrization methods save many compilation runs.

REFERENCES

1. "IEEE Standard VHDL Language Reference Manual," IEEE Std. 1076-1987, The Institute of Electrical and Electronic Engineers, Inc., 1988.
2. Lipsett, L., C. Schaefer, and C. Ussery, "VHDL: Hardware Description and Design," Klewer Academic Publishing, Boston, 1988.

PROBLEMS

5.1. Write a function for the carry output of a full-adder.

5.2. Write a function for the sum output of a full-adder.

5.3. Write a function, *inc_bits*, that returns the 4-bit increment of its 4-bit input vector. Write Boolean expressions for the four bits of the output.

5.4. Using the carry and sum functions of Problems 5.1 and 5.2 write a functional description of a full-adder. Use an entity declaration with *a*, *b* and *ci* inputs and *s* and *co* outputs. In the *functional* architecture of this entity include the necessary functions. Use 21 ns and 18 ns delays for the sum and carry outputs, respectively. The solution to this problem depends on code developed in Problems 5.1 and 5.2.

5.5. The *apply_data* procedure in Figure 5.4 causes a transaction on its target every 500 ns even if the data on this line does not change from one time interval to another. Modify this procedure to remove unnecessary transactions.

5.6. Write a procedure, *apply_bit*, such that bits of a 24-bit wide string input to the procedure are applied to its target signal according to the specified time interval. Make sure no unnecessary transactions occur on the target of the procedure. A sample call to this procedure is shown here:

```
apply_bit (target, "110001000100001111001010", 300 NS);
```

5.7. Using *bin2int* and *int2bin*, write a function, *inc_bin*, that uses a binary input parameter and returns a binary value. The return value is the increment of the input parameter.

5.8. Write the package declaration and package body such that it includes the sum and carry of Problems 5.1 and 5.2, *inc_bits* of problem 5.3, *apply_bit* of problem 5.6, and *inc_bin* of problem 5.7. Use *additional_utilities* for the name of this package. The solution to this problem depends on code developed in Problems 5.1, 5.2, 5.3, 5.6 and 5.7.

5.9. Use the *apply_bit* procedure in the *additional_utilities* package in Problem 5.8 in a test bench for the full-adder in Problem 5.4. Use test vectors to test the full-adder for all eight input combinations. The solution to this problem depends on code developed in Problems 5.1, 5.2, 5.3, 5.6, 5.7 and 5.8.

5.10. Write an entity declaration and an *average_delay* architecture for an Exclusive-OR gate with a *tplh* of 9 ns and *tphl* of 7 ns. The entity declaration should contain generics for the timing parameters with the specified default values.

5.11. Use the XOR gate of Problem 5.10 and the basic gates of Figure 5.18 to write a gate level description for a full-adder. Use a configuration specification with generic map aspects to override the default values of the timing parameters of all gates with 11 ns. The solution to this problem depends on code developed in Problem 5.10.

5.12. Use the *apply_bit* procedure of the *additional_utilities* package in Problem 5.8 in a test bench for testing the full-adder in Problem 5.4 and the full-adder in Problem 5.11 in parallel. Declare two signals in this test bench to show the differences of the sum and carry outputs of the two versions of the full-adder. Use *difference_sum* and *difference_carry* for these signals, and use the XOR operation for subtracting the like signals. The solution to this problem depends on code developed in Problems 5.1, 5.2, 5.3, 5.6, 5.7, 5.8, 5.10 and 5.11.

5.13. Write a description for a full-adder using 2-input NAND and XOR gates. In this description, do not include the configuration specification.

5.14. Write a configuration declaration on top of the full-adder in Problem 5.13 to bind the components of this design with the XOR gate of Problem 5.10 and the gates of Figure 5.18. Specify 11 ns in this configuration declaration for timing generic parameters of all gates. The solution to this problem depends on code developed in Problems 5.10 and 5.13.

5.15. Develop a test bench for the full-adder of Problem 5.14. The solution to this problem depends on code developed in Problems 5.10, 5.13 and 5.14.

5.16. Use generate statements to describe an 8-bit adder using the full-adders in Problem 5.13. Write a configuration declaration on top of this adder for binding the underlaying gate components of the full-adder to the XOR gate of Problem 5.10 and the gates of Figure 5.18. Using this configuration declaration, specify the timing parameters as shown below:

Gate	tplh	tphl
NAND2	10 ns	11 ns
XOR	11 ns	13 ns

The solution to this problem depends on code developed in Problems 5.10 and 5.13.

5.17. Use the configured adder of Problem 5.16 in a test bench testing it for worst case delay. The solution to this problem depends on code developed in Problems 5.10, 5.13 and 5.16.

5.18. Write a procedure that assigns consecutive binary numbers to its OUT BIT_VECTOR lines. The parameters of the procedure are an 8-bit *target* output and a TIME *period*. When called, it will assign sequential binary numbers from 0 to 255 to its *target* signal output. These numbers are distanced by the amount of the constant associated with the *period* parameter. You can use the utilities of the *basic_utilities* package.

5.19. Design an 8-bit odd-parity checker using the XOR gate in Problem 5.10. Use generate statements and wire the gates for minimum delay. Use the default delay values of the XOR gate. Write a test bench for testing all the input combinations of this circuit. You may use the procedure developed in Problem 5.18. The solution to this problem depends on code developed in Problems 5.10 and 5.18.

5.20. Show the gate level implementation of a master-slave JK flip-flop. Use the gates in Figure 5.18, and write a configuration declaration on top of the flip-flop. Use reasonable delay values and avoid oscillation by using different delay values for the two cross-coupled gates.

CHAPTER
6

UTILITIES
FOR HIGH
LEVEL
DESCRIPTIONS

The previous two chapters discussed issues related to interconnecting, configuring, and testing hardware structures. In parallel with that, the VHDL constructs that support these tasks were also presented. For higher level hardware descriptions, however, more advanced utilities than those introduced thus far are needed. This chapter is devoted to the presentation of such issues. The two major topics covered in this chapter are types and attributes. Section 1 discusses type declaration and usage. This is followed by issues related to the type of subprogram parameters and operator operands. The last two sections discuss predefined and user-defined attributes.

Unlike the two previous chapters, this chapter does not develop complete and evolutionary examples. Instead, it presents isolated examples, some of which are improvements of the examples of Chapters 4 and 5. In order to develop more useful examples, VHDL constructs that are not necessarily related to types or attributes are also introduced as concepts are presented. In addition to making the examples in this chapter more interesting, this prepares the reader for the higher level descriptions presented in Chapters 7 and 8.

The development of the *basic_utilities* package begun in Chapter 5 continues in this chapter as we make improvements and add more utilities to the package. The examples in this chapter assume users have this package in their WORK design library.

6.1 TYPE DECLARATIONS AND USAGE

VHDL is a strongly typed language. Type declarations must be used for definition of objects and their types. Operations in VHDL are defined for specific types of operands. The STANDARD package in the STD library defines basic types such as BIT or INTEGER; other types also can be defined. Basic operators also can be defined to perform operations on operands of these new types. The general classes of types we will discuss in this chapter include the *scalar*, *composite*, and *file* types.

6.1.1 Enumeration Type for Multi-Value Logic

The basic scalar type is enumeration. This is defined as a set of all possible values that such a type can have. The BIT type of the STANDARD package is an enumeration of '0' and '1', and the BOOLEAN type of this package is an enumeration of FALSE and TRUE. CHARACTER, also in this package, is defined as the set of 128 ASCII characters. Other enumeration types can be defined by the use of the type declaration construct. For example, to define a four-value logic type which takes values '0', '1', 'Z', and 'X', the following declaration is needed:

```
TYPE qit IS ('0', '1', 'Z', 'X');
```

When this type is declared in the declarative part of an architecture, or if it is made visible to a design by inserting a use clause, then *qit* can be used to declare objects that can assume one of the four possible values, '0', '1', 'Z', or 'X'. The examples in this and the following chapters assume users have this type declaration included in the *basic_utilities* package in their WORK library. As BIT is used for *b*inary dig*it*s, we will use *qit* for the *q*uad-dig*it* system, and later *tit* for *t*rinary dig*it*s.

Figure 6.1 shows syntax details of the above type declaration. Enclosed in parentheses are four enumeration elements that are separated by commas. This forms the enumeration type definition which, together with the TYPE keyword, the *qit* identifier, and the IS keyword, forms a type declaration for declaring *qit*. Instead of using single characters enclosed in quotes, enumeration elements can be identifiers formed by a string of characters. For example, individual instruction mnemonics can be used as enumeration elements to declare an instruction set in a computing machine.

6.1.1.1 MODELING A FOUR-VALUE INVERTER. In the four-value logic system described above, '0' and '1' are for low and high logic values, respectively. The 'Z' value is for the high impedance or open value, and the 'X' value is unknown. Input to output mapping of an inverter in this value system is shown in Figure 6.2. As shown in the figure, inverting an unknown input 'X' results in an unknown, while a high impedance input is treated as a '1' and results in a '0' output. Figure 6.3 shows the entity declaration and the architecture body of an inverter that uses this logic value system.

The *qit* type is made visible to the description in Figure 6.3 when we specify the use of the package that contains it. This visibility enables us to use *qit* for the

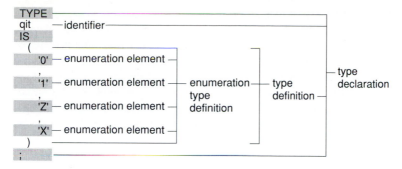

FIGURE 6.1
Syntax details of a type declaration.

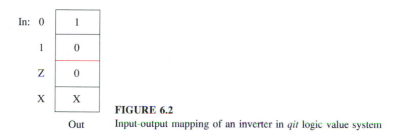

FIGURE 6.2
Input-output mapping of an inverter in *qit* logic value system

```
USE  WORK.basic_utilities.ALL;
-- FROM  PACKAGE  USE:  qit
ENTITY  inv_q  IS
    GENERIC  (tplh : TIME := 5 NS; tphl : TIME := 3 NS);
    PORT  (i1 : IN  qit; o1 : OUT  qit);
END  inv_q;
--
ARCHITECTURE  double_delay  OF  inv_q  IS
BEGIN
    o1 <= '1' AFTER tplh  WHEN i1 = '0' ELSE
          '0' AFTER tphl  WHEN i1 = '1' OR i1 = 'Z' ELSE
          'X' AFTER tplh;
END  double_delay;
```

FIGURE 6.3
VHDL description of an inverter in *qit* logic value system.

type of the ports on the *inv_q* entity. The architectural description in Figure 6.3 uses a conditional signal assignment statement for implementing the table in Figure 6.2. This statement enables us to use different delay values for the rise and the fall propagation delays. The *tplh* generic parameter (the larger of the two delay parameters) is used for the gate delay value when the input is unknown. This gives the 'X' output the worst case propagation.

The conditional signal assignment in Figure 6.3 is a concurrent statement, and can only appear in concurrent bodies of VHDL. Figure 6.4 shows the syntax details for this statement. As shown in this figure, a conditional signal assignment consists of several conditional waveforms and a mandatory default nonconditional waveform. The conditions are evaluated sequentially in the order in which they are listed. If a condition evaluates to TRUE, its corresponding waveform is assigned to the target signal and all other assignments that follow it are ignored. If none of the conditions are satisfied, the nonconditional waveform, i.e., 'X' AFTER tplh in the example in Figure 6.4 is assigned to the left hand side signal.

6.1.1.2 MODELING A FOUR-VALUE NAND GATE.

A two-input NAND gate in the *qit* logic values system can be modeled according to the input-output mapping shown in Figure 6.5.

Figure 6.6 shows the VHDL description for an interface and an architecture of a *nand2_q* entity. The input and output ports of this entity are of the *qit* type, whose declaration is included in the *basic_utilities* package. A conditional signal assignment in the statement part of the *double_delay* architecture of the *nand2_q* entity is used for implementing the table in Figure 6.4. As in the previous example, the open input is treated as '1', and the gate in Figure 6.6 responds to 'Z' and '1' input values in exactly the same manner. The behavior of a gate when its input is open depends on the technology in which the gate is implemented, and our assumption that 'Z' and

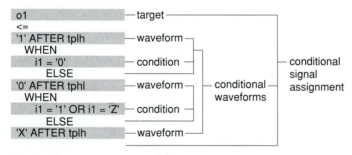

FIGURE 6.4
Syntax details of a conditional signal assignment.

In1:	0	1	Z	X
In2: 0	1	1	1	1
1	1	0	0	X
Z	1	0	0	X
X	1	X	X	X

Out

FIGURE 6.5
Input-output mapping of a NAND gate in *qit* logic value system.

```
USE  WORK.basic_utilities.ALL;
-- FROM  PACKAGE  USE: qit
ENTITY  nand2_q  IS
    GENERIC (tplh : TIME := 7 NS; tphl : TIME := 5 NS);
    PORT (i1, i2 : IN qit; o1 : OUT qit);
END  nand2_q;
--
ARCHITECTURE  double_delay  OF  nand2_q  IS
BEGIN
    o1 <= '1' AFTER tplh WHEN i1 = '0' OR i2 = '0' ELSE
          '0' AFTER tphl WHEN (i1 = '1' AND i2 = '1') OR
                              (i1 = '1' AND i2 = 'Z') OR
                              (i1 = 'Z' AND i2 = '1') OR
                              (i1 = 'Z' AND i2 = 'Z') ELSE
          'X' AFTER tplh;
END  double_delay;
```

FIGURE 6.6
VHDL description of a NAND gate in *qit* logic value system.

'1' are equivalent is not always true. For example, if an NMOS gate input becomes open, that input keeps its value for a few milliseconds before it becomes zero. This is due to the discharging of the input capacitance of such structures. This behavior can easily be modeled using RC circuit models connected to each of the inputs of a NAND description. The output of an RC circuit becomes '0' a few milliseconds after its input has become 'Z'. Modeling an NMOS NAND gate is left as an exercise.

6.1.1.3 INITIAL VALUES OF ENUMERATION TYPES. With declaration of objects, an initial value can optionally be specified using the initial value expression that follows the := symbol. If this symbol and its following expression are not present in the declaration of an object, a default initial value that depends on the type of the object is used. For the enumeration types, this value is the left-most enumeration element. For the gates in Figures 6.3 and 6.6, '0', which is the left-most element of the *qit* type, is the initial value for all the input and output ports. Had we used the 'Z', '0', '1', 'X' ordering for the definition of the *qit* type, default initial values of all the objects of this type would have been 'Z'.

6.1.2 Using Real Numbers for Timing Calculations

Besides the enumeration type, other types of the scalar classes are the INTEGER and REAL types. Both of these types are defined in the STANDARD package. The exact range of these types is implementation dependent, but they generally range from a small negative number to a large positive number depending on the word size of the host machine. For the INTEGER type, these numbers are restricted to integers.

We will use a load dependent model of a CMOS inverter in order to demonstrate the use of REAL and INTEGER numbers and their relationship to each other. The inverter contains its own pull-up and pull-down resistance values, and adjusts its delays according to the load capacitance at its output node. This capacitance value is passed to the inverter model by use of the generic parameters. A CMOS inverter with equivalent resistance

Corresponding to the composition aspect in Figure 6.7 are the *inv_rc* entity declaration and the *double_delay* architectural description for this entity, shown in Figure 6.8. The *inv_rc* entity contains a generic formal parameter of REAL type and two ports of *qit* type. The entity declaration part of this figure specifies the *rpu* and *rpd* constants and their values. Declaring these constants in the entity declaration causes them to be visible to all architectures that are written for this entity.

The declarative part of the *double_delay* architecture in Figure 6.8 defines the *tplh* and *tphl* constants in terms of the pull-up or the pull-down resistances and the load capacitance. The constructs used for these declarations are constant declarations that contain expressions for their values. Since all the generics and constants are defined at the initialization time, expressions based on these parameters can be used for the initial values of objects or for the values of other constants.

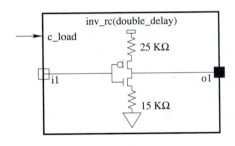

FIGURE 6.7
Composition aspect of an inverter with RC timing.

```
USE  WORK.basic_utilities.ALL;
-- FROM  PACKAGE  USE:  qit
ENTITY  inv_rc  IS
    GENERIC  (c_load : REAL := 0.066E-12);   -- Farads
    PORT  (i1 : IN qit; o1 : OUT qit);
    CONSTANT  rpu : REAL := 25000.0;   -- Ohms
    CONSTANT  rpd : REAL := 15000.0;   -- Ohms
END  inv_rc;
--
ARCHITECTURE  double_delay  OF  inv_rc  IS
    CONSTANT  tplh : TIME := INTEGER ( rpu * c_load * 1.0E15) * 3 FS;
    CONSTANT  tphl : TIME := INTEGER ( rpd * c_load * 1.0E15) * 3 FS;
BEGIN
    o1 <= '1' AFTER tplh WHEN i1 = '0' ELSE
          '0' AFTER tphl WHEN i1 = '1' OR i1 = 'Z' ELSE
          'X' AFTER tplh;
END  double_delay;
```

FIGURE 6.8
An inverter model with RC timing parameters.

Because of the types of the *tplh* and *tphl* constants, the result of the evaluation of their constant value expressions must be of type TIME. A constant of type TIME can be formed by multiplying an integer number by a valid unit of this type. Since the resistance and capacitance values are of the REAL type, their multiplication result is a floating point number. A floating point number must be converted to an integer and it must be given a unit of TIME in order to be used for an object of type TIME. For this reason, in the constant value expressions of the *double_delay* architecture of *inv_rc*, we have used explicit REAL to INTEGER type conversion and have multiplied the resulting integer by an appropriate time unit. Explicit type conversions, such as those demonstrated here, can be done for closely related types.

Consider the constant expression for the *tplh* constant. This expression converts the multiplication of *rpu* and *c_load* to an integer by use of the explicit type conversion. Before this type conversion takes place, however, the RC product is multiplied by a factor of 1E15. This is done because normal pull resistance and load capacitance multiplications result in small fractions and converting these small floating point numbers to the INTEGER type results in zero. The 1E15 factor is compensated for by using the femtosecond (FS = 1E-15 s) time unit for the overall expression. Multiplication by a factor of 3 is also included in the constant expression of the *tplh* constant. This factor is used to account for the exponentiality of the waveforms. We are approximating the delay values that are based on exponential waveforms by linear RC equations. An exponential function takes about 3*RC to complete its transition from one value to another.

The *double_delay* architecture body of the *inv_rc* entity is similar to that in Figure 6.3. This architecture assumes resistance values in ohms and capacitance values in farads. In the next section we illustrate the use of units for such parameters.

6.1.3 Physical Types and RC Timing

Physical types in VHDL are another type in the scalar class. Values of a physical type are used with units defined in the type definition. Type TIME is a physical type that is defined in the STANDARD package and it is used for measuring time. The units of this type have been defined as FS, PS, NS, US, MS, SEC, MIN, and HR. Other physical types for measuring other quantities such as distance, temperature, resistance, and capacitance can also be defined.

Figure 6.9 shows the definition of *capacitance* as a type for measuring capacitance. This definition consists of the name of the physical type, a range constraint, a base unit declaration (declaration of *ffr*), and several secondary unit declarations (declarations of *pfr* to *kfr*). The units for this type range from *ffr* (femto-farads) to *kfr* (kilo-farads). The base unit is *ffr*, and all other units are defined in terms of this unit. Other units can be added to this type, provided they are multiples of the base unit. Only integer numbers can be used for the bounds of the range constraint of a physical type. Since we have specified 0 to 1E16 for the range constraint, negative capacitance values and values larger than 1E16 base units cannot be assigned to an object of type *capacitance*, although larger values of this type may be used in expressions. Another example of a physical type definition is that of *resistance*, as shown in Figure 6.10.

```
┌TYPE capacitance IS RANGE 0 TO 1E16
├UNITS
│     ffr;   -- Femto Farads (base unit)
│     pfr = 1000 ffr;
│     nfr = 1000 pfr;
│     ufr = 1000 nfr;
│     mfr = 1000 ufr;
│     far = 1000 mfr;
│     kfr = 1000 far;
└END UNITS;
```

FIGURE 6.9
Type definition for defining the *capacitance* physical type.

As defined by this type, an object of type *resistance* can have units ranging from *l_o* (milli-ohms = $10^{-3}\Omega$) to *g_o* (giga-ohms = $10^{9}\Omega$).

To illustrate the use of the *capacitance* and the *resistance* physical types, we show them in an alternative description for the *inv_rc* inverter. (The definitions for these types are assumed to be included in the *basic_utilities* package; if they are included, the definitions are available to designs that have a use clause specifying application of the *basic-utilities* package.)

Figure 6.11 shows an entity declaration and an architectural description for the *inv_rc* that takes advantage of the *resistance* and the *capacitance* physical types. Except for the types of the generics and the constants, this description is the same as that in Figure 6.8. The *inv_rc* entity declaration in Figure 6.11 has a generic parameter of type *capacitance*. This declaration also defines the pull-up and pull-down resistances in terms of the *resistance* type. The *double_delay* architecture of the *inv_rc* uses two constant declarations for declaring propagation delay parameters and assigning constant values to them. The expression evaluating the constant value for *tplh* uses *rpu* and *c_load* to evaluate the low-to-high propagation delay. In the first set of parentheses in the constant expression of this parameter, the *rpu* parameters are divided by the base unit for the *resistance* physical type. This results in an integer representing the value of *rpu* in terms of *l_o* ($10^{-3}\Omega$). Similarly, in the second set of parentheses, *c_load* is divided by the *capacitance* base unit. This converts any capacitance value that is

```
┌TYPE resistance IS RANGE 0 TO 1E16
├UNITS
│     l_o;   -- Milli-Ohms (base unit)
│     ohms = 1000 l_o;
│     k_o = 1000 ohms;
│     m_o = 1000 k_o;
│     g_o = 1000 m_o;
└END UNITS;
```

FIGURE 6.10
Type definition for defining the *resistance* physical type.

```
USE  WORK.basic_utilities.ALL;
-- FROM PACKAGE USE: qit, resistance, capacitance
ENTITY inv_rc IS
    GENERIC (c_load : capacitance := 66 ffr);
    PORT (i1 : IN qit; o1 : OUT qit);
    CONSTANT rpu : resistance := 25000 ohms;
    CONSTANT rpd : resistance := 15000 ohms;
END inv_rc;
--

ARCHITECTURE double_delay OF inv_rc IS
    CONSTANT tplh : TIME := (rpu / 1 l_o) * (c_load / 1 ffr) * 3 FS 1000;
    CONSTANT tphl : TIME := (rpd / 1 l_o) * (c_load / 1 ffr) * 3 FS 1000;
BEGIN
    o1 <= '1' AFTER tplh WHEN i1 = '0' ELSE
          '0' AFTER tphl WHEN i1 = '1' OR i1 = 'Z' ELSE
          'X' AFTER tplh;
END double_delay;
```

FIGURE 6.11

Using *resistance* and *capacitance* physical types in the description of an inverter.

associated with the *c_load* generic parameter to an integer representing the amount of the capacitance in *ffr* (10^{-15} farads). Multiplying these two sets of parentheses results in an integer RC value which is scaled up by a factor of 10^{18}. Using FS (10^{-15} s) and dividing the *tplh* constant expression by 1000 compensates for the use of *l_o* and the *ffr* units. As shown in the description in Figure 6.8, a factor of 3 is used in order to account for the exponentiality of the waveforms. The constant expression for the *tphl* delay parameter is similar to that of the *tplh*. Dividing a physical type by one of its units removes the type from it and converts it to an integer. For best precision, the base unit should be used. Had we divided *rpu* by *k_o* instead of *l_o*, *rpu* values would have been rounded off to the smallest *k_o* values.

The VHDL multiplication operator is defined for multiplying integer and floating point numbers. It is also valid to multiply an integer or a floating point number by a physical type. Multiplication of two physical types, however, is not defined for the standard multiplication operator. Dividing the *resistance* and *capacitance* physical types by their base units enabled the use of the standard multiplication operator in the timing equations in Figure 6.11.

6.1.4   Array Declarations

The VHDL language includes constructs that can be used to declare multi-dimensional array types; these array types can then be used to declare objects. Array elements must all be of the same type. Arrays can be indexed with the normal integer indexing or indexed using the elements of an enumeration type. Arrays can be unconstrained, meaning that their range can be left unspecified.

A VHDL array type declaration begins with the keyword TYPE. The declaration specifies the name of the type that is being declared, the range of the array, and the type of each element in the array. Figure 6.12 shows the declarations of *qit_nibble*, *qit_byte*, *qit_word*, *qit_4by8*, and *qit_nibble_by_8*. The elements of *qit_nibble*, *qit_byte*, *qit_word*, and *qit_4by8* are of the previously defined *qit* type, and the type of the eight elements of *qit_nibble_by_8* is *qit_nibble* defined in the first line of the figure.

Once types declared in Figure 6.12 become visible to a design, they can be used to declare objects. For example, an 8-bit *qit* signal should be declared as:

```
SIGNAL sq8 : qit_byte := " ZZZZZZZZ";
```

The initial values of the eight lines of *sq8* signal are all 'Z'. For the individual bits of *sq8*, the 'Z' value overrides '0', which is the default initial value for the *qit* type. Recall that the left-most element is the default initial value in an enumeration type, which was '0' in the declaration of *qit*.

Figure 6.13 shows the syntax details of the type declaration used to define the *qit_byte* type in Figure 6.12. This declaration specifies the range of the arrays and the type of its elements. The range defines the upper and the lower bounds of the array. The DOWNTO descending range specification causes the left most bit and the right most bit of an object of type *qit_byte* to have indices of 7 and 0, respectively.

Figure 6.12 also shows the declaration of a two-dimensional array type, namely *qit_4by8*. This declaration uses two range specifications separated by commas. The first is a descending range and the second is an ascending range. The index (3,0), therefore, references the upper left bit of an object of type *qit_4by8*.

Referencing an element or groups of elements in an array can be achieved by indexing or by using slice specifications. To reference an array element by indexing, an

```
TYPE  qit_nibble IS  ARRAY  ( 3  DOWNTO 0 )  OF  qit;
TYPE  qit_byte IS  ARRAY  ( 7  DOWNTO 0 )  OF  qit;
TYPE  qit_word IS  ARRAY  ( 15  DOWNTO 0 )  OF  qit;
TYPE  qit_4by8 IS  ARRAY  ( 3  DOWNTO 0, 0  TO 7 )  OF  qit;
TYPE  qit_nibble_by_8 IS  ARRAY  ( 0  TO 7 )  OF  qit_nibble;
```

FIGURE 6.12
Declaring array types.

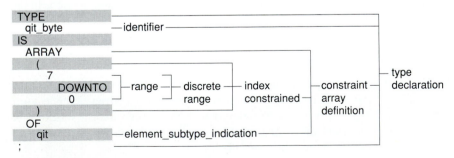

FIGURE 6.13
Syntax details of an array type declaration.

index for each of the ranges in the array must be specified. To reference an array slice, a discrete range should be specified. Figure 6.14 shows signal declaration and several valid assignments to signals of the types declared in Figure 6.12. The first declaration in Figure 6.14a declares *sq1* as a scalar of type *qit*. The next three declarations define *sq4*, *sq8*, and *sq16* as one-dimensional arrays of *qit*. The *sq_4_8* array is a 4-by-8 two-dimensional array of *qit*, and finally the *sq_nibble_8* signal is a one-dimensional array of size 8, whose elements are the *qit_nibble* type. The first signal assignment in Figure 6.14b assigns a slice of *sq16* to all of *sq8*. The second assignment assigns all of *sq4* to a slice of *sq16*. The next assignment indexes a bit of the *sq_4_8* two-dimensional *qit* array and it assigns this bit to the *sq1* signal. Multi-dimensional arrays such as *sq_4_8* can only be indexed and cannot be sliced. Therefore, it is more appropriate to use one-dimensional arrays of vectors such as those of *sq_nibble_8* type for declaring hardware memories. Figure 6.14b shows as assignment of nibble number two of the *sq_nibble_8* to the *sq4* signal. The next assignment, in Figure 6.14b shows an assignment for the right rotation of the *sq8* signal and the last assignment reverses the *sq8* bits and assigns them to the *sq4* signal. Reversing the order of bits is accomplished by concatenating the individual bits of *sq8* as is illustrated graphically in Figure 6.15.

Slicing an array with a range in the opposite direction of its declared range is considered to be a constraint error.

6.1.4.1 INITIALIZING MULTI-DIMENSIONAL ARRAYS.
Initial values for a one-dimensional array type signal must be placed in a set of parentheses and should follow the := symbol in the signal declaration. The initial values of individual array elements should be separated by commas. Nested sets of parentheses should be used

```
SIGNAL sq1  :  qit;
SIGNAL sq4  :  qit_nibble;
SIGNAL sq8  :  qit_byte;
SIGNAL sq16 :  qit_word;
SIGNAL sq_4_8 :  qit_4by8;
SIGNAL sq_nibble_8 :  qit_nibble_by_8;
```
                          (a)

```
sq8  <= sq16 (11 DOWNTO 4);              -- middle 8 bit slice of sq16 to sq8;
sq16 (15 DOWNTO 12) <= sq4;              -- sq4 into left 4 bit slice of sq16;
sq1  <= sq_4_8 (0, 7);                   -- lower right bit of sq_4_8 into sq1;
sq4  <= sq_nibble_8 (2);        -- third nibble (number 2) of sq_nibble_8 into sq4;
sq8  <= sq(0) & sq8 (7 DOWNTO 1);                       -- right rotate sq8;
sq4  <= sq8(2) & sq8(3) & sq8(4) & sq8(5);           -- reversing sq8 into sq4;
```
                          (b)

FIGURE 6.14
Various forms of signal declarations and signal assignments based on signal declarations of Figure 6.12, (a) signal declarations, (b) valid signal assignments.

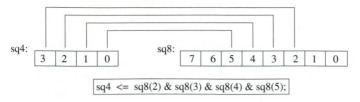

FIGURE 6.15
Referencing bits of a vector; reversing bits of *sq8* and assigning them to *sq4*.

for multi-dimensional arrays. In this case, the top level set of parentheses corresponds to the left-most range of the array.

Figure 6.16 shows initialization of the *sq_4_8* signal whose type is defined to be *qit_4by8* in Figure 6.12. The initial values of this array type signal are specified in a nesting of parenthesized sets of values. Shown in separate rows, the deepest level of nestings correspond to the 0 TO 7 range of *sq_4_8*. Since the left most range of the array is 3 DOWNTO 0, four such rows are needed to initialize all the elements in the array.

6.1.4.2   NON INTEGER INDEXING. In most languages, array indexing is done only with integers. VHDL allows the use of any type indication for index definition of arrays. Referring to Figure 6.13, the 7 DOWNTO 0 range was used for the definition of the array in this figure. Instead of using a range, a type indication can be used for the discrete range of an array. If an enumeration type is used for the discrete range specification of an array, the array must be indexed using the enumeration elements of this type. As an example, consider the following declaration of the *qit_2d* array:

```
TYPE qit_2d IS ARRAY (qit, qit) OF qit;
```

This is a two-dimensional array, that has *qit* type elements. The *qit* type-marks also constitute the two discrete ranges of this array. Therefore, the enumeration elements of *qit* must be used to access elements in the *qit_2d* array. The two-input NAND gate description in Figure 6.17 uses this array for describing a NAND gate in the *qit* logic value system. For this and other examples in this chapter, we assume that the *qit_2d* type is included in the *basic_utilities* package, and can become visible by application of the use clause as shown in Figure 6.17.

```
SIGNAL sq_4_8 : qit_4by8 :=
            (
        ( '0', '0', '1', '1', 'Z', 'Z', 'X', 'X' ),
        ( 'X', 'X', '0', '0', '1', '1', 'Z', 'Z' ),
        ( 'Z', 'Z', 'X', 'X', '0', '0', '1', '1' ),
        ( '1', '1', 'Z', 'Z', 'X', ' X', '0', '0' )
            );
```

FIGURE 6.16
Initializing a two-dimensional array.

```
USE  WORK.basic_utilities.ALL;
-- FROM PACKAGE USE: qit, qit_2d
ENTITY  nand2_q  IS
    GENERIC (tplh : TIME := 7 NS; tphl : TIME := 5 NS);
    PORT (i1, i2 : IN qit; o1 : OUT qit);
END nand2_q;
--
ARCHITECTURE  average_delay  OF  nand2_q  IS
   CONSTANT  qit_nand2_table : qit_2d := (
                                ('1','1','1','1'),
                                ('1','0','0','X'),
                                ('1','0','0','X'),
                                ('1','X','X','X'));
BEGIN
    o1  <= qit_nand2_table (i1, i2) AFTER (tplh + tphl) / 2;
END average_delay;
```

FIGURE 6.17
Using *qit* enumeration type for the discrete range of a two-dimensional array.

Figure 6.17 also shows the *nand2_q* entity and the *average_delay* architecture
for this entity. Types *qit* and *qit_2d* are visible to this architecture. Since *qit* has
four enumeration elements, the *qit_2d* is a 4-by-4 array with its rows and columns
indexed as '0', '1', 'Z', and 'X'. In the declarative part of the *average_delay* architecture
in *nand2_q*, the *qit_nand2_table* is declared as a constant array of type *qit_2d* and
it is initialized according to the two-input NAND gate input-output mapping shown
in Figure 6.5. The statement part of this architecture consists of a signal assignment
whose right hand side is a look-up into the *qit_nand2_table*.

6.1.4.3 UNCONSTRAINED ARRAYS. VHDL allows the declaration of unconstrained
arrays. This is particularly useful for developing generic descriptions or designs. The
bounds of unconstrained arrays used for formal parameters are determined according
to the actual parameters that are associated with them. The standard BIT_VECTOR
is an unconstrained one-dimensional array of BITs. In the STANDARD package, this
type is declared as shown here:

```
TYPE BIT_VECTOR IS ARRAY (NATURAL RANGE <>) OF BIT;
```

This declaration defines BIT_VECTOR as an array with type BIT elements, and
specifies that it can be indexed by any range of natural numbers. NATURAL, also
declared in the STANDARD package is a type for numbers ranging from 0 to the
largest allowable integer. Another unconstrained array in the STANDARD package is
the STRING type. This type is an unconstrained array of characters; when indexing
it, positive numbers should be used.

Similar to the declaration we used to define BIT_VECTOR, we can define an
unconstrained array of integers as shown here:

```
TYPE integer_vector IS ARRAY (NATURAL RANGE <>) OF INTEGER;
```

Figure 6.18 shows syntax details for this type declaration. The index definition of this array (which is read as "natural range box") indicates that for range specification of objects of this type or for other type declarations that are based on this type, any descending or ascending range of natural numbers can be used.

To illustrate the use of unconstrained arrays, a more general version of the *apply_data* procedure than that developed in Chapter 5 (Figure 5.15b) is shown in Figure 6.19. The *target* and the *values* formal parameters of this procedure are declared as unconstrained arrays of BITs and INTEGERs, respectively. The *target* parameter uses the predefined BIT_VECTOR type and the *values* parameter uses the *integer_vector* in Figure 6.18. To specify the range of the intermediate variable, *buf*, and the range of the for loop, we have used *target*'RANGE and *values*'RANGE, respectively. The *buf* variable stores the binary result of this procedure before assigning it to *target*. When an actual signal is associated with the *target* formal parameter, *target* becomes an array signal whose range is the same as that of the actual parameter. This range is then passed on to *buf*, making it a variable whose range is the same as the range of the actual parameter associated with *target*. The use of *values*'RANGE enables the *apply_data* procedure to loop for all the integers in the array associated with the

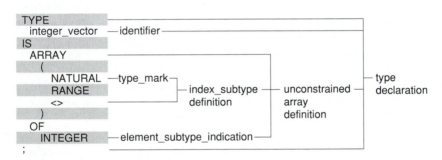

FIGURE 6.18
Syntax details of an unconstrained array declaration.

```
PROCEDURE apply_data (
      SIGNAL target : OUT BIT_VECTOR;
      CONSTANT values : IN integer_vector; CONSTANT period : IN TIME)
IS
      VARIABLE buf : BIT_VECTOR (target' RANGE);
BEGIN
      FOR i IN values' RANGE LOOP
          int2bin (values(i), buf);
          target <= TRANSPORT buf AFTER i * period;
      END LOOP;
END apply_data;
```

FIGURE 6.19
A generic version of the *apply_data* procedure.

values formal parameter. For example, in calling *apply_data*, if concatenation of 20 integers is associated with the *values* parameter, then the loop range becomes 0 TO 19. Each time through the loop, one of these integers is converted to its equivalent binary number and assigned to *values*. To make it possible to use this procedure in our designs, we first add the *integer_vector* type definition to the *basic_utilities* package declaration. Next, in the *basic_utilities* package body, we replace the *apply_data* procedure in Figure 5.15b with the new *apply_data* procedure in Figure 6.19. The declaration of the *apply_data* procedure in the *basic_utilities* package declaration (see Figure 5.15a) must be modified to conform to the new version of this procedure.

Another use of unconstrained arrays is in the design of generic hardware structures. Figure 6.20 shows an *n*-bit comparator that uses unconstrained arrays for its input signals. This comparator is based on the *bit_comparator* in Chapter 4 (see Figure 4.12). The entity declaration of the *n_bit_comparator* is similar to that of the *nibble_comparator* in Figure 4.17, except that the range of the input BIT_VECTORs is not specified. The *iterative* architecture of the *n_bit_comparator* is similar to that of

```
ENTITY n_bit_comparator IS
    PORT (a, b : IN BIT_VECTOR; gt, eq, lt : IN BIT;
            a_gt_b, a_eq_b, a_lt_b : OUT BIT);
END n_bit_comparator;
--
ARCHITECTURE structural OF n_bit_comparator IS
    COMPONENT comp1
        PORT (a, b, gt, eq, lt : IN BIT; a_gt_b, a_eq_b, a_lt_b OUT BIT);
    END COMPONENT;
    FOR ALL : comp1 USE ENTITY WORK.bit_comparator (gate_level);
    CONSTANT n : INTEGER := a' LENGTH;
    SIGNAL im : BIT_VECTOR ( 0 TO (n-1)*3-1);
BEGIN
    c_all: FOR i IN 0 TO n-1 GENERATE
        l: IF i = 0 GENERATE
            least: comp1 PORT MAP (a(i), b(i), gt, eq, lt,
                                    im(0), im(1), im(2) );
        END GENERATE;
        m: IF i = n-1 GENERATE
            most: comp1 PORT MAP (a(i), b(i), im(i*3-3), im(i*3-2), im(i*3-1),
                                    a_gt_b, a_eq_b, a_lt_b);
        END GENERATE;
        r: IF i > 0 AND i < n-1 GENERATE
            rest: comp1 PORT MAP (a(i), b(i), im(i*3-3), im(i*3-2), im(i*3-1),
                                    im(i*3+0), im(i*3+1), im(i*3+2) );
        END GENERATE;
    END GENERATE;
END structural;
```

FIGURE 6.20
An n-bit comparator, wiring *n* number of one-bit comparators.

the *nibble_comparator* in Figure 4.22, except that the value of constant *n* is defined as the length of the *a* operand, using the 'LENGTH attribute. Associating an instance of a component with the *n_bit_comparator* in Figure 6.20 causes association of fixed size signals with its *a* and *b* inputs. When this happens, the length and the range of the parameters in this entity are known, and constant *n* has a fixed integer value. The generate statement in the *structural* architecture of *n_bit_comparator* uses *n* to instantiate the appropriate number of *bit_comparator*s. For the *n*-bit comparator to function properly, the *a* and *b* inputs must be of the same size. Furthermore, the range of these vectors must be descending and the indices of their right most bits must be zero.

The test bench in Figure 6.21 uses the generic *apply_data* procedure for testing a 6-bit comparator. The test bench associates 6-bit arrays with the input ports of the *n_bit_comparator* in Figure 6.20, which makes this variable-size comparator a 6-bit comparator. The *apply_data* procedure is called twice to assign values to the *a* and *b* inputs of the comparator under test. Since *a* and *b* are 6-bit signals, the *apply_data* procedure converts its input integers to 6-bit binary numbers. The two calls to this procedure use a different number of concatenated integers.

6.1.5   File Type and External File I/O

File declarations can be used to define a file type. A data type is associated with an identifier that is defined as a file type. This data type is the type of the data contained

```
 ┌ENTITY n_bit_comparator_test_bench IS
 └END n_bit_comparator_test_bench ;
    --
 │ USE WORK.basic_utilities.ALL;
 │  -- FROM PACKAGE USE: apply_data which uses integer_vector
 ┌ARCHITECTURE procedural OF n_bit_comparator_test_bench IS
 │    COMPONENT comp_n PORT (a, b : IN bit_vector;
 │                             gt, eq, lt : IN BIT;
 │                             a_gt_b, a_eq_b, a_lt_b : OUT BIT);
 │    END COMPONENT;
 │    FOR a1 : comp_n USE ENTITY WORK.n_bit_comparator(structural);
 │    SIGNAL a, b : BIT_VECTOR (5 DOWNTO 0);
 │    SIGNAL eql, lss, gtr : BIT;
 │    SIGNAL vdd : BIT := '1';
 │    SIGNAL gnd : BIT := '0';
 ├BEGIN
 │    a1: comp_n PORT MAP (a, b, gnd, vdd, gnd, gtr, eql, lss);
 │    apply_data (a, 00&15&57&17, 500 NS);
 │    apply_data (b, 00&43&14&45&11&21&44&11, 500 NS);
 └END procedural;
```

FIGURE 6.21
Using generic *apply_data* procedure for testing *n_bit_comparator*.

in files of the specified type. The following statement declares *logic_data* as a file type whose contents are of the predefined CHARACTER type:

```
TYPE logic_data IS FILE OF CHARACTER;
```

This file type can be used in a file declaration to declare input and output files of this type. A file declaration uses an identifier for a file name, specifies its type as an existing file type, and associates it with a host system file name. Consider, for example, the following file declaration:

```
FILE input_logic_value_file : logic_data IS IN "input.dat";
```

This declaration specifies that *input_logic_value_file* is an input file object of type *logic_data*, as declared above, and it associates this file with the host system *input.dat* file. Data read from this file is in ASCII (elements of CHARACTER) form, and an object of the CHARACTER type must be associated with the operand that is used for reading from this file.

VHDL provides three operations, READ, WRITE, and ENDFILE for the file types. READ takes a file name and an object of the file data type as its argument. It reads the next data from the file and places it in its data argument. The arguments of the WRITE operation are similar to those of the READ operation. This operation writes data into the specified file. The ENDFILE operation takes a file name as its argument and returns TRUE if a subsequent READ cannot be done from the file. READ and WRITE operations are procedure calls, while ENDFILE is a function call.

As an example of file type declaration and external file I/O, consider the *assign_bits* procedure in Figure 6.22. This procedure reads CHARACTER type data from a specified host system input file, transforms this data into appropriate BIT type values, and assigns the bit values to its output signal. Each assignment is delayed from its previous assignment by the amount of time specified in the *period* TIME type parameter. In general, the function of this procedure is similar to that of the *apply_data* procedure in Chapter 5, or the modified version of it shown in Figure 6.19. Instead of converting integers and assigning them to a multi-bit *target* signal, the *target* parameter of the *assign_bits* procedure is a one-bit scalar, and its corresponding data is read from a file.

The declaration of *logic_data* file type must be visible to the procedure in Figure 6.22. The formal parameters of the *assign_bits* procedure consist of a BIT type output *target*, a STRING type input parameter for the host system file name, and a *period* of type TIME. In the declarative part of this procedure, the temporary variable, *char*, is declared for use as a buffer for characters read from the input file and the *input_value_file* is declared as the input file. The purpose of the *current* variable is to keep a record of timing. The *input_value_file* is associated with the host system file name that is passed to this procedure via the *file_name* formal parameter. In the statement part of the *assign_bits* procedure, a while loop uses the ENDFILE file operation to determine if more characters exist in the input file. In this case, the next character will be read from the file into the *char* buffer. If *char* is a '0' or a '1', *current* will be incremented by *period* and appropriate assignments, based on the value of *char*, will be made to the *target* signal. Note that *char* contains data of the CHARACTER type and cannot directly be assigned to *target* which is type BIT. The inner if statement of

```
-- File Type   logic_data is Visible
┌PROCEDURE assign_bits (
│      SIGNAL target : OUT BIT; file_name : IN STRING; period : IN TIME)
├IS
│      VARIABLE char : CHARACTER;
│      VARIABLE current : TIME := 0 NS;
│      FILE input_value_file : logic_data IS IN file_name;
├BEGIN
│      WHILE NOT ENDFILE (input_value_file) LOOP
│          READ (input_value_file, char);
│          IF char = '0' OR char = '1' THEN
│              current := current + period;
│              IF char = '0' THEN
│                  target <= TRANSPORT '0' AFTER current;
│              ELSIF char = '1' THEN
│                  target <= TRANSPORT '1' AFTER current;
│              END IF;
│          END IF;
│      END LOOP;
└END assign_bits;
```

FIGURE 6.22
A procedure for reading characters from a file and assigning them to a BIT type.

the *assign_bits* procedure converts '0' and '1' elements that belong to the CHARAC-
TER enumeration type to like elements for the BIT enumeration type. Literals like
'0' and '1' that are used in more than one enumeration type are said to be overloaded.

As with the *apply_data* procedure, the *assign_bits* procedure and its corresponding declarations become part of our design utilities when they are added to the *ba-
sic_utilities* package. Declaration of this procedure and the *logic_data* file declaration
will be placed in the *basic_utilities* package declaration. The subprogram body in
Figure 6.22 is also entered in the corresponding body of this package. When this has
been done a design can read binary data from a system file by making this procedure
call:

    assign_bits (a_signal, "unix_file.bit", 1500 NS);

A procedure call for the *assign_bits* procedure in a concurrent body of VHDL, for
example, the statement part of an architecture, is executed once at the beginning of
the simulation run. When *assign_bits* is called, it reads the entire *unix_file.bit* and
assigns '0's and '1's to the *a_signal* output of the procedure. If this procedure is called
a multiple number of times with the same file name, each time it is called reading
begins from the top of the file and the same data is re-read. This is because the file
declaration is contained in the declarative part of the procedure and a new file object
is declared each time it is called. This re-reading can be avoided if a file object is
declared outside of a procedure and then passed to the procedure that reads a file.

The next section shows an example for reading *qit* type data from an input
file. The VHDL standard TEXTIO package also provides several file types and their

corresponding read and write procedures. Chapter 8 illustrates the use of this standard VHDL package.

6.2 SUBPROGRAM PARAMETER TYPES AND OVERLOADING

In VHDL, subprograms with the same name and different types of parameters or results are distinguished from each other. A name used by more than one such subprogram is said to be overloaded. Overloading is a useful mechanism for using the same name for subprograms that perform the same operation on data of different types. VHDL allows overloading of user defined subprograms, standard functions, and operators.

Our first examples for overloading show how to define the essential logical operators for the *qit* type defined in the previous section. Figure 6.23 shows logic tables for AND, OR and inversion operations in the *qit* logic value system. As before, the high impedance 'Z' value is treated as a '1' by all three functions. If one input of the AND function is '0', the output is '0' even if the other input is unknown ('X'). Similarly, if at least one input of the OR function is '1', the output becomes '1'. The NOT table is a repetition of the logic value table for the inverter in Section 6.1, and is shown here for completeness. Figure 6.24 shows the declaration and definition of "AND", "OR", and "NOT" functions according to the tables in Figure 6.23. These definitions overload the corresponding VHDL operators that are defined for the BIT and the BOOLEAN types. In the declarations in Figure 6.24a, declarations of *qit*, *qit_2d*, and *qit_1d*, as well those for the "AND", "OR" and "NOT" functions are shown. The *qit_2d* and *qit_1d* arrays are used by the function definitions and must be visible to them. For the declarations and definitions of the functions that overload the operators, for example, the "AND" function overloading the AND operator, the operator symbol enclosed in double quotes must be used for the function name. Figure 6.24b shows the subprogram bodies for the functions declared in Figure 6.24a. The declarative part of each function consists of a constant declaration that sets a local array of type *qit* according to its corresponding table in Figure 6.23. A return statement constitutes the statement part of each of these functions. This statement returns the value of a table entry that is indexed by the input(s) of the function. The constant tables for the two input "AND" and "OR" functions are the *qit_2d* type, and the "NOT" function is the *qit_1d* type.

When a design uses AND, OR or NOT operators with BIT or BOOLEAN operands, the standard VHDL operators are used. If, however, the operand types of these operators are of the *qit* type, the functions in Figure 6.24 are used if they are visible to the design. For the examples that follow, we assume that the contents of Figure 6.24a are included in the *basic_utilities* package declaration and that the subprogram bodies in Figure 6.24b are included in the *basic_utilities* package body. Type declarations that are only used internally to a package do not have to be included in the package declaration; it is sufficient to declare them in the package body. Although types *qit_2d* and *qit_1d* fit this category, i.e., they are only used inside the *basic_utilities* package, we include them in the *basic_utilities* package declaration for possible future use, thus making them visible to all designs that use this package.

a:	0	1	Z	X
b: 0	0	0	0	0
1	0	1	1	X
Z	0	1	1	X
X	0	X	X	X

$$z = a \cdot b$$

(a)

a:	0	1	Z	X
b: 0	0	1	1	X
1	1	1	1	1
Z	1	1	1	1
X	X	1	1	X

$$z = a + b$$

(b)

a: 0	1
1	0
Z	0
X	X

$$z = a'$$

(c)

FIGURE 6.23
Tables for the basic logic functions in the *qit* four value logic system, (a) AND function, (b) OR function, (c) NOT function.

Figure 6.25 shows entity declaration and architecture bodies for a NOT, a two-input NAND, and a three-input NAND gate in the *qit* logic value system. These structures use the overloaded AND and NOT operators. The *inv_q*, *nand2_q*, and the *nand3_q* descriptions shown in this figure are similar to the parameterized gate models in Figure 5.18 in Chapter 5. The types of the input and output ports in the descriptions in Chapter 5 are of type BIT, and those in Figure 6.25 are of type *qit*. Because of this difference, the overloaded AND and NOT operators of Figure 6.24 are used by the *average_delay* architectures in the *inv_q*, *nand2_q*, and *nand3_q* entities instead of the standard VHDL operators. Unlike the *nand2* description in Chapter 5, the NAND function is not used by the *nand2_q* description because we have not provided an overloading function for the NAND operator. Using the NAND operator with operands of type *qit* is incorrect.

```
TYPE qit IS ('0', '1', 'Z', 'X');
TYPE qit_2d IS ARRAY (qit, qit) OF qit;
TYPE qit_1d IS ARRAY (qit) OF qit;

--

FUNCTION "AND" (a, b : qit) RETURN qit;
FUNCTION "OR" (a, b : qit) RETURN qit;
FUNCTION "NOT" (a : qit) RETURN qit;
```

(a)

```
FUNCTION "AND" (a, b : qit) RETURN qit IS
    CONSTANT qit_and_table : qit_2d := (
                                ('0','0','0','0'),
                                ('0','1','1','X'),
                                ('0','1','1','X'),
                                ('0','X','X','X'));
BEGIN
    RETURN qit_and_table (a, b);
END "AND";
--
FUNCTION "OR" (a, b : qit) RETURN qit IS
    CONSTANT qit_or_table : qit_2d := (
                                ('0','1','1',',X'),
                                ('1','1','1','1'),
                                ('1','1','1','1'),
                                (',X','1','1',',X'));
BEGIN
    RETURN qit_or_table (a, b);
END "OR";
--
FUNCTION "NOT" (a : qit) RETURN qit IS
    CONSTANT qit_not_table : qit_1d := ('1','0','0',' X');
BEGIN
    RETURN qit_not_table (a);
END "NOT";
```

(b)

FIGURE 6.24
Overloading basic logical functions for the *qit* four value logic system, (a) function declarations and other necessary declarations, (b) definition of functions.

For the next example of overloading, consider the expressions used for calculating the *tplh* and *tphl* delay parameters in the *double_delay* architecture of the *inv_rc* entity in Figure 6.11. Physical type to integer conversions, and integer to physical type conversions were done in these expressions because the VHDL multiplication operator is not defined for multiplying two physical types. By overloading this operator as shown in Figure 6.26, it can be made to accept *resistance* as the type of its first

```
USE  WORK.basic_utilities.ALL;
 -- FROM PACKAGE USE: qit, "NOT"
ENTITY inv_q IS
     GENERIC (tplh : TIME := 5 NS; tphl : TIME := 3 NS);
     PORT (i1 : IN qit; o1 : OUT qit);
END inv_q;
 --
ARCHITECTURE average_delay OF inv_q IS
BEGIN
     o1 <= NOT i1 AFTER (tplh + tphl) / 2;
END average_delay;


USE  WORK.basic_utilities.ALL;
 -- FROM PACKAGE USE: qit, "AND"
ENTITY nand2_q IS
     GENERIC (tplh : TIME := 6 NS; tphl : TIME := 4 NS);
     PORT (i1, i2 : IN qit; o1 : OUT qit);
END nand2_q;
 --
ARCHITECTURE average_delay OF nand2_q IS
BEGIN
     o1 <= NOT ( i1 AND i2 ) AFTER (tplh + tphl) / 2;
END average_delay;


USE  WORK.basic_utilities.ALL;
 -- FROM PACKAGE USE: qit, "AND"
ENTITY nand3_q IS
     GENERIC (tplh : TIME := 7 NS; tphl : TIME := 5 NS);
     PORT (i1, i2, i3 : IN qit; o1 : OUT qit);
END nand3_q;
 --
ARCHITECTURE average_delay OF nand3_q IS
BEGIN
     o1 <= NOT ( i1 AND i2 AND i3) AFTER (tplh + tphl) / 2;
END average_delay;
```

FIGURE 6.25
Basic gates in the *qit* logic value system using overloaded AND and OR operators.

operand (left of the operator), *capacitance* as the type of its second operand (right of the operator), and produce results of type TIME.

The "*" overloading function uses the definition of *resistance* and *capacitance* physical types. In the statement part of this function, *resistance* and *capacitance* physical types are neutralized to equivalent integers and the result of multiplying these integers is multiplied by the appropriate unit of type TIME. This time expression is returned as the result of the function. By adding the declaration and the subprogram body in Figure 6.26 to the *basic_utilities* package, the "*" function can use *capaci-*

```
...
FUNCTION "*" (a : resistance; b : capacitance) RETURN TIME;
                    (a)
```

```
FUNCTION "*" (a : resistance; b : capacitance) RETURN TIME IS
BEGIN
    RETURN  ( ( a / 1 l_o) * ( b / 1 ffr ) * 1 FS ) / 1000;
END "*";
                    (b)
```

FIGURE 6.26
Overloading the multiplication operator for returning TIME when multiplying *resistance* and *capacitance* physical types, (a) function declaration, (b) the "*" subprogram body.

tance and *resistance* definitions from this package, and it becomes visible to designs that use this package. The *double_delay* architecture of *inv_rc* shown in Figure 6.27, uses the overloaded multiplication operator for calculating *tplh* and *tphl* propagation delays. The first multiplication operator in the constant value expressions of *tplh* and *tphl* is associated with the function in Figure 6.26. The other multiplication operator uses the standard VHDL operator. As shown, types *qit*, *resistance*, and *capacitance*, as well as the "*" function are visible to the description in Figure 6.27.

The final example in this section discusses overloading the *assign_bits* procedure in Figure 6.22. The overloading is done so that this procedure can accept data files containing *qit* type information and produce *qit* data on its output signal of type *qit*. In Figure 6.22, the name *assign_bits* is used to designate a procedure that reads ASCII data from a file, ignoring non '0' or '1' data, and then places the filtered data on a

```
USE WORK.basic_utilities.ALL;
-- FROM PACKAGE USE: qit, capacitance, resistance, "*"
ENTITY inv_rc IS
    GENERIC (c_load : capacitance := 66 ffr);
    PORT (i1 : IN qit; o1 : OUT qit);
    CONSTANT rpu : resistance := 25 k_o;
    CONSTANT rpd : resistance := 15 k_o;
END inv_rc;
--
ARCHITECTURE double_delay OF inv_rc IS
    CONSTANT tplh : TIME := rpu * c_load * 3;
    CONSTANT tphl : TIME := rpd * c_load * 3;
BEGIN
    o1 <= '1' AFTER tplh WHEN i1 = '0' ELSE
          '0' AFTER tphl WHEN i1 = '1' OR i1 = 'Z' ELSE
          ',X' AFTER tplh;
END double_delay;
```

FIGURE 6.27
Using the overloaded multilplication operator in the *double_delay* architecture of *inv_rc*.

BIT type output signal. Figure 6.28 shows an *assign_bits* procedure that uses *qit* for the type of its first parameter and accepts the elements of the *qit* type from its input file. The *qit* version of the *assign_bits* procedure requires visibility of the enumeration type, *qit*, in addition to the file type, *logic_data*. The parameters of this procedure consist of an output signal of type *qit*, a STRING type input file name, and a *period* of type TIME. As in the description in Figure 6.22, this description uses *char* and *current* for temporary storage of input data and time of assignment, respectively.

When this procedure is called, a host system file is associated with the *file_name* parameter. As long as there are unread characters in this file, the procedure extracts a character from the file and increments the *current* variable by *period*. A case statement maps an extracted character to the appropriate *qit* element, and assigns this element to the output *target* signal. This mapping, which is implemented by choosing alternatives of a case statement, converts '0', '1' and uppercase or lowercase 'X' and 'Z' characters in the input file to the corresponding *qit* type enumeration elements. If the value of *char* does not match any of the case alternative

```
TYPE qit IS ('0', '1', 'Z', ',X');
TYPE logic_data IS FILE OF CHARACTER;
PROCEDURE assign_bits (SIGNAL target : OUT qit;
                             file_name : IN STRING; period : IN TIME);
```
(a)

```
PROCEDURE assign_bits (
     SIGNAL target : OUT qit; file_name : IN STRING; period : IN TIME)
IS
     VARIABLE char : CHARACTER;
     VARIABLE current : TIME := 0 NS;
     FILE input_value_file : logic_data IS IN file_name;
BEGIN
     WHILE NOT ENDFILE (input_value_file) LOOP
          READ (input_value_file, char);
          current := current + period;
          CASE char IS
               WHEN '0' => target <= TRANSPORT '0' AFTER current;
               WHEN '1' => target <= TRANSPORT '1' AFTER current;
               WHEN 'Z' | 'z' => target <= TRANSPORT 'Z' AFTER current;
               WHEN ',X' | 'x' => target <= TRANSPORT ',X' AFTER current;
               WHEN OTHERS => current := current - period;
          END CASE;
     END LOOP;
END assign_bits;
```
(b)

FIGURE 6.28
Overloading the *assign_bits* procedure for accepting and producing *qit* data, (a) procedure declaration and other necessary declarations, (b) the subprogram body.

choices, the last case statement alternative causes the *current* time tracking variable to decrement by *period*. Decrementing *current* and reading the next character from the file causes characters that cannot be mapped to the elements of *qit* to be ignored.

The two different *assign_bits* procedures shown in Figures 6.22 and 6.28 can co-exist in the same library or even in the same package, for example, the *basic_utilities* package. In this case, the two procedures are said to be overloading each other. When the *assign_bits* procedure is called, the appropriate procedure is used based on the type of the first parameter in the association list of the procedure call statement.

This is the first time we have encountered a sequential case statement, so it is appropriate to elaborate on this construct. The syntax details of the case statement in Figure 6.28 are illustrated in Figure 6.29. The expression that follows the CASE keyword is checked against the choice(s) of all the case statement alternatives. When a match is found, the sequence of statements that follow the arrow is executed. If the value of the expression is not equal to any of the choices in the case statement alternatives, the case statement alternative with OTHERS as its choice is executed. Case statements must be complete, which means that all

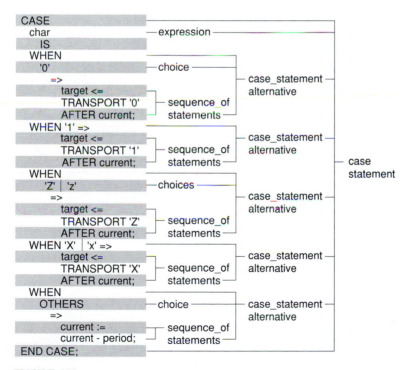

FIGURE 6.29
Syntax details of a sequential case statement.

```
USE WORK.basic_utilities.ALL;
-- FROM PACKAGE USE: qit, capacitance, resistance, assign_bits (Fig 6.30)
ENTITY tester IS
END tester;
--
ARCHITECTURE input_output OF tester IS
    COMPONENT inv
        GENERIC (c_load : capacitance := 11 ffr);
        PORT (i1 : IN qit; o1 : OUT qit);
    END COMPONENT;
    FOR ALL : inv USE ENTITY WORK.inv_rc(double_delay);
    SIGNAL a, z : qit;
BEGIN
    assign_bits (a, "data.qit", 500 NS);
    i1 : inv PORT MAP (a, z);
END input_output;
```

FIGURE 6.30
Calling the overloaded *assign_bits* for testing an inverter.

possible choices of an expression must be accounted for. The use of OTHERS
is necessary only if the prior case statement alternatives do not cover all possible values of the case expression. In this example, OTHERS covers for all ASCII
characters except '0', '1', 'Z', 'z', 'X', and 'x'. The case statement alternative that
uses OTHERS for its choice must be the last such statement in the case statement.

We close this section by presenting a test bench for the *double_delay* architecture
of *inv_rc* (Figure 6.27). The test bench shown in Figure 6.30 calls the *assign_bits*
procedure for reading the test data from an external file. Since the *a* signal of type *qit*
is associated with the first formal parameter of *assign_bits*, the procedure in Figure 6.28
will be used, rather than the one shown in Figure 6.22, whose first formal parameter is
the BIT type. The second parameter in the procedure call association list is a constant
string ("*data.qit*") that is associated with the *file_name* formal parameter that is used
for the file name of the host system. Calling this procedure causes the use of *qit* data
from the *data.qit* file in the generation of a waveform on signal *a*.

6.3 OTHER TYPES AND TYPE RELATED ISSUES

Subtypes, records, and aliases are type related issues that can be used for hardware
modeling and design. This section is devoted to the description of these topics.

6.3.1 Subtypes

For a previously defined type, subtypes consisting of the subsets of the values of
the original type can be defined. The original type is called the base type and it is
fully compatible with all its subtypes. In VHDL, all types are subtypes of themselves.
Because of this, the word "subtype" is used to refer to all declared types and subtypes.

Subtypes are used when a subset of a previously defined type is to be utilized and when compatibility with the base type is to be preserved. For example, consider defining *compatible_nibble_bits* as:

```
SUBTYPE compatible_nibble_bits IS BIT_VECTOR ( 3 DOWNTO 0);
```

This declaration makes objects that are declared as *compatible_nibble_bits* compatible with other objects whose base types are BIT_VECTOR. As a counter example, consider the declaration of *nibble_bits* as:

```
TYPE nibble_bits IS ARRAY ( 3 DOWNTO 0 ) OF BIT;
```

If an object of type *nibble_bits* is to be assigned to a 4-bit BIT_VECTOR object, or if such objects are to be used in an expression, the use of explicit type conversions from *nibble_bits* to BIT_VECTOR or vice versa is required.

A subtype can be declared to have a range of enumeration elements of an enumeration type. For example, the following subtype declaration defines *ten_value_logic* as a subtype whose elements are integers between 0 and 9:

```
SUBTYPE ten_value_logic IS INTEGER RANGE 0 TO 9;
```

Objects of type *ten_value_logic* can be used in the same expressions with INTEGER type objects without requiring any form of a type conversion.

The definition of a general multi-level logic value system, that the definition of other logic value systems can be based on is an important application of this concept. For example, based on our *qit* type, subtypes such as *tit* and *bin* can be defined as shown here:

```
SUBTYPE tit IS qit RANGE '0' TO 'Z';
SUBTYPE bin IS qit RANGE '0' TO '1';
```

According to these declarations, the *tit* type is a three-value logic system that contains enumeration elements of '0', '1', and 'Z'and the *bin* type is a two-value logic which contains '0'and '1'. The base type for both of these subtypes is *qit*.

Assigning an object of a smaller subtype, e.g., *bin*, to an object of a larger subtype, e.g., *qit*, can be done directly and there is no need for any type conversion. The opposite is also possible, except that if an out of range value is assigned to the object of the smaller subtype, a simulation warning message will be issued.

In our example, the *bin* subtype contains all the enumeration elements of the predefined BIT type. These two types, however, are not compatible, so type conversion is required for assignments or operations that involve these two types.

6.3.2 Record Types

Arrays are composite types whose elements are all the same type. Records are also of the composite class, but they can consist of elements of different types. A record type definition consists of the declaration of the elements of the record that is bracketed between the RECORD keyword and the END RECORD keywords. Each record element declaration declares one or more identifiers and their types.

For example, consider an instruction format for a simple computer that has eight operations, four addressing modes, and an address space of 2^{11} words. Figure 6.31a shows the instruction format and the type declarations for these three fields. The opcode is an enumeration type whose elements are the instruction mnemonics, the addressing mode is an integer ranging from 0 to 3, and the address is an 11-bit BIT_VECTOR. In Figure 6.31b, the *instruction_format* type is declared as a record that contains three fields of *opc*, *mde*, and *adr* of types *opcode*, *mode*, and *address*, respectively. A signal of type *instruction_format*, shown in Figure 6.31c, is declared and the fields of this signal (*instr*) are initialized to *nop*, 0, and "00000000000". Figure 6.31d shows three signal assignments assigning values to the *instr* signal fields.

6.3.3 Alias Declaration

An object, an indexed part of it, or a slice of it can be given alternative names by using an alias declaration. This declaration can be used for signals, variables, or constants, and it can define new identifiers of the same class and type.

As an example, consider a flag register that is declared as a 4-bit BIT_VECTOR with a descending 3 DOWNTO 0 range. Starting with the most significant bit, the bits

```
|  15 14 13  |  12 11  |    10 09 08 07 06 05 04 03 02 01 00  |
```

opcode	mode	address

```
|---------------------------instruction_format---------------------------|
```

```
TYPE  opcode  IS  (sta,  lda,  add,  sub,  and,  nop,  jmp,  jsr);
TYPE  mode  IS  RANGE  0  TO  3;
TYPE  address  IS  BIT_VECTOR  (10  DOWNTO  0);
```
                    (a)

```
TYPE  instruction_format  IS  RECORD
   opc  :  opcode;
   mde  :  mode;
   adr  :  address;
END  RECORD;
```
                    (b)

```
SIGNAL  instr  :  instruction_format  :=  (nop,  0,  "00000000000");
```
                    (c)

```
instr.opc  <=  lda;
instr.mde  <=  2;
instr.adr  <=  "00011110000";
```
                    (d)

FIGURE 6.31
Record type, (a) three fields of an instruction, (b) declaration of instruction format, (c) a signal of record type, (d) referencing fields of a record type signal.

of this register are carry, overflow, negative, and zero flags. The declarations shown below specify aliases for each of the bits in the flag register:

```
ALIAS c_flag : BIT IS flag_register (3)
ALIAS v_flag : BIT IS flag_register (2)
ALIAS n_flag : BIT IS flag_register (1)
ALIAS z_flag : BIT IS flag_register (0)
```

With these declarations, the equivalent identifiers can be used instead of indexing the *flag_register*. An alias declaration specifies an identifier, its type, and the name of an object the identifier becomes an alias of.

For an example of using an alternative name for a slice of an array, consider the address field of the *instruction_format* in Figure 6.31. This 11-bit address can consist of a 3-bit page address and an 8-bit offset address as shown in Figure 6.32a. The alias declarations in Figure 6.32b equate *page* to the three most significant bits of the address field of an instruction and *offset* to its eight least significant bits. Figure 6.32c shows signal assignment to *page* and *offset* aliases. These assignments result in assigning an 11-bit address to the *adr* field of *instr*.

6.4 PREDEFINED ATTRIBUTES

Predefined attributes in VHDL provide functions for more efficient coding or mechanisms for modeling hardware characteristics. Attributes can be applied to arrays, types and signals and they have the following format:

```
array_or_type_or_signal_name' ATTRIBUTE_NAME
```

When reading this, the single quote (') is read as **tick**.

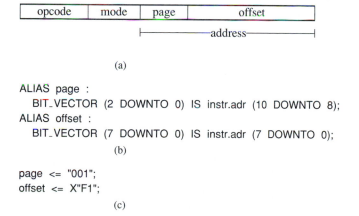

(a)

```
ALIAS page :
  BIT_VECTOR (2 DOWNTO 0) IS instr.adr (10 DOWNTO 8);
ALIAS offset :
  BIT_VECTOR (7 DOWNTO 0) IS instr.adr (7 DOWNTO 0);
```
(b)

```
page <= "001";
offset <= X"F1";
```
(c)

FIGURE 6.32
Alias declaration, (a) page and offset addresses, (b) alias declaration for the page and offset parts of the address, (c) assignments to page and offset parts of address.

This section discusses array, type, and signal attributes. All the predefined attributes are listed and categorically discussed. Examples are shown only for key attributes, however, other attributes are used in examples in the chapters that follow.

6.4.1 Array Attributes

Array attributes are used to find range, length, or boundaries of arrays. These attributes can only be used with array objects. Figure 6.33 shows all the predefined array attributes in VHDL and presents an example of each one. The examples are based on the *sq_4_8* signal declared in Figure 6.14a. The type of this signal is *qit_4by8*, as shown in Figure 6.12, which is a two-dimensional array with one range specified as 3 DOWNTO 0 and the other as 0 TO 7. A parenthesized number can follow array attributes. For multi-dimensional arrays, this number indicates the index range of the array, while for one-dimensional arrays it defaults to 1.

The examples in the previous chapters used 'RANGE and 'LENGTH attributes. More examples, based on *array_x* being an array object with ascending range, are shown here:

Condition *array_x*'LEFT < *array_x*'RIGHT is true.

Range *array_x*'LEFT TO *array_x*'RIGHT is equivalent to *array_x*'RANGE.

Expression *array_x*'HIGH - *array_x*'LOW + 1 is equivalent to *array_x*'LENGTH.

Result of *array_x* (*array_x*'LOW) is the value of *array_x* in its lowest index.

Attribute	Description	Example	Result
'LEFT	Left bound	sq_4_8'LEFT(1)	3
'RIGHT	Right bound	sq_4_8'RIGHT sq_4_8'RIGHT(2)	0 7
'HIGH	Upper bound	sq_4_8'HIGH(2)	7
'LOW	Lower bound	sq_4_8'LOWS(2)	0
'RANGE	Range	sq_4_8'RANGE(2) sq_4_8'RANGE(1)	0 TO 7 3 DOWNTO 0
'REVERSE_RANGE	Reverse Range	sq_4_8'REVERSE_RANGE(2) sq_4_8'REVERSE_RANGE(1)	7 DOWNTO 0 0 TO 3
'LENGTH	Length	sq_4_8'LENGTH	4

FIGURE 6.33
Predefined array attributes. The type of *sq_4_8* is *qit_4by8* in Figure 6.12.

6.4.2 Type Attributes

Type attributes are used for accessing elements of defined types and are only valid for nonarray types. Although several type and array attributes use the same names, it is important to realize that their meanings may be different. For example, when applied to an enumeration type, the 'RIGHT type attribute results in the right most enumeration element of that type. Attributes 'BASE, 'LEFT, 'RIGHT, 'HIGH, and 'LOW can be applied to any scalar type while attributes 'POS, 'VAL, 'SUCC, 'PRED, 'LEFTOF, and 'RIGHTOF can only be used with an integer type, an enumeration type, or a physical type. For example, using 'VAL(2) with an enumeration type results in the enumeration element in position 2 for this type. The positions of enumeration elements are numbered from left to right starting with 0.

Figure 6.34 shows a tabular list of all type attributes in VHDL and presents an example of each one. All examples refer to the *qit* and *tit* types that were defined in earlier sections of this chapter. The results of attributes 'LEFT, 'RIGHT, 'HIGH, and 'LOW correspond to the values of the types or subtypes that they are applied to, while the 'POS, 'VAL, 'SUCC, 'PRED, 'LEFTOF, and 'RIGHTOF attributes perform the specified functions on the base of the subtype. For example, *tit*'POS('X') results in 3, which is the position of 'X'in the *qit* type. Notice that 'X'is not even contained in the *tit* subtype.

6.4.3 Signal Attributes

Signal attributes are used for objects in the signal class of any type. Such attributes are used for finding events, transactions, or timing of events and transactions on signals. These attributes are most useful for modeling hardware properties.

Attributes 'STABLE, 'EVENT, 'LAST_EVENT, and 'LAST_VALUE deal with events occurring on a signal. For example, when 'EVENT is used with a signal, the result is true (BOOLEAN TRUE) when an event occurs on that signal, that is, the value of the signal changes. Attributes 'QUIET, 'ACTIVE, 'LAST_ACTIVE, and 'TRANSACTION have to do with the transactions that occur on a signal. For example, *s_signal*'ACTIVE is true when a transaction occurs on the *s_signal*, even if the transaction does not cause a change of value on this signal.

Results of the attributes 'DELAYED, 'STABLE, 'QUIET, and 'TRANSACTION are signals and can be used like signal objects. For example, *s_signal*'DELAYED' STABLE is only valid because *s_signal*'DELAYED results in a signal to which the 'STABLE signal attribute can be applied.

Figure 6.35 presents a list of the signal attributes and gives a simple example for each one, showing the kind and type of the result. Also shown in this figure is a box indicating whether the attribute deals with transactions or events on a signal.The *s1* signal used in the examples is assumed to be a scalar signal of type BIT. Signal attributes are time dependent, which means that their values may change continuously during simulation. Figure 6.36 shows an example waveform on *s1*, and the result of using various attributes with this BIT type signal. The waveform shown here includes transactions and events. Each transaction is indicated by a shaded area (▧) of δ duration

Attribute	Description	Example	Result
'BASE	Base of type	tit'BASE	qit
'LEFT	Left bound of type or subtype.	tit'LEFT qit'LEFT	'0' '0'
'RIGHT	Right bound of type or subtype.	tit'RIGHT qit'RIGHT	'Z' 'X'
'HIGH	Upper bound of type or subtype.	INTEGER'HIGH tit'HIGH	Large 'Z'
'LOW	Lower bound of type or subtype.	POSITIVE'LOW qit'LOW	1 '0'
'POS(V)	Position of value V in *base* of type.	qit'POS('Z') tit'POS('X')	2 3
'VAl(P)	Value at Position P in *base* of type.	qit'VAL(3) tit'VAL(3)	'X' 'X'
'SUCC(V)	Value, after value V in *base* of type.	tit'SUCC('Z')	'X'
'PRED(V)	Value, before value V in *base* of type.	tit'PRED('1')	'0'
'LEFTOF(V)	Value, left of value V in *base* of type.	tit'LEFTOF('1') tit'LEFTOF('0')	'0' Error
'RIGHTOF(V)	Value, right of value V in *base* of type.	tit'RIGHTOF('1') tit'RIGHTOF('Z')	'Z' 'Z'

FIGURE 6.34
Predefined type attributes. *qit* and *tit* are enumeration types.

on the waveform. Events occur when a transaction causes the value of *s1* to change. Those attributes whose results are of the type of signal that they are applied to (type BIT for signal *s1*) are shown by logical waveforms and those with BOOLEAN or BIT results (independent of type of *s1*) are indicated with a block (■) for TRUE or '1' and a space (_) for FALSE or '0'. Attributes that result in a signal are shown in the **bold** font.

Common applications of signal attributes include edge detection, pulse width verification, glitch detection, and level mode analysis. For example, the 'STABLE

Attribute	T/E	Example	Kind	Type
Description				
'DELAYED	–	sl'DELAYED(5 NS)	SIGNAL	As *sl*
A copy of *sl*, but delayed by 5 NS. If no parameter or 0, delayed by δ. Equivalent to TRANSPORT delay of *s*1.				
'STABLE	EV	s1'STABLE(5 NS)	SIGNAL	BOOLEAN
A signal that is TRUE if *S1* has not changed in the last 5 NS. If used with no parameter or 0, the resulting signal is TRUE if *sl* has not changed in the current simulation time.				
'EVENT	EV	s1'EVENT	Value	BOOLEAN
If *sl* changes in the current simulation cycle, *sl*'EVENT will be TRUE for this cycle (δ time).				
'LAST_EVENT	EV	s1'LAST_EVENT	Value	Time
The amount of time since the last value change on *sl*. If *sl*'EVENT is TRUE, the value of *sl*'LAST_EVENT is 0.				
'LAST_VALUE	EV	s1'LAST_VALUE	VALUE	As *sl*
The value of *sl* before the most recent event occurs on it.				
'QUIET	TR	s1'QUIET(5 NS)	SIGNAL	BOOLEAN
A signal that is TRUE if no transaction has been placed on *sl* in the last 5 NS. If no parameter of 0, for current simulation cycle is assumed.				
'ACTIVE	TR	s1'ACTIVE	VALUE	BOOLEAN
If *sl* has had a transaction in the current simulation cycle, *sl*'ACTIVE will be TRUE for this simulation cycle, for δ time.				
'LAST_ACTIVE	TR	s1'LAST_ACTIVE	VALUE	TIME
The amount of time since the last transaction occurred on *sl*. If *sl*'ACTIVE is TRUE, *sl*'LAST_ACTIVE is 0.				
'TRANSACTION	TR	s1'TRANSACTION	SIGNAL	BIT
A signal that toggles each time a transaction occurs on *sl*.				

FIGURE 6.35
Predefined signal attributes. Signal *s* is assumed to be of type BIT.

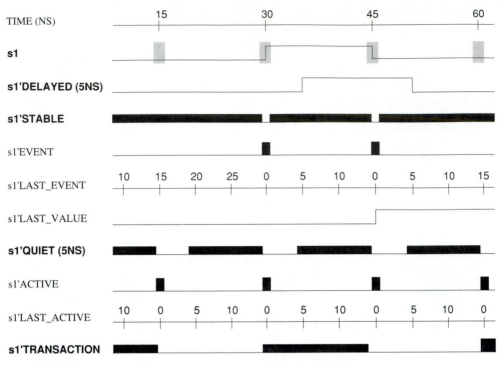

FIGURE 6.36
Results of signal attributes when applied to the BIT type signal, *s1*.

attribute in an edge trigger flip-flop can check for a change in the value of the clock, that is, an edge of a clock. Let us consider the description of the falling-edge D-type flip-flop in Figure 6.37. The statement part of this description consists of a conditional signal assignment which conditionally assigns the D-input to a temporary signal, *tmp*. If a new value is assigned to this signal, it will be assigned to the output after a delay of 8 NS. The condition of the conditional signal assignment becomes TRUE if 1) *c* is *zero*, and 2) *c* has *not* been *stable* during the current simulation cycle. In other words, the condition is TRUE if *c* changes, and this change causes it to be 0. Clearly, this condition detects the falling edge of *c* in the current simulation cycle. The *tmp* signal receives *d* on the falling edge of the clock; otherwise, *tmp* remains unchanged.

Although *c*'EVENT and NOT *c*'STABLE are equivalent in most cases, since the latter generates a signal, its use is recommended in concurrent statements.

As another example in the use of signal assignments, consider the *brief_t_flip_flop* in Figure 6.38. This is the description of a toggle flip-flop that toggles only when a positive pulse longer that 20 NS appears on its *t* input. As in the previous example, a conditional signal assignment assigns one of the two possible values to the *tmp* signal, which is then assigned to the output. The *tmp* signal, which stores the internal state

```
ENTITY  brief_d_flip_flop  IS
    PORT  (d, c  :  IN  BIT;  q  :  OUT  BIT);
END  brief_d_flip_flop;
--
ARCHITECTURE  falling_edge  OF  brief_d_flip_flop  IS
    SIGNAL  tmp  :  BIT;
BEGIN
    tmp  <=  d  WHEN  (c  =  '0'  AND  NOT  c'  STABLE)  ELSE  tmp;
    q  <=  tmp  AFTER  8  NS;
END  falling_edge;
```

FIGURE 6.37
A simple falling edge flip-flop using signal attributes.

```
ENTITY  brief_t_flip_flop  IS
    PORT  (t  :  IN  BIT;  q  :  OUT  BIT);
END  brief_t_flip_flop;
--
ARCHITECTURE  toggle  OF  brief_t_flip_flop  IS
    SIGNAL  tmp  :  BIT;
BEGIN
    tmp  <=  NOT  tmp  WHEN  (
            (t  =  '0'  AND  NOT  t'  STABLE)  AND  (t'  DELAYED'  STABLE(20 NS))
                        )  ELSE  tmp;
    q  <=  tmp  AFTER  8  NS;
END  toggle;
```

FIGURE 6.38
A simple toggle flip-flop using signal attributes.

of the flip-flop, is assigned to the complement of itself when the two conditions are TRUE. The first condition is the falling edge of t (t='0'AND NOT t'STABLE), which is the same as the condition in the example in Figure 6.37. The second condition is TRUE if t, before this last fall, has been stable for 20 NS. The operation t'DELAYED evaluates to a signal that is delayed from t by 0 NS and, therefore, it does not include the change that just occurred on it. If this delayed signal has been stable for at least 20 NS, then we can conclude that the width of the positive pulse on t has been at least 20 NS.

6.5 USER-DEFINED ATTRIBUTES

In addition to the predefined attributes, VHDL allows definition and use of user-defined attributes. Such attributes do not have simulation semantics, so it is up to the user to define them and use them in accordance with the way they are defined.

User-defined attributes may be applied to the elements of what is referred to as the entity class in VHDL. The entity class consists of entities, architectures, configurations, procedures, functions, packages, types, subtypes, constants, signals, variables, components, and labels. Before an attribute can be used, it has to be declared using an attribute declaration. An attribute declaration identifies a name as an attribute with a given type. For example, the following declaration declares *sub_dir* as an attribute that can take values of STRING type:

```
ATTRIBUTE sub_dir : STRING;
```

If the above declaration is made visible to a description, it can be associated with any of the elements of the entity class mentioned above, i.e., entity, architecture, configuration, etc. For example, in order to associate the *sub_dir* attribute with the *brief_d_flip_flop* entity in Figure 6.37, this attribute specification must appear in the declarative part of that entity:

```
ATTRIBUTE sub_dir OF brief_d_flip_flop : ENTITY IS "/user/vhdl";
```

The expression *brief_d_flip_flop'sub_dir*, anywhere in an architecture of the *brief_d_flip_flop* entity, evaluates to *"/user/vhdl"*.

Figure 6.39 shows two attribute definitions and usages. A package called *utility_attributes* declares attributes *sub_dir* and *delay*. The *sub_dir* attribute has a STRING

```
PACKAGE utility_attributes IS
    TYPE timing IS RECORD
        rise, fall : TIME;
    END RECORD;
    ATTRIBUTE delay : timing;
    ATTRIBUTE sub_dir : STRING;
END utility_attributes;
--
USE WORK.utility_attributes.ALL;
-- FROM PACKAGE USE: delay, sub_dir
ENTITY brief_d_flip_flop IS
    PORT (d, c : IN BIT; q : OUT BIT);
    ATTRIBUTE sub_dir OF brief_d_flip_flop : ENTITY IS "/user/vhdl";
    ATTRIBUTE delay OF q : SIGNAL IS (8 NS, 10 NS);
END brief_d_flip_flop;
--
ARCHITECTURE attributed_falling_edge OF brief_d_flip_flop IS
    SIGNAL tmp : BIT;
BEGIN
    tmp <= d WHEN ( c= '0' AND NOT c' STABLE ) ELSE tmp;
    q <= '1' AFTER q'delay.rise WHEN tmp = '1' ELSE
         '0' AFTER q'delay.fall;
END attributed_falling_edge;
```

FIGURE 6.39
Associating attributes to entities and signals.

type, and the type of the *delay* attribute is *timing* which is a record consisting of two fields of type TIME. The entity declaration of *brief_d_flip_flop*, also shown in Figure 6.39, makes use of both attributes defined in this package. In the declarative part of this entity, where both attributes have become visible by applying the use statement, the attributes are associated with the entity itself and with the output of this entity. In the statement part of the *attributed_falling_edge* architecture of the *brief_d_flip_flop* entity, the *rise* and *fall* fields of the *delay* attribute of the *q* output are used in calculating the delay values on this output.

An attribute specification for associating a user-defined attribute with an entity class can appear in any declarative part in which the attribute and the entity it is being applied to are visible. For example, in Figure 6.39, the attribute specification that associates *delay* with the *q* output could appear in the declarative part of the *attributed_falling_edge* architecture. In the same example, it is also worthwhile noting that if the *delay* attribute is to be applied to other signals, those signals should be listed along with *q*, separated by commas. If an attribute is to be applied to all visible signals, the keyword ALL can replace the list of individual signals. The keyword OTHERS can also be used to apply the attribute to all entity classes that have not been specified above it.

Values of user-defined attributes can be used in expressions or on the right hand side of assignments, but no assignments can be made to them.

6.6   PACKAGING BASIC UTILITIES

Chapter 5 introduced a package that we referred to as *basic_utilities*. This chapter added utility types, definitions, and subprograms to this package. We used this package in most of the examples in this chapter and we will continue using it and adding to it in the next two chapters. The present form of the *basic_utilities* package is shown for reference in Figure 6.40. In addition to items whose addition to this package were explicitly specified in the text of Chapters 5 and 6, the package also includes the *qit_vector*, *tit_vector*, and *tit* types and subtype. The *qit_vector* and *tit_vector* types are unconstrained arrays of *qit* and *tit*, respectively.

6.7   SUMMARY

This chapter presented tools for high level descriptions. Declaration of types and the usage of objects of various types were covered in the first part of the chapter. In the context of describing type related issues, we introduced the unconstrained array and file type. Unconstrained arrays are utilities in the language that not only make hardware descriptions very flexible; they are also very useful for software processes and programs. The basic I/O presented in this chapter showed a simple way to read or write from files. The overloading which is related to types was discussed next. This subject was discussed for user-defined subprograms as well as for the VHDL operators. Our emphasis on operator overloading was on the logic and hardware-

```
PACKAGE basic_utilities IS
   TYPE qit IS ('0', '1', 'Z', ',X');
   TYPE qit_2d IS ARRAY (qit, qit) OF qit;
   TYPE qit_1d IS ARRAY (qit) OF qit;
   TYPE qit_vector IS ARRAY (NATURAL RANGE <>) OF qit;
   SUBTYPE tit IS qit RANGE '0' TO 'Z';
   TYPE tit_vector IS ARRAY (NATURAL RANGE <>) OF tit;
   TYPE integer_vector IS ARRAY (NATURAL RANGE <>) OF INTEGER;
   TYPE logic_data IS FILE OF CHARACTER;
   TYPE capacitance IS RANGE 0 TO 1E16
   UNITS
      ffr;   -- Femto Farads (base unit)
      pfr = 1000 ffr;
      nfr = 1000 pfr;
      ufr = 1000 nfr;
      mfr = 1000 ufr;
      far = 1000 mfr;
      kfr = 1000 far;
   END UNITS;
   TYPE resistance IS RANGE 0 TO 1E16
   UNITS
      l_o;   -- Milli-Ohms (base unit)
      ohms = 1000 l_o;
      k_o = 1000 ohms;
      m_o = 1000 k_o;
      g_o = 1000 m_o;
   END UNITS;
   FUNCTION fgl (w, x, gl : BIT) RETURN BIT;
   FUNCTION feq (w, x, eq : BIT) RETURN BIT;
   PROCEDURE bin2int (bin : IN BIT_VECTOR; int : OUT INTEGER);
   PROCEDURE int2bin (int : IN INTEGER;   bin : OUT BIT_VECTOR);
   PROCEDURE apply_data ( SIGNAL target : OUT BIT_VECTOR;
        CONSTANT values : IN integer_vector;   CONSTANT period : IN TIME);
   PROCEDURE assign_bits ( SIGNAL s : OUT BIT; file_name : IN STRING; period : IN TIME);
   PROCEDURE assign_bits ( SIGNAL s : OUT qit; file_name : IN STRING; period : IN TIME);
   FUNCTION "AND" (a, b : qit) RETURN qit;
   FUNCTION "OR" (a, b : qit) RETURN qit;
   FUNCTION "NOT" (a : qit) RETURN qit;
   FUNCTION "*" (a : resistance; b : capacitance) RETURN TIME;
END basic_utilities;
```

FIGURE 6.40
Present form of the *basic-utilities* package. (*continued*)

related operators, but by overloading the multiplication operator we indicated that any operator can be overloaded for any type of operand. Predefined attributes in VHDL can be looked upon as operators or predefined functions. The difference, however, is that such attributes apply to nonobjects as well as signal objects in the language. In

```
┌PACKAGE BODY basic_utilities IS
│   ┌FUNCTION "AND" (a, b : qit) RETURN qit IS
│   │   CONSTANT qit_and_table : qit_2d := (
│   │                               ('0','0','0','0'),
│   │                               ('0','1','1',',X'),
│   │                               ('0','1','1',',X'),
│   │                               ('0',',X',',X',',X'));
│   ├BEGIN
│   │   RETURN qit_and_table (a, b);
│   └END "AND";
│   ┌FUNCTION "OR" (a, b : qit) RETURN qit IS
│   │   CONSTANT qit_or_table : qit_2d := (
│   │                               ('0','1','1','X'),
│   │                               ('1','1','1','1'),
│   │                               ('1','1','1','1'),
│   │                               ('X','1','1','X'));
│   ├BEGIN
│   │   RETURN qit_or_table (a, b);
│   └END "OR";
│   ┌FUNCTION "NOT" (a : qit) RETURN qit IS
│   │   CONSTANT qit_not_table : qit_1d := ('1','0','0',' X');
│   ├BEGIN
│   │   RETURN qit_not_table (a);
│   └END "NOT";
│   ┌FUNCTION "*" (a : resistance; b : capacitance) RETURN TIME IS
│   ├BEGIN
│   │   RETURN   ( ( a / 1 l_o) * ( b / 1 ffr ) * 1 FS ) / 1000;
│   └END "*";
│   ┌FUNCTION fgl (w, x, gl : BIT) RETURN BIT IS
│   ├BEGIN
│   │   RETURN   (w AND gl) OR (NOT x   AND   gl) OR (w   AND   NOT x);
│   └END fgl;
│   ┌FUNCTION feq (w, x, eq : BIT) RETURN BIT IS
│   ├BEGIN
│   │   RETURN   (w AND x AND eq) OR (NOT w   AND   NOT x   AND   eq);
│   └END feq;
│   ┌PROCEDURE bin2int (bin : IN BIT_VECTOR; int : OUT INTEGER) IS
│   │   VARIABLE result: INTEGER;
│   ├BEGIN
│   │   result := 0;
│   │   FOR i IN bin'RANGE LOOP
│   │     IF bin(i) = '1'THEN   result := result + 2**i;
│   │     END IF;
│   │   END LOOP;
│   │   int := result;
│   └END bin2int;
```

FIGURE 6.40
Present form of the *basic-utilities* package. (*continued*)

```
PROCEDURE int2bin (int : IN INTEGER;   bin : OUT BIT_VECTOR) IS
   VARIABLE tmp : INTEGER;
BEGIN
   tmp := int;
   FOR i IN 0 TO (bin'LENGTH - 1) LOOP
      IF (tmp MOD 2  =  1) THEN   bin (i) := '1';
      ELSE bin (i) := '0';
      END IF;
      tmp := tmp / 2;
   END LOOP;
END int2bin;
PROCEDURE apply_data ( SIGNAL target : OUT BIT_VECTOR;
   CONSTANT values : IN integer_vector; CONSTANT period : IN TIME)
IS
   VARIABLE buf : BIT_VECTOR (target'RANGE);
BEGIN
   FOR i IN values'RANGE LOOP
      int2bin (values(i), buf);
      target <= TRANSPORT buf AFTER i * period;
   END LOOP;
END apply_data;
PROCEDURE assign_bits (
   SIGNAL s : OUT BIT; file_name : IN STRING; period : IN TIME)
IS
   VARIABLE char : CHARACTER;
   VARIABLE current : TIME := 0 NS;
   FILE input_value_file : logic_data IS IN file_name;
BEGIN
   WHILE NOT ENDFILE (input_value_file) LOOP
      READ (input_value_file, char);
      IF char = '0' OR char = '1' THEN
         current := current + period;
         IF char = '0' THEN
            s <= TRANSPORT '0' AFTER current;
         ELSIF char = '1' THEN
            s <= TRANSPORT '1' AFTER current;
         END IF;
      END IF;
   END LOOP;
END assign_bits;
```

FIGURE 6.40
Present form of the *basic-utilities* package (*continued*).

modeling, hardware behavior attributes are very useful, as we will see in the following, chapters. Finally in this chapter, we presented the *basic_utilities* package. Elements of this package are useful for hardware modeling and the creation of the package demonstrates the importance of packaging capability in VHDL.

```
PROCEDURE assign_bits (
    SIGNAL s : OUT qit; file_name : IN STRING; period : IN TIME)
IS
    VARIABLE char : CHARACTER;
    VARIABLE current : TIME := 0 NS;
    FILE input_value_file : logic_data IS IN file_name;
BEGIN
    WHILE NOT ENDFILE (input_value_file) LOOP
        READ (input_value_file, char);
        current := current + period;
        CASE char IS
            WHEN '0' => s <= TRANSPORT '0' AFTER current;
            WHEN '1' => s <= TRANSPORT '1' AFTER current;
            WHEN 'Z' | 'z' => s <= TRANSPORT 'Z' AFTER current;
            WHEN 'X' | 'x' => s <= TRANSPORT 'X' AFTER current;
            WHEN OTHERS => current := current - period;
        END CASE;
    END LOOP;
END assign_bits;
END basic_utilities;
```

FIGURE 6.40
Present form of the *basic-utilities* package.

REFERENCES

1. "IEEE Standard VHDL Language Reference Manual," IEEE Std 1076-1987, The Institute of Electrical and Electronic Engineers, Inc., 1988.
2. Lipsett, L., C. Schaefer, and C. Ussery, "VHDL: Hardware Description and Design," Klewer Academic Publishing, Boston, 1988.

PROBLEMS

6.1. Write an entity declaration and a *double_delay* architecture for an XOR gate in the *qit* logic value system. Use a conditional signal assignment. Use a *tplh* of 9 ns and a *tphl* of 7 ns.

6.2. Write an entity declaration and an architecture for an RC circuit in the *qit* logic value system. The circuit has an input and an output. The output follows the input for '0', '1' or 'X' input values. If the input becomes 'Z', the output holds its old value for several milliseconds (use 8 ms).

6.3. Use the RC circuit in Problem 2 to describe an NMOS two-input NAND gate.
    The solution to this problem depends on code developed in Problem 6.2.

6.4. Show type definition for the *distance* physical type, ranging from microns to meters.

6.5. Write a procedure, *apply_bit*, such that bits of an unconstrained string input to the procedure are applied to its target signal according to the specified time interval. Make sure no unnecessary transactions occur on the target of the procedure. A sample call to this procedure is shown here:

```
apply_bit (target, "1100010001000011111001010", 300 NS);
```

6.6. Using *bin2int* and *int2bin*, write a function, *inc_qits*, that returns the increment of its *qit_vector* input parameter. The output of the function should be *qit_vector* type, and values 'X' and 'Z' should be treated as '1'. Use unconstrained arrays so that your function works regardless of the size of the input.

6.7. Use the concatenation operator to develop a complete VHDL description for an 8-bit logic shifter. The circuit has a 2-bit control input c. The value of $c=00$ is for no-operation, $c=01$ is for right rotate, $c=10$ is for left rotate, and $c=11$ is for arithmetic right shift. The data input and output of the circuit are of the *qit_vector* type, and their mapping is determined by the bits of c.

6.8. Write a procedure that assigns consecutive binary numbers to its OUT BIT_VECTOR lines. The procedure should have a *target* output that is an unconstrained array, and a TIME *period*. When called with an n-bit argument, it should assign sequential binary numbers from 0 to $2^n - 1$ to its *target* signal output. These numbers are distanced by the amount of the constant associated with the *period* parameter. For example, if called with a 2-bit vector and a *period* of 100 NS, then the target will receive this data:

"00", "01" AFTER 100 NS, "10" AFTER 200 NS, "11" AFTER 300 NS;

You can use all the procedures and utilities in the *basic_utilities* package.

6.9. Show the overloading function for the XOR operator for the *qit* logic value system.

6.10. Write an unconstrained odd parity checker function. The input is of *qit_vector* type and the output of *qit* type. Treat values 'Z' and 'X' as '1'. The function returns the XOR results of all its input bits.

6.11. Use the function in Problem 6.10 in an architecture for functional description of a parity checker circuit.

6.12. Speed is distance/time. Write the physical type for speed. Overload the division operator to evaluate speed when it is used for dividing distance by time (see Problem 6.4).

6.13. Rewrite the *int2bin* procedure such that it functions properly for any size output, declared with any range, and in any direction. Treat the left bit of the output as the most significant bit and the right-most bit as the least significant. Bit 3 is the MSB for a BIT_VECTOR ranging from 3 TO 10 associated with the output and the LSB is bit 10.

6.14. Rewrite the *bin2int* procedure such that it functions properly for any size output, declared with any range, and in any direction. Treat the left bit of the input as the most significant bit, and the right most bit as the least significant. Bit 3 is the MSB for a BIT_VECTOR ranging from 3 TO 10 associated with the input of this procedure and the LSB is bit 10.

6.15. Write an expression for detecting the falling edge on a clock that is the *qit* type. Falling edge occurs only when the clock makes a transition from '1' to '0'.

6.16. The 'TRANSACTION attribute toggles when a transaction occurs on its parameter. Write an expression such that it causes the value of signal e to toggle when an *event* occurs on a. Using this expression in the following VHDL code, show and justify all transactions and events that occur on the a, t, and e signals.

```
ARCHITECTURE challenging  OF transaction_vs_event IS
    SIGNAL  a : BIT := '1';
    SIGNAL  t, e : BIT := '0';
BEGIN
    a <= '0', '1' AFTER 10 NS, '0' AFTER 12 NS, '0' AFTER 14 NS;
    t <= a' TRANSACTION;
    e <= toggle_when_event_on_a__expression;
END challenging;
```

6.17. Use conditional signal assignments to describe a toggle flip-flop in *qit* logic value system. The output toggles when a complete positive pulse ('0' to '1' to '0') appears on the input.

6.18. Repeat Problem 6.7 for unconstrained input and output vectors. The output of the shifter should become all 'X' if the value of c is anything but "00", "01", "10", or "11". Take advantage of array attributes.

6.19. Use an array of BITS as shown below to model a master-slave *jk* flip-flop.

```
ARRAY(BIT, BIT, BIT) OF BIT
```

Use j, k and q values for the indices of this array, and let the array represent the next state of the flip-flop. In the declarative part of the architecture of the flip-flop declare a constant (for example, *jk-table*) of the type of the array shown above. Initialize this constant to appropriate next values of a *jk* flip-flop. In the statement part of the architecture of the flip-flop look up next q values by indexing the jk table using j, k and present q values.

CHAPTER

7

DATAFLOW DESCRIPTIONS IN VHDL

The middle ground between structural and behavioral descriptions is the dataflow or register transfer level of abstraction as we defined it in Chapter 1. Descriptions at this level specify flow of data through the registers and buses of a system. This flow is controlled by external signals that can be generated by other dataflow machines. Signal assignments constitute the primary VHDL constructs for description of hardware at the dataflow level. These constructs allow controlled movement of data through registers and buses. Various forms of controlled signal assignments, that is, *conditional*, *selected*, and *guarded* assignments, can be used for explicit clock control and handshaking specifications, and to make selections from among several sources.

This chapter discusses the forms of signal assignments not presented in the previous chapters. We also will demonstrate the use of signal assignments for data selection, clock control, and enabling registers and buses. The subject of concurrent assignment of values to signals is related to the various forms of signal assignments and is also dealt with in this chapter.

7.1 MULTIPLEXING AND DATA SELECTION

In a digital system, various forms of hardware structures are used for the selection and placement of data into buses or registers. The simplest form of data selection is the AND-OR logic shown in Figure 7.1.

174

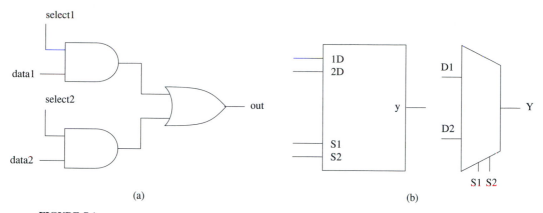

FIGURE 7.1
Basic data selection hardware, (a) logic diagram, (b) symbols.

This structure selects *data1* or *data2*, depending on the values of *select1* and *select2*. Other forms of hardware for the selection of data may consist of a wired connection of tri-state gate outputs, or a parallel connection of MOS transmission gates. Data selection is also referred to as multiplexing and the hardware that performs this task is called a multiplexer. Figure 7.1b shows two multiplexer symbols for the hardware of Figure 7.1a. In addition to the selection of data through a multiplexer, clocking is also often used to enable the acceptance of data by a register or memory structure. As shown in Figure 7.2, this scheme requires enabling of the *clock* signal by the use of an AND gate. On the rising edge of the clock, the data at the *d_input* of the flip-flop is loaded into the flip-flop, only when the *enable* input is active.

The two schemes for multiplexing and clock enabling can also be combined, as shown in Figure 7.3. In this case, data is loaded into the register on the edge of the clock when the clock is enabled and the data is selected by the input multiplexer.

Structures such as those described above can be described in VHDL using various forms of signal assignments.

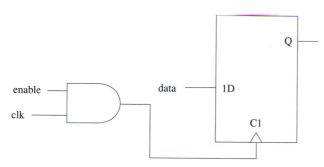

FIGURE 7.2
Selection of data by clock enabling.

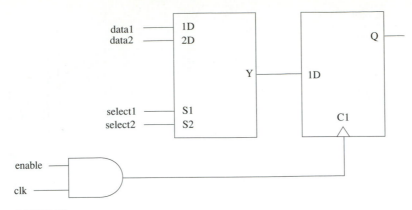

FIGURE 7.3
Multiplexing and clock enabling.

7.1.1 General Multiplexing

A 1-bit 8-to-1 multiplexer with eight select inputs is shown in Figure 7.4. The output of this structure becomes equal to one of the eight inputs when a corresponding select input is active. The symbol shown here does not specify what occurs if more than one select input is active, however, this usually depends on the hardware used for implementing the multiplexer.

The VHDL description that corresponds to this multiplexer is shown in Figure 7.5. This description uses the *qit* logic value system that is defined in the *basic_utilities* package. The ports of the system consist of eight data inputs, eight select inputs, and one output. Although an array of *qit* could be used for the ports, for a

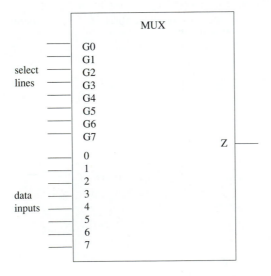

FIGURE 7.4
An eight-to-one multiplexer.

```
USE  WORK.basic_utilities.ALL;
-- FROM  PACKAGE  USE: qit, qit_vector
ENTITY  mux_8_to_1  IS
    PORT ( i7, i6, i5, i4, i3, i2, i1, i0 : IN qit;
              s7, s6, s5, s4, s3, s2, s1, s0 : IN qit; z : OUT qit );
END  mux_8_to_1;
--
ARCHITECTURE dataflow OF mux_8_to_1 IS
    SIGNAL sel_lines : qit_vector ( 7 DOWNTO 0);
BEGIN
    sel_lines <= s7&s6&s5&s4&s3&s2&s1&s0;
    WITH sel_lines SELECT
        z <= '0' AFTER 3 NS  WHEN  "00000000",
              i7 AFTER 3 NS  WHEN  "10000000" | "Z0000000",
              i6 AFTER 3 NS  WHEN  "01000000" | "0Z000000",
              i5 AFTER 3 NS  WHEN  "00100000" | "00Z00000",
              i4 AFTER 3 NS  WHEN  "00010000" | "000Z0000",
              i3 AFTER 3 NS  WHEN  "00001000" | "0000Z000",
              i2 AFTER 3 NS  WHEN  "00000100" | "00000Z00",
              i1 AFTER 3 NS  WHEN  "00000010" | "000000Z0",
              i0 AFTER 3 NS  WHEN  "00000001" | "0000000Z",
              'X' WHEN OTHERS;
END dataflow;
```

FIGURE 7.5
VHDL description for the eight-to-one multiplexer.

closer correspondence to the symbol in Figure 7.4, all inputs are declared as individual *qit* type lines.

In the *dataflow* architecture of the multiplexer, the *sel_lines* intermediate signal of the *qit_vector* type holds the concatenation of the eight select inputs. This 8-bit vector is then used in a selected signal assignment to select '0', 'X', or one of the eight data inputs to be assigned to the z output. If none of the select lines are active (*sel_lines* is "00000000"), a '0' will be scheduled for the z output after 3 nanoseconds. A data input, i.e., $i7, i6, i5, i5, i4, i3, i2, i1$ or $i0$, will be assigned to the z output if its corresponding select line, i.e., $s7, s6, s5, s4, s3, s2, s1$ or $s0$, is '1' or 'Z'. As in the gates discussing Chapter 6, we are treating open inputs as logic value '1'. Finally, the output of the multiplexer becomes 'X' or unknown if more than one select input is active, or if an 'X'appears on any of the select lines.

The syntax details of the selected signal assignment in Figure 7.5 are illustrated in Figure 7.6. The WITH keyword begins this language construct, and is followed by an expression. The possible values of this expression form the choices of the selected waveforms of the selected signal assignment. In our example, the expression is the 8-bit *sel_lines* signal. The next part of this construct consists of a left hand side target and the right hand side selected waveforms. For the target, ten waveforms are specified. Each of these waveforms is conditioned by one or more of the choices of the *sel_lines* expression. For the '0' AFTER 3 NS waveform, only one choice is specified, which

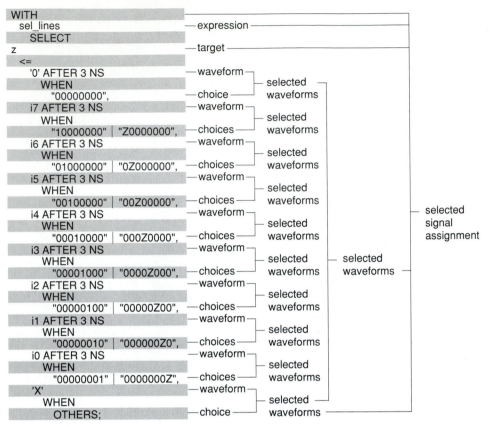

```
WITH
  sel_lines                           — expression
  SELECT
z                                     — target
  <=
    '0' AFTER 3 NS                    — waveform
      WHEN                                         selected
        "00000000",                   — choice      waveforms
    i7 AFTER 3 NS                     — waveform
      WHEN                                         selected
        "10000000" | "Z0000000",      — choices     waveforms
    i6 AFTER 3 NS                     — waveform
      WHEN                                         selected
        "01000000" | "0Z000000",      — choices     waveforms
    i5 AFTER 3 NS                     — waveform
      WHEN                                         selected
        "00100000" | "00Z00000",      — choices     waveforms
    i4 AFTER 3 NS                     — waveform
      WHEN                                         selected
        "00010000" | "000Z0000",      — choices     waveforms
    i3 AFTER 3 NS                     — waveform
      WHEN                                         selected     selected
        "00001000" | "0000Z000",      — choices     waveforms    waveforms
    i2 AFTER 3 NS                     — waveform
      WHEN                                         selected
        "00000100" | "00000Z00",      — choices     waveforms
    i1 AFTER 3 NS                     — waveform
      WHEN                                         selected
        "00000010" | "000000Z0",      — choices     waveforms
    i0 AFTER 3 NS                     — waveform
      WHEN                                         selected
        "00000001" | "0000000Z",      — choices     waveforms
    'X'                               — waveform
      WHEN                                         selected
        OTHERS;                       — choice       waveforms
```

selected signal assignment

FIGURE 7.6
Syntax details of a selected signal assignment.

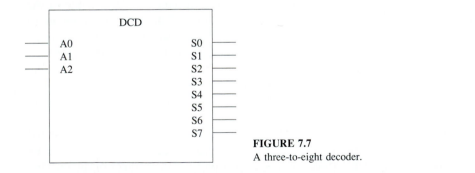

FIGURE 7.7
A three-to-eight decoder.

is the value of *sel_lines*, "00000000". For the waveforms that contain the data input signals (*i7* through *i0*), two choices separated by a vertical bar are specified. For the last waveform choice, i.e., 'X', OTHERS is used. This choice represents all possible values of the *sel_lines* signal that have not been explicitly specified. Choices used with the selected signal assignment must form a complete set of all possible values of the expression of this statement. The use of OTHERS eliminates the need to individually list all 65,536 ($= 4^8$) values of the *sel_lines* 8-bit *qit_vector*.

For another example of the use of the selected signal assignment construct, consider the 3-to-8 decoder in Figure 7.7. This decoder has a 3-bit address input and eight output lines. An output, i, becomes active (high) when the decimal equivalent of the input address is equal to i. As before, we treat 'Z' input value as logic '1'.

The VHDL description for this unit is shown in Figure 7.8. The elements of all inputs and outputs are of type *qit*. A single selected signal assignment, the target of which is the 8-bit output, *so* (selected output), is used for decoding the input. The right hand side of this assignment consists of selected waveforms that set the bits of the output according to the three bits of the input address. For the input bits, both '1' and 'Z' are taken as logic '1'. For each waveform, all possible combinations of 'Z's and '1's have been used as choices. The last waveform causes all bits of the output to become 'X' if any of the address bits is unknown. As in the previous example, the use of OTHERS with the last waveform reduces the amount of coding that would have been required if we were to list all possible values of the 3-bit long *qit* type address.

For a multiplexer with a decoded input, the decoder in Figure 7.8 can be used with the multiplexer in Figure 7.5. For large multiplexers and binary decoders which have regular input to output mappings, behavioral constructs can be used to simplify the descriptions. Specifying input-output values in a tabular form, such as in the

```
USE  WORK.basic_utilities.ALL;
-- FROM  PACKAGE  USE:  qit_vector
ENTITY  dcd_3_to_8  IS
     PORT ( adr : IN  qit_vector (2 DOWNTO 0);
     so : OUT  qit_vector (7 DOWNTO 0));
END  dcd_3_to_8;
--
ARCHITECTURE  dataflow  OF  dcd_3_to_8  IS
BEGIN
    WITH  adr  SELECT
        so <= "00000001" AFTER 2 NS WHEN "000",
              "00000010" AFTER 2 NS WHEN "00Z" | "001",
              "00000100" AFTER 2 NS WHEN "0Z0" | "010",
              "00001000" AFTER 2 NS WHEN "0ZZ" | "0Z1" | "01Z" | "011",
              "00010000" AFTER 2 NS WHEN "100" | "Z00",
              "00100000" AFTER 2 NS WHEN "Z0Z" | "Z01" | "10Z" | "101" ,
              "01000000" AFTER 2 NS WHEN "ZZ0" | "Z10" | "1Z0" | "110",
              "10000000" AFTER 2 NS WHEN "ZZZ" | "ZZ1" | "Z1Z" | "Z11" |
                                         "1ZZ" | "1Z1" | "11Z" | "111",
              "XXXXXXXX" WHEN OTHERS;
END  dataflow;
```

FIGURE 7.8
VHDL description for the three-to-eight decoder.

descriptions in Figures 7.5 and 7.8, is most useful when describing circuits with random input to output mapping. For example, a seven-segment decoder can easily be described using a selected signal assignment.

7.1.2   Guarded Signal Assignments

Using conditional signal assignments for the description of edge trigger flip-flops was discussed in Chapter 6. Figure 7.9a provides a more complete example than the one in Figure 6.37. The corresponding circuit notation, illustrating the dependencies of the *c* and *d* inputs, is shown in Figure 7.9b. The *assigning* architecture of the *d_flipflop* entity specifies that the value of the *d* input is assigned to the *internal_state* signal on the rising edge of the clock. If this assignment causes the value of *internal_state* to change, the new value is assigned to *q* after *delay1*, and its complement to *qb* after *delay2*. The conditional assignment to the *internal_state* specifies that this signal receives its own value when an event other than the rising edge of the clock occurs on the *d* or *c* inputs. This feedback of information causes extra transactions on the internal state of the flip-flop, which may not be an accurate representation of the actual

```
ENTITY d_flipflop IS
   GENERIC (delay1: TIME := 4 NS; delay2 : TIME :=5 NS);
   PORT (d, c : IN BIT; q, qb : OUT BIT);
END d_flipflop;
--
ARCHITECTURE assigning OF d_flipflop IS
   SIGNAL internal_state : BIT;
BEGIN
   internal_state <=d WHEN (c='1' AND NOT c'STABLE) ELSE internal_state;
   q <=internal_state AFTER delay1;
   qb <=NOT internal_state AFTER delay2;
END assigning;
```
(a)

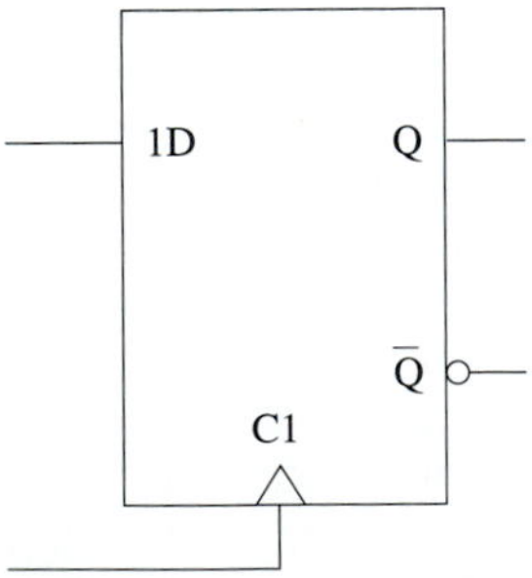

(b)

FIGURE 7.9
A basic flip-flop, that is, just a simple extension of the flip-flop in Figure 6.39, (a) VHDL description, (b) logic symbol.

hardware. This problem can be remedied by using what is referred to as a guarded signal assignment. A guarded signal assignment uses the keyword GUARDED on the right hand side of the assignment arrow, as shown here:

```
target <= GUARDED waveforms__or__conditional_waveforms__or__selected_waveforms;
```

Such an assignment executes only when a Boolean signal, GUARD, is TRUE. When GUARD is FALSE, the assignment does not execute even if events occur on the right hand side waveforms. In this case the right hand side is said to be disconnected from the left hand side target signal.

The GUARD signal can either be explicitly defined, or it can be provided implicitly by the use of a block statement with a guard expression. The *guarding* architecture of *d_flipflop*, shown in Figure 7.10, uses the latter method to define the GUARD signal. As in the *assigning* architecture in *d_flipflop* in Figure 7.9a, the architecture in Figure 7.10 describes the positive edge trigger flip-flop in Figure 7.9b. On the rising edge of the clock, the expression in the parentheses that follows the BLOCK keywords becomes TRUE. The value of this expression corresponds to that of the implicit GUARD signal, and it is used by the guarded signal assignments that assign values to the *q* and *qb* outputs. The value of the *d* input and its complement will be scheduled for *q* and *qb* when GUARD is TRUE. When GUARD is FALSE, *q* and *qb* are disconnected from their respective drivers, namely *d* and NOT *d*.

Figure 7.11 shows the syntax details of the block statement used in the *guarding* architecture of the *d_flipflop* entity. As shown, a block statement must begin with a label. This label may be used for gaining visibility into the block. The guard expression of the block is optional, and if used, defines an implicit GUARD signal that controls all the guarded assignments that appear in the statement part of the block. The statement part of the block may contain any number of concurrent statements and the entire block statement is considered a concurrent statement. Therefore, it is possible to nest block statements.

We have used the *assigning* and *guarding* architectures of the *d_flipflop* entity to demonstrate the use of conditional and guarded signal assignments when controlling assignment of values to signals. Parallel simulation of these two architectures is useful in understanding the timing details of the assignments used in them. A test bench for this purpose is shown in Figure 7.12.

```
ARCHITECTURE guarding OF d_flipflop IS
BEGIN
   ff: BLOCK ( c = '1' AND NOT c'STABLE )
   BEGIN
      q <= GUARDED d AFTER delay1;
      qb <= GUARDED NOT d AFTER delay2;
   END BLOCK ff;
END guarding;
```

FIGURE 7.10
The *guarding* architecture for the *d_flipflop* entity.

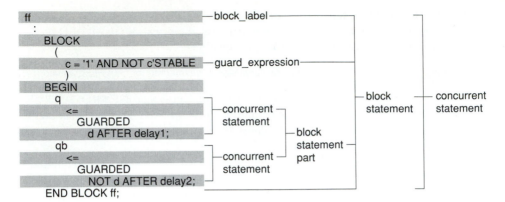

FIGURE 7.11
Syntax details of a guarded block statement with guarded signal assignments.

```
ENTITY flipflop_test IS END flipflop_test;
--
ARCHITECTURE input_output OF flipflop_test IS
    COMPONENT
        flop PORT (d, c : IN BIT; q, qb : OUT BIT);
    END COMPONENT;
    FOR c1 : flop USE ENTITY WORK.d_flipflop (assigning);
    FOR c2 : flop USE ENTITY WORK.d_flipflop (guarding);
    SIGNAL dd, cc, q1, q2, qb1, qb2 : BIT;
BEGIN
    cc <= NOT cc AFTER 400 NS WHEN NOW < 2 US ELSE cc;
    dd <= NOT dd AFTER 1000 NS WHEN NOW < 2 US ELSE dd;
    c1: flop PORT MAP (dd, cc, q1, qb1);
    c2: flop PORT MAP (dd, cc, q2, qb2);
END input_output;
```

FIGURE 7.12
A test bench for testing *assigning* and *guarding* architectures of *d_flipflop*.

In this description, the *c1* instance of the declared *flop* component is associated with the *assigning* architecture of the *d_flipflop* entity, and the *c2* instance of *flop* is associated with the *guarding* architecture of this circuit. Periodic waveforms with different periods are generated for the clock (*cc*) and data (*dd*) inputs of both architectures. The outputs of the *assigning* architecture are *q1* and *qb1* and those of the *guarding* architecture are *q2* and *qb2*.

A conditional signal assignment generates a periodic waveform on *cc*. Every time *cc* changes, this assignment is executed, causing the complement of the new value of *cc* to be scheduled for *cc* after 400 ns. When the simulation time exceeds 2 us, the value of *cc* is assigned to itself, causing all future events to diminish on this signal. The predefined function, NOW, returns the simulation time and can be used like any other function. This method of generating a periodic signal is compact, and we will continue to use it in our sequential circuit examples.

Figure 7.13 shows simulation results in the test bench in Figure 7.12. In addition to the inputs and outputs of the *assigning* and *guarding* architectures of *d_flipflop* (*q1*, *qb1* for *assigning* in Figure 7.9, and *q2*, *qb2* for *guarding* in Figure 7.10), this report shows the *internal_state* signal of the *assigning* architecture (shown as *c1:state*) and the implied GUARD signal of the *ff* block of the *guarding* architecture (shown as *c2.ff:GUARD*). The report shows all transactions that occur on the displayed signals. Dots (.) indicate no transaction. In the time column, *delta* symbols (δ) following time values indicate simulation cycles at which events or transactions occur on any of the observed signals.

TIME (ns)				SIGNALS				
	cc	dd	q1	q2	qb1	qb2	c1: state	c2.ff: GUARD
0000	'0'	'0'	'0'	'0'	'0'	'0'	'0'	FALSE
$+\delta$	...	...	...	...	...	...	'0'	......
004	...	...	'0'	...	...	...	...	......
0005	...	...	...	...	'1'	...	...	......
0400	'1'	...	...	...	...	...	...	TRUE
$+\delta$	...	...	...	...	...	...	'0'	FALSE
$+\delta$	...	...	...	...	...	...	'0'	......
0404	...	...	...	'0'	...	...	...	......
0405	...	...	...	...	...	'1'	...	......
0800	'0'	...	...	...	...	...	...	FALSE
$+\delta$	...	...	...	...	...	...	'0'	FALSE
$+\delta$	...	...	...	...	...	...	'0'	......
1000	...	'1'	...	...	...	...	...	......
$+\delta$	...	...	...	...	...	...	'0'	......
1200	'1'	...	...	...	...	...	...	TRUE
$+\delta$	...	...	...	...	...	...	'1'	FALSE
$+\delta$	...	...	...	...	...	...	'1'	FALSE
1204	...	...	'1'	'1'	...	...	...	......
1205	...	...	...	...	'0'	'0'	...	......
1600	'0'	...	...	...	...	...	...	FALSE
$+\delta$	...	...	...	...	...	...	'1'	FALSE
$+\delta$	...	...	...	...	...	...	'1'	......
2000	'1'	'0'	...	...	...	...	...	TRUE
$+\delta$	'1'	'0'	...	...	...	...	'0'	FALSE
$+\delta$	...	...	...	...	...	...	'0'	......
2004	...	...	'0'	'0'	...	...	...	......
2005	...	...	...	...	'1'	'1'	...	......

FIGURE 7.13
Simulation results of the *input_output* architecture of the *flipflop_test* entity in Figure 7.12. All transactions are observed.

As expected, the *cc* and *dd* inputs toggle between '0'and '1' every 400 and 1000 ns, respectively. These inputs cause the same *events* on the outputs of the two architectures of the *d_flipflop* entity. There are, however, differences in the *transactions* that occur on the outputs, and in what occurs internally to these circuits. We discuss these differences and the justification for the events and transactions on various signals of architectures in Figure 7.9 and 7.10 in the following paragraphs.

The '0' transaction at 4 ns on the *q1* output of the *c1* instance of *flop* (associated with the *assigning* architecture of *d_flipflop*) is due to the initial execution of the statement that assigns *internal_state* of this circuit to its *q* output; this assignment is delayed and appears 4 ns later as a transaction on *q1*. Since the *guarding* architecture of *d_flipflop* does not use an intermediate signal, initializations occur directly on its outputs (*q2* and *qb2*) at time zero.

The transaction at 404 ns on *q2* is due to the fact that the guard expression of the *guarding* architecture is TRUE at 400 ns. This causes the value of input *d* to be assigned to *q2*, even if it does not cause a change in the value of this output. In the *assigning* architecture, the *internal_state* signal isolates such transactions from the outputs.

Internal to the *assigning* architecture of *d_flipflop*, every change in the clock results in two transactions on the *internal_state* signal. For the rising edge of the clock (at 400, 1200 and 2000 ns), one transaction occurs when condition *c='1' AND NOT c'STABLE* of the conditional signal assignment of Figure 7.9 becomes TRUE; at this time the value of *d* is assigned to the *internal_state* signal. The other transaction occurs when this condition becomes FALSE; at this time the value of *internal_state* is assigned to itself. On the falling edge of the clock (at 800 and 1600 ns), the change in *c* causes two events on *c'STABLE* which in turn cause the conditional signal assignment to be executed in two consecutive simulation cycles. In both these cycles, however, the *internal_signal* receives its own value.

The simulation report in Figure 7.13 indicates that the implied GUARD signal that is internal to the *guarding* architecture of *d_flipflop* (associated with the *c2* instance of *flop*) receives transactions on each edge of the clock. On the rising edge, this signal becomes TRUE for exactly one *delta* time. The guarded assignments of the *guarding* architecture execute only during this time; this causes *q* and *qb* to receive *d* and *NOT d*, respectively.

7.1.3 Nesting Guarded Blocks

The block statement in Figure 7.11 is a concurrent statement, as indicated in the syntax details. The statement part of the block statement can contain other concurrent statements. When nesting these statements, the implied GUARD signal within an inner block statement is defined by the guard expression of this statement only, and guard expressions do not automatically accumulate. For a GUARD signal to contain conditions of all its enclosing block statements, explicit ANDing of these expressions must be done.

For an example of nesting block statements, consider the *d_flipflop* in Figure 7.14. As indicated by the circuit notation, the *d* input will be clocked into the

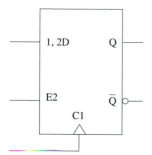

FIGURE 7.14
A positive edge trigger flip-flop with enable input.

flip-flop if the rising edge of the clock occurs while the enabling input is active. If either of these two conditions is not satisfied, the q and qb outputs remain unchanged. The VHDL description for this flip-flop is shown in Figure 7.15.

The entity declaration of *de_flipflop* uses the BIT type d, e, and c input ports for the data, enable, and clock inputs, respectively. The statement part of the *guarding* architecture of *de_flipflop* uses a block statement, labeled *edge*, for which the rising edge of the clock forms its guard expression. The *gate* block statement forms the statement part of the outer *edge* block statement. The *(e = '1' AND GUARD)* expression is the guard expression of the *gate* block. In this expression, GUARD refers to the implied GUARD signal outside the *gate* block and inside the *edge* block. Within the *gate* block, the GUARD signal is equivalent to:

   (e = '1') AND (c = '1' AND NOT c'STABLE).

The guarded assignments to q and qb signals occur only when this signal is TRUE.

```
_ENTITY de_flipflop IS
    GENERIC (delay1 : TIME := 4 NS; delay2 : TIME := 5 NS);
    PORT (d, e, c : IN BIT; q, qb : OUT BIT);
└END de_flipflop;
  --
┌ARCHITECTURE guarding OF de_flipflop IS
├BEGIN
    ┌edge: BLOCK ( c = '1' AND NOT c'STABLE )
    ├BEGIN
        ┌gate: BLOCK ( e = '1' AND GUARD )
        ├BEGIN
                q <= GUARDED d AFTER delay1;
                qb <= GUARDED NOT d AFTER delay2;
        └END BLOCK gate;
    └END BLOCK edge;
└END guarding;
```

FIGURE 7.15
VHDL description for the positive edge trigger flip-flop with enable input in Figure 7.14.

A study of the simulation of the *guarding* architecture of *de_flipflop* illustrates important timing issues. The test bench in Figure 7.16 is used for this purpose. The *c1* label in the statement part of the *input_output* architecture of the *flipflop_test* entity is bound to the *guarding* architecture of *de_flipflop*. The *q1* and *qb1* signals are the outputs of this flip-flop.

Figure 7.17 shows all the transactions that occur on the inputs and outputs of this flip-flop between 0 and 3.2 microseconds. While *ee* is active, *dd* and its complement are assigned to the outputs of the *de_flipflop* on the rising edge of the clock. When *ee* becomes '0' at 2200 ns, the guard expression for the inner block of the *de_flipflop* becomes FALSE, and subsequent rising edges of *cc* do not effect its outputs. The drivers of the outputs are disconnected from them when the *ee* signal is zero.

Another event that deserves attention is the changing of clock at 2000 ns. This event occurs exactly at the same time that *dd* changes from '1' to '0'. At time 2000 ns, for a *delta* duration; the expression *c = '1' AND NOT c'STABLE* is TRUE. In this δ time duration, the data input of the flip-flop has a new value, '0'. Since at this time the implied GUARD signal that controls assignments into *q* and *qb* is TRUE, the values that are scheduled for these targets are based on this new value of the *dd* input. Therefore, the *q1* and *qb1* outputs will change to '0' and '1' at 2004 ns and 2005 ns, respectively.

7.1.4 Resolving Between Several Driving Values

Up to this point in the book, we have only discussed signals that correspond to simple circuit nodes. Multiple concurrent assignments cannot be made on such signals. This is analogous to driving a circuit node with more than one gate output. In hardware, this usually results in smoke or an unknown value; correspondingly, in VHDL it results in an error message. Figure 7.18 shows the *smoke_generator* architecture for an example entity.

```
ENTITY flipflop_test IS END flipflop_test;
--
ARCHITECTURE input_output OF flipflop_test IS
    COMPONENT
        ff1 PORT (d, e, c : IN BIT; q, qb : OUT BIT);
    END COMPONENT;
    FOR c1 : ff1 USE ENTITY WORK.de_flipflop (guarding);
    SIGNAL dd, ee, cc, q1, qb1 : BIT;
BEGIN
    cc <= NOT cc AFTER 400 NS WHEN NOW < 3 US ELSE cc;
    dd <= NOT dd AFTER 1000 NS WHEN NOW < 3 US ELSE dd;
    ee <= '1', '0' AFTER 2200 NS;
    c1: ff1 PORT MAP (dd, ee, cc, q1, qb1);
END input_output;
```

FIGURE 7.16
A test bench for testing the *guarding* architectures of *de_flipflop*.

TIME	SIGNALS				
(ns)	cc	ee	dd	q1	qb1
0000	'0'	'0'	'0'	'0'	'0'
δ	...	'1'	...	...	...
0400	'1'	...	...	...	...
0404	...	...	...	'0'	...
0405	...	...	...	...	'1'
0800	'0'	...	...	...	...
1000	...	...	'1'	...	...
1200	'1'	...	...	...	...
1204	...	...	...	'1'	...
1205	...	...	...	...	'0'
1600	'0'	...	...	...	...
2000	'1'	...	'0'	...	...
2004	...	...	...	'0'	...
2005	...	...	...	...	'1'
2200	...	'0'	...	...	...
2400	'0'	...	...	...	...
2800	'1'	...	...	...	...
3000	...	...	'1'	...	...
δ	...	...	'1'	...	...
3200	'0'	...	...	...	...
δ	'0'	...	...	...	...

FIGURE 7.17
Simulation results of the *input_output* architecture of the *flipflop_test* entity of Figure 7.16. All transactions are observed.

```
USE  WORK.basic_utilities.ALL;
-- FROM PACKAGE USE: qit
ENTITY y_circuit IS
     PORT (a, b, c, d : IN qit; z : OUT qit);
END y_circuit;
--
ARCHITECTURE smoke_generator OF y_circuit IS
     SIGNAL circuit_node : qit;
BEGIN
     circuit_node <= a;
     circuit_node <= b;
     circuit_node <= c;
     circuit_node <= d;
     z <= circuit_node;
END smoke_generator;
```

FIGURE 7.18
Multiple sources for a simple signal. This results in an error message.

This description has an internal node to which the four inputs, a, b, c, and d are assigned. These assignments are concurrent, which causes four simultaneous driving values for the *circuit_node*; the description makes no provision for a resolution between these multiple values. For example, the *smoke_generator* architecture of *y_circuit* does not specify what the *circuit_node* value becomes if the value on the a input is '1' and the values of all other inputs are '0'.

This problem can be remedied by including a function name in the declaration of the *circuit_node* signal. This function gets called for the resolution of the multiple sources of this signal. An example for such a declaration is shown here:

    SIGNAL circuit_node : anding qit;

This declaration makes *circuit_node* a resolved signal, for which the name *anding* specifies a resolution function. The *anding* function is called each time an event occurs on any of the sources of the *circuit_node* signal. When called, this function returns a *qit* value that becomes the value for the *circuit_node*. As the name implies, the *anding* resolution function is expected to return the ANDing of all its sources. Figure 7.19 shows the *anding* resolution function.

This function uses *qit*, *qit_vector*, and the overloaded "AND" from the *basic_utilities* package. The parameter of a resolution function must be an array whose elements have the same type as the value that the function returns. The concatenation of all sources of a resolved signal are associated with the parameter of the resolution function of this signal. For the *anding* function, *qit* is the type of the value that it returns and *qit-vector* is the type of its parameter. This function can be used for resolving a *qit* type value for a *qit* type target signal from any number of *qit* type driving values.

In the declaration part of the *anding* function in Figure 7.19, the *accumulate* variable is declared and initialized to '1'. In the statement part of this function, a loop statement ANDs together all elements of the *drivers* parameter. The overloaded "AND" ANDs *accumulate* with each element of *drivers* according to the four value AND table in Chapter 6 (see Figure 6.23).

Figure 7.20 shows the *wired_and* architecture of the *y_circuit* entity. In its declaration part, this architecture defines the *anding* function and uses it for declaring

```
-- USE qit, qit_vector, "AND" from basic_utilities
FUNCTION anding (drivers : qit_vector) RETURN qit IS
    VARIABLE accumulate : qit := '1';
BEGIN
    FOR i IN drivers'RANGE LOOP
        accumulate := accumulate AND drivers(i);
    END LOOP;
    RETURN accumulate;
END anding;
```

FIGURE 7.19
The *anding* resolution function ANDs all its drivers.

```
USE  WORK.basic_utilities.ALL;
-- FROM  PACKAGE  USE:  qit
ARCHITECTURE  wired_and  OF  y_circuit  IS
    FUNCTION  anding  (drivers  :  qit_vector)  RETURN  qit  IS
        VARIABLE  accumulate  :  qit  :=  '1';
    BEGIN
        FOR  i  IN  drivers'RANGE  LOOP
            accumulate  :=  accumulate  AND  drivers(i);
        END  LOOP;
        RETURN  accumulate;
    END  anding;
    SIGNAL  circuit_node  :  anding  qit;
BEGIN
    circuit_node  <=  a;
    circuit_node  <=  b;
    circuit_node  <=  c;
    circuit_node  <=  d;
    z  <=  circuit_node;
END  wired_and;
```

FIGURE 7.20
Multiple sources for a simple signal. This results in ANDing all sources.

the *circuit_node* signal. Four assignments in the statement part of this architecture cause the concatenation of the values of *a*, *b*, *c*, and *d* signals to be associated with the *drivers* formal parameter of the *anding* function. An event on any of these inputs causes the *anding* function to be called for a new resolved value. The VHDL language does not specify the order in which multiple sources of a resolved signal are concatenated.

7.1.4.1 REVISITING MULTIPLEXER. Figure 7.21 shows an alternative description for the 8-to-1 multiplexer of Section 7.1.1. In the *multiple_assignments* architecture of *mux_8_to_1* in Figure 7.21, each data input is ANDed with its corresponding select line, and the result of this operation is assigned to the temporary signal *t*. Eight assignments to this signal generate eight concurrent drivers for it. Signal *t* is a resolved signal and it uses the *oring* subprogram for its resolution function. As indicated in the declaration part of the *multiple_assignments* architecture, the *oring* function ORs together the elements of its array input and returns the result. Since the concatenation of the drivers of signal *t* is associated with the array parameter of the *oring* function, the value this function returns is the OR result of these eight drivers. This value is assigned to the *t* signal which is then assigned to the *z* output of the multiplexer. The final result is that the *z* output is assigned to the OR combination of the data inputs ANDed with their respective select inputs. The OR operator of the resolution function and the AND operators in the statement part of the *multiple_assignments* architecture of the *mux_8_to_1* entity use OR and AND functions that are overloaded for *qit* operands.

```
USE  WORK.basic_utilities.ALL;
-- FROM PACKAGE USE: qit
ARCHITECTURE  multiple_assignments  OF  mux_8_to_1  IS
    FUNCTION  oring ( drivers : qit_vector) RETURN  qit  IS
        VARIABLE  accumulate : qit := '0';
    BEGIN
        FOR  i  IN  drivers'RANGE  LOOP
            accumulate := accumulate  OR  drivers(i);
        END  LOOP;
        RETURN  accumulate;
    END  oring;
    SIGNAL  t : oring  qit;
BEGIN
    t <= i7  AND  s7;
    t <= i6  AND  s6;
    t <= i5  AND  s5;
    t <= i4  AND  s4;
    t <= i3  AND  s3;
    t <= i2  AND  s2;
    t <= i1  AND  s1;
    t <= i0  AND  s0;
    z <= t;
END  multiple_assignments;
```

FIGURE 7.21
Implementing the eight-to-one multiplexer using eight concurrent assignments.

The declaration of signal t specifies that the type of this signal is a subtype of *qit*, for which *oring* is the subtype indication. Instead of the syntax used in Figure 7.21, this *qit* subtype can be declared as a new subtype and used to declare resolved signals. The following statement shows how to define *ored_qit* as an *oring* subtype of *qit*:

```
SUBTYPE  ored_qit  IS  oring  qit;
```

Using *ored_qit*, any number of resolved signals that use *oring* for their resolution function may be declared. Declaring t is shown here as an example:

```
SIGNAL  t : ored_qit;
```

For declaring a vector of *oring* resolved signals, the *ored_qit_vector* type definition shown here is needed:

```
TYPE  ored_qit_vector  IS  ARRAY ( NATURAL  RANGE  <> ) OF  ored_qit;
```

The following statement defines *t_byte* as an 8-bit signal; each element of this signal uses *oring* for resolving between the multiple values assigned to it.

```
SIGNAL  t_byte : ored_qit_vector ( 7  DOWNTO  0 );
```

7.1.4.2 PACKAGING RESOLUTION FUNCTIONS. The *anding* and *oring* resolution functions are useful when an implicit or explicit AND or OR gate exists at a node where several drivers meet. Often, however, wiring several nodes of BIT or *qit* type does not result in either of these two functions. A third function, *wiring*, is useful for the representation of wiring several signals into a common node. For this purpose, we will use the two operand *wire* function shown in Figure 7.22.

This function describes the behavior of a node that has two *qit* type signals connected to it. Figure 7.23 shows the *wire* function table for *qit* type inputs. As shown in this table, if the two inputs are equal, the *wire* value will be the same as the inputs. Value 'Z' on either of the inputs is absorbed by a stronger value ('0', '1', or 'X'), and conflicting non 'Z' values on the inputs result in 'X' value for the *wire* value.

A resolution function that resolves a single value from multiple *qit* type values that drive a node is called *wiring*, and it is shown in Figure 7.24.

An architecture that uses this function must define it in its declarative part or else use a library that contains it. We can now add this and the other two functions described in this chapter to the body of the *basic_utilities* package. For the *wiring* function and its related types to be visible when the *basic_utilities* package is used, the declaration of this package must include the declarations shown in Figure 7.25. Similar declarations for the *anding* and *oring* functions are needed for the visibility of the functions and their related types.

Other useful resolution functions for our *basic_utilities* package are *anding* and *oring* for the BIT type. Such functions overload their similarly named functions of

```
FUNCTION wire (a, b : qit) RETURN qit IS
    CONSTANT qit_wire_table : qit_2d := (
                              ('0','X','0','X'),
                              ('X','1','1','X'),
                              ('0','1','Z','X'),
                              ('X','X','X','X'));
BEGIN
    RETURN qit_wire_table (a, b);
END wire;
```

FIGURE 7.22
The *wire* function for modeling wiring two *qit* type nodes.

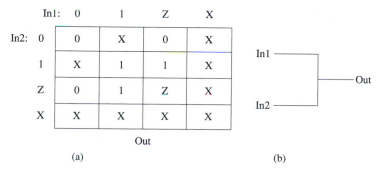

In1:	0	1	Z	X
In2: 0	0	X	0	X
1	X	1	1	X
Z	0	1	Z	X
X	X	X	X	X

Out

(a)   (b)

FIGURE 7.23
The *wire* function for *qit* type operands, (a) input-output mapping, (b) circuit notation.

```
FUNCTION wiring ( drivers : qit_vector) RETURN qit IS
    VARIABLE accumulate : qit := 'Z';
BEGIN
    FOR i IN drivers'RANGE LOOP
        accumulate := wire (accumulate, drivers(i));
    END LOOP;
    RETURN accumulate;
END wiring;
```

FIGURE 7.24
The *wiring* resolution function for *qit* type operands.

```
FUNCTION wiring ( drivers : qit_vector) RETURN qit;
SUBTYPE wired_qit IS wiring qit;
TYPE wired_qit_vector IS ARRAY (NATURAL RANGE <>) OF wired_qit;
```

FIGURE 7.25
Necessary declarations for visibility of the *wiring* resolution function and its related types and subtypes.

the *qit* type. Figure 7.26 shows an *oring* function with a BIT_VECTOR operand and a BIT type return value. Figure 7.26a presents the declarations for visibility of the *oring* function and its related types.

7.1.5   MOS Implementation of Multiplexer

Assigning multiple values to a resolved signal generates multiple drivers for such signals; these drivers then participate in the determination of a final value for the resolved signal. Guarded assignments can also be used for assigning values to a resolved signal. In this case, only those values that are on the right hand side of signal

```
FUNCTION oring ( drivers : BIT_VECTOR) RETURN BIT;
SUBTYPE ored_bit IS oring BIT;
TYPE ored_bit_vector IS ARRAY (NATURAL RANGE <>) OF ored_bit;
```
                            (a)

```
FUNCTION oring ( drivers : BIT_VECTOR) RETURN BIT IS
    VARIABLE accumulate : BIT := '0';
BEGIN
    FOR i IN drivers'RANGE LOOP
        accumulate := accumulate OR drivers(i);
    END LOOP;
    RETURN accumulate;
END oring;
```
                            (b)

FIGURE 7.26
The *oring* resolution function for the BIT type operands, (a) necessary type and subtype definitions for the *basic_utilities* package, (b) definition of function.

assignments with TRUE GUARD signal values participate in the determination of the final value of the target signal. A driver of a guarded signal assignment whose GUARD signal is FALSE is said to be "turned off." Description of an MOS multiplexer illustrates these issues.

A multiplexer can be efficiently implemented through the use of a MOS switch element. The behavior of a multiplexer implemented this way, however, is different from that of the AND-OR logic discussed in the previous section. Figure 7.27 shows an 8-bit NMOS multiplexer. A CMOS multiplexer uses transmission gates instead of the pass transistors shown in this figure, and it behaves in a similar fashion.

The multiplexer consists of eight pass transistors connected in parallel. The gates of the transistors constitute the eight multiplexer select lines ($s0$ through $s7$) and their sources are the data inputs ($i0$ through $i7$). The output of the multiplexer is taken from the common drain of the transistors. A '1' on the gate of a transistor turns the transistor on and causes the common drain to be driven by the value at the source of the transistor. If an si value is '1' and it becomes 'Z', the charge at the gate of the transistor keeps the transistor conducting (ON) for a few milliseconds. We therefore treat 'Z' at this input as '1'. When several transistors are conducting simultaneously, the common drain is driven by more than one source.

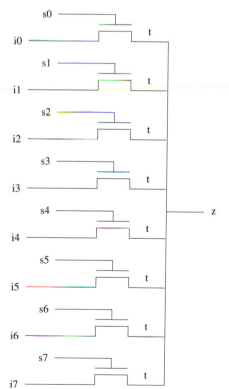

FIGURE 7.27
An NMOS eight-to-one multiplexer. The CMOS version uses transmission gates instead of pass transistors.

A block statement, like the one shown in Figure 7.28 properly describes the behavior of a transistor in the structure shown in Figure 7.27. An i_i input drives t only when s_i is '1'or 'Z'.

An NMOS version of the *mux_8_to_1* eight bit multiplexer uses eight block statements similar to those in Figure 7.28. The description of this multiplexer, shown in Figure 7.29, conditionally connects the i_i inputs to the internal t node. The inputs that are connected to node t are wired together at this node according to the *wire* logic detailed in Figure 7.23.

The *wired_qit* subtype of the *basic_utilities* package is used to declare the t signal. This declaration causes the multiple values assigned to this signal to be resolved according to the *wiring* function in Figure 7.24. The keyword BUS in the declaration of t specifies the kind of this signal—this will become clearer in the discussion that follows.

When an event occurs on any of the inputs in the description presented in Figure 7.29, or on any of the eight implied GUARD signals of the guarded block

```
         .
         .
         .
 ⎡b_i  : BLOCK ( s_i  =  '1'  OR  s_i  =  'Z')
 │ BEGIN
 │      t  <=  GUARDED  i_i;
 ⎣END  BLOCK;
         .
         .
         .
```

FIGURE 7.28
A block statement modeling a transmission gate.

```
 │ USE  WORK.basic_utilities.ALL;
 │ --  FROM  PACKAGE  USE:  wired_qit
 ⎡ARCHITECTURE  multiple_guarded_assignments  OF  mux_8_to_1  IS
 │      SIGNAL  t  :  wired_qit  BUS;
 ⎢BEGIN
 │      b7: BLOCK (s7  =  '1'  OR  s7  =  'Z')  BEGIN   t  <=  GUARDED  i7;  END  BLOCK;
 │      b6: BLOCK (s6  =  '1'  OR  s6  =  'Z')  BEGIN   t  <=  GUARDED  i6;  END  BLOCK;
 │      b5: BLOCK (s5  =  '1'  OR  s5  =  'Z')  BEGIN   t  <=  GUARDED  i5;  END  BLOCK;
 │      b4: BLOCK (s4  =  '1'  OR  s4  =  'Z')  BEGIN   t  <=  GUARDED  i4;  END  BLOCK;
 │      b3: BLOCK (s3  =  '1'  OR  s3  =  'Z')  BEGIN   t  <=  GUARDED  i3;  END  BLOCK;
 │      b2: BLOCK (s2  =  '1'  OR  s2  =  'Z')  BEGIN   t  <=  GUARDED  i2;  END  BLOCK;
 │      b1: BLOCK (s1  =  '1'  OR  s1  =  'Z')  BEGIN   t  <=  GUARDED  i1;  END  BLOCK;
 │      b0: BLOCK (s0  =  '1'  OR  s0  =  'Z')  BEGIN   t  <=  GUARDED  i0;  END  BLOCK;
 │      z  <=  t;
 ⎣END  multiple_guarded_assignments;
```

FIGURE 7.29
The *mutliple_guarded_assignments* architecture of the *mux_8_to_1* entity. The entity declaration is shown in Figure 7.5.

statements, the *wiring* resolution function is called. Concatenation of the i_i values whose corresponding GUARD signal is TRUE, i.e., the corresponding s_i's are either '1' or 'Z', is associated with the formal parameter in this function. The *wiring* function resolves a value based on these active i_i inputs. This value becomes the value of the output of the multiplexer.

An interesting situation arises when all the drivers of t are disconnected from it, and that is that all eight implied GUARD signals are FALSE. In this case, because of the BUS keyword is used in the declaration of t, the wiring resolution function is called with a NULL input parameter. The definition of the *wiring* function (see Figure 7.24) specifies that the initial value of the *accumulate* variable ('Z') is returned as the function value if the entire loop statement in the statement part of this function is skipped due to a NULL range. The end result is that the t signal receives a 'Z' value if all the s_i inputs of the multiplexer are '0'. Note that the pass transistor hardware we are modeling behaves in exactly the same way. If all the gate inputs in Figure 7.27 are '0', the common node, z, will be floating (i.e., high impedance).

The use of BUS in the declaration of t makes it a guarded signal. A resolved signal is guarded if its kind, i.e., BUS or REGISTER, is specified in its declaration. Events and transactions on the BUS and REGISTER kind of signals are exactly the same as long as at least one driver is turned on. If an event turns off the last active driver of a guarded signal, the resolution function is called for BUS signals with a NULL parameter; however, it will not be called if the kind of signal is REGISTER. After all the drivers are turned off, the latter kind of signals retain their last driven value.

As the name implies, the REGISTER signal kinds are useful for modeling register structures. Due to the charge at the gate input of MOS logic gates, connecting an inverter to the output of a transistor structure, such as the multiplexer, causes the data at this output to retain its value after all the transistors driving the node are turned off. This structure, shown in Figure 7.30, is a MOS half-register with multiplexed input.

Node t in Figure 7.30 can hold an undriven value for several milliseconds. Since the clock frequency and the rate of updating data is much higher than milliseconds, half-registers can be used for data storage in many applications.

Figure 7.31 shows a VHDL description for the *multiplexed_half_register* circuit. In the *guarded_assignments* architecture of this figure, the guarded signal t is declared with a *wired_qit* subtype and REGISTER kind. Since the *wired_qit* subtype is defined as a *wiring* subtype of *qit*, multiple *qit* type values driving node t are resolved by the *wiring* function. If all drivers are turned off, node t and node z retain their values indefinitely.

7.1.5.1 DELAYING DISCONNECTIONS. VHDL allows the time delay specification to be used in the disconnection of drivers of a guarded signal. As with other signals, the placement of values on guarded signals can be done by using an AFTER clause in the signal assignment statement. For example, in order to delay the assignment of the $i5$ input of the multiplexer in Figure 7.29 to signal t, the following statement should replace the block statement labeled $b5$:

```
b5: BLOCK (s5 = '1' OR s5 = 'Z')
        BEGIN   t <= GUARDED i5 AFTER 4 NS; END BLOCK;
```

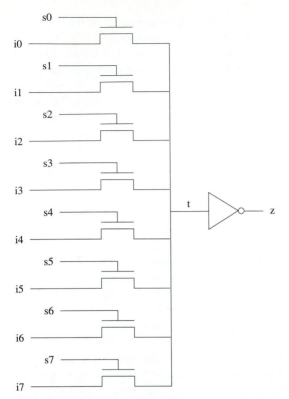

FIGURE 7.30
An NMOS half-register with multiplexed input.

With this replacement, if *i5* changes value while the guard expression of the *b5* block is TRUE, the new value of *i5* will be assigned to *t* after 4 ns. Similarly, if the guard expression changes from FALSE to TRUE, after a 4 ns delay, the value of *i5* will be assigned to *t* at the time of guard expression turning to TRUE. It should be evident from this discussion that the 4 nanosecond delay only applies when a driver is connected, or is being connected, and does not apply when a driver is disconnected from a guarded signal.

A disconnection specification statement can be used to specify the disconnection delay for a guarded signal within a guarded signal assignment. Such a statement contains the name of the signal, its type, and a time expression that specifies the disconnection delay value. To demonstrate the application of this statement, consider the *multiple_guarded_assignments* architecture of *mux_8_to_1* in Figure 7.29. To delay disconnection of the *t* drivers, the following statement should be added to the declarative part of this architecture:

    DISCONNECT t : wired_qit AFTER 6 NS;

With the inclusion of this statement, if a *t* driver, e.g., *i6*, *i5* or *i4*, is turned off because its guard expression becomes FALSE, the effect of this driver remains on *t* for 6 nanoseconds after it has been turned off. The overall effect of this is that the

```
USE  WORK.basic_utilities.ALL;
-- FROM  PACKAGE  USE:  qit,  wired_qit
ENTITY  multiplexed_half_register  IS
    PORT (i7,  i6,  i5,  i4,  i3,  i2,  i1,  i0  :  IN  qit;
          s7,  s6,  s5,  s4,  s3,  s2,  s1,  s0  :  IN  qit;  z  :  OUT  qit );
END  multiplexed_half_register;
--
ARCHITECTURE  guarded_assignments  OF  multiplexed_half_register  IS
    SIGNAL  t  :  wired_qit  REGISTER;
BEGIN
    b7:  BLOCK  (s7 = '1'  OR  s7 = 'Z')  BEGIN    t <=  GUARDED  i7;  END  BLOCK;
    b6:  BLOCK  (s6 = '1'  OR  s6 = 'Z')  BEGIN    t <=  GUARDED  i6;  END  BLOCK;
    b5:  BLOCK  (s5 = '1'  OR  s5 = 'Z')  BEGIN    t <=  GUARDED  i5;  END  BLOCK;
    b4:  BLOCK  (s4 = '1'  OR  s4 = 'Z')  BEGIN    t <=  GUARDED  i4;  END  BLOCK;
    b3:  BLOCK  (s3 = '1'  OR  s3 = 'Z')  BEGIN    t <=  GUARDED  i3;  END  BLOCK;
    b2:  BLOCK  (s2 = '1'  OR  s2 = 'Z')  BEGIN    t <=  GUARDED  i2;  END  BLOCK;
    b1:  BLOCK  (s1 = '1'  OR  s1 = 'Z')  BEGIN    t <=  GUARDED  i1;  END  BLOCK;
    b0:  BLOCK  (s0 = '1'  OR  s0 = 'Z')  BEGIN    t <=  GUARDED  i0;  END  BLOCK;
    z <=  NOT  t  AFTER  8  NS;
END  guarded_assignments;
```

FIGURE 7.31

The *multiple_guarded_assignments* architecture of the *multiplexed_half_register* entity. The entity declaration is shown in Figure 7.5.

output of the multiplexer changes to 'Z' 6 nanoseconds after the last source has been turned off.

The declarative part of an architecture can contain disconnection statements for any number of guarded signals that the designer declares within that architecture. If a disconnection is specified for several signals of the same type, the signal names should appear in a list separated by commas (this is referred to as a guarded signal list) following the DISCONNECT keyword. The ALL keyword used for the signal list implies that the disconnection specification applies to all signals of the type specified. If OTHERS is used in place of the signal list, the disconnection specification applies to signals of the specified type for which disconnection has not been specified in the statements above this statement.

7.1.5.2 A RECOMMENDATION. If resolved nonguarded signals (with no kind specified) are used on the left hand side of guarded assignments, the implied GUARD signals controlling these assignments that become FALSE do not turn off the corresponding drivers. Instead, the value of the driver when it was active continues to be used as a driving value, even when the driver is turned off. The author recommends the use of a guarded signal on the left hand side of guarded assignments if there are multiple such assignments to the signal. In most cases, the drivers that are left on the output of resolved nonguarded signals at the time that their corresponding guard has become false, complicates the analysis of a circuit.

7.1.6 A General Multiplexer

While the multiplexers developed to this point in the chapter demonstrate many language concepts, they do not necessarily use the most efficient coding techniques offered by VHDL. A code-efficient multi-bit multiplexer that uses guarded blocks is shown in Figure 7.32. The iterative description of the *mux_n_to_1* entity in this figure declares data inputs and select lines as unconstrained arrays of *qit*. The port clause specifies the type and kind of the output *z* as *wired_qit* and BUS, respectively. As before, the *wired_qit* of the *basic_utilities* package, defined as a *wiring* subtype of *qit*, is used to specify the resolution of the multiplexer output node.

The architecture in Figure 7.32 uses a generate statement to generate as many guarded block statements as there are elements in the parameter associated with the *i* input of the *mux_n_to_1* entity. The b_j block encloses a guarded assignment of input i_j to the guarded output, *z*. The description expects the ranges of *i* and *s* inputs to be the same.

A simple test bench is presented in Figure 7.33 for the multi-bit multiplexer to illustrate how a *qit* type can be associated with the *z* formal parameter of the *mux_n_to_1* entity. This is, of course, possible because *wired_qit* is a subtype of *qit*— as stated earlier, types and subtypes are completely compatible. This compatibility, however, does not exist between *qit_vector* and *wired_qit_vector*, since the latter is defined as a new type. These types are closely related and the designer can convert them from one type to the other, using the type conversion methods discussed in Chapter 6 (Section 6.1.2).

The simulation run of the *mux_tester* shown in Figure 7.34 verifies the correctness of the description of *mux_n_to_1*. At time 0, the output is 'Z', since none of the four select lines are active. At 15000 ns, the output becomes 'X' because a

```
USE  WORK.basic_utilities.ALL;
-- FROM PACKAGE USE: qit, qit_vector, wired_qit
ENTITY mux_n_to_1 IS
    PORT (i, s : IN qit_vector; z : OUT wired_qit BUS);
END mux_n_to_1;
--
ARCHITECTURE multiple_guarded_assignments OF mux_n_to_1 IS
BEGIN
    bi: FOR j IN i'RANGE GENERATE
        bj: BLOCK (s(j) = '1' OR s(j) = 'Z')
        BEGIN
            z <= GUARDED i(j);
        END BLOCK;
    END GENERATE;
END multiple_guarded_assignments;
```

FIGURE 7.32

The *mutliple_guarded_assignments* architecture of the *mux_n_to_1* entity. The circuit is a general n-bit multiplexer.

```
USE  WORK.basic_utilities.ALL;
ENTITY  mux_tester  IS
END  mux_tester;
  --
ARCHITECTURE  input_output  OF  mux_tester  IS
    COMPONENT  mux  PORT  (i, s : IN  qit_vector; z : OUT  wired_qit  BUS);
    END  COMPONENT;
    FOR  ALL : mux  USE
        ENTITY  WORK.mux_n_to_1  (multiple_guarded_assignments);
    SIGNAL  ii, ss : qit_vector (3  DOWNTO  0) := "0000";
    SIGNAL  zz : qit;
BEGIN
    ii <= "1010" AFTER 10 US, "Z100" AFTER 20 US, "0011" AFTER 30 US;
    ss <= "0010" AFTER 05 US, "1100" AFTER 15 US, "000Z" AFTER 25 US;
    mm : mux  PORT  MAP  (ii, ss, zz);
END  input_output;
```

FIGURE 7.33

A test bench for the *guarded_assignments* architecture of *mux_n_to_1* entity. This entity is used as a 4-bit multiplexer.

TIME (ns)	SIGNALS ii(3:0)	ss(3:0)	zz
00000	"0000"	"0000"	'0'
δ	......	......	'Z'
05000	......	"0010"	...
δ	......	......	'0'
10000	"1010"	......	...
δ	......	......	'1'
15000	......	"1100"	...
δ	......	......	'X'
20000	"Z100"	......	...
δ	......	......	'1'
25000	......	"000Z"	...
δ	......	......	'0'
30000	"0011"	......	...
δ	......	......	'1'

FIGURE 7.34

Simulation results of the *input_output* architecture of the *mux_tester* entity in Figure 7.33, testing the *mux_n_to_1* circuit. All events are observed.

'1' and a '0' (bits 3 and 2) are simultaneously driving the output node. Events on the *zz* output of the multiplexer occur δ time after events on its inputs. This is due to the signal assignment to the *z* output in the statement part of the *guarded_assignments* architecture of the *mux_n_to_1* entity in Figure 7.32. Had we not declared the *z* port of this entity as a guarded signal, an intermediate guarded signal, such as *t* in the description of *mux_8_to_1* multiplexer, would have been required. This signal would delay assignments to the output by 2δ. An interested reader can verify by simulation that the output of the *mux_8_to_1* circuit in Figure 7.29 is 2δ behind its input.

7.2   STATE MACHINE DESCRIPTION

State diagrams are used to graphically represent state machines. An important part of digital systems, state machines can appear explicitly in a digital system for the control and sequencing of events, or they can be embedded in sequential components, such as counters and shift-registers. At the dataflow level, where we separate control and data of a hardware system, the design and description of state machines for implementing the control unit become important. VHDL provides convenient constructs to describe various forms of state machines at various levels of abstraction. At the dataflow level, description of a state machine has a close correspondence to the state diagram of the machine. We will use block statements, signal assignments, and guarded assignments in this section to accurately describe state machines in VHDL.

7.2.1   A Sequence Detector

A sequence detector is a classical example of an application of state machines in hardware. Figure 7.35 shows the state diagram for a sequence detector that continuously searches for the 1011 sequence on its x input. This diagram is a Mealy machine, which means that the output is a function of the input while the machine is in a stable state.

The states of this machine are labeled according to the significant input sequences they detect. For example, in the reset state, if a '1' followed by a '0' appears on the x input, the machine moves to the *10* state.

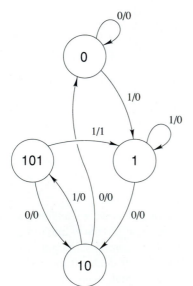

FIGURE 7.35
A 1011 mealy sequence detector. State names indicate detected sequences.

The VHDL description in Figure 7.36 corresponds to the state diagram of the 1011 detector. The entity declaration of this circuit has two BIT type inputs, *x* and *clk*, and an output, *z*. The architectural description of the *detector* is called *singular_state_machine*, indicating that it can only have one active state at any given time.

The declarative part of the *singular_state_machine* architecture of *detector* contains the *state* enumeration type definition, the enumeration elements of which are the state designators of the state machine in Figure 7.35. This is followed by the *state_vector* type definition that defines an unconstrained array of *state*, which is then followed by the *one_of* resolution function. The last declaration in this declarative part indicates that *current* is a guarded resolved signal of type *state*. The kind of this sig-

```
ENTITY detector IS
    PORT (x, clk : IN BIT; z : OUT BIT);
END detector;
ARCHITECTURE singular_state_machine OF detector IS
    TYPE state IS (reset, got1, got10, got101);
    TYPE state_vector IS ARRAY (NATURAL RANGE <>) OF state;
    FUNCTION one_of (sources : state_vector) RETURN state IS
    BEGIN
        RETURN sources(sources'LEFT);
    END one_of;
    SIGNAL current : one_of state REGISTER := reset;
BEGIN
    clocking : BLOCK (clk = '1' AND NOT clk'STABLE)
    BEGIN
        s1: BLOCK ( current = reset AND GUARD )
        BEGIN
            current <= GUARDED got1 WHEN x = '1' ELSE reset;
        END BLOCK s1;
        s2: BLOCK ( current = got1 AND GUARD )
        BEGIN
            current <= GUARDED got10 WHEN x = '0' ELSE got1;
        END BLOCK s2;
        s3: BLOCK ( current = got10 AND GUARD )
        BEGIN
            current <= GUARDED got101 WHEN x = '1' ELSE reset;
        END BLOCK s3;
        s4: BLOCK ( current = got101 AND GUARD)
        BEGIN
            current <= GUARDED got1 WHEN x = '1' ELSE got10;
            z <= '1' WHEN ( current = got101 AND x = '1') ELSE '0';
        END BLOCK s4;
    END BLOCK clocking;
END singular_state_machine;
```

FIGURE 7.36
VHDL description of 1011 detector. Only one simultaneous active state.

nal is REGISTER and it uses the *one_of* resolution function. This resolution function chooses one of the driving values of *current* for assignment to this signal. Shortly it becomes clear that *current* has only one driving value at any one time; the use of 'LEFT in the statement part of the *one_of* function, therefore, returns just that one value.

The statement part of the architecture in Figure 7.36 consists of the *clocking* block statement that uses the rising edge of *clk* for its guard expression. Nested in this block statement are four block statements that correspond to the states of the state machine. We refer to these blocks (labeled *s1*, *s2*, *s3* and *s4*) as state blocks. The implied GUARD signal within each of these inner state blocks is TRUE if *current* equals the state designator, i.e., *reset*, *got1*, *got10*, or *got101* of that state; and if the guard expression of the outer *clocking* block statement is also TRUE. The *current* signal represents the current active state of the state machine. Initially, this signal is equal to *reset*. In this initial state on the rising edge of the clock, the implied GUARD signal in the *s1* block becomes TRUE. Depending on the value of *x*, the guarded signal assignment within this block assigns *got1* or *reset* to the *current* signal. If *current* becomes *got1*, the next rising edge of the clock sets *current* to *got10* or *got1* depending on the value of *x*. The edges of the clock cause assignment of values to *current* according to the state diagram in Figure 7.35. When *current* is equal to *got101*, the signal assignment in the *s4* block assigns a '1' to the *z* output if *x* is '1'. This statement does not use the guard expression of the *s4* block; therefore, it can be placed anywhere in the statement part of the *detector* architecture. In our description, the place of this statement corresponds to its activating state.

Since there are four concurrent signal assignments that use *current* for their targets, this signal is declared as a resolved signal. The logic that we used to describe the *singular_state_machine* architecture of the *detector* entity does not allow any more than one driver for this signal at any one time. As soon as a new value is assigned to *current*, the guard expression that allows this assignment to take place becomes FALSE, causing the removal of the previous driving value from it. This leaves the *current* signal with only one active driver at any one time, and the 'LEFT in the *one_of* function returns that one driver.

7.2.2   Allowing Multiple Active States

Although a standard finite state machine is defined for one active state at any given time, the ability to handle multiple active states enables us to describe pipeline and multiple state machines. An alternative description for the state machine in Figure 7.35 is shown in Figure 7.37. The states of the machine are represented by the elements of the declared *s* signal. As shown in Figure 7.26, declaration of *s* as an *ored_bit_vector* makes *s(1)*, *s(2)*, *s(3)*, and *s(4)* resolved signals of type BIT and the *oring* resolution function. This declaration also specifies that *s* is a guarded signal of REGISTER kind, *s(1)* is initialized to '1', and *s(2)* through *s(4)* are initially '0'.

The statement part of the *multiple_state_machine* architecture of *detector* contains the *clocking* block statement for the clock edge detection. Nested in this block statement are four block statements that use the elements of *s* in their guard expressions and they correspond to the states of the state machine in Figure 7.35. In a state

```
USE  WORK.basic_utilities.ALL;
-- FROM  PACKAGE  USE:  ored_bit_vector
ARCHITECTURE  multiple_state_machine  OF  detector  IS
    SIGNAL  s  :  ored_bit_vector  (1  TO  4)  REGISTER  :=  "1000";
BEGIN
    clocking : BLOCK (clk = '1' AND NOT clk'STABLE)
    BEGIN
        s1: BLOCK (s(1) = '1'  AND  GUARD)
        BEGIN
            s(1) <= GUARDED '1' WHEN  x = '0' ELSE '0';
            s(2) <= GUARDED '1' WHEN  x = '1' ELSE '0';
        END BLOCK s1;
        s2: BLOCK (s(2) = '1'  AND  GUARD)
        BEGIN
            s(3) <= GUARDED '1' WHEN  x = '0' ELSE '0';
            s(2) <= GUARDED '1' WHEN  x = '1' ELSE '0';
        END BLOCK s2;
        s3: BLOCK (s(3) = '1'  AND  GUARD)
        BEGIN
            s(1) <= GUARDED '1' WHEN  x = '0' ELSE '0';
            s(4) <= GUARDED '1' WHEN  x = '1' ELSE '0';
        END BLOCK s3;
        s4: BLOCK (s(4) = '1'  AND  GUARD)
        BEGIN
            s(3) <= GUARDED '1' WHEN  x = '0' ELSE '0';
            s(2) <= GUARDED '1' WHEN  x = '1' ELSE '0';
            z <= '1' WHEN (s(4) = '1' AND x = '1') ELSE '0';
        END BLOCK s4;
        s <= GUARDED "0000";
    END BLOCK clocking;
END multiple_state_machine;
```

FIGURE 7.37
VHDL description of 1011 detector. More than one state can simultaneously be active.

block, other states become active based on the input conditions. Since four separate signals (elements of *s*) are used to specify current active states, any number of these states can be active simultaneously. Because the *oring* resolution function is associated with the elements of *s*, one or more assignments to an element of *s* are able to activate that state.

The expected behavior of a state machine description is that each state dies out after it conditionally activates its next states(s). Since our state signals are of the REGISTER kind, this does not happen automatically. If all the drivers of an element of *s* are turned off, the *oring* resolution function is not called and the signal retains its previous value. In order to keep at least one driver active and cause all elements of *s* to become '0' after they cause activation of other states, we drive all elements of *s* with '0's on the edge of each clock. This is achieved by the last guarded signal assignment in the statement part of the architecture in Figure 7.37. On the rising edge of each clock, the '0' on an element of s is ORed with all other values that drive this signal. If this '0' is the only driver for that element, it causes the value to become '0'. On the other hand, if this element is activated by other '1's, the '0' will have no effect on the value that is assigned to the s element.

7.2.3   Outputs of Mealy and Moore Machines

Mealy and Moore machines make their state transitions in exactly the same way. The state transitions portion of the description styles presented in Figures 7.36 and 7.37 apply to Moore machines as well as Mealy machines. The main difference between these machines is the way they assign values to the outputs.

In a Mealy machine, inputs and states of the machine participate in the formation of conditions for assigning values to the outputs. In a Moore machine, the states alone are used in conditional signal assignments to the output signals. In either machine, several states can provide values for the output signals. This requires either resolved output signals using a resolution function such as *oring*, or it requires a single conditional or selected signal assignment to assign value to each unresolved output. The advantage of using resolved outputs is that assignments to the outputs can be placed in the description next to the state making the assignment, instead of combining all conditions into a condition for a single signal assignment.

7.3   OPEN COLLECTOR GATES

The concept of resolution functions and resolved signals is very useful for modeling various bus forms. A bussing structure formed by connecting the outputs of open collector gates is very common. Figure 7.38a shows an open collector NAND gate, and Figure 7.38b shows a 74LS03 package that consists of four such gates.

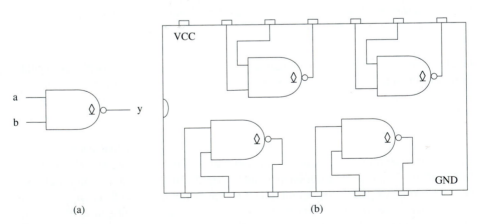

(a)   (b)

FIGURE 7.38
Open collector NAND gate, (a) A two-input NAND gate, (b) TTL 74LS03 SSI package.

Figure 7.39 shows the VHDL description of an open collector two-input NAND gate. This description uses the *qit* type and the overloaded AND operator from the *basic_utilities* package. The simple test bench in Figure 7.40a and the simulation report in Figure 7.40b indicate that the *open_output* architecture of *nand2* operates as expected. The output node is 'Z' if any of the inputs is '0'; otherwise it is '0'.

Figure 7.41 shows the VHDL description for the TTL 74LS03 package. The *structural* architecture of the *sn7403* entity instantiates four *open_output* architectures of *nand2*. As shown in the simulation of an individual NAND gate, if an output is used without a pull-up resistor, its value is either '0' or 'Z'. We now demonstrate how resolution functions can be used to model pull-up resistors.

In general, the function of a pull-up resistor is to produce a '1' if none of its drivers is '0', and to produce a '0' if at least one driver is '0'. For the *qit* type, this function is the same as the *anding* function that we described earlier in Section 7.1.4.2 of this chapter. Therefore, we can use the following declaration for modeling a circuit node that is connected to a five-volt supply through a pull-up resistor:

    SIGNAL pull_up : anded_qit;

Associating this signal with an output port of an open collector gate is equivalent to connecting that output to a pull-up resistor in hardware.

The gate level design in Figure 7.42 illustrates the use of pull-up resistors. This circuit uses four NAND gates of a 74LS03 package for implementing an Exclusive-NOR function. Gates *g1* and *g2* serve as inverters for inverting the *aa* and the *bb* inputs. In order to be able to use these outputs for the inputs of other gates, they have been pulled up by *pull_up_1* and *pull_up_2* resistors. These outputs are used for the inputs of *g3* and *g4* gates; the outputs of these gates are tied together to the *pull_up_3* resistor. The resulting Boolean expression on the *yy* output is:

$$yy = (aa' . bb)' . (bb' . aa)' = (aa \oplus bb)'$$

```
USE  WORK.basic_utilities.ALL;
-- FROM PACKAGE USE: qit, "AND"
ENTITY nand2 IS
    PORT (a, b : IN qit; y : OUT qit);
    CONSTANT tplh : TIME := 10 NS;
    CONSTANT tphl : TIME := 12 NS;
END nand2;
--
ARCHITECTURE open_output OF nand2 IS
BEGIN
    y <= '0' AFTER tphl WHEN (a AND b) = '1' ELSE
         'Z' AFTER tplh WHEN (a AND b) = '0' ELSE
         'X' AFTER tphl;
END open_output;
```

FIGURE 7.39
VHDL description of a NAND gate with open collector output.

```
ENTITY test_nand2 IS END test_nand2;
    --
USE WORK.basic_utilities.ALL;
-- FROM PACKAGE USE: qit, assign_bits
ARCHITECTURE input_output OF test_nand2 IS
    COMPONENT nand2 PORT (a, b : IN qit; y : OUT qit); END COMPONENT;
    FOR ALL : nand2 USE ENTITY WORK.nand2 (open_output);
    SIGNAL aa, bb, yy : qit;
BEGIN
    assign_bits (aa, "qit_data", 500 NS);
    assign_bits (bb, "qit_data", 750 NS);
    c1: nand2 PORT MAP (aa, bb, yy);
END input_output;
```

(a)

TIME	SIGNALS		
(ns)	aa	bb	yy
0000	'0'	'0'	'0'
0010	...	...	'Z'
1000	'1'	...	...
1500	...	'1'	...
1512	...	...	'0'
2500	'0'	...	...
2510	...	...	'Z'
3000	'Z'	...	...
3012	...	...	'0'
3750	...	'0'	...
3760	...	...	'Z'
4000	'0'	...	...
4500	'1'	'Z'	...
4512	...	...	'0'
5000	'0'	...	...
5010	...	...	'Z'
5500	'Z'	...	...
5512	...	...	'0'
6000	...	'0'	...
6010	...	...	'Z'
6750	...	'1'	...
6762	...	...	'0'
7500	...	'0'	...
7510	...	...	'Z'
8250	...	'Z'	...
8262	...	...	'0'

(b)

FIGURE 7.40
Testing the open-collector NAND gate of Figure 7.39, (a) test bench using external file data, (b) simulation report. All events are observed.

```
USE  WORK.basic_utilities.ALL;
-- FROM PACKAGE USE: qit
ENTITY sn7403 IS
    PORT (a1, a2, a3, a4, b1, b2, b3, b4 : IN qit; y1, y2, y3, y4 : OUT qit);
END sn7403;
   --

ARCHITECTURE structural OF sn7403 IS
    COMPONENT nand2 PORT (a, b : IN qit; y : OUT qit); END COMPONENT;
    FOR ALL : nand2 USE ENTITY WORK.nand2 (open_output);
BEGIN
    g1: nand2 PORT MAP ( a1, b1, y1 );
    g2: nand2 PORT MAP ( a2, b2, y2 );
    g3: nand2 PORT MAP ( a3, b3, y3 );
    g4: nand2 PORT MAP ( a4, b4, y4 );
END structural;
```

FIGURE 7.41
VHDL description of TTL 74LS03 which contains four open collector NAND gates.

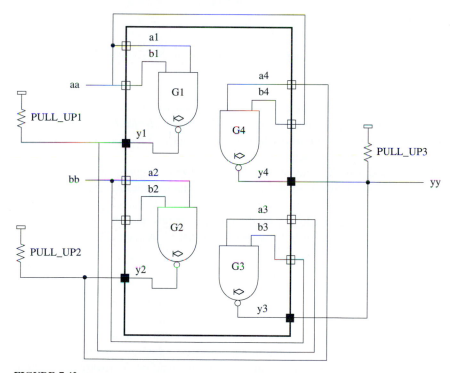

FIGURE 7.42
Implementing XNOR logic using open collector NAND gates.

The VHDL description in Figure 7.43 specifies the wiring in Figure 7.42 and it provides test data to the *aa* and the *bb* inputs.

```
USE WORK.basic_utilities.ALL;
-- FROM PACKAGE USE: qit, anded_qit
ENTITY test_xnor IS END test_xnor;
    --
ARCHITECTURE input_output OF test_xnor IS
    COMPONENT sn7403
        PORT (a1, a2, a3, a4, b1, b2, b3, b4 : IN qit; y1, y2, y3, y4 OUT qit);
    END COMPONENT;
    FOR ALL : sn7403 USE ENTITY WORK.sn7403 (structural);
    SIGNAL aa, bb : qit;
    SIGNAL pull_up_1, pull_up_2, pull_up_3 : anded_qit := 'Z';
BEGIN
    aa <=
        '1', '0' AFTER 10US, '1' AFTER 30US, '0' AFTER 50US, 'Z' AFTER 60US;
    bb <= '0', '1' AFTER 20US, '0' AFTER 40US, 'Z' AFTER 70US;
    c1: sn7403 PORT MAP (
        aa,          bb,              pull_up_1,      pull_up_2,
        aa,          bb,              bb,             aa,
        pull_up_1,   pull_up_2,       pull_up_3,      pull_up_3);
END input_output;
```

FIGURE 7.43
Wiring and testing XNOR function implemented by four open collector NAND gates. The circuit is shown in Figure 7.42.

In this figure, nodes connected to the pull-up resistors in Figure 7.42 are associated with signals whose subtype indications are *anded_qit*. *Pull_up_3* of this type has two drivers which are ANDed by the *anding* resolution function. This function is implied in the *anded_qit* declaration.

Figure 7.44 shows the simulation result of the *input_output* architecture of the *test_xnor* entity. This figure shows the values of the inputs, outputs, and the intermediate nodes of XNOR logic every 2 microseconds. The 'Z' values produced by the individual gates are translated to ',1', by the *pull_up* signals and do not appear in the simulation report. This behavior is consistent with that of the actual hardware.

7.4   A GENERAL DATAFLOW CIRCUIT

Application of dataflow descriptions is not limited to specification of bussing structures and state machines described in previous sections. Hardware descriptions at this level can be used to describe a complete sequential circuit consisting of registers, combinational units, and buses. Using an example, we show how word specification of a clocked sequential circuit can be translated into its dataflow hardware description.

The circuit to design is a sequential comparator that keeps a modulo-16 count of matching consecutive data set pairs. The circuit uses an 8-bit *data*, a *clk*, and a *reset* input. The 4-bit output is called *matches*. If on any two consecutive rising edges of the clock, the same data appears on *data*, then the output will be incremented by 1. The synchronous reset of the circuit resets the output count to zero.

TIME (us)	SIGNALS				
	aa	bb	pull_up_1	pull_up_2	pull_up_3
00	'1'	'0'	'0'	'0'	'0'
02	'1'	'0'	'0'	'1'	'0'
04	'1'	'0'	'0'	'1'	'0'
06	'1'	'0'	'0'	'1'	'0'
08	'1'	'0'	'0'	'1'	'0'
10	'0'	'0'	'0'	'1'	'0'
12	'0'	'0'	'1'	'1'	'1'
14	'0'	'0'	'1'	'1'	'1'
16	'0'	'0'	'1'	'1'	'1'
18	'0'	'0'	'1'	'1'	'1'
20	'0'	'1'	'1'	'1'	'1'
22	'0'	'1'	'1'	'0'	'0'
24	'0'	'1'	'1'	'0'	'0'
26	'0'	'1'	'1'	'0'	'0'
28	'0'	'1'	'1'	'0'	'0'
30	'1'	'1'	'1'	'0'	'0'
32	'1'	'1'	'0'	'0'	'1'
34	'1'	'1'	'0'	'0'	'1'
36	'1'	'1'	'0'	'0'	'1'
38	'1'	'1'	'0'	'0'	'1'
40	'1'	'0'	'0'	'0'	'1'
42	'1'	'0'	'0'	'1'	'0'
44	'1'	'0'	'0'	'1'	'0'
46	'1'	'0'	'0'	'1'	'0'
48	'1'	'0'	'0'	'1'	'0'
50	'0'	'0'	'0'	'1'	'0'
52	'0'	'0'	'1'	'1'	'1'
54	'0'	'0'	'1'	'1'	'1'
56	'0'	'0'	'1'	'1'	'1'
58	'0'	'0'	'1'	'1'	'1'
60	'Z'	'0'	'1'	'1'	'1'
62	'Z'	'0'	'0'	'1'	'0'
64	'Z'	'0'	'0'	'1'	'0'
66	'Z'	'0'	'0'	'1'	'0'
68	'Z'	'0'	'0'	'1'	'0'
70	'Z'	'Z'	'0'	'1'	'0'

FIGURE 7.44
Simulation results for testing XNOR implementation using open collector NAND gates. Results are observed at 2 us intervals.

The hardware implementation of this circuit, using standard parts, requires a register for holding the old data, a comparator for comparing new and old data, a counter for keeping the count, and perhaps a few logic gates used as "glue logic." At the dataflow level, however, there is no need to be concerned with the component level details of this circuit; rather, flow of data between registers and buses can be captured directly in a VHDL description of this unit.

```
USE  WORK.basic_utilities.ALL;
-- FROM  PACKAGE  USE:  bin2int,  int2bin
ENTITY  sequential_comparator  IS
      PORT (data : IN BIT_VECTOR (7 DOWNTO 0); clk, reset : IN BIT;
                  matches : OUT BIT_VECTOR (3 DOWNTO 0));
END  sequential_comparator;
      --
ARCHITECTURE  dataflow  OF  sequential_comparator  IS
      FUNCTION  inc  (x : BIT_VECTOR)  RETURN  BIT_VECTOR  IS
            VARIABLE  i : INTEGER;
            VARIABLE  t : BIT_VECTOR  (x'RANGE);
      BEGIN
            bin2int  (x, i);
            i := i + 1;  IF  i >= 2**x'LENGTH  THEN  i := 0;  END  IF;
            int2bin  (i, t);
            RETURN  t;
      END  inc;
      SIGNAL  buff : BIT_VECTOR (7 DOWNTO 0);
      SIGNAL  count : BIT_VECTOR (3 DOWNTO 0);
BEGIN
      edge:  BLOCK  (clk = '0' AND NOT clk'STABLE)
      BEGIN
            buff <= GUARDED data;
            count <= GUARDED "0000" WHEN reset = '1' ELSE
                              inc (count) WHEN data = buff ELSE count;
      END  BLOCK;
      matches <= count;
END  dataflow;
```

FIGURE 7.45
Dataflow description of the sequential comparator circuit.

The VHDL description for the *sequential_comparator* is shown in Figure 7.45. The *dataflow* architecture of this circuit uses the *inc* function for incrementing the 4-bit output counter. This function takes advantage of the *bin2int* and *int2bin* procedures in the *basic_utilities* package. In the statement part of the architecture in Figure 7.45, a guarded block statement detects the falling edge of the clock. On this edge, the new data on the *data* input lines is clocked into the 8-bit buffer. Also on the same edge of the clock, the count signal is incremented if the new data and the previous data are equal. Loading *buff* and incrementing *count* are done by concurrent signal assignments and take place simultaneously. A careful study of timing, however, reveals that the condition for incrementing *count* uses the old data in *buff*. The following paragraph elaborates on this timing issue.

If in a simulation cycle at time t, clock makes a 1 to 0 transition, data on the *data* input lines is assigned to *buff*. The new data in *buff* will not be available until $t+\delta$. At time t, the old data in *buff* is compared with what appears on *data* at time t. If these data sets are equal, the *count* signal is incremented. The result of this incrementing becomes available on *count* at $t+\delta$, which is the same time that the new data appears on *buff*. The assignment of *count* to the *matches* output causes this output to lag behind the internal count by another *delta*.

Figure 7.46 shows the sequence of events in the *sequential_comparator*. Understanding timing and clocking is essential in the understanding of dataflow, to be able to use this level of abstraction for the description of systems.

TIME (ns)	reset	clk	data(7:0)	SIGNALS buff(7:0)	count(3:0)	matches
0000	'0'	'0'	"00000000"	"00000000"	"0000"	"0000"
δ	...	...	....	....	......	"0000"
0200	...	...	"11110101"	....	......	......
0500	...	'1'	....	....	......	......
1000	...	'0'	....	....	......	......
δ	...	...	....	"11110101"	"0000"	......
1200	...	...	"01010110"	....	......	......
1500	...	'1'	....	....	......	......
1700	...	...	"11111110"	....	......	......
2000	...	'0'	....	....	......	......
δ	...	...	....	"11111110"	"0000"	......
2500	...	'1'	....	....	......	......
3000	...	'0'	....	....	......	......
δ	...	...	....	"11111110"	"0001"	......
δ	...	...	....	....	......	"0001"
3200	...	...	"01010100"	....	......	......
3500	...	'1'	....	....	......	......
3700	...	...	"00010001"	....	......	......
4000	...	'0'	....	....	......	......
δ	...	...	....	"00010001"	"0001"	......
4200	...	...	"10010110"	....	......	......
4500	...	'1'	....	....	......	......
5000	...	'0'	....	....	......	......
δ	...	...	....	"10010110"	"0001"	......
5500	...	'1'	....	....	......	......
6000	...	'0'	....	....	......	......
δ	...	...	....	"10010110"	"0010"	......
δ	...	...	....	....	......	"0010"
6500	...	'1'	....	....	......	......
7000	...	'0'	....	....	......	......
δ	...	...	....	"10010110"	"0011"	......
δ	...	...	....	....	......	"0011"
7500	...	'1'	....	....	......	......
8000	...	'0'	....	....	......	......
δ	...	...	....	"10010110"	"0100"	......
δ	...	...	....	....	......	"0100"
8500	...	'1'	....	....	......	......

FIGURE 7.46

Simulation results for testing dataflow architecture of *sequential_comparator*. All transactions are observed.

7.5 UPDATING BASIC UTILITIES

The *basic_utilities* package was used extensively in the examples in this chapter. We specified the addition of several resolution functions and their related type definitions to this package. Another useful function to have in this package is the *inc* function from the *sequential_comparator* example. For reference, the contributions added to the *basic_utilities* package in this chapter are shown in Figure 7.47.

7.6 SUMMARY

This chapter presented signal assignments, guarded assignments, and resolution functions, which are considered to be among the most important hardware related constructs in the VHDL language. We focused on resolution functions and how they can be used to model various bussing structures and registers. Various forms of sig-

```
PACKAGE basic_utilities IS
    .
    .
    .
    FUNCTION wire (a, b : qit) RETURN qit;
    --
    FUNCTION oring ( drivers : qit_vector) RETURN qit;
    SUBTYPE ored_qit IS oring qit;
    TYPE ored_qit_vector IS ARRAY (NATURAL RANGE <>) OF ored_qit;
    --
    FUNCTION anding ( drivers : qit_vector) RETURN qit;
    SUBTYPE anded_qit IS anding qit;
    TYPE anded_qit_vector IS ARRAY (NATURAL RANGE <>) OF anded_qit;
    --
    FUNCTION wiring ( drivers : qit_vector) RETURN qit;
    SUBTYPE wired_qit IS wiring qit;
    TYPE wired_qit_vector IS ARRAY (NATURAL RANGE <>) OF wired_qit;
    --
    FUNCTION oring ( drivers : BIT_VECTOR) RETURN BIT;
    SUBTYPE ored_bit IS oring BIT;
    TYPE ored_bit_vector IS ARRAY (NATURAL RANGE <>) OF ored_bit;
    --
    FUNCTION anding ( drivers : BIT_VECTOR) RETURN BIT;
    SUBTYPE anded_bit IS anding bit;
    TYPE anded_bit_vector IS ARRAY (NATURAL RANGE <>) OF anded_bit;
    --
    FUNCTION inc (x : BIT_VECTOR) RETURN BIT_VECTOR;
END basic_utilities;
```

FIGURE 7.47
Resolution functions and *inc* function added to the *basic_utilities* package in Chapter 7. (*continued*)

```
┌─PACKAGE  BODY  basic_utilities  IS
│      .
│      .
│      .
│   ┌─FUNCTION  wire  (a,  b  :  qit)  RETURN  qit  IS
│   │      CONSTANT  qit_and_table  :  qit_2d  :=  (
│   │                              ('0','X','0','X'),
│   │                              ('X','1','1','X'),
│   │                              ('0','1','Z','X'),
│   │                              ('X','X','X','X'));
│   ├─BEGIN
│   │      RETURN  qit_and_table  (a,  b);
│   └─END  wire;
│   ┌─FUNCTION  oring  (  drivers  :  qit_vector)  RETURN  qit  IS
│   │      VARIABLE  accumulate  :  qit  :=  '0';
│   ├─BEGIN
│   │      FOR  i  IN  drivers'RANGE  LOOP
│   │          accumulate  :=  accumulate  OR  drivers(i);
│   │      END  LOOP;
│   │      RETURN  accumulate;
│   └─END  oring;
│   ┌─FUNCTION  anding  (  drivers  :  qit_vector)  RETURN  qit  IS
│   │      VARIABLE  accumulate  :  qit  :=  '1';
│   ├─BEGIN
│   │      FOR  i  IN  drivers'RANGE  LOOP
│   │          accumulate  :=  accumulate  AND  drivers(i);
│   │      END  LOOP;
│   │      RETURN  accumulate;
│   └─END  anding;
│   ┌─FUNCTION  wiring  (  drivers  :  qit_vector)  RETURN  qit  IS
│   │      VARIABLE  accumulate  :  qit  :=  'Z';
│   ├─BEGIN
│   │      FOR  i  IN  drivers'RANGE  LOOP
│   │          accumulate  :=  wire  (accumulate,  drivers(i));
│   │      END  LOOP;
│   │      RETURN  accumulate;
│   └─END  wiring;
```

FIGURE 7.47
Resolution functions and *inc* function added to the *basic_utilities* package in Chapter 7. (*continued*)

nal assignments in VHDL provide tools for describing complex bussing structures in register transfer level descriptions.

The first part of this chapter presented forms of signal assignments that had not been encountered in the examples in previous chapters. Guarded signal assignment and the concept of disconnection, or turning off a source, were presented next. This prepared the way for describing resolution functions, multiple drivers of signals, and guarded signals. Although VHDL only requires resolution of signals with multiple

```
FUNCTION oring ( drivers : BIT_VECTOR) RETURN BIT IS
    VARIABLE accumulate : BIT := '0';
BEGIN
    FOR i IN drivers'RANGE LOOP
        accumulate := accumulate OR drivers(i);
    END LOOP;
    RETURN accumulate;
END oring;
FUNCTION anding ( drivers : BIT_VECTOR) RETURN BIT IS
    VARIABLE accumulate : BIT := '1';
BEGIN
    FOR i IN drivers'RANGE LOOP
        accumulate := accumulate AND drivers(i);
    END LOOP;
    RETURN accumulate;
END anding;
FUNCTION inc (x : BIT_VECTOR) RETURN BIT_VECTOR IS
    VARIABLE i : INTEGER;
    VARIABLE t : BIT_VECTOR (x'RANGE);
BEGIN
    bin2int (x, i);
    i := i + 1; IF i >= 2**x'LENGTH THEN i := 0; END IF;
    int2bin (i, t);
    RETURN t;
END inc;
END basic_utilities;
```

FIGURE 7.47
Resolution functions and *inc* function added to the *basic_utilities* package in Chapter 7.

concurrent sources, in general a resolved signal is a better representation of a circuit node. In VHDL, a regular signal retains its value indefinitely—this behavior is different from a hardware node that loses its value as soon as its driver is removed. A resolved signal, on the other hand, can be made to act in exactly the same way as a hardware circuit node. A resolution function for such a node can be written to match its technology-dependent behavior. The resolution functions developed in this chapter are typical of the way buses function in a digital system. Hardware designers develop their own libraries of resolution functions, based on the design styles and the technologies they are working with. The last part of this chapter presented a dataflow description for an entire system. This demonstrated that signal assignments, resolution functions, and guarded block statements are applicable to high level designs as well as to low level buses or flip-flops.

REFERENCES

1. Wakerly, J. F., "Digital Design Principles and Practices," Prentice-Hall Inc., Englewood Cliffs, N.J., 1990.

2. Hill, F. J., and G. R. Peterson, "Digital Systems: Hardware Organization and Design," 3rd ed., John Wiley and Sons, New York, 1987.

3. "IEEE Standard VHDL Language Reference Manual," IEEE Std 1076-1987, The Institute of Electrical and Electronic Engineers, Inc., 1988.

4. Lipsett, L., C. Schaefer, and C. Ussery, "VHDL: Hardware Description and Design," Klewer Academic Publishing, Boston, 1988.

5. Armstrong, J. R., "Chip-Level Modeling with VHDL," Prentice-Hall Inc., Englewood Cliffs, N.J., 1988.

PROBLEMS

7.1. Write functions *qit2bit* and *bit2qit* for converting an unconstrained *qit_vector* to a BIT_VECTOR, and an unconstrained BIT_VECTOR to a *qit_vector*, respectively. Take advantage of arrays with noninteger indices for converting from one base type to another.

7.2. Use a selected signal assignment to describe a BCD to seven-segment decoder. Use *qit* as the base type of all elements of inputs and outputs. You may use the functions you created in Problem 7.1.

7.3. Write a description for an 8-to-1 multiplexer with a 3-bit decoded input in the *qit* logic value system. Take advantage of the functions you prepared in Problem 7.1.

7.4. Wire the multiplexer in Figure 7.5 and the decoder of Figure 7.8 to generate a multiplexer with decoded input.

7.5. A decoder with an enable input is easily cascadable. Write a VHDL description for a 3-to-8 decoder with an active low enable input and an active high enable input. When disabled, all outputs have to be 0. Use the *qit* logic value system.

7.6. Write a VHDL description for wiring two of the decoders in Problem 7.5 to implement a 4-to-16 decoder.

7.7. Use guarded signal assignments to describe a simple latch with *q* and NOT *q* outputs that functions the same as a latch formed by cross-coupled NOR gates with clocked inputs. Use reasonable delay values.

7.8. Use two of the latches in Problem 7.7 and necessary logic operations to describe a master-slave JK flip-flop.

7.9. Use guarded block statements to describe an 8-bit shift register. The structure has a serial input for right shifting the data and a single serial output. All activities are synchronized with the leading edge of the clock.

7.10. Write a description for a universal 8-bit shift register with a 2-bit mode select input, an 8-bit parallel data input, and an 8-bit data output. The unit performs a right shift if the mode is 01, left shift if the mode is 10, and a parallel load of the eight bit input if the mode is 11. All activities are synchronized with the leading edge of the clock.

7.11. Write a description for a clocked T-type flip-flop. If *T* is '1' on the rising edge of the clock, the outputs of the flip-flop toggle. Use the *qit* logic value system.

7.12. Write a VHDL description for a rising edge trigger D-type flip-flop with asynchronous set and reset inputs and two outputs. Label the data, clock, set and reset inputs *d*, *c*, *s* and *r*, respectively. Active *s* or *r* inputs override the clocked values on the *d* input; *s* and *r* cannot simultaneously be active. Changes on *d* without the rising edge of *c* have no effect on the *q* and *qb* outputs of the flip-flop. Use delay parameters *sq_delay*, *rq_delay*, and *cq_delay* for setting, resetting, and clocking the flip-flop, respectively. Develop a test bench for testing this flip-flop. Generate a simple periodic clock using a conditional signal assignment.

7.13. Given the following description, show waveforms on $x1$, $x2$ and *diff* in a timing diagram. Explain the reason for different waveforms on $x1$ and $x2$.

```
ENTITY find_out IS END find_out;
    --
ARCHITECTURE comparing OF find_out IS
    SIGNAL c, x1, x2, diff : BIT := '0';
BEGIN
    c <= '0', '1' AFTER 60 NS, '0' AFTER 120 NS;
    x1 <= '1' AFTER 6 NS WHEN c'EVENT ELSE x1;
    x2 <= '1' AFTER 6 NS WHEN NOT c'STABLE ELSE x2;
    diff <= x1 XOR x2;
END comparing;
```

7.14. A resolution function, named *majority*, resolves to the majority of '1's or '0's on its inputs. If there are more ones ('1's) than zeros, the function generates a '1' output. If there are more zeros ('0's) than ones, the function generates a '0' output. If the number of '1's and '0's are equal the output will be 'E'. A) Declare all necessary types, and write the description of the *majority* function. B) Declare types and subtypes that can be used for declaring signals that can take advantage of this resolution function. C) Package all of the above, and show how a single-bit signal *candidate* and a 16-bit signal *candidate_16* should be declared such that placement of multiple values on these signals will resolve according to the *majority* function.

7.15. A resolution function, named *all_same*, resolves all '1's on its sources to '1' and all '0's to zero. This function generates 'E', indicating an error condition if conflicting values are placed at its sources. A) Declare all necessary types, and write the description of the *all_same* function. B) Declare types and subtypes that can be used for declaring signals that can take advantage of this resolution function. C) Package all of the above, and show how a single-bit signal *x* and a 16-bit signal *x16* should be declared such that placement of multiple values on these signals will resolve according to the *all_same* function. D) What actual hardware construct behaves like the *all_same* function?

7.16. Ten controlled sources ($s(i)$ where i is 1 to 10) that range between -25 and $+25$ volts are connected to the sources of 10 parallel MOS transistors. The common drain of these transistors is node n. Each source, $s(i)$, is controlled by a control line, $c(i)$, that is connected to the gate of the MOS transistors. Control line voltages also range between -25 to $+25$. A control line, $c(i)$, turns its corresponding transistor on, i.e., causes it to conduct which in turn causes node n be driven by source $s(i)$ when $c(i)$ is greater than or equal to $+5$ volts. The on-resistance of the parallel transistors is 10 KΩ. Node n is also connected to a 25 V supply through a 10 KΩ pull-up resistor. At any time, any number of controlled sources may be active. A) Write a resolution function that returns the voltage at node n depending on the value and number of active sources. B) In a test architecture, declare a resolved guarded signal (node n) whose resolution function is that in Part A. Use guarded block statements to conditionally drive this signal (node n) with up to 10 sources, each of which can take a value between -25 and $+25$. This is analogous to connecting 10 parallel MOS transistors to node n and applying various voltages to the sources of these transistors. Use a generate statement instead of 10 individual block statements.

7.17. Use a block statement, a resolution function, a conditional signal assignment, and a disconnection specification to model a tri-state noninverting buffer. The gate has data and enable inputs x and e, and output z. When e is '1', the z output is driven by x; otherwise, the output is in the high impedance state. The inputs and outputs are of type *qit* and output is a guarded signal. Use the three delay values *tp_e_z_float*, *tp_x_z_high*, and *tp_x_z_low* where: *tp_e_z_float* is for e changing to '0' and causing the output to disconnect from the input; *tp_x_z_high* is for e equal to '1'and x changing to '1' causing the output to become '1', or when x is '1' and e changes to '1'; and *tp_x_z_low* is for e equal to '1' and x changing to '0' causing the output to become '0', or when x is '0' and e changes to '1'. Use '0' and '1' values for the inputs, and map 'X' and 'Z' into '0' and '1', respectively. Use two such buffers for implementing a 2-to-1 multiplexer.

7.18. Design a Mealy sequence detector and develop a tester for this circuit. The circuit monitors its x input for the 10110 sequence. When this sequence is found, the z output becomes '1'. A valid data bit is one that coincides with the rising edge of the clock, c. Make sure that you understand the behavior of a Mealy machine output. A) Write a VHDL dataflow description for this sequence detector. B) Show a test bench that tests this circuit for the 10110110101 sequence on the x input. Use a periodic clock.

7.19. Accurately model the circuit shown below in VHDL at the dataflow level. This circuit uses positive edge triggered D flip-flop. Flip-flop 1 has an asynchronous reset in addition to the synchronous D input. The reset input has priority over the clock input. Write a complete VHDL description at the dataflow level for modeling this circuit. Your description should include an ENTITY and an ARCHITECTURE.

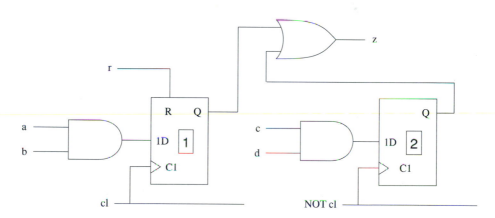

7.20. Write the complete VHDL description for a Moore machine detecting 10111 or 11001. The circuit continuously monitors its x input. When in five consecutive clock pulses either sequence is found, the z output becomes '1' and stays at this level for a complete clock pulse. Write a VHDL dataflow description for this sequence detector. Show a test bench that tests this circuit for the 10110010111001 10100 sequence on the x input. Use a periodic clock.

7.21. Write the complete VHDL description for a circuit with an input x and two outputs, $z1$ and $z2$. The circuit consists of two concurrent Mealy machines. The $z1$ output becomes '1' when a 1011 sequence is found on the input, and the $z2$ output becomes '1' when a 110 sequence is found x. Your description should be capable of having multiple active states.

7.22. Write a VHDL description for a Moore state machine with resetting capability. While continuously searching for 1011 on the data input x, if the reset input, r, becomes '1', the circuit returns to a reset state. In this state, all previously received data will be ignored and a complete 1011 is required before the output becomes '1'. While not reset, circuit responds to overlapping valid sequences.

7.23. Describe a synchronous shifter circuit with a left serial input, *lsi*, and an 8-bit shift register. The circuit synchronously resets when a '1' appears on its reset input. After a reset, for every five clock pulses, a data bit from the *lsi* input is shifted into the 8-bit register. You may use utilities of the *basic_utilities* package.

CHAPTER
8

BEHAVIORAL
DESCRIPTION
OF HARDWARE

Most hardware characteristics can be described by the methods and techniques presented in the previous chapters. Although the emphasis has been on the structural and dataflow descriptions, we have also shown how subprograms can be used to represent hardware modules at the behavioral level. The use of such constructs, however, has mainly been for nonhardware processes.

In this chapter, the emphasis is on behavioral descriptions of hardware components. We show how a hardware unit can be described by its input/output mapping without specifying its technology, netlist, or even its data path.

The chapter begins by presenting key VHDL constructs for behavioral descriptions of concurrent bodies. This is followed by a description of high level constructs for handshaking, timing, and formatted I/O. Next, we present a complete design using standard MSI parts. The behavioral description of these parts will be described in detail. A configuration declaration and a test bench complete the design and testing of this MSI-based design.

8.1 PROCESS STATEMENT

A simple signal assignment in the statement part of an architecture is a *process* which is always active and executing concurrent with other processes within the same architecture. This process has a single target, and executes when an event occurs on one of the signals on its right hand side. Therefore, it is said to be sensitive to signals on the right hand side of the signal assignment. A different kind of a process is a process statement which is also active at all times, executing concurrently with other processes, but can be made sensitive to selected signals.

A process statement can assign values to more than one signal and can contain sequential statements. This statement begins with the PROCESS keyword and ends with END PROCESS. As shown in Figure 8.1, a process statement has a declarative part and a statement part. All constructs allowed in the declarative and statement parts of subprograms can be used in process statements. The semantics of subprograms and the sequential statements used within them, however, are different from those in the process statements.

8.1.1 Declarative Part of a Process

Variable, file, or constant objects can be declared in the declarative part of a process. Such objects are only visible to the process within which they are declared. Signals and constants declared in the declarative part of an architecture that encloses a process statement can be used inside a process. Such signals are the only means of communication between different processes.

Initialization of objects declared in a process is done only once at the beginning of a simulation run. These objects stay alive for the entire simulation run. This way a variable declared in a process can be used to hold memory status or the internal state of a hardware system. Note that initializations in a subprogram are performed each time the subprogram is called.

8.1.2 Statement Part of a Process

The statement part of a process is sequential, always active, and it executes in zero time. The following paragraphs and examples will elaborate on these concepts.

Only sequential statements are allowed in the statement part of a process. These statements provide high level program flow control for assignment of values to signals and variables. For selection and assignment of values to signals, if, loop or case statements can be used. Although the syntax of many concurrent and sequential statements is the same, in general, concurrent statements are not allowed in the statement

```
PROCESS
    ┌─────────────────────┐
    │ declarative_part    │
    ├─────────────────────┤
    │ ...                 │
    └─────────────────────┘
BEGIN
    ┌─────────────────────┐
    │ statement_part      │
    ├─────────────────────┤
    │ ...                 │
    └─────────────────────┘
END     PROCESS;
```

FIGURE 8.1
A process statement block diagram.

part of a process statement. Conditional and selected signal assignments are strictly concurrent, and they cannot be used in a process statement.

Program flow inside a process starts at the beginning of its statement part and proceeds toward the end of this part. Statements reached by the program flow are executed sequentially in zero time. Consider, for example, the partial code in Figure 8.2. In this example, the assignment of a to x is executed before assigning b to y. Both assignments schedule values to their left hand side targets, which will appear one *delta* time later.

Figure 8.3 shows another partial code in which assignment of values to x and y use 10 ns and 6 ns delays, respectively. When the flow of program reaches the first assignment, the value of a is scheduled for x after 10 ns. Following the execution of this statement, the signal assignment assigning b to y is executed. As the result of this execution, the value of b is scheduled for the y target after 6 ns. The end result is that the y signal receives the value of b 4 ns sooner than x receives a, even though the scheduling of the former was done after that of the latter.

Another partial code, demonstrating the availability of data assigned to signals, is shown in Figure 8.4. In this figure, we assume that the value of x is '0' be-

```
┌ARCHITECTURE  sequentiality_demo  OF  partial_process  IS
├BEGIN
│     ┌PROCESS
│     ├BEGIN
│     │   ...
│     │   x  <=  a;
│     │   y  <=  b;
│     │   ...
│     └END  PROCESS;
└END  sequentiality_demo;
```

FIGURE 8.2
Sequentiality in process statements. The amount of real time between the execution of one statement and the next is zero. Both statements occur in one simulation cycle.

```
┌ARCHITECTURE  execution_time_demo  OF  partial_process  IS
├BEGIN
│     ┌PROCESS
│     ├BEGIN
│     │   ...
│     │   x  <=  a  AFTER  10  NS;
│     │   y  <=  b  AFTER  6  NS;
│     │   ...
│     └END  PROCESS;
└END  execution_time_demo;
```

FIGURE 8.3
Partial code for demonstration of zero execution time of a process statement.

```
ARCHITECTURE  data_availability_demo  OF  partial_process  IS
BEGIN
    PROCESS
    BEGIN
        ...
        x <= '1';
        IF x = '1' THEN
            perform   action_1
        ELSE
            perform   action_2
        END  IF;

        ...
    END  PROCESS;
END  data_availability_demo;
```

FIGURE 8.4
Partial code for demonstrating delay in assignment of values to signals.

fore the flow of the program reaches the signal assignment that uses x on the left
hand side. Execution of this statement causes '1' to be scheduled for the x target
after a δ delay. The if statement in this figure is executed immediately after the
execution of the signal assignment. Since these two statements are executed during the same simulation cycle (in zero time), the new value of x is not available
when the if statement is executed. The condition of this statement, therefore, will
not be satisfied and *action_2* is performed. Had x been a variable, the symbol :=
would have to be used to assign a value to it, and its new value, '1', would be
available when the if statement is executed. In that case, *action_1* would have been
performed.

The statement part of a process is always active. When the program flow reaches
the last sequential statement of this part the execution returns to the first statement in
the statement part and continues. This behavior is different from that of subprograms;
in subprogram execution, the subprogram terminates when the flow of the program
reaches the last statement in its statement part. In fact, a procedure with an infinite
loop in its statement parts behaves the same as a process statement.

8.1.3   Sensitivity List

A process statement is always active and executes at all times if not suspended. A
mechanism for suspending and subsequently conditionally activating a process is the
use of sensitivity list. Following a PROCESS keyword, a list of signals in parentheses
can be specified; this list is called the sensitivity list, and the process is activated
when an event occurs on any of these signals. When the program flow reaches the
last sequential statement, the process becomes suspended, although alive, until another event occurs on a signal that it is sensitive to. Regardless of the events on the
sensitivity list signals, processes are executed once at the beginning of the simulation
run.

The signal assignment of Figure 8.5a is considered to be a process and it is equivalent to the process statement in Figure 8.5b. These two processes are only activated when an event occurs on *b*, and they become suspended after the new value of *b* is scheduled for *a*.

8.1.4   A First Process Example

Figure 8.6 shows the logic symbol for a D-type flip-flop with asynchronous active-high set and reset inputs. The VHDL description in Figure 8.7 corresponds to this D-type flip-flop. The description demonstrates concurrency of processes, sensitivity lists, and several process related timing issues.

The behavioral architecture of the *d_sr_flipflop* in Figure 8.7 uses an internal state to record the status of the current memory. The statement part of this architecture includes three concurrent processes, one of which is a process statement sensitive to inputs *rst*, *set* and *clk*. When an event occurs on any of these signals, the *dff* process becomes active. This process uses an if statement to schedule a value for *state*. When the value of *state* changes, the signal assignments to *q* and *qb* become active, causing these outputs to receive their values after one δ delay. From the time that values are scheduled for the *state* signal to the time that *state* changes, all three processes are suspended.

The if statement in the statement part of the *dff* process gives a higher priority to the asynchronous inputs than to the clock. If, for example, the clock edge appears while the *set* input is high, value of '1' on the *state* signal will be reinstated. This description makes no provisions for the illegal case of *set* and *rst* both being '1' simultaneously.

```
...              PROCESS
...              BEGIN
a <= b;              a <= b;
...              END PROCESS;
    (a)              (b)
```

FIGURE 8.5
A simple process with sensitivity list, (a) signal assignment, (b) equivalent process statement.

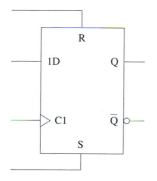

FIGURE 8.6
A positive edge trigger D-Type flip-flop with asynchronous set and reset inputs.

```
ENTITY d_sr_flipflop IS
    GENERIC (sq_delay, rq_delay, cq_delay : TIME := 6 NS);
    PORT (d, set, rst, clk : IN BIT; q, qb : OUT BIT);
END d_sr_flipflop;
--
ARCHITECTURE behavioral OF d_sr_flipflop IS
    SIGNAL state : BIT := '0';
BEGIN
    dff: PROCESS (rst, set, clk)
    BEGIN
    IF set = '1' THEN
        state <= '1' AFTER sq_delay;
    ELSIF rst = '1' THEN
        state <= '0' AFTER rq_delay;
    ELSIF clk = '1' AND clk'EVENT THEN
        state <= d AFTER cq_delay;
    END IF;
    END PROCESS dff;
    q <= state;
    qb <= NOT state;
END behavioral;
```

FIGURE 8.7
VHDL description for the flip-flop of Figure 8.6.

Since the internal state of the flip-flop is realized by use of a signal, there are always two simulation cycles between input and output changes; one for assignment of values to *state*, and one for assigning *state* or its complement to the outputs. If the delay values, i.e., *sq_delay*, *rq_delay*, and *cq_delay* are nonzero, the first δ delay (the delay for the assignment of values to *state*) will be absorbed in the nonzero delay values, and only the second δ delay appears on the output.

Another architecture for the *d_sr_flipflop* entity is shown in Figure 8.8. For zero delay parameter values, this architecture reduces the δ delays between inputs and outputs to only one *delta*. For nonzero delay parameters, no δ delay will appear on the outputs. Comparison of the two models of *d_sr_flipflop* is useful in understanding signals and variables in process statements.

The variable declared in the declarative part of *dff* process in Figure 8.8 holds the internal state of the flip-flop. When this process is suspended, *state* retains the value assigned to it in the last activation of the process. Because *state* is a variable, no delays are associated with it and no delays can be specified with its assignment. Therefore, we have averaged the three delay parameters and used a single delay value for assigning *state* and its complement to *q* and *qb*, respectively.

It is probably obvious to the reader that the *average_delay_behavioral* archi-tecture for a D-type flip-flop is less accurate than the one shown in Figure 8.7, but avoiding the extra δ delay may be important in some applications. Figure 8.9 shows the results of simultaneous simulation of the two models, illustrating δ delay differ-ences between them. For a better illustration of δ delays, we have avoided real time

```
ARCHITECTURE average_delay_behavioral OF d_sr_flipflop IS
BEGIN
    dff: PROCESS (rst, set, clk)
    VARIABLE state : BIT := '0';
    BEGIN
    IF  set = '1'  THEN
        state := '1';
    ELSIF  rst = '1'  THEN
        state := '0';
    ELSIF  clk = '1'  AND  clk'EVENT  THEN
        state := d;
    END  IF;
    q  <=  state AFTER (sq_delay + rq_delay + cq_delay)/3;
    qb  <=  NOT state AFTER (sq_delay + rq_delay + cq_delay)/3;
    END  PROCESS  dff;
END average_delay_behavioral;
```

FIGURE 8.8
Alternative architecture for *d_sr_flipflop* entity; reducing δ delay by one.

differences between the two models by using equal values for the three timing parameters. This way, average values for the *average_delay_behavioral* and the individual values for the *behavioral* architectures are equal.

The simulation report in this figure shows the two architectures tested for asynchronous setting (*ss*='1' at 200 ns), asynchronous resetting (*rr*= '1' at 1400 ns), and clocking them with *dd*='1' and *dd*='0' (at 2500 ns and 3500 ns, respectively). In all these cases, *q* and *qb* of the *behavioral* architecture (*q1* and *qb1*) receive their values one delta time after their corresponding physical delay values. However, for the *average_delay_behavioral*, the only delays seen on the outputs (*q2* and *qb2*) are the physical delays that are equal to the average of the three delay parameters.

8.1.5   Syntax Details of Process Statements

Figure 8.10 shows the syntax details for the process statement used in the description of Figure 8.8. The label of a process, which precedes this statement, is optional, but, if used, it should also be placed at the end of the process statement. The sensitivity list is also optional and it can contain any number of signals that are visible outside of the process. Objects declared inside a process cannot be used in its sensitivity list for that process.

As shown in Figure 8.10, only sequential statements are allowed in the statement part of a process, whereas, the process statements themselves are considered concurrent statements. This implies that processes cannot be nested. Where nesting of behavioral sequential bodies is necessary, procedures can be called from processes. It is, of course, possible to nest procedures since procedure calls are both concurrent and sequential statements.

TIME (ns)	SIGNALS							
	ss	rr	cc	dd	q1	q2	qb1	qb2
0000	'0'	'0'	'0'	'0'	'0'	'0'	'0'	'0'
δ	...	...	...	...	...	...	'1'	...
0006	...	...	...	...	...	...	...	'1'
0200	'1'	...	...	...	...	...	...	...
0206	...	...	...	...	...	'1'	...	'0'
δ	...	...	...	...	'1'	...	'0'	...
0500	...	...	'1'	...	...	...	...	...
1000	...	...	'0'	...	...	...	...	...
1200	'0'	...	...	...	...	...	...	...
1400	...	'1'	...	...	...	...	...	...
1406	...	...	...	...	...	'0'	...	'1'
δ	...	...	...	...	'0'	...	'1'	...
1500	...	...	'1'	...	...	...	...	...
2000	...	...	'0'	...	...	...	...	...
2200	...	'0'	...	...	...	...	...	...
2400	...	...	...	'1'	...	...	...	...
2500	...	...	'1'	...	...	...	...	...
2506	...	...	...	...	...	'1'	...	'0'
δ	...	...	...	...	'1'	...	'0'	...
3000	...	...	'0'	...	...	...	...	...
3300	...	...	...	'0'	...	...	...	...
3500	...	...	'1'	...	...	...	...	...
3506	...	...	...	...	...	'0'	...	'1'
δ	...	...	...	...	'0'	...	'1'	...
4000	...	...	'0'	...	...	...	...	...

FIGURE 8.9
Simultaneous simulation of *behavioral* and *average_delay_behavioral* architectures of *d_sr_flipflop*. All events are observed.

8.1.6 Behavioral Flow Control Constructs

As stated previously, software-like program flow control constructs such as if, loop, and case statements are considered sequential statements, and can appear only in subprograms and processes. Although the semantics of a process statement as a whole are different from those in a subprogram, the semantics of individual sequential statements (among them, program flow control statements) are equivalent. Most such constructs have been described in relation to subprograms in the previous chapters. Statements related to flow control that we have not encountered in the examples in previous chapters are the loop statement without iteration scheme, exit statement, and the next statement.

The loop statement without an iteration scheme, i.e., without FOR or WHILE, is an infinite loop. The only way to exit from this loop is to use an exit statement. For example, the loop shown in Figure 8.11 terminates only when x is equal to 25. If this condition does not occur, the looping continues indefinitely.

Next and exit statements can be used within loop statements. A next statement reached by the program flow within a loop causes the rest of the loop to be skipped

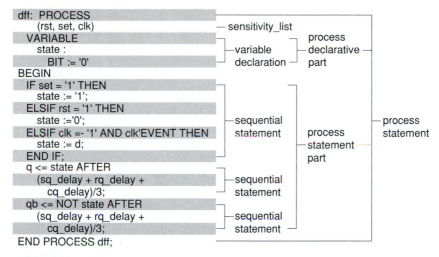

```
dff: PROCESS
      (rst, set, clk)                          — sensitivity_list
      VARIABLE                                                  process
         state :                              ┌variable       ┌declarative —
             BIT := '0'                       └ declaration   └ part
BEGIN
      IF set = '1' THEN                       ┐
         state := '1';                        │
      ELSIF rst = '1' THEN                    ┤sequential        ┐process
         state :='0';                         │statement         │statement
      ELSIF clk =- '1' AND clk'EVENT THEN     │        process   │
         state := d;                          │        ┤statement │
      END IF;                                 ┘        └ part     │
      q <= state AFTER                        ┐                   │
         (sq_delay + rq_delay +               ┤sequential         │
             cq_delay)/3;                     ┘statement          │
      qb <= NOT state AFTER                    ┐                  │
         (sq_delay + rq_delay +                ┤sequential        │
             cq_delay)/3;                      ┘statement         ┘
END PROCESS dff;
```

FIGURE 8.10
Syntax details of a process statement with sensitivity list, declarative part, and statement part.

```
┌long_running : LOOP
│    ...
│    IF  x  =  25  THEN  EXIT;
│    END  IF;
│    ...
└END  LOOP  long_running;
```

FIGURE 8.11
Partial code for demonstrating exiting from a potentially infinite loop.

and the next iteration to be taken. An exit statement causes the termination of the loop that it applies to. Both statements can be used optionally with a loop label and a condition, as presented here:

> NEXT loop_label WHEN condition;

The if statement of Figure 8.11 can be replaced with the exit statement shown here:

> EXIT WHEN x = 25;

If the optional loop label of the next or the exit statements is not included, the next or exit statements apply to their innermost enclosing loop. Inclusion of this label, however, enables the application of these statements to selected outer loops. Consider the partial code in Figure 8.12.

While in the *loop_2* loop, if after the execution of *sequential_ statement_4* con-*dition_1* is TRUE, the next statement causes the remainder of *loop_2* and *loop_1* loops

```
loop_1 : FOR i IN 5 TO 25 LOOP
    sequential_statement_1;
    sequential_statement_2;
    loop_2 : WHILE j <= 90 LOOP
        sequential_statement_3;
        sequential_statement_4;
        NEXT loop_1 WHEN condition_1;
        sequential_statement_5;
        sequential_statement_6;
    END LOOP loop_2;
END LOOP loop_1;
```

FIGURE 8.12
Partial code for demonstrating conditional next statements in a loop.

to be skipped, and the next iteration of *loop_1* is taken. Therefore, the value of *i* is incremented and the *sequential_statement_1* is executed after the execution of the next statement.

8.2   ASSERTION STATEMENT

The assertion statement is a useful statement for observing activity in a circuit or defining constraints or conditions in the way a circuit operates. The general format of this statement is:

```
ASSERT assertion_condition REPORT "reporting_message" SEVERITY severity_level;
```

The statement is said to "occur" when the Boolean *assertion_condition* expression becomes FALSE. At this point, the *reporting_message* is issued, and the simulator takes the action specified by the *severity_level* parameter. The latter parameter can be NOTE, WARNING, ERROR or FAILURE. The ERROR or FAILURE severity levels cause the simulation to stop after issuing the *reporting_message* and a simulation error or failure message. The other two *severity_levels* cause appropriate messages to be issued and the simulation to continue. The REPORT keyword and its following *reporting_message*, as well as the SEVERITY keyword and *severity_level*, are optional parts of the assertion statement. If the REPORT is not present, only the system messages are issued, and the absence of the SEVERITY keyword and its accompanying *severity_level* defaults to the ERROR severity level. The exact series of actions taken by different severity level parameters is simulation-dependent.

8.2.1   Sequential Use of Assertion Statements

Sequential and concurrent VHDL bodies can use assertion statements. A sequential assertion statement issues the *reporting_message* if its *assertion_condition* is FALSE when the program flow reaches the statement. Figure 8.13 shows an example illustrating this use of the assertion statement.

```
┌ARCHITECTURE behavioral OF d_sr_flipflop IS
│   │ SIGNAL state : BIT := '0';
├BEGIN
│   ┌dff: PROCESS (rst, set, clk)
│   ├BEGIN
│   │       ┌ASSERT
│   │       │    (NOT (set = '1' AND rst = '1'))
│   │       ├REPORT
│   │       │    "set and rst are both 1"
│   │       └SEVERITY NOTE;
│   │       ┌IF set = '1' THEN
│   │       │    state <= '1' AFTER sq_delay;
│   │       ├ELSIF rst = '1' THEN
│   │       │    state <= '0' AFTER rq_delay;
│   │       ├ELSIF clk = '1' AND clk'EVENT THEN
│   │       │    state <= d AFTER cq_delay;
│   │       └END IF;
│   └END PROCESS dff;
│   │ q <= state;
│   │ qb <= NOT state;
└END behavioral;
```

FIGURE 8.13
A modified *behavioral* architecture of *d_sr_flipflop*, checking for simultaneous assertion of *set* and *rst*.

In the modified *behavioral* architecture of the *d_sr_flipflop* in this figure, the assertion statement checks to see if the *set* and *rst* inputs are simultaneously active. Obviously, this case is undesirable, and a good model should be able to detect it. When simulating this *behavioral* architecture of *d_sr_flipflop*, if *set* and *rst* are both 1 at the same time, the message "set and rst are both 1" is issued and the simulation continues execution with the if statement that follows the assertion statement. The condition in this statement specifies that the statement issues the message when *NOT (set='1' AND rst='1')* becomes FALSE. In other words, the assertion statement occurs when the expression *(set='1' AND rst='1')* becomes TRUE.

Because of the negation associated with the condition of assertion statements, they can be somewhat confusing, so care must be taken when writing this condition. The expression "ASSERT condition ..." reads as "make sure that this condition is satisfied; otherwise, ...". Therefore, it is clear that a good case must be used as the condition of the statement. The problem arises, however, in the many situations where the good cases are too many to list, and it is easier to write the complement of the unwanted case. For checking errors, then, we will always use *ASSERT(NOT(unwanted_cases))*. After cancelling the two negations, this is equivalent to *ASSERT(wanted_cases)*. For cases in which grouping good cases is as easy as grouping unwanted cases, this negation is not necessary. For example, this statement stops the simulation when *numb* becomes negative:

```
ASSERT numb >= 0;
```

8.2.2 Concurrent Assertion Statements

For cases where violation of constraints must be continuously checked and reported, concurrent assertion statements should be used. These cases include checking of timing constraints such as pulse width, setup time, and hold time. A concurrent assertion statement can be placed in the statement part of an architecture or in the statement part of an entity declaration; we will show the latter shortly. In either case, it is observed at all times and it occurs when an event causes its condition to become FALSE.

Figure 8.14 shows setup and hold times for a positive edge trigger clocked D-type flip-flop. The setup time is the minimum required time between changes on the data input and the triggering edge of the clock. An expression for checking this timing constraint can be based on this statement:

> When (clock changes from zero to 1)$^{--1}$, if the (data input has not been stable at least for the amount of the setup time)$^{--2}$, then a setup time violation has occurred.

The VHDL expression corresponding to this statement is:

```
(clock = '1' AND   NOT clock'STABLE)--1
AND
(NOT data'STABLE (setup_time))--2
```

The numbered parentheses sets around the above statements indicate the corresponding VHDL code in the expression. The setup time is violated when the expression becomes TRUE or when its complement becomes FALSE. Thus, the assertion statement for checking and reporting a setup time violation should use the *assertion_condition* shown here:

> NOT ((clock = '1' AND   NOT clock'STABLE) AND (NOT data'STABLE (setup_time)))

The hold time, also shown in Figure 8.14, is the minimum time that data input of a flip-flop should stay stable after the effective edge of the clock. The following statement describes the circumstances that violate this timing constraint:

> When (there is a change on the data input)$^{--1}$, if the (logic value on the clock is '1')$^{--2}$ and the (clock has got a new value more recent than the amount of hold time)$^{--3}$, then a hold time violation has occurred.

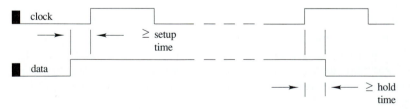

FIGURE 8.14
Setup and hold times for a positive edge trigger D-Type flip-flop.

The VHDL expression based on this statement is:

```
(data'EVENT)--1
AND
(clock = '1')--2
AND
(NOT clock'STABLE (hold_time))--3
```

The condition for the assertion statement that would issue a message when hold time is violated should be as shown here:

```
NOT ((data'EVENT) AND (clock = '1') AND (NOT clock'STABLE (hold_time)))
```

Figure 8.15 shows a new entity declaration for the *d_sr_flipflop* that was first described in Figure 8.7. This entity declaration uses *setup* and *hold* generic timing parameters. In the statement part of this entity declaration, two assertion statements check for setup and hold time violations. Each statement issues an appropriate message if a violation occurs, and also causes the issuance of a system warning message.

The effect of placing these statements in the statement part of the entity declaration is exactly the same as using them in the statement part of an architecture for this entity. The difference is that the statements in the entity statement part apply to all architectures, rather than the one that contains them. For completeness, the *behavioral* architecture of Figure 8.13 is also included in Figure 8.15. This description is a fairly complete model for a rising edge D-type flip-flop with asynchronous set and reset inputs.

We have shown that assertion statements can be used in concurrent and sequential bodies of VHDL. It must be noted, however, that sequential assertion statements execute only when program flow reaches them. For example, if an assertion statement for checking the minimum pulse width on the *d* input is placed in the *dff* process statement in Figure 8.15, in most cases it fails to report violations of this kind. This is because the *dff* process is not sensitive to this input and glitches on *d* do not activate this process. This will not be seen by the assertion statement, so the glitches go undetected.

8.3   SEQUENTIAL WAIT STATEMENTS

The wait statement is a highly behavioral construct for modeling delays, handshaking, and hardware dependencies. This statement comes in four different forms and can be used only in procedures and processes that do not have the optional sensitivity list. When a program flow reaches a wait statement, the process or procedure that encloses it is suspended. The sequential body resumes after the conditions specified by the wait statement are met.

Four forms of the wait statement are shown here:

```
WAIT  FOR    waiting_time;
WAIT  ON     waiting_sensitivity_list;
WAIT  UNTIL  waiting_condition;
WAIT;
```

```
ENTITY d_sr_flipflop IS
    GENERIC (sq_delay, rq_delay, cq_delay : TIME := 6 NS;
             setup, hold : TIME := 4 NS);
    PORT (d, set, rst, clk : IN BIT; q, qb : OUT BIT);
BEGIN
    ASSERT
        (NOT (clk = '1' AND clk'EVENT AND NOT d'STABLE(setup) ))
    REPORT
        "setup time violation"
    SEVERITY WARNING;
    ASSERT
        (NOT (d'EVENT AND clk = '1' AND NOT clk'STABLE(hold) ))
    REPORT
        "Hold time violation"
    SEVERITY WARNING;
END d_sr_flipflop;
--
ARCHITECTURE behavioral OF d_sr_flipflop IS
    SIGNAL state : BIT := '0';
BEGIN
    dff: PROCESS (rst, set, clk)
    BEGIN
        ASSERT
            (NOT (set = '1' AND rst = '1'))
        REPORT
            "set and rst are both 1"
        SEVERITY NOTE;
        IF set = '1' THEN
            state <= '1' AFTER sq_delay;
        ELSIF rst = '1' THEN
            state <= '0' AFTER rq_delay;
        ELSIF clk = '1' AND clk'EVENT THEN
            state <= d AFTER cq_delay;
        END IF;
    END PROCESS dff;
    q <= state;
    qb <= NOT state;
END behavioral;
```

FIGURE 8.15
A complete D-flip-flop description, using assertion statements for illegal set-reset combinations, and setup and hold time violations.

WAIT FOR causes suspension of a sequential body until the *waiting_time* elapses. The suspension caused by WAIT ON is resumed when an event occurs on any of the signals in the *waiting_sensitivity_list*. If a sequential body is suspended by a WAIT UNTIL, that body is resumed when the Boolean *waiting_condition* turns from FALSE to TRUE. If the flow of program reaches a WAIT UNTIL when the *waiting_condition* is TRUE, suspension occurs, and resumption does not occur until condition turns from TRUE to FALSE and then from FALSE to TRUE. The fourth form of wait statement, WAIT, suspends a process forever.

The sensitivity list of a process statement is equivalent to a WAIT ON statement placed at the end of the statement part of the process. The *waiting_sensitivity_list* in this statement is the list of signals that would appear in the process sensitivity list. Therefore, the sensitivity list provides a simple, yet limited way of suspending and activating a process; the more general method is the use of wait statements. The two methods cannot be combined.

8.3.1   A Behavioral State Machine

Chapter 7 presented two methods for describing state machines. A more behavioral method that uses process statements and wait constructs is shown here. The example we use is the Moore implementation of the 1011 detector discussed in the previous chapter, whose state diagram is shown in Figure 8.16. As shown in this diagram, the output becomes '1' and stays '1' for a complete clock cycle when the 1011 sequence appears on the x input on four consecutive clock edges.

Figure 8.17 shows the VHDL description for this sequence detector. The enumeration literals of the *state* type, declared in the declarative part of the *behavioral_state_machine* architecture of *moore_detector*, correspond to the state designators of the state machine. The *current* signal of *state* type is initialized to *reset* and it is used in the statement part of this architecture for containing the present active state of the machine. A process statement forms the statement part and a case statement in

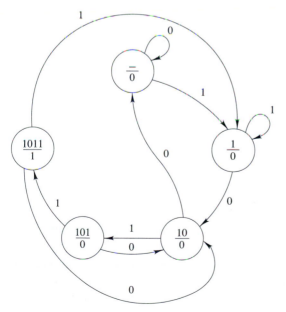

FIGURE 8.16

A Moore machine state diagram for detecting 1011 sequence.

```
ENTITY moore_detector IS
    PORT (x, clk : IN BIT; z : OUT BIT);
END moore_detector;
    --
ARCHITECTURE behavioral_state_machine OF moore_detector IS
    TYPE state IS (reset, got1, got10, got101, got1011);
    SIGNAL current : state := reset;
BEGIN
    PROCESS
    BEGIN
        CASE current IS
        WHEN reset =>
            WAIT UNTIL clk = '1';
            IF x = '1' THEN current <= got1;
            ELSE current <= reset;
            END IF;
        WHEN got1 =>
            WAIT UNTIL clk = '1';
            IF x = '0' THEN current <= got10;
            ELSE current <= got1;
            END IF;
        WHEN got10 =>
            WAIT UNTIL clk = '1';
            IF x = '1' THEN current <= got101;
            ELSE current <= reset;
            END IF;
        WHEN got101 =>
            WAIT UNTIL clk = '1';
            IF x = '1' THEN current <= got1011;
            ELSE current <= got10;
            END IF;
        WHEN got1011 =>
            z <= '1';
            WAIT UNTIL clk = '1';
            IF x = '1' THEN current <= got1;
            ELSE current <= got10;
            END IF;
        END CASE;
        WAIT FOR 1 NS;
        z <= '0';
    END PROCESS;
END behavioral_state_machine;
```

FIGURE 8.17
VHDL description of the 1011 sequence detector in Figure 8.16, using process and wait statements.

this part contains one case alternative for each of the states of the state machine. A case alternative sets the value of the output (if any), waits for the edge of the clock, and depending on the inputs, sets the *current* signal to the next active state.

Following the case statement, a wait statement suspends the enclosing process statement for 1 ns, and after resumption of this process the z output is set to zero and the case statement is executed again. The reason for this 1 ns wait is to create a delay between setting *current* and using it in the case expression. Since *current* is a signal, the new value assigned to it will be available in the next simulation cycle (δ time later), and the 1 ns delay gives enough time for the new value to settle and be used by the case expression. If this wait statement were not present, assigning a new value to *current* and re-execution of the case statement would take place during the same simulation cycle, causing the old value of *current* to be reused by the case expression. The following statement instead of the "WAIT FOR 1 NS;" statement would also serve this purpose:

```
WAIT  ON    current 'TRANSACTION  ;
```

The former, however, provides a realistic time delay between state and output changes. Following the wait statement, the assignment of '0' to the output signal, z, is necessary to reset this signal so that it can conditionally be assigned a '1' depending on the next state of the machine. Individual states had to have specific assignment of values to the output if the statement assigning '0' to z was to be removed.

The above description style is an accurate representation for state machines. It is easy to read, can be used for Mealy and Moore machine representations, and uses convenient behavioral constructs for state transitions. However, due to the use of a case statement and a single signal for active state representation, only one state can be active simultaneously. We use the style with concurrent block statements, presented in Chapter 7, when multiple active states are needed.

The above discussion illustrates the use of wait statements for describing state machines, and demonstrates several complex timing issues of VHDL. Because the individual states of the style presented here are controlled by separate wait statements, this description offers flexibility in the control of timing beyond standard state machine requirements. Alternatively, a state machine can be more easily described by a process statement that is sensitive to the events on the clock. In the statement part of such a process, an if statement detects the correct edge of the clock, and a case statement similar to the one in Figure 8.17 implements the branching of the states. Assignment of values to the output should be done outside of the process statement using a conditional signal assignment. In such a description, detection of the clock edge is done only once outside of the case statement, instead of within each state as it was done in Figure 8.17. This issue is dealt with in Problem 8.4 at the end of this chapter. Problem 8.5 deals with adding reset capability to a state machine. For this purpose, an if statement, following the case statement can be used to set the current state of the machine to a reset state if a resetting condition is satisfied.

8.3.2 Two Phase Clocking

A very common clocking scheme in MOS circuits is two-phase nonoverlapping clocking. This scheme insures input to output isolation in master-slave registers, and eliminates many charge sharing problems. Figure 8.18 shows generation of a second clock phase, *c2*, from a periodic first phase, *c1*. We are assuming the period of *c1* is 1 us with a 500 ns duty cycle.

The *phase2* process in this figure stays suspended while *c1* is '1'. Ten nanoseconds after *c1* changes from '1' to '0', *c2* becomes '1', and the process goes into suspension again for 480 ns. While suspended, *c2* stays at '1'. When *phase2* resumes, it assigns a zero to *c2*, and becomes suspended again, waiting for *c1* to change from '1' to '0'. This process continues until it is suspended indefinitely due to lack of events on *c1*. Figure 8.19 shows a timing diagram that results from a periodic waveform on *c1*.

8.3.3 Implementing Handshaking

Asynchronous communication between systems is done by handshaking. Handshaking refers to the signaling that occurs between two systems as one transfers data to the other. When a system prepares data for transfer to another system, the sending system informs the receiving system that the data is ready. When the receiving system accepts the data, it informs the sending system it has received it.

Handshaking can be fully responsive or partially responsive. In a fully responsive process, all events on the handshaking signals of one system occur in response

```
...
phase2: PROCESS
BEGIN
     WAIT  UNTIL  c1  =  '0';
     WAIT  FOR  10  NS;
     c2  <=  '1';
     WAIT  FOR  480  NS;
     c2  <=  '0';
END  PROCESS  phase2;
...
```

FIGURE 8.18
Partial code for generation of second phase of a two phase nonoverlapping clocking.

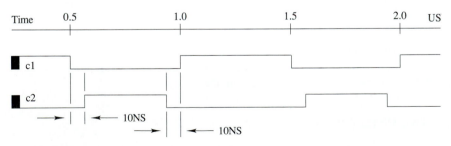

FIGURE 8.19
Two nonoverlapping phases of clock, *c2* generated by the *phase2* process in Figure 8.18.

to events on the signals of the other system as they communicate. Handshaking requires at least one signal for this specific purpose and can use as many as six for a two-way, fully responsive communication. Exchanging data without handshaking is called nonresponsive communication. Figure 8.20 shows a fully responsive two-line handshaking process for transfering data on *data_lines* from system *A* to system *B*.

System *A* places valid data on *data_lines* and informs system *B* of this new data by raising the *data_ready* line. When system *B* is ready to accept data, it does so, and it informs system *A* that it has accepted data by raising *accepted*. When system *A* sees that data on *data_lines* are no longer needed by system *B*, it removes valid data from *data_lines*, and lowers the *data_ready* line. System *B* acknowledges this, and informs system *A* that it can accept new data by lowering its *accepted* signal.

A variation of this system can include a third handshaking line used by system *B* to inform system *A* that it is ready to accept new data. Fully responsive handshaking is performed when no assumptions are possible as to the relative speed of the communicating systems. Other less responsive handshakings can be done in which the *data_ready* line returns to zero after a fixed amount of time, instead of waiting for *accepted* to become '1'.

Figure 8.21 shows the corresponding VHDL code for the handshaking process in Figure 8.20. Partial code sections in this figure are sequentially executed by system *A* and *B* when they need to talk to each other. In all forms of handshaking, various forms of wait statements are very useful and descriptive.

For a comprehensive example of modeling handshaking in VHDL, consider *system_i* that works as an interface between *system_a* and *system_b*, as depicted in Figure 8.22. *System_a* uses handshaking to provide 4-bit data, and *system_b* uses handshaking to receive 16-bit data. The interface *system_i* accumulates four data nibbles that it receives from *system_a* and it makes a 16-bit data available to system *system_b*. The first nibble received from *system_a* forms the least significant four bits of the data that becomes available for *system_b*. *System_i* is capable of talking to *system_a* and *system_b* simultaneously. It should be possible for *system_i* to be involved in transmitting the previously accumulated data to *system_b*, while accumulating a new 16-bit data from *system_a*.

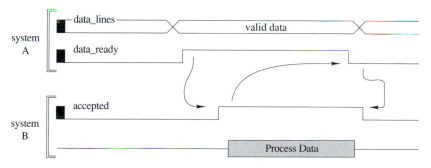

FIGURE 8.20
Signals of a fully responsive two-line handshaking.

```
          ⌈   -- start the following when ready to send data
          |   data_lines <= newly_prepared_data;
System    |   data_ready <= '1';
  A       |   WAIT UNTIL accepted = '1';
          |   data_ready <= '0';
          |   --can use data_lines for other purposes
          ⌊
```

```
          ⌈   -- start the following when ready to accept data
          |   WAIT UNTIL data_ready = '1';
System    |   accepted <= '1';
  B       |   -- start processing the newly received data
          |   WAIT UNTIL data_ready = '0';
          |   accepted <= '0';
          ⌊
```

FIGURE 8.21
VHDL code for fully responsive two line handshaking.

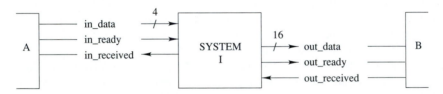

FIGURE 8.22
Interfacing *system_a* and *system_b*. *System_i* uses handshaking to talk to both systems.

When *system_a* has a nibble ready on the *in_data* lines, it places a '1' on the *in_ready* line. The data and the *in_ready* line stay valid until this system sees a '1' on its *in_received* input. The interface *system_i* waits in an idle state looking for *in_ready* to become '1'. When this happens, it receives data from *in_data* and acknowledges that it has received the data by placing a '1' on *in_received*. The interface holds *in_received* active until *in_ready* becomes '0'. On the other side, *system_i* talks to *system_b* by providing data on the *out_data* output bus, and by activating the *out_ready* line, informs the other system of the new data. When *system_b* receives the data, it places a '1' on the *out_received* line, and holds this line active until *system_i* deactivates its *out_ready* output.

The VHDL description for *system_i* is shown in Figure 8.23. This implementation has three handshaking involvements; one for talking to *system_a*, one for talking to *system_b*, and the third for communication between the transmitting and receiving parts of *system_i*.

The *a_talk* process waits for *in_ready* to become '1', it receives data, and it places it in the part of the *word_buffer* indicated by *count*. When this is complete, it indicates that data has been accepted by placing a '1' on *in_received* (statement following END CASE). This line stays active until *system_a* deactivates the *in_ready*

```
ENTITY system_i IS
   PORT (in_data : IN BIT_VECTOR (3 DOWNTO 0);
      out_data : OUT BIT_VECTOR (15 DOWNTO 0);
      in_ready, out_received : IN BIT; in_received, out_ready : OUT BIT);
END system_i;
--
ARCHITECTURE waiting OF system_i IS
      SIGNAL buffer_full, buffer_picked : BIT := '0';
      SIGNAL word_buffer : BIT_VECTOR (15 DOWNTO 0);
BEGIN
   a_talk: PROCESS
         VARIABLE count : INTEGER RANGE 0 TO 4 := 0;
   BEGIN
      WAIT UNTIL in_ready = '1';
      count := count + 1;
      CASE count IS
         WHEN 0 => NULL;
         WHEN 1 => word_buffer (03 DOWNTO 00) <= in_data;
         WHEN 2 => word_buffer (07 DOWNTO 04) <= in_data;
         WHEN 3 => word_buffer (11 DOWNTO 08) <= in_data;
         WHEN 4 => word_buffer (15 DOWNTO 12) <= in_data;
                     buffer_full <= '1';
                     WAIT UNTIL buffer_picked = '1';
                     buffer_full <= '0';
                     count := 0;
      END CASE;
      in_received <= '1';
      WAIT UNTIL in_ready = '0';
      in_received <= '0';
   END PROCESS a_talk;
   b_talk: PROCESS
   BEGIN
      IF buffer_full = '0' THEN WAIT UNTIL buffer_full = '1'; END IF;
      out_data <= word_buffer;
      buffer_picked <= '1';
      WAIT UNTIL buffer_full = '0';
      buffer_picked <= '0';
      out_ready <= '1';
      WAIT UNTIL out_received = '1';
      out_ready <= '0';
   END PROCESS b_talk;
END waiting;
```

FIGURE 8.23
VHDL model for the interface between systems *A* and *B* in Figure 8.22.

line. In accumulating data in the *word_buffer*, if the data received is the forth nibble (choice 4 of the case alternative), the *a_talk* process asserts the *buffer_full* internal handshaking signal to indicate that data is ready to be transmitted to *system_b*. This line stays active until the buffer has been received by the *b_talk* process as indicated by the *buffer_picked* signal issued by *b_talk*. When the buffer is picked, the nibble count is set to zero and *word_buffer* starts being refilled. While waiting for the buffer to be picked, *system_i* keeps *system_a* waiting by not issuing the *in_received* signal.

The *b_talk* process waits for a full buffer. This waiting is implemented by the first if statement in this process which causes the process to continue if *buffer_full* is '1'. The if statement is used so that the WAIT UNTIL does not hold the process, if *buffer_full* is already '1' when this statement is reached. Remember that the "WAIT UNTIL buffer_full = '1'" statement resumes the process only when *buffer_full* changes from '0' to '1'. When this process finds a full buffer, it assigns it to the *out_data* output lines, and causes the resumption of *a_talk* by setting *buffer_picked* to '1'. This line returns to zero only when *a_talk* acknowledges that it knows a buffer has been received. At this time, *b_talk* communicates with *system_b* for sending the 16-bit data on *out_data* to this system. When *system_b* acknowledges the reception of data by raising its *out_received* line, the *b_talk* process deactivates *out_ready* and returns to the beginning of its statement part.

In the *a_talk* process, the *count* variable keeps a count of the number of nibbles received. Since *count* is not needed across processes, it is declared as a variable in *a_talk*. According to the declaration of this variable, the only values it can take are integers between 0 and 4. The program flow never reaches the case statement when *count* is zero and considering this alternative is unnecessary. However, the case statement requires coverage of all choices or OTHERS to be used; therefore, we have covered the *count* value of zero by a NULL case alternative.

8.4 FORMATTED ASCII I/O OPERATIONS

Basic unformatted input/output to external files was described in Chapter 6. The methods described used primitive VHDL file operations and can be used with any data type. VHDL also supports a TEXTIO package which includes types and procedures for ASCII line oriented input or output. This package is in the STD Library, and is shown in Appendix F.

The TEXTIO package defines a LINE type which is used for all file readings and writings. The file type provided by this package is TEXT and it defines files of ASCII strings. Procedures defined in this package for handling input/output are READ, READLINE, WRITE, and WRITELINE. In addition, function ENDFILE provides a mechanism for checking the status of a file.

The READLINE(f,l) procedure reads a line of file *f* and places it in buffer *l*. The READ(l,v,...) reads a value *v* of its type from *l*. The WRITE(l,v,...) writes the value *v* to LINE *l* and WRITELINE(f,l) writes *l* to file *f*. Function ENDFILE(f) returns TRUE if the end of FILE is reached. READ and WRITE procedures are valid for values of types BIT, BIT_VECTOR, BOOLEAN, CHARACTER, INTEGER, REAL,

STRING, and TIME. Other parameters of these procedures include orientation, size, and unit if *v* is of type TIME.

For reading from a file, after READLINE reads a line, data can be extracted from the line (or buffer) using READ. This can continue until the entire buffer is consumed. For writing to a file, a LINE type variable is filled with data using WRITE and the line is written to the file using WRITELINE.

8.4.1 Basic Screen Output

In our first ASCII I/O example, we develop a debugging mechanism for resolution functions and apply this mechanism to one of the resolution functions in Chapter 7. Knowing the driving values of a resolved signal's drivers gives an insight into a resolution function for debugging and learning purposes.

Figure 8.24 shows the *one_of* resolution function we used to implement a Mealy state machine in Chapter 7 (*singular_state_machine* of Figure 7.36). The double vertical lines in this figure indicate the new code being added to observe the active drivers of the signals that are resolved by this resolution function.

The *one_of* function uses types and procedures from the TEXTIO package in the standard STD library and these utilities are made visible to it by the application of the use statement in the description in Figure 8.24. In the declarative part of this function, variable *l* of type LINE is declared to act as a buffer for outputting strings.

```
USE STD.TEXTIO.ALL;
...
TYPE state IS (reset, got1, got10, got101);
TYPE state_vector IS ARRAY (NATURAL RANGE <>) OF state;
FUNCTION one_of (sources : state_vector) RETURN state IS
    VARIABLE l : LINE;
    FILE flush : TEXT IS OUT "/dev/tty";
    VARIABLE state_string : STRING (1 TO 7);
BEGIN
    FOR i IN sources'RANGE LOOP
        CASE sources(i) IS
            WHEN reset  => state_string := "reset  ";
            WHEN got1   => state_string := "got1   ";
            WHEN got10  => state_string := "got10  ";
            WHEN got101 => state_string := "got101 ";
        END CASE;
        WRITE (l, state_string, LEFT, 7);
    END LOOP;
    WRITELINE (flush, l);
    RETURN sources(sources'LEFT);
END one_of;
```

FIGURE 8.24
A resolution function that writes its active drivers each time it is called.

The *flush* file is declared as an output text file with the logical file name of */dev/tty*. In the Unix operating system, this logical name refers to the standard output or screen. A for loop in the statement part of the *one_of* function translates all the active states to their corresponding strings. These strings are appended to the end of the *l* buffer by the WRITE procedure call. The keyword LEFT specifies the left justification of this string when it is appended to *l* and the number 7 specifies its length in characters. When strings corresponding to all active states have been appended to *l*, this buffer is displayed by the WRITELINE procedure call.

When the *one_of* resolution function is called, the file declaration in its declarative part is initialized, and the list of active states is displayed. A time stamp can also be generated by writing the value returned by the NOW function to *l*. This provides additional information as to when the function is called and is also a useful debugging feature. The example that follows illustrates this.

8.4.2 A Display Procedure

The procedure shown in Figure 8.25 has two signal parameters. When called, it displays the current simulation time and the new value of its signal parameter that has just changed.

The declarative part of this procedure is the same as that in Figure 8.24. The file declaration initializes *flush* every time the procedure is called. In its statement part, a call to the WRITE procedure writes the current simulation time, sized to eight characters and using nanosecond units, to *l*. The if statement following this procedure call appends the new value of the signal that has had an event and a *filler* string to *l*. The filler string is used in place of the value of the signal that has been stable. At the end, the WRITELINE procedure call writes this assembled buffer (*l*) to the screen.

```
PROCEDURE display (SIGNAL value1, value2 : BIT) IS
   FILE flush : TEXT IS OUT "/dev/tty";
   VARIABLE filler : STRING (1 TO 3) := " ..";
   VARIABLE l : LINE;
BEGIN
   WRITE (l, NOW, RIGHT, 8, NS);
   IF value1'EVENT THEN
      WRITE (l, value1, RIGHT, 3);
      WRITE (l, filler, LEFT, 0);
   ELSE
      WRITE (l, filler, LEFT, 0);
      WRITE (l, value2, RIGHT, 3);
   END IF;
   WRITELINE (flush, l);
END display;
```

FIGURE 8.25
A display procedure for displaying time and value of a signal that has just changed.

Using 0 for the size parameter in the procedure call that writes *filler* to *l* results in a minimum use of space for this string.

Figure 8.26 shows a two-phase clock generator that uses the *phase2* process of Section 8.3.2 for generating a second clock phase, *c2*, from *c1*, and uses the *display* procedure for displaying these nonoverlapping clock phases. The use statement at the beginning of this description provides the *display* procedure with its needed visibility into the standard TEXTIO package. A concurrent procedure call in the statement part of the *input_output* architecture of *two_phase_clock* entity calls the *display* procedure when an event occurs on *c1* or *c2*.

8.4.3   Simulation Report

In order to have the ability to to generate a simulation report in which new output lines are appended to the end of a file, we must insure that the file initialization, unlike the previous two examples, is done only once at the beginning of the report generation. This implies that for this purpose, a file declaration must be placed in a process statement or in the statement part of an architecture, or if declared in a subprogram, the entire report must be generated in one subprogram call. The same thing applies to an input file. Reinitialization of an input file causes the next READLINE to be done from its beginning.

For the procedure in Figure 8.25 to write into a file, it either has to be called from a process statement with a declared file passed to it, or else the task this procedure

```
USE STD.TEXTIO.ALL;
ENTITY two_phase_clock IS END two_phase_clock;
--
ARCHITECTURE input_output OF two_phase_clock IS
   -- procedure of Figure 8.25 goes here
   SIGNAL c1 : BIT := '1';
   SIGNAL c2 : BIT := '0';
BEGIN
   phase1: c1 <= NOT c1 AFTER 500 NS WHEN NOW < 4 US ELSE c1;
   phase2: PROCESS
   BEGIN
      WAIT UNTIL c1 = '0';
      WAIT FOR 10 NS;
      c2 <= '1';
      WAIT FOR 480 NS;
      c2 <= '0';
   END PROCESS phase2;
   display (c1, c2);
END input_output;
```

FIGURE 8.26
Using *display* procedure for displaying two nonoverlapping clock phases.

performs should be placed in a process statement. We have used the latter alternative for generating a simulation report for the *two-phase-clock* circuit.

The description in Figure 8.27 repeats the clock description and adds to it the *writing* process for writing BIT values of *c1* and *c2* to the logical *clock.out* file. This new section of code is made to stand out by the double vertical lines. The *flush* file is initialized at the beginning of the simulation and stays open for the entire simulation run. For every event on *c1* or *c2*, a new line is appended to the *clock.out* file. The complete run of the *input-output* architecture of *two-phase-clock* in Figure 8.27 generates the report shown in Figure 8.28 in the *clock.out* file.

Figure 8.29 shows another example for using TEXTIO to generate a simulation report. The example we are using is the familiar *two-phase-clock* circuit, and in the

```
USE STD.TEXTIO.ALL;
ENTITY two_phase_clock IS END two_phase_clock;
--
ARCHITECTURE input_output OF two_phase_clock IS
    SIGNAL c1 : BIT := '1';
    SIGNAL c2 : BIT := '0';
BEGIN
    phase1: c1 <= NOT c1 AFTER 500 NS WHEN NOW < 4 US ELSE c1;
    phase2: PROCESS
    BEGIN
        WAIT UNTIL c1 = '0';
        WAIT FOR 10 NS;
        c2 <= '1';
        WAIT FOR 480 NS;
        c2 <= '0';
    END PROCESS phase2;
    writing: PROCESS (c1, c2)
        FILE flush : TEXT IS OUT "clock.out";
        VARIABLE filler : STRING (1 TO 3) := " ..";
        VARIABLE I : LINE;
    BEGIN
        WRITE (I, NOW, RIGHT, 8, NS);
        IF c1'EVENT THEN
            WRITE (I, c1, RIGHT, 3);
            WRITE (I, filler, LEFT, 0);
        ELSE
            WRITE (I, filler, LEFT, 0);
            WRITE (I, c2, RIGHT, 3);
        END IF;
        WRITELINE (flush, I);
    END PROCESS writing;
END input_output;
```

FIGURE 8.27
The *input-output* architecture of *two-phase-clock* circuit with a process statement for generating a simulation report.

0	ns	..	0
500	ns	0	..
510	ns	..	1
990	ns	..	0
1000	ns	1	..
1500	ns	0	..
1510	ns	..	1
1990	ns	..	0
2000	ns	1	..
2500	ns	0	..
2510	ns	..	1
2990	ns	..	0
3000	ns	1	..
3500	ns	0	..
3510	ns	..	1
3990	ns	..	0
4000	ns	1	..

FIGURE 8.28
File generated by running the *input_output* architecture in Figure 8.27.

figure, double vertical lines indicate new code. The *input_output* architecture of this figure generates an ASCII time plot with 5 ns time resolution.

A *print_tick* signal activates the *plotting* process every 5 ns. The output file (*clock4.out*), a header (*header*), *l*, and the *append_wave_slice* procedure are declared in the declarative part of the process. In its statement part, at the start of simulation when NOW equals zero, the header line is written to the beginning of the output file. After this line, every 5 nanoseconds a new line is written to the output file containing the simulation time and string representation for the values and transitions of *c1* and *c2*. String representations are appended to *l* by the *append_wave_slice* procedure. The "| " and " |" strings represent low and high, respectively; they are low and high wave slices if turned 90° in the counterclockwise direction. The transition strings are used when the last event on the signal associated with the *s* parameter of the *append_wave_slice* procedure is more recent than the print resolution. This is done by the first if statement in the statement part of this procedure. The "s'LAST_VALUE /= s" expression in the condition part of the if statement causes "| " and " |" strings to be used at the beginning of simulation, while s'LAST_EVENT continues to be zero and less than the print resolution.

Figure 8.30 shows a portion of the file generated by running the description of Figure 8.29. This file can easily be turned into a continuous waveform by simple editing on a personal computer. VHDL allows the first 128 ASCII characters, but does not support ASCII extensions, which include line and edge segments ($| \llcorner \neg \ulcorner \lrcorner$). Such characters are needed for a continuous waveform.

Figure 8.29 illustrates a method by which a subprogram can be used to input or output to an already declared open file (file *flush* in that figure). Alternatively, a file object can be passed to a function or procedure as a subprogram parameter. The following statements illustrate subprogram declarations for passing file objects to

```
ARCHITECTURE input_output OF two_phase_clock IS
    ...
    SIGNAL print_tick : BIT := '0';
    CONSTANT print_resolution : TIME := 5 NS;
BEGIN
    --phase1: and phase2: processes remain the same as
              those shown in Figure~8.27.
    print_tick <= NOT print_tick AFTER print_resolution WHEN NOW <= 2 US
                  ELSE print_tick;
    plotting: PROCESS (print_tick, c1, c2)
        FILE flush : TEXT IS OUT "clock4.out";
        VARIABLE header : STRING (1 TO 18) := "          c1    c2   ";
        VARIABLE l : LINE;
        PROCEDURE append_wave_slice (SIGNAL s : BIT) IS
            CONSTANT lo_value : STRING (1 TO 3) := "|  ";
            CONSTANT hi_value : STRING (1 TO 3) := "  |";
            CONSTANT lo_to_hi : STRING (1 TO 3) := ".-+";
            CONSTANT hi_to_lo : STRING (1 TO 3) := "+-.";
        BEGIN
            IF s'LAST_EVENT < print_resolution AND s'LAST_VALUE /= s
            THEN
                IF s = '1' THEN
                    WRITE (l, lo_to_hi, RIGHT, 5);
                ELSE
                    WRITE (l, hi_to_lo, RIGHT, 5);
                END IF;
            ELSE
                IF s = '1' THEN
                    WRITE (l, hi_value, RIGHT, 5);
                ELSE
                    WRITE (l, lo_value, RIGHT, 5);
                END IF;
            END IF;
        END append_wave_slice;
    BEGIN
        IF NOW = 0 US THEN
            WRITE (l, header, LEFT, 0);
            WRITELINE (flush, l);
        END IF;
        WRITE (l, NOW, RIGHT, 8, NS);
        append_wave_slice (c1);
        append_wave_slice (c2);
        WRITELINE (flush, l);
    END PROCESS plotting;
END input_output;
```

FIGURE 8.29
Generating an ASCII plot file with five ns time resolution.

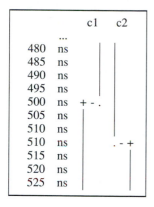

FIGURE 8.30
Partial plot generated by the *plotting* process of Figure 8.29.

procedures for reading or writing from open files:

```
PROCEDURE reading_from_file (VARIABLE in_file : IN TEXT;
                              ... other parameters ...);

PROCEDURE writing_to_file (VARIABLE out_file : OUT TEXT;
                              ... other parameters ...);
```

This method offers a more modular description for subprograms using external files. Note that in this case, the variable of type LINE can be declared in the subprogram and calls to READLINE or WRITELINE should be done in the corresponding subprograms.

8.5   MSI BASED DESIGN

This section shows the design of an overall system using standard parts. The parts we use are from the 74LS00 logic family while the example circuit is a variation of the sequential comparator in Chapter 7.

The design strategy is as follows: after an initial understanding of the functionality of the circuit we are to design, we partition it into several functional components and the components are mapped into standard parts. If such a mapping is not possible, more partitioning is done. Once the standard parts are chosen, they are assembled to perform the necessary functions and wired together to form the implementation of the system.

8.5.1   Top Level Partitioning

The circuit shown in the block diagram in Figure 8.31 keeps a modulo-16 count of consecutive equal data bytes on *data_in*. It has synchronous active low clear and load inputs, *clear_bar* and *load_bar*. The *clear_bar* input clears the output count and the *load_bar* loads the *count_in* into the counter.

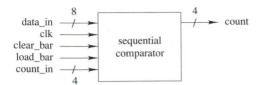

FIGURE 8.31
Block diagram of the sequential comparator circuit.

Figure 8.32 shows the partitioning of this circuit into a register, a comparator pair, and a counter. The register component keeps the most recent data byte. The comparator pair compares the incoming data on *data_in* with the old data in the register and asserts its output if the two data bytes are equal. This output enables the synchronous counting of the counter.

The MSI components that most closely correspond to this partitioning are the 74LS85 4-bit magnitude comparator, the 74LS377 8-bit register, and the 74LS163 4-bit binary counter, all shown in Figure 8.33.

The 74LS85 has three outputs that indicate the relation of values of the 4-bit inputs. The $P<Q$ outputs become '1' when input P is less than input Q, likewise the $P>Q$ output becomes '1' when P is greater than Q. When the two inputs are equal, the values on $<$, $=$, and $>$ inputs appear on their corresponding output lines.

The 74LS377 is a positive edge trigger 8-bit register with an active low enable input. If this input is low on the edge of the clock, data is clocked into the register.

The 74LS163 is a 4-bit binary counter with a synchronous active low parallel load and reset inputs. The counting is enabled when loading is disabled and count enable inputs $G3$ and $G4$ are high. When the count reaches 15, the $5CT=15$ output becomes '1' and the next clock starts the count from 0.

8.5.2   Description of Components

For describing the necessary components of the sequential comparator circuit, and in general for describing any of the 74LS parts, we use the *qit* type of the *basic_utilities* package for the logic value system. The 'Z' value of this system is needed to describe components with three-state outputs, and the 'X' value can be used to show illegal, unknown, or uninitialized logic values. We have extended the *basic_utilities* package

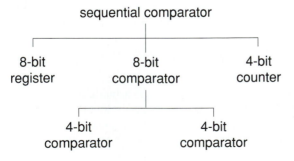

FIGURE 8.32
Partitioning sequential comparator circuit into smaller functional components.

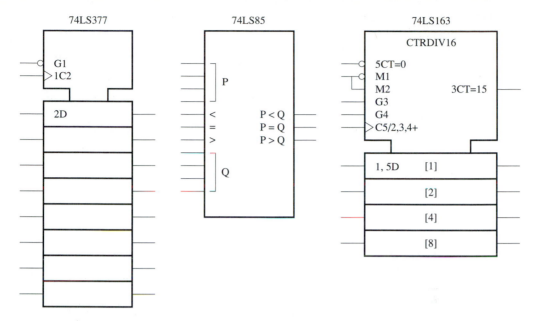

FIGURE 8.33
Standard MSI parts for the implementation of sequential comparator according to the partitioning of Figure 8.32.

to include *qit* conversion procedures and other necessary utilities. The final form of this package is shown in Appendix A.

The VHDL description for the 74LS85 4-bit magnitude comparator is shown in Figure 8.34. Unlike the comparator descriptions in Chapter 4, this description is purely behavioral and its functionality rather than its hardware details is evident from its model. The *qit2int* procedure in *basic_utilities* package converts *qit* type inputs to integers so that the relational operators of VHDL ($= < > >= <= \not=$) can be used for their comparison. Since the outputs are nonresolved and non-guarded signals, they retain their values and only change these values when new values are assigned to them. Therefore, we have assigned new values to all output signals any time an input changes.

Figure 8.35 shows the VHDL description for the 74LS377 register. This description is at the dataflow level and uses a guarded signal assignment for assigning the 8-bit input vector to the *q8* output. An explicit GUARD signal is used instead of the standard practice of using implicit GUARD signal of a block statement. This is done to demonstrate the equivalency of these two methods. GUARD is TRUE on the edge of the clock when *q_bar* (enable input of register) is low. We are assuming the clock is never 'Z', and we have not worked this situation in the edge detection.

A description for the 4-bit binary counter is presented in Figure 8.36. The *counting* process statement in the behavioral description of the *ls163_counter* uses a variable for the internal storage of the count value. When an event occurs on *clk* (any edge), this process becomes active. If this event causes *clk* to be '1' *(rising edge*

```
USE WORK.basic_utilities.ALL;
ENTITY ls85_comparator IS
    GENERIC (prop_delay : TIME := 10 NS);
    PORT (a, b : IN qit_vector (3 DOWNTO 0);   gt, eq, lt : IN qit;
          a_gt_b, a_eq_b, a_lt_b : OUT qit);
END ls85_comparator;
--
ARCHITECTURE behavioral OF ls85_comparator IS
BEGIN
    PROCESS (a, b, gt, eq, lt)
        VARIABLE ai, bi : INTEGER;
    BEGIN
        qit2int (a, ai);
        qit2int (b, bi);
        IF ai > bi THEN
            a_gt_b <= '1' AFTER prop_delay;
            a_eq_b <= '0' AFTER prop_delay;
            a_lt_b <= '0' AFTER prop_delay;
        ELSIF ai < bi THEN
            a_gt_b <= '0' AFTER prop_delay;
            a_eq_b <= '0' AFTER prop_delay;
            a_lt_b <= '1' AFTER prop_delay;
        ELSIF ai = bi THEN
            a_gt_b <= gt AFTER prop_delay;
            a_eq_b <= eq AFTER prop_delay;
            a_lt_b <= lt AFTER prop_delay;
        END IF;
    END PROCESS;
END behavioral;
```

FIGURE 8.34
Behavioral description of the 74LS85 4-Bit magnitude comparator.

```
USE WORK.basic_utilities.ALL;
ENTITY ls377_register IS
    GENERIC (prop_delay : TIME := 7 NS);
    PORT (clk, g_bar : IN qit; d8 : IN qit_vector (7 DOWNTO 0);
          q8 : OUT qit_vector (7 DOWNTO 0));
END ls377_register;
--
ARCHITECTURE dataflow OF ls377_register IS
    SIGNAL GUARD : BOOLEAN;
BEGIN
    GUARD <= NOT clk'STABLE AND clk = '1' AND (g_bar = '0');
    q8 <= GUARDED d8 AFTER prop_delay;
END dataflow;
```

FIGURE 8.35
Dataflow description of the 74LS377 8-bit clocked register.

```
USE  WORK.basic_utilities.ALL;
ENTITY  ls163_counter  IS
   GENERIC (prop_delay : TIME := 12 NS);
   PORT (clk, clr_bar, ld_bar, enp, ent : IN qit;
            abcd : IN qit_vector (3 DOWNTO 0);
            q_abcd : OUT qit_vector (3 DOWNTO 0); rco : OUT qit);
END  ls163_counter;
--

ARCHITECTURE  behavioral  OF  ls163_counter  IS
BEGIN
      counting : PROCESS (clk)
         VARIABLE  internal_count : qit_vector (3 DOWNTO 0) := "0000";
      BEGIN
        IF (clk = '1') THEN
            IF (clr_bar = '0') THEN
                internal_count := "0000";
            ELSIF (ld_bar = '0') THEN
                internal_count := abcd;
            ELSIF (enp = '1' AND ent = '1') THEN
                internal_count := inc (internal_count);
                IF (internal_count = "1111") THEN
                    rco <= '1' AFTER prop_delay;
                ELSE
                    rco <= '0';
                END IF;
            END IF;
            q_abcd <= internal_count AFTER prop_delay;
        END IF;
      END PROCESS counting;
END behavioral;
```

FIGURE 8.36
Behavioral description of the 74LS163 4-bit synchronous counter.

detection), the internal count is either loaded with the input value, set to zero, or incremented depending on load, clear, and enable control lines. The carry out (*rco*) output becomes '1' when the count reaches "1111". The *internal_count* variable is assigned to the *q_abcd* output in the statement part of the *counting* process.

8.5.3   Design Implementation

Figure 8.37 shows the composition aspect of the sequential comparator. This implementation is accomplished according to the partitioning shown in Figure 8.32, which uses two 74LS85 packages for realizing an 8-bit comparator, a 74LS377 for the register, and a 74LS163 for the counter. The figure shows an entity declaration to specify the wiring of components, and a configuration declaration (rounded rectangle) for bindings and generic parameter specifications.

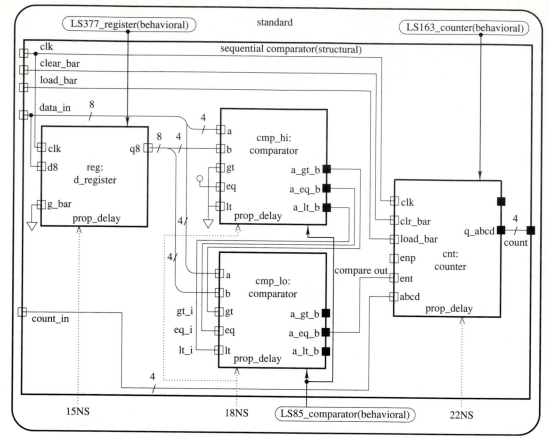

FIGURE 8.37
Composition aspect of the sequential comparator.

The VHDL description for the sequential comparator circuit is shown in Figure 8.38. In the statement part of the entity declaration of *sequential_comparator*, an assertion statement issues warning messages whenever short glitches are observed on the clock input of the circuit. The declarative part of the *structural* architecture of *sequential_comparator* declares the necessary components and the statement part of this architecture specifies their wirings.

The *standard* configuration in Figure 8.39 associates the components of this design with the 74LS parts and specifies timing parameters of these parts. The configured *structural* architecture of the *sequential_comparator* should be referenced by CONFIGURATION *library.standard* where *library* is the name of the library that this configuration is compiled in.

Figure 8.40 shows a simple test bench for verifying the basic operations of *sequential_comparator*. The configuration specification in this figure indicates that the *mfi* instance of *seq_comp* is associated with the configuration declaration in Figure 8.39.

```
USE  WORK.basic_utilities.ALL;
ENTITY  sequential_comparator  IS
    PORT (data_in : IN qit_vector (7 DOWNTO 0);
          clk, clear_bar, load_bar : IN qit;
          count_in : IN qit_vector (3 DOWNTO 0);
          count : OUT qit_vector (3 DOWNTO 0) );
BEGIN
    ASSERT  NOT
        ((clk='0' AND NOT clk'STABLE) AND NOT clk'DELAYED'STABLE (1 US))
        REPORT "Minimum Clock Width Violation" SEVERITY WARNING;
END  sequential_comparator;

--

ARCHITECTURE  structural  OF  sequential_comparator  IS
    COMPONENT  d_register
        PORT (clk, g_bar : IN qit; d8 : IN qit_vector (7 DOWNTO 0);
              q8 : OUT qit_vector (7 DOWNTO 0));
    END COMPONENT;
    COMPONENT  comparator
        PORT (a, b : IN qit_vector (3 DOWNTO 0);   gt, eq, lt : IN qit;
              a_gt_b, a_eq_b, a_lt_b : OUT qit);
    END COMPONENT;
    COMPONENT  counter
        PORT (clk, clr_bar, ld_bar, enp, ent : IN qit;
              abcd : IN qit_vector (3 DOWNTO 0);
              q_abcd : OUT qit_vector (3 DOWNTO 0); rco : OUT qit);
    END COMPONENT;
    SIGNAL gnd : qit := '0'; SIGNAL vdd : qit := '1';
    SIGNAL old_data : qit_vector (7 DOWNTO 0);
    SIGNAL compare_out : qit;
    SIGNAL gt_i, eq_i, lt_i : qit;
BEGIN
    reg: d_register PORT MAP (clk, gnd, data_in, old_data);
    cmp_lo: comparator PORT MAP (data_in (3 DOWNTO 0),
                old_data (3 DOWNTO 0), gnd, vdd, gnd, gt_i, eq_i, lt_i);
    cmp_hi: comparator PORT MAP (data_in (7 DOWNTO 4),
                old_data (7 DOWNTO 4), gt_i, eq_i, lt_i, OPEN, compare_out, OPEN);
    cnt: counter PORT MAP (clk, clear_bar, load_bar, vdd, compare_out,
                count_in, count, OPEN);
END  structural;
```

FIGURE 8.38
Structural implementation of the sequential comparator.

8.6 SUMMARY

This chapter presented descriptions of hardware at the behavioral level and discussed how a process statement can be used to describe the main functionality of a module. In the early part of the chapter, syntax and semantics for various forms of this construct were described. We then showed how process statements are used to describe control-

```
USE WORK.ALL;
CONFIGURATION standard OF sequential_comparator IS
    FOR structural
        FOR reg : d_register
            USE ENTITY WORK.ls377_register (dataflow)
            GENERIC MAP (prop_delay => 15 NS);
        END FOR;
        FOR ALL : comparator
            USE ENTITY WORK.ls85_comparator (behavioral)
            GENERIC MAP (prop_delay => 18 NS);
        END FOR;
        FOR cnt : counter
            USE ENTITY WORK.ls163_counter (behavioral)
            GENERIC MAP (prop_delay => 22 NS);
        END FOR;
    END FOR;
END standard;
```

FIGURE 8.39
Configuring the *structural* architecture of the *sequential_comparator* entity.

```
USE WORK.basic_utilities.ALL;
ENTITY test_sequential_comparator IS END test_sequential_comparator;
--
ARCHITECTURE input_output OF test_sequential_comparator IS
    COMPONENT seq_comp
    PORT (data_in : IN qit_vector (7 DOWNTO 0);
            clk, clear_bar, load_bar : IN qit;
            count_in : IN qit_vector (3 DOWNTO 0);
            count : OUT qit_vector (3 DOWNTO 0) );
    END COMPONENT;
    FOR mfi : seq_comp USE CONFIGURATION WORK.standard;
    SIGNAL data : qit_vector (7 DOWNTO 0);
    SIGNAL ck, cl_bar, ld_bar : qit;
    SIGNAL cnt : qit_vector (3 DOWNTO 0);
    SIGNAL cnt_out : qit_vector (3 DOWNTO 0);
BEGIN
    ck <= NOT ck AFTER 2 US WHEN NOW <= 70 US ELSE ck;
    cl_bar <= '1', '0' AFTER 60 US;
    ld_bar <= '1', '0' AFTER 50 US, '1' AFTER 55 US;
    cnt <= "1111", "1011" AFTER 40 US, "0111" AFTER 55 US;
    data <= "00000000", "01110111" AFTER 3 US, "10101100" AFTER 5 US,
            "01010100" AFTER 25 US;
    mfi : seq_comp PORT MAP (data, ck, cl_bar, ld_bar, cnt, cnt_out);
END input_output;
```

FIGURE 8.40
Test bench for testing the *standard* configuration of *sequential_comparator*.

ling hardware, handshaking, and file I/O. Various forms of wait statements were extensively used in these descriptions.

Although behavioral level constructs of VHDL provide a convenient method for describing very complex hardware, a hardware designer can completely describe a digital circuit without having to use these constructs. Behavioral descriptions can be read and understood by nontechnical managers and others who are not very familiar with VHDL.

REFERENCES

1. "IEEE Standard VHDL Language Reference Manual," IEEE Std 1076-1987, The Institute of Electrical and Electronic Engineers, Inc., 1988.
2. Lipsett, L., C. Schaefer, and C. Ussery, "VHDL: Hardware Description and Design," Klewer Academic Publishing, Boston, 1988.
3. Armstrong, J. R., "Chip-Level Modeling with VHDL," Prentice-Hall Inc., Englewood Cliffs, N.J., 1988.

PROBLEMS

8.1. Write a VHDL description for a D-type flip-flop with a d input, asynchronous set and reset inputs, with q and qb outputs. Use three delay parameters for set-input to q, reset-input to q, and d-input to q (as in Figure 8.7). Your description should have only one *delta* delay between the input and output changes and for the nonzero delay values the delta delay should not appear on the output.

8.2. Write an assertion statement to issue a warning message if a negative pulse shorter than 1 us appears on the input clock.

8.3. Write an assertion statement to issue a warning message if the frequency of the observing clock is lower that 100 KHz. If the clock is too slow in some MOS circuits, the circuit loses information. Assume symmetrical clock pulses.

8.4. An equivalent description for the Moore state machine in Figure 8.17 is shown here in Figure 8.41. Modify this description to one for a Mealy machine detecting the same sequence. Write a test bench and compare the Mealy and Moore machine outputs.

8.5. Write a behavioral description for a Mealy machine that continuously monitors its x input for the 11010 sequence. When the sequence is found, the output becomes '1', and it returns to '0' with the clock. The circuit has a synchronous reset input that resets the circuit to its initial state when it becomes '1'. Use the style presented in Problem 8.4.

8.6. Write a description for an asynchronous circuit that generates one positive pulse for every two complete positive pulses that appear on its input. Use wait statements and processes.

8.7. Write a behavioral description for a divide-by-n circuit in which n is passed to it via a generic parameter. The circuit has an x input and a z output. For every n positive pulse on x, one positive pulse should appear on z.

8.8. Generate two phases of a clock using a single triggering signal as its input as shown below. Width of the short pulses on the triggering signal determine the time that both phases are zero. Use wait and process statements.

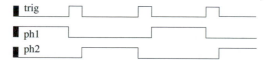

```
ENTITY moore_detector IS
    PORT (x, clk : IN BIT; z : OUT BIT);
END moore_detector;
--
ARCHITECTURE behavioral_state_machine OF moore_detector IS
    TYPE state IS (reset, got1, got10, got101, got1011);
    SIGNAL current : state := reset;
BEGIN
    PROCESS (clk)
    BEGIN
        IF clk = '1' THEN
            CASE current IS
            WHEN reset =>
                IF x = '1' THEN current <= got1;
                ELSE current <= reset;
                END IF;
            WHEN got1 =>
                IF x = '0' THEN current <= got10;
                ELSE current <= got1;
                END IF;
            WHEN got10 =>
                IF x = '1' THEN current <= got101;
                ELSE current <= reset;
                END IF;
            WHEN got101 =>
                IF x = '1' THEN current <= got1011;
                ELSE current <= got10;
                END IF;
            WHEN got1011 =>
                IF x = '1' THEN current <= got1;
                ELSE current <= got10;
                END IF;
            END CASE;
        END IF;
    END PROCESS;
    z <= '1' WHEN current = got1011 ELSE '0';
END behavioral_state_machine;
```

FIGURE 8.41
Moore state machine; equivalent to description given in Figure 8.17.

8.9. Write a behavioral description for modeling an asynchronous circuit. The circuit has inputs x and y, and output z. If a 0-to-1 transition on x is immediately followed by a 1-to-0 transition on y (with no other transitions on either input between these two transitions), the output becomes '1'. The output stays high until either x changes to '0' or y changes to '1'. Use process and wait statements.

8.10. Write a process to output a 4-bit BIT_VECTOR signal in hexadecimal. When an event occurs on the signal, the process becomes active, and it writes the time and the hexadecimal representation of the signal to an output file. To test this process, use it in a description of a synchronous binary up-counter, and output the counter output to a file named *hex.out*. You may use the utilities in the *basic_utilities* package. The statement shows a simple implementation of the binary counter:

```
count <= inc (count) WHEN clk = '1' AND clk'EVENT ELSE count;
```

8.11. Write a procedure (*print_hex*) to convert an unconstrained BIT_VECTOR to a string of hexadecimal digits and print it to a declared file. The subprogram declaration should be specified this way:

```
PROCEDURE print_hex (VARIABLE hex : OUT TEXT;   bin : BIT_VECTOR);
```

In this declaration, *hex* is the open text file object to which writing is to be done, and *bin* is the binary data to be printed. Use this procedure in a description of a synchronous binary up-counter to verify its functioning. Use the method suggested in Problem 8.10 to implement the counter.

8.12. Write a procedure for reading hexadecimal data from a text file. When the procedure is called, it reads a new line from the file. Each line consists of time and hex data separated by a space. The hex data needs to be converted to binary data and then assigned to a target signal parameter in the procedure at the specified time. The subprogram declaration should be stated this way:

```
PROCEDURE assign_hex (SIGNAL bin : OUT BIT_VECTOR;
VARIABLE success : OUT BOOLEAN; VARIABLE hex_data : IN TEXT);
```

When the procedure is called, it reads a line of a file object passed to it via the *hex_data* parameter and assigns the data read from the file to the *bin* signal. If an end-of-file is reached and the reading is not successful, the *success* output of the procedure becomes FALSE. To verify the behavior of this procedure, use it in a process statement and assign the values read from a test file to a signal output in your test description.

8.13. A 4-bit shift register has a *mode*, a *serial_input*, and *clock* inputs as well as four *parallel_input* lines. The four lines of outputs are *parallel_output*. When *mode* is high, the shift register is in the right-shift mode and on the falling edge of the *clock*, the *serial_input* is clocked into the shift register. When *mode* is low, on the falling edge of the *clock*, the *parallel_input* is loaded into the shift register. A) For this shift register, write an *entity* with a *generic* delay. With this delay proper output appears on the *parallel_output* the falling edge of the clock. B) Write the pure *behavioral* architectural body for this shift register. Be sure to use the *generic* delay for the final output.

8.14. Use a process statement to develop a behavioral description for a Toggle flip-flop. The flip-flop has a single *t* input and two *q* and *nq* outputs. After the rising edge of the *t* input, the two outputs will be complemented. The *q* output has a low-to-high propagation delay of *q_tplh* and a high-to-low propagation delay of *q_tphl*. The *nq* output has a low-to-high propagation delay of *nq_tplh* and a high-to-low propagation delay of *nq_tphl*. Pass the propagation delays as generic parameters and use them in your behavioral description. Write the complete description using the entity declaration shown here:

```
ENTITY t_ff IS
    GENERIC( q_tplh, q_tphl, nq_tplh, nq_tphl : TIME);
    PORT (t : IN BIT; q, nq OUT BIT);
END t_ff;
```

8.15. In this problem you will configure and use the T flip-flop of the previous problem. Write a description of an *n*-bit *t_register* using *t_ff*s of Problem 8.14. For the *t_register*, write a configuration declaration that uses the behavioral *t_ff* with *q_tplh, q_tphl, nq_tplh, nq_tphl* delay values of 2 ns, 4 ns, 3 ns, and 5 ns, respectively. The output of a T flip-flop has a frequency half of that of its input. Two cascaded T flip-flops can be used as a divide by four circuit. Use two configured *t_register*s to build a parallel 8-bit divide-by-4 circuit.

8.16. In this problem you will use a 10 value logic system of integers ranging between 0 and 9. When an input reaches value 0, it is considered low and when it reaches 9, it is considered high. A) Define the ten value type using the integer base type. B) Write a description of an inverter using this value system. When the input reaches the low level (0), the output starts switching to high, and linearly changes from 0 to 9 in 30 ns. When the input reaches the high level (9), the output starts switching to low and linearly changes from 9 to 0 in 20 ns. You need not be concerned about the input changing too fast for the output to respond. Model linear changes on the output only, considering only extreme low and high values at the input of the inverter.

8.17. Use the 10 value logic system in the previous problem to model waveform dependencies in logic gates. Model an inverter with an input threshold value of 5, so that the inverter starts switching to its high state when the input state crosses 5 in the downward direction and starts switching to its low state when its input crosses the threshold (5) in the upward direction. Complete transitions of the output of the inverter from high state (9) to low state (0) take 20 ns (2 ns each state), while the transitions from low to high takes 30 ns (3 ns each state). The output should respond to changes on the input while making a transition, i.e., if the input switches from state 5 to 6 while the output is making a low-to-high transition, the direction of the output should change. This is not an easy problem. Also, you can easily modify this problem to make the speed of the output depend on the speed of the input.

8.18. Develop a behavioral model of an 8-bit sequential multiplier. The 4-bit version of this multiplier was discussed in Chapter 1 (Section 1.2.2). Use the same interface and signaling as the multiplier in Chapter 1, i.e., use *dataready*, *busy* and *done*. The circuit receives two 8-bit operands when the input *dataready* becomes '1'. This causes the multiplication process to begin and the *busy* flag to become active. Using the add-shift method, the multiplier takes one or two clock pulses for each bit of the multiplicand. When the process is completed, *done* becomes '1' for one clock period and *busy* returns to zero. The circuit receives two operands from its *inputbus*, and produces the result on its 8-bit *result* output. Your behavioral description of this circuit should model it at the clock level. That is, the number of clock pulses that the behavioral model takes for multiplication of two numbers should be the same as that of an actual circuit using the add-shift method.

CHAPTER
9

CPU
MODELING
AND
DESIGN

Concepts of VHDL, the syntax and semantics of its constructs, and various ways that a hardware component can be described in VHDL were discussed in the previous chapters. No additional VHDL constructs are presented in this chapter; instead we will use the constructs of earlier chapters to describe a simple 8-bit processor. A CPU structure represents a large class of digital systems and its description involves the use of many important constructs of VHDL.

This chapter begins by introducing and describing a CPU example at a high level of abstraction, then capturing this high level information in a behavioral VHDL description. Following that, the data path of this machine and its structural details is designed and the information is then used to develop the dataflow description for our example CPU. The last part of this chapter develops a test bench for testing the behavioral or dataflow models. Various descriptions of this CPU are presented in Appendix D. The end-of-chapter problems suggest ways for enhancing the capabilities of this processor as well as improving its test bench.

9.1 DEFINING A COMPREHENSIVE EXAMPLE

The CPU that we use in this chapter is *a* reduced processor, which we refer to as PAR-1 (pronounced and written as "Parwan"). Parwan, first developed to teach computer hardware to novice logic design students, employs a reduced hardware requirement and a simple instruction set. The implementation of the machine in terms of MSI and SSI parts was illustrated for this purpose. Later, a senior design project for students in a VLSI design course capitalized on this processor. Using standard public-domain CAD tools, Parwan was designed as a full custom VLSI chip (see Figure 9.1) and fabricated at the Massachusetts Microelectronics Center (M^2C). Because of its reduced architecture and simple instruction set, it is easier to explore the hardware details of Parwan and students are able to see the inner workings of a CPU down to its transistors and gates.

We will use Parwan to illustrate the use of VHDL as a language for modeling and design of CPU-like architectures. The use of this simple architecture enables us to show modeling styles and applications of hardware description languages without overshadowing these concepts with the complexity of an architecture.

The behavioral description of Parwan, presented later in this chapter, is written according to the functionality of this CPU as it is first described to a user, or in our case to a student. Its dataflow description considers register transfer level hardware details and utilizes the same partitioning previously employed when generating the layout shown in Figure 9.1. The actual chip, its dataflow description, and its behavioral description all have the same functionality and input/output ports.

9.2 PARWAN CPU

Because of the size of its data registers and buses, Parwan is generally considered to be an 8-bit processor. This machine has an 8-bit external data bus and a 12-bit address bus. It has the basic arithmetic and logical operations and several jump and branch instructions, along with direct and indirect addressing modes. Parwan also has a simple subroutine call instruction and an input interrupt that resets the machine.

9.2.1 Memory Organization of Parwan

Parwan is capable of addressing 4096 bytes of memory through its 12-bit address bus (*adbus*). This memory is partitioned into sixteen pages of 256 bytes each. As shown in Figure 9.2, the four most significant bits of *adbus* constitute the page address and its eight least significant bits are the offset. In this figure, and in the future examples of this chapter, we use hexadecimal numbers for the addresses. We separate page and offset parts of the address by a colon. In spite of the 16 pages of memory partitioning the Parwan's memory is treated as a contiguous 4K memory and page crossing is done automatically. This memory is also used for communication with input and output devices. Due to its memory mapped I/O, Parwan does not have separate I/O instructions.

9.2.2 Instruction Set

With two addressing modes, Parwan has a total of 23 instructions, as summarized in Figure 9.3. The main and only CPU data register is the accumulator, which is

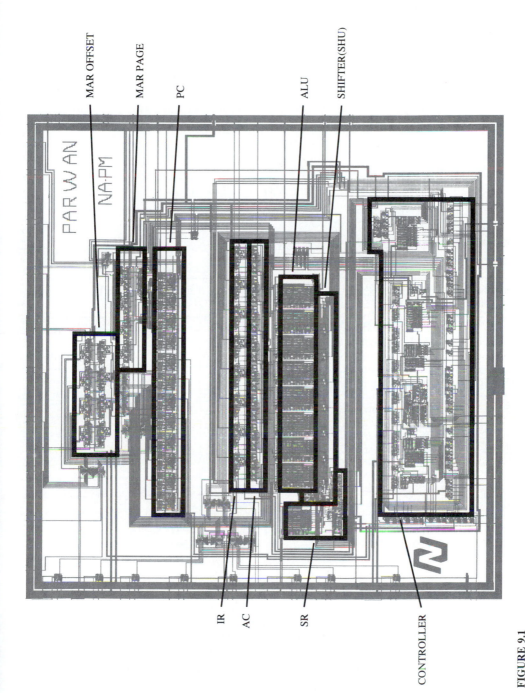

MAR OFFSET

MAR PAGE

PC

ALU

SHIFTER(SHU)

PARWAN

NA-PM

IR

AC

SR

CONTROLLER

FIGURE 9.1
VLSI Implementation of Parwan, fabricated at Massachusetts Microelectronics Center.

261

ADDRESS:

1	1	0	0	0	0	0	0	0	0	0	0
1	0	9	8	7	6	5	4	3	2	1	0

Page	Offset

MEMORY:

7 | 6 | 5 | 4 | 3 | 2 | 1 | 0

0:00 - 0:FF	page 0 ..
1:00 - 1:FF	page 1 ..
2:00 - 2:FF	page 2 ..
∘	∘
∘	∘
∘	∘
E:00 - E:FF	page 14 ..
F:00 - F:FF	page 15 ..

FIGURE 9.2
Page and offset Parts of Parwan addresses.

Instruction Mnemonic	Brief Description	ADDRESSING			FLAGS	
		Bits	Scheme	Indirect	use	set
LDA loc	Load AC w/(loc)	12	FULL	YES	----	--zn
AND loc	AND AC w/(loc)	12	FULL	YES	----	--zn
ADD loc	Add (loc) to AC	12	FULL	YES	-c--	vczn
SUB loc	Sub (loc) from AC	12	FULL	YES	-c--	vczn
JMP adr	Jump to adr	12	FULL	YES	----	----
STA loc	Store AC in loc	12	FULL	YES	----	----
JSR tos	Subroutine to tos	8	PAGE	NO	----	----
BRA_V adr	Branch to adr if V	8	PAGE	NO	v---	----
BRA_C adr	Branch to adr if C	8	PAGE	NO	-c--	----
BRA_Z adr	Branch to adr if Z	8	PAGE	NO	--z-	----
BRA_N adr	Branch to adr if N	8	PAGE	NO	---n	----
NOP	No operation	-	NONE	NO	----	----
CLA	Clear AC	-	NONE	NO	----	----
CMA	Complement AC	-	NONE	NO	----	--zn
CMC	Complement carry	-	NONE	NO	-c--	-c--
ASL	Arith shift left	-	NONE	NO	----	vczn
ASR	Arith shift right	-	NONE	NO	----	--zn

FIGURE 9.3
Summary of Parwan instructions.

used in conjunction with most instructions. This machine has *overflow, carry, zero,* and *negative* flags (v, c, z, and n). These flags may be modified by specific flag instructions or by the instructions that alter the contents of the accumulator.

The *lda* instruction loads the accumulator with the contents of memory, while the *and, add,* and *sub* instructions access memory for an operand, perform the specified operation (ANDing, adding, and subtracting), and load the results in the accumulator.

Flags *z* and *n* are set or reset based on the results of *lda*, *and*, *add*, and *sub*. Instructions *add* and *sub* also influence *v* and *c* flags (overflow and carry), depending on the outcome of the corresponding operations. The *sta* instruction stores the contents of accumulator into the specified memory location. Execution of the *jmp* instruction causes the next instruction to be received from the address specified by the instruction. Instructions *lda*, *and*, *add*, *sub*, *jmp*, and *sta* use 12-bit addresses, and can be used with the indirect addressing mode. We refer to these instructions as having a full-addressing scheme.

The addressing scheme of *jsr* and branch instructions is page-addressing. These instructions can only point to the page that they appear in. The *jsr* instruction with an 8-bit *tos* (top of subroutine) address causes the next instruction to be received from memory location *tos+1* of the current page. At the end of a subroutine, a return from subroutine can be accomplished by an indirect jump to *tos*. Four branch instructions, *bra_v*, *bra_c*, *bra_z*, and *bra_n* cause the next instruction to be received from the specified location of the current page if the respective flags *v*, *c*, *z*, or *n* are set.

Instructions *nop*, *cla*, *cma*, *cmc*, *asl*, and *asr* are nonaddress instructions and perform operations on the internal registers of the CPU flags. The *nop* instruction performs no operation, *cla* clears the accumulator, *cma* complements the accumulator, *cmc* complements the *c* flag, and *asl* and *asr* cause arithmetic left or right shift of the contents of accumulator. When shifting left, the most significant bit of the accumulator is shifted into the carry flag, and the overflow flag is set if the sign of accumulator changes. The *asr* instruction extends the sign of accumulator and shifts out its least significant bit. Both shift instructions affect the zero and negative flags.

9.2.3   Instruction Format

As shown in Figure 9.3, there are three groups of Parwan instructions. Full-address instructions requiring two bytes can access all of Parwan's memory and be used with indirect addressing. Page-address instructions requiring two bytes can access the current page, but cannot use indirect addressing. The third group, which are nonaddress instructions, do not use the memory for their operands. Figure 9.4 shows the opcodes and format of these instructions.

9.2.3.1   FULL ADDRESS INSTRUCTIONS. The opcode specifying the operation of a full-address instruction is formed by the three most significant bits of the first byte. The next bit (bit number 4) specifies direct or indirect addressing modes (0 for direct, 1 for indirect), and the other four bits (the least significant four) contain the page number of the operand of the instruction. The second byte of a full-address instruction specifies the offset address, which together with the page address, completes a 12-bit address for the operand. Figure 9.5 shows the formation of a complete 12-bit address for this group of Parwan instructions.

9.2.3.2   PAGE ADDRESS INSTRUCTIONS. Figure 9.6 shows the format for *jsr* and branch instructions. These instructions reference memory within the page where they appear. The opcode of *jsr* is 110 and the other five bits of the first instruction byte

Instruction Mnemonic	Fields and Bits		
	Opcode 7 6 5	D/I 4	3 2 1 0
LDA loc	0 0 0	0/1	page adr
AND loc	0 0 1	0/1	page adr
ADD loc	0 1 0	0/1	page adr
SUB loc	0 1 1	0/1	page adr
JMP adr	1 0 0	0/1	page adr
STA loc	1 0 1	0/1	page adr
JSR tos	1 1 0	-	- - - -
BRA_V adr	1 1 1	1	1 0 0 0
BRA_C adr	1 1 1	1	0 1 0 0
BRA_Z adr	1 1 1	1	0 0 1 0
BRA_N adr	1 1 1	1	0 0 0 1
NOP	1 1 1	0	0 0 0 0
CLA	1 1 1	0	0 0 0 1
CMA	1 1 1	0	0 0 1 0
CMC	1 1 1	0	0 1 0 0
ASL	1 1 1	0	1 0 0 0
ASR	1 1 1	0	1 0 0 1

FIGURE 9.4
Parwan instruction opcodes.

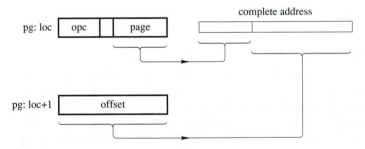

FIGURE 9.5
Addressing in full-address instructions.

are ignored. The opcode field of a branch instruction contains 111. Bit 4 is always 1 and its least significant bits specify the condition for a branch. The second byte of *jsr* and branch instructions specify the jump address within the current page.

For a branch example, consider the instruction shown in Figure 9.7. At location 0D on page 5, a *bra_c* causes the next instruction to be received from location 6A of page 5 if the carry flag is set, or from location 0F of page 5 if the carry flag is zero. Figure 9.8 shows the execution of a *jsr* instruction at location 5:11. The byte at location 5:12 specifies that the subroutine begins at location 33 of the current page (5:33). The first location of a subroutine is reserved for the return address, and the programmer is not allowed to use it for program information, i.e., code or data. The

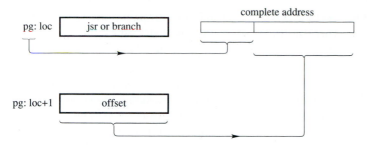

complete address

pg: loc | jsr or branch |

pg: loc+1 | offset |

FIGURE 9.6
Addressing in page-address instructions.

programmer is required to use an indirect jump instruction at the end of a subroutine to return from it. Figure 9.8 shows a *jmp-indirect* instruction at locations 5:55 and 5:56. After the execution of *jsr*, the return address (the address of the instruction that follows *jsr* in memory, which in this example is location 5:13) is placed in the first location of the subroutine (location 5:33). The indirect jump at location 5:55 causes the program flow to return to location 5:13 after the subroutine completes.

MEMORY

	...
5:0D	1 1 1 1 0 1 0 0
5:0E	6 A
5:0F	...

FIGURE 9.7
A branch instruction.

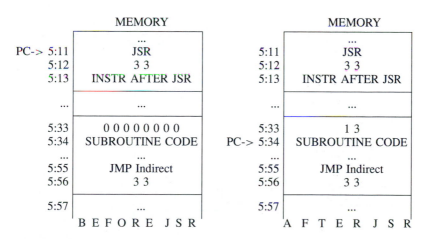

	MEMORY
	...
PC-> 5:11	JSR
5:12	3 3
5:13	INSTR AFTER JSR
	...
5:33	0 0 0 0 0 0 0 0
5:34	SUBROUTINE CODE
	...
5:55	JMP Indirect
5:56	3 3
5:57	...

B E F O R E   J S R

	MEMORY
	...
5:11	JSR
5:12	3 3
5:13	INSTR AFTER JSR
	...
5:33	1 3
PC-> 5:34	SUBROUTINE CODE
	...
5:55	JMP Indirect
5:56	3 3
5:57	...

A F T E R   J S R

FIGURE 9.8
An example for the execution of *jsr*. Memory and *pc*, before and after *jsr*.

9.2.3.3 NONADDRESS INSTRUCTIONS. Nonaddress instructions are the last group of Parwan instructions. These instructions occupy one byte whose most significant four bits are 1110. The other 4-bits specify *nop, cla, cma, cmc, asl,* or *asr.*

9.2.3.4 INDIRECT ADDRESSING IN PARWAN. If bit 4 of the first byte of a full-address instruction is '1', the address specified by this instruction is the indirect address of the operand. Indirect addressing uses a 12-bit address to receive an 8-bit offset from the memory. This offset, together with the page number of the indirect address, makes a complete address for the actual operand of the instruction.

Figure 9.9 shows an example of indirect addressing in Parwan. It is assumed that a full-address instruction with indirect addressing is in locations 0:25 and 0:26. The 12-bit address of this instruction (6:35) points to 1F in the memory which is used with page number 6 to form 6:1F as the actual address of the operand.

9.2.4 Programming in Parwan Assembly

For a better understanding of Parwan instructions, consider the program shown in Figure 9.10. The assembly code of this figure adds ten data bytes which are stored in memory starting from location 4:25, and stores the result at 4:03. The code begins at location 0:15 and assumes constants 25, 10, and 1 are stored in 4:00, 4:01, and 4:02, respectively. Although Parwan does not have an immediate addressing mode, series of shifts and adds can generate any necessary constant. Modifying this processor to handle immediate addressing mode is dealt with in a series of problem at the end of the chapter.

9.3 BEHAVIORAL DESCRIPTION OF PARWAN

A more compact and far less ambiguous description of the behavior of Parwan than the "word" description of the previous section can be developed using VHDL. This section presents such a behavioral description for our 8-bit machine. The interface description

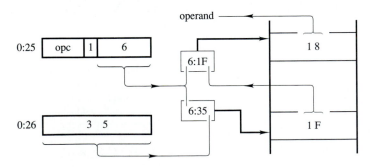

FIGURE 9.9
An example for indirect addressing in Parwan.

```
                           -- load 25 in 4:00
                           -- load 10 in 4:01
                           -- load 01 in 4:02
0:15    cla                -- clear accumulator
0:16    asl                -- clears carry
0:17    add, i     4:00    -- add bytes
0:19    sta        4:03    -- store partial sum
0:1B    lda        4:00    -- load pointer
0:1D    add        4:02    -- increment pointer
0:1F    sta        4:00    -- store pointer back
0:21    lda        4:01    -- load count
0:23    sub        4:02    -- decrement count
0:25    bra_z      :2D     -- end if zero count
0:27    sta        4:01    -- store count back
0:29    lda        4:03    -- get partial sum
0:2B    jmp        0:17    -- go for next byte
0:2D    nop                -- adding completed
```

FIGURE 9.10
An example program for Parwan CPU.

of this machine is kept at the hardware level, using bits for external control signals and memory and data buses.

9.3.1 Timing and Clocking

The interface of our behavioral description includes a clock signal which is not used. This signal is included for compatibility with the actual chip and with the dataflow model that we develop later in this chapter. The timing of the behavioral model is independent of the clock and may not necessarily match those of the actual chip and the more realistic models.

Timing is introduced in a behavioral model when reading or writing from or to the memory. This timing is only for synchronization with the memory in order that the same memory model can be used for the behavioral as well as other more detailed models. Parwan uses a static memory with an active high read and write lines.

9.3.2 Packages

When describing Parwan at the behavioral level, we use the *basic_utilities* package presented in the previous chapters. This package is compiled and placed in a design library named *cmos*. Another library called *par_library* contains packages that include utilities which are needed to describe Parwan and do not appear in the *basic_utilities* package.

9.3.2.1 PAR_UTILITIES PACKAGE. The first of two packages appearing in *par_library* is *par_utilities*, whose package declaration is shown in Figure 9.11. This package

```
LIBRARY cmos;
USE cmos.basic_utilities.ALL;
--
PACKAGE par_utilities IS
    FUNCTION "XOR" (a, b : qit) RETURN qit ;
    FUNCTION "AND" (a, b : qit_vector) RETURN qit_vector;
    FUNCTION "OR" (a, b : qit_vector) RETURN qit_vector;
    FUNCTION "NOT" (a : qit_vector) RETURN qit_vector;
    SUBTYPE nibble IS qit_vector (3 DOWNTO 0);
    SUBTYPE byte IS qit_vector (7 DOWNTO 0);
    SUBTYPE twelve IS qit_vector (11 DOWNTO 0);
    SUBTYPE wired_nibble IS wired_qit_vector (3 DOWNTO 0);
    SUBTYPE wired_byte IS wired_qit_vector (7 DOWNTO 0);
    SUBTYPE wired_twelve IS wired_qit_vector (11 DOWNTO 0);
    SUBTYPE ored_nibble IS ored_qit_vector (3 DOWNTO 0);
    SUBTYPE ored_byte IS ored_qit_vector (7 DOWNTO 0);
    SUBTYPE ored_twelve IS ored_qit_vector (11 DOWNTO 0);
    CONSTANT zero_4 : nibble := "0000";
    CONSTANT zero_8 : byte := "00000000";
    CONSTANT zero_12 : twelve := "000000000000";
    FUNCTION add_cv (a, b : qit_vector; cin : qit) RETURN qit_vector;
    FUNCTION sub_cv (a, b : qit_vector; cin : qit) RETURN qit_vector;
    FUNCTION set_if_zero (a : qit_vector) RETURN qit;
END par_utilities;
```

FIGURE 9.11
Declarations of *par_utilities* package of *par_library*.

uses the *basic_utilities* package of the *cmos* library and includes several type and function declarations.

Subtypes *nibble*, *byte*, and *twelve* are *qit_vectors* of 4, 8, and 12 *qit*s long. Types *wired_nibble* (*ored_nibble*), *wired_byte* (*ored_byte*), and *wired_twelve* (*ored_twelve*) are resolved *qit_vectors* using the *wiring* (*oring*) resolution functions of the *basic_utilities* package. Function "XOR" of the *par_utilities* package overloads the XOR operator for *qit* operands. Functions "AND", "OR" and "NOT" overload their corresponding functions in the *basic_utilities* package for *qit_vector* operands. Recall that the *basic_utilities* package overloads basic logical operators with functions for *qit* type operands.

The *par_utilities* package also includes *add_cv* and *sub_cv* functions. These functions perform the respective addition or subtraction on their n *qit* long *qit_vector* operands and return a *qit_vector* of length $n+2$. The two most significant *qit*s of the result (positions $n+1$ and n) are the overflow and carry indicators. The last function in the package in Figure 9.11 is *set_if_zero*, which returns a '1' if its unconstrained *qit_vector* parameter contains all zeros. Figure 9.12 shows the body of the *par_utilities* package.

9.3.2.2 PAR_PARAMETERS PACKAGE. Another package in the *par_library* is *par_parameters*. This package, shown in Figure 9.13, defines bit patterns for opcodes

```
PACKAGE BODY par_utilities IS
    FUNCTION "XOR" (a, b : qit) RETURN qit IS
        CONSTANT qit_or_table : qit_2d := (
            ('0','1','1','X'), ('1','0','0','X'), ('1','0','0','X'), ('X','X','X','X'));
    BEGIN   RETURN qit_or_table (a, b);
    END "XOR";
    FUNCTION "AND" (a,b : qit_vector) RETURN qit_vector IS
        VARIABLE r : qit_vector (a'RANGE);
    BEGIN
        loop1: FOR i IN a'RANGE LOOP
            r(i) := a(i) AND b(i);
        END LOOP loop1;   RETURN r;
    END "AND";
    FUNCTION "OR" (a,b: qit_vector) RETURN qit_vector IS
        VARIABLE r: qit_vector (a'RANGE);
    BEGIN
        loop1: FOR i IN a'RANGE LOOP
            r(i) := a(i) OR b(i);
        END LOOP loop1;   RETURN r;
    END "OR";
    FUNCTION "NOT" (a: qit_vector) RETURN qit_vector IS
        VARIABLE r: qit_vector (a'RANGE);
    BEGIN
        loop1: FOR i IN a'RANGE LOOP
            r(i) := NOT a(i);
        END LOOP loop1;   RETURN r;
    END "NOT";
```

FIGURE 9.12
Body of the *par_utilities* package of *par_library* library. (*continued on following page*)

and groups of instructions. In naming opcodes, we avoid VHDL reserved words and use names that are similar to Parwan mnemonics. The *par_parameters* package is primarily used for the readability of behavioral descriptions of Parwan components. In all cases, bit patterns equivalent to the defined constants could be used as well.

9.3.3   Interface Description of Parwan

The interface of the Parwan behavioral description, described according to the fabricated chip in Figure 9.1, is pin-compatible with its dataflow description. The declarative part of the entity in this CPU uses signals whose types are *qit*, *qit_vector*, or their resolved subtypes. Although using string type for the inputs and outputs of Parwan would simplify instruction representation and decoding at the behavioral level, it would also require different types of input and output signals for different Parwan models. For consistency between various models and the actual hardware this feature has been avoided.

Figure 9.14 shows the interface description of Parwan. This description uses the *basic_utilities* package from the *cmos* library, and *par_utilities* and *par_parameters*

```
FUNCTION add_cv (a, b : qit_vector; cin : qit) RETURN qit_vector IS
    VARIABLE r, c: qit_vector (a'LEFT + 2 DOWNTO 0);   -- extra r bits: msb overflow,
                                                              next carry
    VARIABLE a_sign, b_sign: qit;
BEGIN
    a_sign := a(a'LEFT);    b_sign := b(b'LEFT);
    r(0) := a(0) XOR b(0) XOR cin;
    c(0) := ((a(0) XOR b(0)) AND cin) OR (a(0) AND b(0));
    FOR i IN 1 TO (a'LEFT) LOOP
        r(i) := a(i) XOR b(i) XOR c(i-1);
        c(i) := ((a(i) XOR b(i)) AND c(i-1)) OR (a(i) AND b(i));
    END LOOP;
    r(a'LEFT+1) := c(a'LEFT);
    IF a_sign = b_sign AND r(a'LEFT) /= a_sign
        THEN r(a'LEFT+2) := '1'; --overflow
    ELSE r(a'LEFT+2) := '0'; END IF;
    RETURN r;
END add_cv;
FUNCTION sub_cv (a, b : qit_vector; cin : qit) RETURN qit_vector IS
    VARIABLE not_b : qit_vector (b'LEFT DOWNTO 0);
    VARIABLE not_c : qit;
    VARIABLE r : qit_vector (a'LEFT + 2 DOWNTO 0);
BEGIN
    not_b := NOT b;    not_c := NOT cin;
    r := add_cv (a, not_b, not_c);
    RETURN r;
END sub_cv;
FUNCTION set_if_zero (a : qit_vector) RETURN qit IS
    VARIABLE zero : qit := '1';
BEGIN
    FOR i IN a'RANGE LOOP
        IF a(i) /= '0' THEN
            zero := '0'; EXIT;
        END IF;
    END LOOP;
    RETURN zero;
END set_if_zero;
END par_utilities;
```

FIGURE 9.12
Body of the *par_utilities* package of *par_library* library. (*continued from previous page*)

from the *par_library* package. The generic clause specifies memory read and write timing parameters, as well as a cycle time and a simulation run time. The cycle time is equivalent to a complete read or write cycle. The port clause in Figure 9.14 contains inputs and outputs of Parwan. The *databus* bidirectional bus is a resolved signal that uses the wiring resolution function of the *basic_utilities* package. This declaration allows multiple sources to drive the bus. For example, in reading from the

```
LIBRARY  cmos;
USE  cmos.basic_utilities.ALL;
---
PACKAGE  par_parameters  IS
    CONSTANT  single_byte_instructions : qit_vector (3 DOWNTO 0) := "1110";
    CONSTANT  cla : qit_vector (3 DOWNTO 0) := "0001";
    CONSTANT  cma : qit_vector (3 DOWNTO 0) := "0010";
    CONSTANT  cmc : qit_vector (3 DOWNTO 0) := "0100";
    CONSTANT  asl : qit_vector (3 DOWNTO 0) := "1000";
    CONSTANT  asr : qit_vector (3 DOWNTO 0) := "1001";
    CONSTANT  jsr : qit_vector (2 DOWNTO 0) := "110";
    CONSTANT  bra : qit_vector (3 DOWNTO 0) := "1111";
    CONSTANT  indirect : qit := '1';
    CONSTANT  jmp : qit_vector (2 DOWNTO 0) := "100";
    CONSTANT  sta : qit_vector (2 DOWNTO 0) := "101";
    CONSTANT  lda : qit_vector (2 DOWNTO 0) := "000";
    CONSTANT  ann : qit_vector (2 DOWNTO 0) := "001";
    CONSTANT  add : qit_vector (2 DOWNTO 0) := "010";
    CONSTANT  sbb : qit_vector (2 DOWNTO 0) := "011";
END par_parameters;
```

FIGURE 9.13
Declaration of the *par_parameters* package of *par_library*.

```
LIBRARY  cmos;
USE  cmos.basic_utilities.ALL;
LIBRARY  par_library;
USE  par_library.par_utilities.ALL;
USE  par_library.par_parameters.ALL;
--
ENTITY  par_central_processing_unit  IS
    GENERIC (read_high_time, read_low_time,
                write_high_time, write_low_time : TIME := 2 US;
                cycle_time : TIME := 4 US; run_time : TIME := 140 US);
    PORT (clk : IN qit;
            interrupt : IN qit;
            read_mem, write_mem : OUT qit;
            databus : INOUT wired_byte BUS := "ZZZZZZZZ"; adbus : OUT twelve
        );
END par_central_processing_unit;
```

FIGURE 9.14
Interface description of Parwan.

memory, the CPU drives the bus with 'Z's, while the memory drives it with the data from the memory. For writing into the memory, the role of the CPU and the memory are reversed. The *databus* declaration also allows multiple peripherals to connect to the CPU.

9.3.4 Parwan Behavioral Architecture

The high level behavioral description of Parwan presented here models this machine from an instruction execution point of view. The functionality of this model is identical to lower level models, e.g., dataflow and gate level, and to the actual hardware. However, this model is by no means perfect. At this stage of design, when the bussing structure of the machine is not known, it is not possible to generate a model that complies with the clock level timing of the actual hardware. Furthermore, we are only modeling the good behavior of Parwan. Unanticipated data inputs, unusually long delays, or faulty inputs can cause the behavioral model to generate responses that are very different from the response of the actual hardware or the lower level models.

Figure 9.15 outlines the *behavioral* architecture of the *par_central_processing_unit*. The description contains a process statement in which the if statements separate various instructions or groups of instructions. The declarative part of the process, shown in Figure 9.16, contains the declarations of temporary variables and buffers.

In the statement part of the process statement in Figure 9.15, an if statement halts the simulation when the *run_time* is reached. Following this statement, a check is made for the interrupt input. Figure 9.17 shows the code that is executed if the interrupt input is '1'. After setting the program counter to zero, the processor waits for one *cycle_time* before checking *interrupt* again.

When the *interrupt* input becomes '0', the first instruction byte is read from the memory. Figure 9.18 shows how the *byte1* variable stores this byte. The wait statement that follows the assignment of '1' to *read_mem*, allows sufficient time for the memory unit to respond to a read request. The wait statement which appears after the signal assignment that resets *read_mem* to zero, stops subsequent '1' values from overwriting the zero value on this signal. The last statement in Figure 9.18 increments the program counter in order to make it ready for reading the next byte.

After reading the first byte of an instruction, the behavioral description in Figure 9.15 checks for those instructions that use only one memory byte. For these instructions, the code of Figure 9.19 is executed. This code checks bits 3 to 0 of the instruction byte for *cla*, *cma*, *cmc*, *asl*, or *asr*, and performs appropriate operations.

For instructions that use two memory bytes, another byte is read from the memory and placed in the *byte2* variable, shown in Figure 9.20. This is followed by the if statements that check for various types of two-byte instructions.

The outline in Figure 9.15 handles the execution of *jsr* as the first two-byte instruction. The code for the execution of this instruction, presented in Figure 9.21, shows that the offset part of the program counter is first written to the top of subroutine. The top of subroutine is a memory location whose page number is the page number that already exists on *adbus* (the current page), and whose offset is taken from the second instruction byte (*byte2*). Transferring the contents of *pc* to this location forms the subroutine return address. In order to prepare the program counter for fetching the next instruction from the subroutine, *pc* is set to the increment of *byte2*. The execution of subroutine instructions continues until the indirect jump at the end of subroutine (which must be put there by the programmer) is reached.

```
┌ARCHITECTURE behavioral OF par_central_processing_unit IS
├BEGIN
│   ┌PROCESS
│   │       ‖     Declare necessary variables; Figure 9.16.
│   ├BEGIN
│   │   _IF NOW > run_time THEN WAIT; END IF;
│   │   ┌IF interrupt = '1' THEN
│   │   │       ‖     Handle interrupt; Figure 9.17.
│   │   ├ELSE   -- no interrupt
│   │   │       ‖     Read first byte into byte1, increment pc; Figure 9.18.
│   │   │   ┌IF byte1 (7 DOWNTO 4) = single_byte_instructions THEN
│   │   │   │       ‖     Execute single-byte instructions; Figure 9.19.
│   │   │   ├ELSE   -- two-byte instructions
│   │   │   │       ‖     Read second byte into byte2, increment pc; Figure 9.20.
│   │   │   │   ┌IF byte1 (7 DOWNTO 5) = jsr THEN
│   │   │   │   │       ‖     Execute jsr instruction, byte2 has address; Figure 9.21.
│   │   │   │   ├ELSIF byte1 (7 DOWNTO 4) = bra THEN
│   │   │   │   │       ‖     Execute bra instructions, address in byte2; Figure 9.22.
│   │   │   │   ├ELSE -- all other two-byte instructions
│   │   │   │   │   ┌IF byte1 (4) = indirect THEN
│   │   │   │   │   │       ‖     Use byte1 and byte2 to get address; Figure 9.23.
│   │   │   │   │   └END IF; -- ends indirect
│   │   │   │   │   ┌IF byte1 (7 DOWNTO 5) = jmp THEN
│   │   │   │   │   │       ‖     Execute jmp instruction; Figure 9.24;
│   │   │   │   │   ├ELSIF byte1 (7 DOWNTO 5) = sta THEN
│   │   │   │   │   │       ‖     Execute sta instruction, write ac; Figure 9.25.
│   │   │   │   │   ├ELSE -- read operand for lda, and, add, sub
│   │   │   │   │   │       ‖     Read memory onto databus; Figure 9.26, top.
│   │   │   │   │   │       ‖     Execute lda, and, add, and sub;  Figure 9.26, middle.
│   │   │   │   │   │       ‖     Remove memory from databus; Figure 9.26, bottom.
│   │   │   │   │   └END IF; -- jmp / sta / lda, and, add, sub
│   │   │   │   └END IF; -- jsr / bra / other double-byte instructions
│   │   │   └END IF; -- single-byte / double-byte
│   │   └END IF; -- interrupt / otherwise
│   └END PROCESS;
└END behavioral;
```

FIGURE 9.15
Outline of the Parwan behavioral description.

```
┌ VARIABLE pc : twelve;
│ VARIABLE ac, byte1, byte2 : byte;
│ VARIABLE v, c, z, n : qit;
└ VARIABLE temp : qit_vector (9 DOWNTO 0);
```

FIGURE 9.16
Variable declarations of the Parwan behavioral model.

```
pc := zero_12;
WAIT FOR cycle_time;
```

FIGURE 9.17
Interrupt handling of the Parwan behavioral model.

```
adbus <= pc;
read_mem <= '1';   WAIT FOR read_high_time;
byte1 := byte (databus);
read_mem <= '0';   WAIT FOR read_low_time;
pc := inc (pc);
```

FIGURE 9.18
Reading the first byte from the memory (part of the Parwan behavioral model).

```
CASE byte1 (3 DOWNTO 0) IS
  WHEN cla =>
    ac := zero_8;
  WHEN cma =>
    ac := NOT ac;
    IF ac = zero_8 THEN z := '1'; END IF;
    n := ac (7);
  WHEN cmc =>
    c := NOT c;
  WHEN asl =>
    c := ac (7);
    ac := ac (6 DOWNTO 0) & '0';
    IF ac = zero_8 THEN z := '1'; END IF;
    n := ac (7);
    IF c /= n THEN v := '1'; END IF;
  WHEN asr =>
    ac := ac (7) & ac (7 DOWNTO 1);
    IF ac = zero_8 THEN z := '1'; END IF;
    n := ac (7);
  WHEN OTHERS => NULL;
END CASE;
```

FIGURE 9.19
Executing single-byte instructions in the behavioral model of Parwan.

The code for the branch instructions follows that of *jsr* in the outline in Figure 9.15. The execution of branch code shown in Figure 9.22 causes the conditional loading of the offset part of the program counter with the contents of *byte2*. Therefore, branching is to the current page only.

```
adbus <= pc;
read_mem <= '1';   WAIT FOR read_high_time;
byte2 := byte (databus);
read_mem <= '0';   WAIT FOR read_low_time;
pc := inc (pc);
```

FIGURE 9.20
Reading the second byte from the memory (part of Parwan behavioral model).

```
databus <= wired_byte (pc (7 DOWNTO 0) );
adbus (7 DOWNTO 0) <= byte2;
write_mem <= '1';   WAIT FOR write_high_time;
write_mem <= '0';   WAIT FOR write_low_time;
databus <= "ZZZZZZZZ";
pc (7 DOWNTO 0) := inc (byte2);
```

FIGURE 9.21
Execution of the *jsr* instruction in the behavioral model of Parwan.

```
IF
   ( byte1 (3) = '1' AND v = '1' ) OR
   ( byte1 (2) = '1' AND c = '1' ) OR
   ( byte1 (1) = '1' AND z = '1' ) OR
   ( byte1 (0) = '1' AND n = '1' )
THEN
   pc (7 DOWNTO 0) := byte2;
END IF;
```

FIGURE 9.22
Execution of branch instructions in the Parwan behavioral model.

If a two-byte instruction is not *jsr* or any of the branch instructions, the *behavioral* architecture of the *par_central_processing_unit* checks for indirect addressing. For indirect addressing (see Figure 9.23), a 12-bit address whose page number comes from the least significant nibble of *byte1* and whose offset is *byte2* is used for addressing the memory and reading the actual offset. This newly read byte replaces the old contents of *byte2*. After execution of the code in Figure 9.23, the least significant nibble of *byte1* contains the page while *byte2* has the offset of the actual address of the operand.

The code for the full-address instructions follows that of indirect addressing shown in Figure 9.15. The first such instruction is *jmp*, which loads the program counter with the 12-bit address that is available from *byte1* and *byte2* variables.

The next full-address instruction is *sta* which writes the accumulator into the memory location specified by the least significant nibble of *byte1* and by *byte2*. Figure 9.25 shows the code for this instruction.

```
adbus (11 DOWNTO 8) <= byte1 (3 DOWNTO 0);
adbus (7 DOWNTO 0) <= byte2;
read_mem <= '1';   WAIT FOR read_high_time;
byte2 := byte (databus);
read_mem <= '0';   WAIT FOR read_low_time;
```

FIGURE 9.23
Handling indirect addressing by the Parwan behavioral model.

```
pc := byte1 (3 DOWNTO 0) & byte2;
```

FIGURE 9.24
Execution of *jmp* instruction in the Parwan behavioral model.

```
adbus <= byte1 (3 DOWNTO 0) & byte2;
databus <= wired_byte (ac);
write_mem <= '1';   WAIT FOR write_high_time;
write_mem <= '0';   WAIT FOR write_low_time;
databus <= "ZZZZZZZZ";
```

FIGURE 9.25
Execution of *sta* instruction in the Parwan behavioral model.

The last group of full-address instructions are *lda*, *and*, *add*, and *sub*. As shown in Figure 9.26, the actual operand is read from the memory and is kept on the *databus* by keeping the *read_mem* signal active for execution of these instructions. A case statement separates these four instructions and performs their corresponding operations. The *read_mem* signal is disabled at the end to indicate to the memory that the *databus* is no longer needed. This causes the memory unit to release the bus by setting it to high impedance.

The process statement in the Parwan behavioral description uses at least one cycle time for the execution of each Parwan instruction. Each time through the process statement, one complete instruction is executed and this may take up to three cycles. Execution of a new instruction begins when the program reaches the beginning of the process statement. A complete behavioral description of Parwan consists of Figures 9.16 to 9.26 which are inserted in their specified places in Figure 9.15. This description is shown in Appendix D.

9.4   PARWAN BUSSING STRUCTURE

The bussing structure of a CPU describes the way its registers and logic units are connected. The first step in the hardware design process of a CPU is the design of this structure. Figure 9.27 shows the bussing structure of Parwan. This diagram is useful

```
adbus (11 DOWNTO 8) <= byte1 (3 DOWNTO 0);
adbus (7 DOWNTO 0) <= byte2;
read_mem <= '1';   WAIT FOR read_high_time;
CASE byte1 (7 DOWNTO 5) IS
  WHEN lda =>
    ac := byte (databus);
  WHEN ann =>
    ac := ac AND byte (databus);
  WHEN add =>
    temp := add_cv (ac, byte (databus), c);
    ac := temp (7 DOWNTO 0);
    c := temp (8);
    v := temp (9);
  WHEN sbb =>
    temp := sub_cv (ac, byte (databus), c);
    ac := temp (7 DOWNTO 0);
    c := temp (8);
    v := temp (9);
  WHEN OTHERS => NULL;
END CASE;
IF ac = zero_8 THEN z := '1'; END IF;
n := ac (7);
read_mem <= '0';   WAIT FOR read_low_time;
```

FIGURE 9.26
Execution of *lda*, *and*, *add*, and *sub* instructions in the Parwan behavioral model.

when performing a detailed study of timing for the individual machine instructions and will be used when developing a dataflow description of Parwan in the next section. In this diagram, names of major buses and registers appear in capital letters, and all other signal names are in lowercase letters. Only signal names to be referenced in this section are shown.

9.4.1   Interconnection of Components

The major components of Parwan are *ac*, *ir*, *pc*, *mar*, *sr*, *alu*, and *shu*. Data flows between these components through buses and hard-wired interconnections. Figure 9.27 uses a hollow triangle to show controlled interconnection of a register or logic unit output to a bus, and uses an arrow for permanent wired connections. For example, the output of *shu*, labeled *obus*, connects to *dbus* only when a signal named *obus_on_dbus* is active. On the other hand, connection of the accumulator output (*ac_out*) to the input of *alu* is hard-wired. In general, connections to buses with multiple sources must be controlled. VLSI implementation of Parwan uses transmission gates for implementing the selection of data on to multi-source buses.

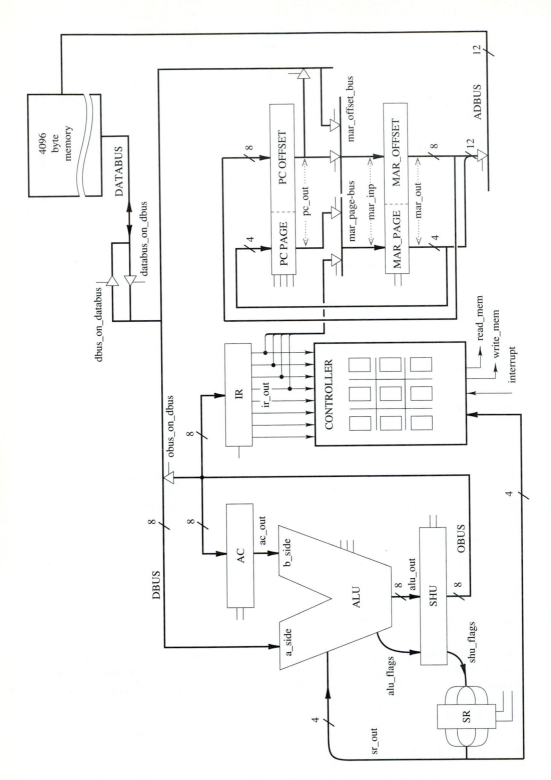

9.4.2 Global View of Parwan Components

Of the seven Parwan components, *ac*, *ir*, *pc*, *mar*, and *sr* are registers, and *alu* and *shu* are combinatorial logic units. Each component has a set of inputs and outputs and several control lines. In addition, register structures have clock inputs that are all connected to the main system clock.

The accumulator, *ac*, is an 8-bit register that provides one operand of *alu*. The instruction register, *ir*, connects to *dbus* through *alu*, and provides instruction bits to the controller, and page address to the address bus (*adbus*). The 12-bit program counter register, *pc*, is a binary up-counter that provides instruction addresses to *adbus* through the memory address register (*mar*). This register is an address buffer. The *mar* and *pc* registers have page and offset parts that are identified by *mar_page*, *pc_page*, *mar_offset*, and *pc_offset*. Page numbers are stored in their four most significant bits.

The arithmetic logic unit, *alu*, is a combinatorial logic unit with two sets of 8-bit inputs, four flag inputs, and three control inputs. The outputs of this unit are connected to the inputs of the *shu* unit. The shifter (*shu*) is also a combinatorial logic unit, and performs right and left shiftings of its 8-bit operand. The status register, *sr*, has four inputs and four outputs. Outputs of this register pass through *alu* and *shu* and circle back to its own inputs. This allows flags to be modified by either one of these logical units.

Figure 9.27 also shows a controller; a unit that generates control signals for the data components and buses. These signals cause the movement of data through system buses, and storage of this data into registers. The controller makes its decisions based on its state, external interrupt, and bits of *ir* and *sr*.

9.4.3 Instruction Execution

The bussing structure in Figure 9.27 provides the necessary registers and the data path for executing the Parwan instructions. Based on an instruction in *ir*, the controller generates control signals in an appropriate order for the proper execution of the instruction. For an illustration of this mechanism, we describe the sequence of events for execution of a *lda* instruction.

Initially, the program counter contains the address of instruction to be fetched. Fetching begins by moving the address from *pc* to *mar* and incrementing *pc*. For this move to take place, the address in *pc* must be placed on *mar_bus* and *mar* must be enabled and clocked. When this is completed, the controller activates the signal that places *mar* on *adbus* and at the same time it asserts *read_mem*. This causes the byte from the memory to appear on *databus*, which must now pass through *dbus*, *alu*, *shu*, and *obus* to reach *ir*. For this purpose, the controller activates the *databus_on_dbus* control signal, instructs *alu* to place its *a_side* on its output, and instructs the shifter

---

FIGURE 9.27
Parwan bussing structure.

unit to place its data input on its output without shifting it. The data on the output of *shu* becomes available for loading into *ir*.

Following an instruction fetch, the controller makes appropriate decisions based on the bits of *ir*. In our example, the most significant bits of *ir* are 0000, indicating a direct address *lda* instruction. To complete the address for the full-address *lda* instruction, the controller causes the current contents of *pc* to be clocked into *mar* and then be placed on *adbus* while it asserts *read_mem*. The byte read from the memory will pass through *dbus* and *mar_bus* to reach the input of *mar_offset* register. At the same time controller activates a signal which will place *ir* on *mar_page* register. Clocking *mar* while its load input is enabled causes the full address of the operand of *lda* to be clocked into this register.

The next read from the memory places the operand of the *lda* instruction on *databus*. This 8-bit data passes through *dbus* and becomes available on the *a_side* of *alu*. The controller instructs *alu* to place its *a_side* input on its output, and it causes *shu* to pass its input to its output without shifting. The *lda* operand now appears on *obus*, the controller enables the loading of *ac*, and on the edge of the clock, the operand of *lda* is clocked into the accumulator.

Execution of other instructions is done in a manner similar to the procedure described for *lda*. For the *and*, *add*, and *sub* instructions, when the operand of instruction becomes available on the *a_side* of *alu*, the controller signals *alu* to perform *and*, *add*, or *sub* operations instead of passing the operand through to the output of *alu*. For indirect addressing, the controller causes an extra read from the memory before performing the operation.

9.5 DATAFLOW DESCRIPTION OF PARWAN

The behavioral description in Section 9.2 presented an unambiguous description of the correct operation of Parwan. Hardware implementation of this machine, or even its bussing structure, is not apparent from the description in Figure 9.15. This section presents a description of Parwan which is closer to its actual hardware. This description consists of the structural interconnection of the data registers and logic units and it uses a dataflow description for the controller. Since the overall description deals with controlling the flow of data through registers and buses, we refer to it as the dataflow description of Parwan.

9.5.1 Data and Control Partitioning

Figure 9.28 shows data and control partitioning that we use for the dataflow description of Parwan. The data section contains the interconnection specification of CPU components. This includes instantiation of individual components and conditional placement of their outputs on appropriate buses. The control section uses external control signals and signals from the data section, and generates signals to control conditional assignments of data into registers or buses of the data section.

Figure 9.29 shows a list of control signals generated by the control section to control data movement in the data section. The names are chosen according to the

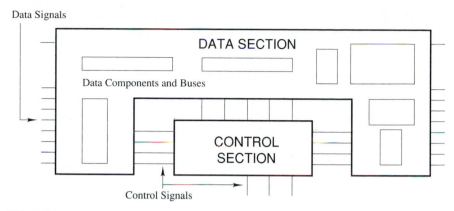

FIGURE 9.28
Data and control sections of Parwan CPU.

RELATED TO:	SIGNAL CATEGORY AND NAME
Register control signals	
AC	load_ac, zero_ac
IR	load_ir
PC	increment_pc, load_page_pc, load_offset_pc,reset_pc
MAR	load_page_mar, load_offset_mar
SR	load_sr, cm_carry_sr
Bus connection control signals	
MAR_BUS	pc_on_mar_page_bus, ir_on_mar_page_bus
	pc_on_mar_offset_bus, dbus_on_mar_offset_bus
DBUS	pc_offset_on_dbus, obus_on_dbus, databus_on_dbus
ADBUS	mar_on_adbus
DATABUS	dbus_on_databus
Logic unit function control signals	
SHU	arith_shift_left, arith_shift_right
ALU	alu_code
Memory control and other external signals	
Etc.	read_mem, write_mem, interrupt

FIGURE 9.29
Inputs and outputs of Parwan control section.

operation that is controlled by the signal. For example, placing the least significant four bits of *ir* into *mar_page* bus is controlled by the *ir_on_mar_page_bus* signal.

9.5.2 Timing of Data and Control Events

Data and control sections are driven by the same clock signal. On the falling edge of this clock, the control section makes its state transition and the registers of the data section accept their new values. Figure 9.30 shows the timing of control signals relative to the circuit clock.

A control signal becomes active on the falling edge of a clock pulse and remains active until the next negative edge. While a control signal is active, logic units of the data section perform their specified operations and their results become available at the inputs of their target registers. When the falling edge of clock arrives, a register, whose load input is enabled, accepts its input. The width of control signals allow for all logic unit and bus propagation delays.

The control section consists of master-slave D-type flip-flops that accept their inputs when the clock becomes '1' and change their outputs when clock returns to '0'. Control flip-flops and data registers are synchronized with the falling edge of the clock.

9.5.3 General Description Methodology

The Parwan description is based on the partitioning in Figure 9.28. The individual components of the data section, shown in Figure 9.27, are independently described at the behavioral or dataflow level. We describe the data section by wiring its components, and bussing component outputs according to the bus structure in Figure 9.27. After the completion of the data section, a state machine description style is used for the description of the control section of Parwan. An overall description wires the data and the control sections.

9.5.4 Description of Components

Components of the data section are *alu*, *shu*, *sr*, *ac*, *ir*, *pc*, and *mar*, and are described in this order. The *basic_utilities* package in the *cmos* library and the *par_utilities* in the *par_library* are used for describing these components. We assume that these components are compiled into the *par_dataflow* VHDL design library.

FIGURE 9.30
Timing of control signals.

9.5.4.1 ARITHMETIC LOGIC UNIT. The *alu* has two 8-bit operands, three select lines, four flag inputs, eight data outputs, and four flag outputs. The three select lines select the operation of *alu* according to the table in Figure 9.31. This figure also shows the flags that may be affected by *alu* operations.

Figure 9.32 shows the logic symbol for Parwan *alu*. This symbol follows the IEEE standard notation. To implement this *alu*, the *alu_operations* package in Figure 9.33 is used in addition to *basic_utilities* and *par_utilities*. This package defines a

S2	S1	S0	OPERATION	FLAGS
0	0	0	a AND b	zn
0	0	1	NOT b	zn
1	0	0	a	zn
1	0	1	b PLUS a	vczn
1	1	0	b	zn
1	1	1	b MINUS a	vczn

FIGURE 9.31
Operations and flags of *alu*.

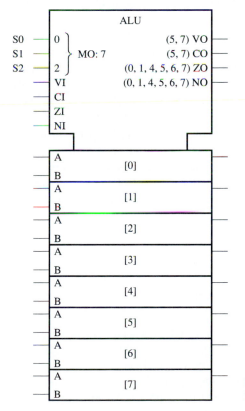

FIGURE 9.32
Logic symbol for Parwan *alu*.

```
LIBRARY cmos;
USE cmos.basic_utilities.ALL;
PACKAGE alu_operations IS
    CONSTANT a_and_b   : qit_vector (2 DOWNTO 0) := "000";
    CONSTANT b_compl   : qit_vector (2 DOWNTO 0) := "001";
    CONSTANT a_input   : qit_vector (2 DOWNTO 0) := "100";
    CONSTANT a_add_b   : qit_vector (2 DOWNTO 0) := "101";
    CONSTANT b_input   : qit_vector (2 DOWNTO 0) := "110";
    CONSTANT a_sub_b   : qit_vector (2 DOWNTO 0) := "111";
END alu_operations;
```

FIGURE 9.33
Package declaration for the *alu_operations* package.

name equivalent for the operation codes of *alu* and is merely used for readability of *alu* code.

Figure 9.34 shows the VHDL description for the Parwan *alu*. The type of the elements of all inputs and outputs is *qit* of the *basic_utilities* package. Types *nibble* and *byte* are defined in *par_utilities* and are used in the entity declaration of the *arithmatic_logic_unit*. In the *behavioral* architecture of *arithmatic_logic_unit*, a case statement selects the *alu* operations based on the 3-bit *code* input. The add and subtract operations use *add_cv* and *sub_cv* functions of *par_utilities*. The most significant bits of the *qit_vector* returned by these functions are the overflow and carry of the corresponding operations. Flag outputs not affected by an *alu* operation are assigned to the values of the input flags.

9.5.4.2 SHIFTER UNIT. Figure 9.35 shows the logic symbol for the shifter unit. This unit has two mode lines that select right or left shift operations, four flag inputs, eight data inputs, four flag outputs, and eight data outputs. A left shift operation moves a '0' into the least significant position of the output, places the shifted input on the output, moves the most significant bit to the carry output, and sets the overflow based on a sign change. A right shift operation extends the sign bit of the input, shifts it one place to the right, and makes it available on the output. Both shift operations can affect negative and zero flag.

The description of *shu* is shown in Figure 9.36. As in *alu*, a single process statement constitutes the statement part of the *behavioral* architecture of the *shifter_unit*. For shifting, the concatenation operator is used to form the shifted pattern, which is assigned to the temporary variable *t*. When no shift operation is specified, the input data and flags are assigned to the outputs of the shifter.

9.5.4.3 STATUS REGISTER UNIT. The status register is a synchronous, negative edge-trigger, 4-bit register. As shown in the logic symbol in Figure 9.37, the data loaded into the flags is synchronously controlled by *load* and *cm_carry* inputs. When *load* is active, all four input flags are loaded into the flag flip-flops, and when *cm_carry* is active, the *c* flag is loaded with the complement of its present value.

```
ENTITY arithmatic_logic_unit IS
    PORT (a_side, b_side : IN byte; code : IN qit_vector (2 DOWNTO 0);
             in_flags : IN nibble; z_out : OUT byte;  out_flags : OUT nibble);
END arithmatic_logic_unit;
--
ARCHITECTURE behavioral OF arithmatic_logic_unit IS
BEGIN
    coding: PROCESS (a_side, b_side, code)
        VARIABLE t : qit_vector (9 DOWNTO 0);
        VARIABLE v, c, z, n : qit;
        ALIAS n_flag_in : qit IS in_flags(0);
        ALIAS z_flag_in : qit IS in_flags(1);
        ALIAS c_flag_in : qit IS in_flags(2);
        ALIAS v_flag_in : qit IS in_flags(3);
    BEGIN
        CASE code IS
            WHEN a_add_b =>
                t := add_cv (b_side, a_side, c_flag_in);
                c := t(8);   v := t(9);   -- other flags are set at the end
            WHEN a_sub_b =>
                t := sub_cv (b_side, a_side, c_flag_in);
                c := t(8);   v := t(9);
            WHEN a_and_b =>
                t (7 DOWNTO 0) := a_side AND b_side;
                c := c_flag_in;   v := v_flag_in;
            WHEN a_input   =>
                t (7 DOWNTO 0) := a_side;
                c := c_flag_in;   v := v_flag_in;
            WHEN b_input   =>
                t (7 DOWNTO 0) := b_side;
                c := c_flag_in;   v := v_flag_in;
            WHEN b_compl =>
                t (7 DOWNTO 0) := NOT b_side;
                c := c_flag_in;   v := v_flag_in;
            WHEN OTHERS => NULL;
        END CASE;
        n := t(7);
        z := set_if_zero (t);
        z_out <= t (7 DOWNTO 0);
        out_flags <= v & c & z & n;
    END PROCESS coding;
END behavioral;
```

FIGURE 9.34
Behavioral description of Parwan arithmatic logic unit.

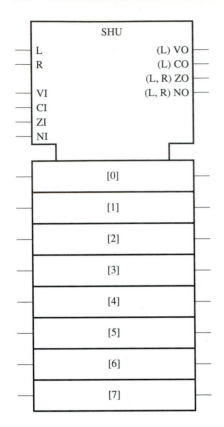

FIGURE 9.35
Logic symbol of Parwan *shu*.

The VHDL description of the status register, shown in Figure 9.38, uses a process statement that is sensitive to the input clock. The *internal_state* variable in the *behavioral* architecture of the *status_register_unit* holds the value of the register. On the falling edge of the clock, this variable is assigned to the nibble output of the status register.

9.5.4.4 ACCUMULATOR. The accumulator of Parwan is an 8-bit register with synchronous loading and zeroing inputs. As shown in Figure 9.39, loading of external data into the register is done on the falling edge of the clock when the *load* input is active and the *zero* input is disabled. Simultaneous activation of the *load* and *zero* inputs causes synchronous resetting of the register.

Figure 9.40 shows the dataflow description of the accumulator. In the *dataflow* architecture of the *accumulator_unit*, when *load* is '1', on the falling edge of *ck*, a guarded signal assignment assigns zero or the *i8* input to the 8-bit output, *o8*.

9.5.4.5 INSTRUCTION REGISTER. The instruction register (*ir*) is an 8-bit synchronous register with an active high load input. The load input enables the clock and causes the register to be loaded on the falling edge of the clock input. The logic symbol of *ir* is shown in Figure 9.41.

```
┌ENTITY  shifter_unit  IS
│   PORT  (alu_side : IN  byte;    arith_shift_left, arith_shift_right : IN  qit;
│              in_flags : IN  nibble; obus\kern1pt_side : OUT  byte;    out\kern1pt_flags : OUT
nibble);
└END  shifter\kern1pt_unit;
--
┌ARCHITECTURE  behavioral  OF  shifter_unit  IS
├BEGIN
│   ┌coding: PROCESS  (alu_side, arith_shift_left, arith_shift_right)
│   │    VARIABLE  t : qit_vector (7 DOWNTO 0);
│   │    VARIABLE  v, c, z, n : qit;
│   │    ALIAS  n_flag_in : qit  IS  in_flags(0);
│   │    ALIAS  z_flag_in : qit  IS  in_flags(1);
│   │    ALIAS  c_flag_in : qit  IS  in_flags(2);
│   │    ALIAS  v_flag_in : qit  IS  in_flags(3);
│   ├BEGIN
│   │    IF  arith_shift_right = '0'  AND  arith_shift_left = '0'  THEN
│   │         t := alu_side (7 DOWNTO 0);
│   │         n := n_flag_in;
│   │         z := z_flag_in;
│   │         c := c_flag_in;
│   │         v := v_flag_in;
│   │    ELSIF  arith_shift_left = '1'  THEN
│   │         t := alu_side (6 DOWNTO 0) & '0';
│   │         n := t (7);
│   │         z := set_if_zero (t);
│   │         c := alu_side (7);
│   │         v := alu_side (6) XOR alu_side (7);
│   │    ELSIF  arith_shift_right = '1'  THEN
│   │         t := alu_side (7) & alu_side (7 DOWNTO 1);
│   │         n := t (7);
│   │         z := set_if_zero (t);
│   │         c := c_flag_in;
│   │         v := v_flag_in;
│   │    END  IF;
│   │    obus_side <= t;
│   │    out_flags <= v & c & z & n;
│   └END PROCESS  coding;
└END  behavioral;
```

FIGURE 9.36
Behavioral description of the Parwan shifter unit.

Figure 9.42 shows the VHDL description of the instruction register that corresponds to its logic symbol. In the *dataflow* architecture of *instruction_register_unit*, a guarded block statement is used to gate the input clock with the *load* input.

9.5.4.6 PROGRAM COUNTER. The program counter is a 12-bit synchronous up-counter with one reset and two load inputs. The *load_page* input synchronously loads

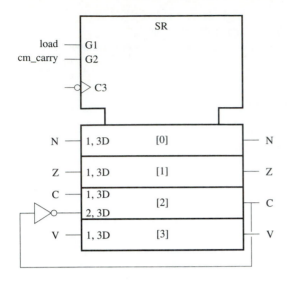

FIGURE 9.37
Logic symbol of the status register.

```
ENTITY  status_register_unit  IS
    PORT (in_flags : IN  nibble;  out_status : OUT  nibble;
           load, cm_carry, ck : IN  qit );
END  status_register_unit;
--
ARCHITECTURE  behavioral  OF  status_register_unit  IS
BEGIN
    PROCESS  (ck)
        VARIABLE  internal_state : nibble := "0000";
        ALIAS  internal_c : qit  IS  internal_state (2);
    BEGIN
        IF  (ck = '0')  THEN
            IF  (load = '1')  THEN
                internal_state := in_flags;
            ELSIF  (cm_carry = '1')  THEN
                internal_c := NOT  internal_c;
            END  IF;
            out_status <= internal_state;
        END  IF;
    END PROCESS;
END  behavioral;
```

FIGURE 9.38
Behavioral description of the Parwan status register.

input data into the most significant four bits and the *load_offset* loads input data into the least significant eight bits of the register. The synchronous reset input resets the entire register. The logic symbol of this unit appears in Figure 9.43.

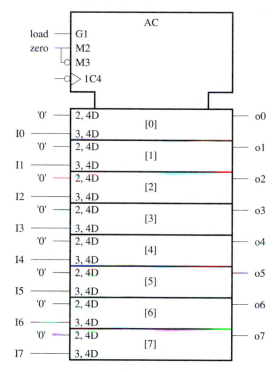

FIGURE 9.39
Logic symbol for the Parwan accumulator.

```
ENTITY accumulator_unit IS
    PORT (i8 : IN byte; o8 : OUT byte; load, zero, ck : IN qit);
END accumulator_unit;
--
ARCHITECTURE dataflow OF accumulator_unit IS
BEGIN
    enable : BLOCK (load = '1')
    BEGIN
        clocking : BLOCK ( (ck = '0' AND NOT ck'STABLE) AND GUARD )
        BEGIN
            o8 <= GUARDED "00000000" WHEN zero = '1' ELSE i8;
        END BLOCK clocking;
    END BLOCK enable;
END dataflow;
```

FIGURE 9.40
Dataflow description of the Parwan accumulator.

The VHDL description of the program counter in Figure 9.44 consists of a process statement that is sensitive to the input clock, *ck*. This code gives the highest priority to *reset*, followed by *increment*, and then by the load inputs. The *behavioral* architecture of the *program_counter_unit* allows for the simultaneous loading of page

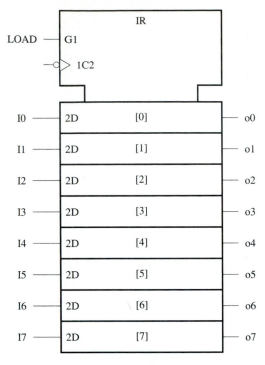

FIGURE 9.41
Logic symbol for the Parwan instruction register.

```
ENTITY instruction_register_unit IS
    PORT (i8 : IN byte; o8 : OUT byte; load, ck : IN qit);
END instruction_register_unit;
--
ARCHITECTURE dataflow OF instruction_register_unit IS
BEGIN
    enable : BLOCK (load = '1')
    BEGIN
        clocking : BLOCK ( (ck = '0' AND NOT ck'STABLE) AND GUARD )
        BEGIN
            o8 <= GUARDED i8;
        END BLOCK clocking;
    END BLOCK enable;
END dataflow;
```

FIGURE 9.42
Dataflow description of the Parwan instruction register.

and offset parts of the register. The *inc* function of the *basic_utilities* package performs the incrementing of the internal state of this description.

9.5.4.7 MEMORY ADDRESS REGISTER. The memory address register (*mar*) is a 12-bit register with two synchronous load inputs. The *load_page* input loads the par-

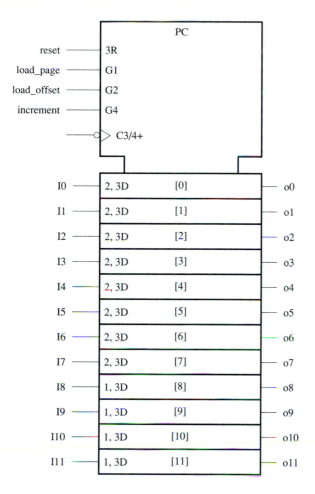

FIGURE 9.43
Logic symbol for the Parwan program counter.

allel data into the most significant nibble of the register and the *load_offset* loads data into its least significant byte. The logic symbol of this unit is presented in Figure 9.45.

Figure 9.46 shows the VHDL description of *mar*. A process statement that is sensitive to events on *ck* constitutes the statement part of the *behavioral* architecture of *memory_address_register*. The if statement in the statement part of this process allows simultaneous loading of *mar* page and offset parts. The *internal_state* that holds the contents of the register is assigned to the output of this unit on the falling edge of each clock pulse.

9.5.5 Data Section of Parwan

We completed our description of the components in the data section of Parwan in the previous section. The data section specifies the interconnection of these components and defines the Parwan's bussing structure. The inputs of this unit are the data bus,

```
ENTITY program_counter_unit IS
    PORT (i12 : IN twelve; o12 : OUT twelve;
            increment, load_page, load_offset, reset, ck : IN qit);
END program_counter_unit;
--
ARCHITECTURE behavioral OF program_counter_unit IS
BEGIN
    PROCESS (ck)
        VARIABLE internal_state : twelve := zero_12;
    BEGIN
        IF (ck = '0' ) THEN
            IF reset = '1' THEN
                internal_state := zero_12;
            ELSIF increment = '1' THEN
                internal_state := inc (internal_state);
            ELSE
                IF load_page = '1' THEN
                    internal_state (11 DOWNTO 8) := i12 (11 DOWNTO 8);
                END IF;
                IF load_offset = '1' THEN
                    internal_state (7 DOWNTO 0) := i12 (7 DOWNTO 0);
                END IF;
            END IF;
            o12 <= internal_state;
        END IF;
    END PROCESS;
END behavioral;
```

FIGURE 9.44
Behavioral description of the Parwan program counter.

the clock signal, and the signals from the control section. Control signals specify the operation of the components in the data section, control their clocking, and enable bussing of data to their inputs. The outputs of the data section are the data and address buses, bits of *ir*, and four status flags. The entity declaration in the Parwan data section (*par_data_path*) is shown in Figure 9.47.

In the port clause of this figure, *databus* is declared as a bidirectional bus that uses the *wiring* resolution function. Bidirectionality enables data in and out of *par_data_path* via this bus and the use of the resolution function allows all devices connected to the bus to drive it simultaneously. A device outputting data via this bus drives it with the output data, while all other devices drive its bits with high impedance 'Z'.

The names of the *par_data_path* control inputs are the same as those we use for the inputs of the control section and the same as those shown in Figure 9.29. A register control signal name is formed by appending the register name to the name of the register signal. For example, *load_page_mar* input of *par_data_path* connects to the *load_page* input of *mar* register in Section 9.5.4.7. A bus connection signal name

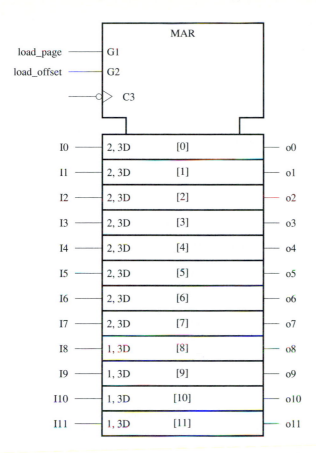

MAR

load_page — G1

load_offset — G2

C3

I0	2, 3D	[0]	o0
I1	2, 3D	[1]	o1
I2	2, 3D	[2]	o2
I3	2, 3D	[3]	o3
I4	2, 3D	[4]	o4
I5	2, 3D	[5]	o5
I6	2, 3D	[6]	o6
I7	2, 3D	[7]	o7
I8	1, 3D	[8]	o8
I9	1, 3D	[9]	o9
I10	1, 3D	[10]	o10
I11	1, 3D	[11]	o11

FIGURE 9.45
Logic symbol for the Parwan
memory address register.

is formed by the source of the bus followed by "*on*" followed by the name of the bus, e.g., *source_on_bus*.

The declarative part of the *structural* architecture of *par_data_path*, in Figure 9.48 includes the declaration of the data section components and the configuration specification of these components. The declared components are bound to their respective descriptions in Section 9.5.4. This declarative part also contains declarations for buses and signals for connecting components of the data section. The 8-bit *dbus* and the 12-bit *mar_bus* are declared as guarded signals which implies selection logic for their multiple sources.

The statement part of the *structural* architecture of *par_data_path*, shown in Figure 9.49, uses component instantiations, signal assignments, and guarded blocks to specify the connections shown in Figure 9.27. The first part of Figure 9.49 shows the connection of *dbus* to the *a_side* of *alu*, *mar_offset_bus*, and to *databus*. Statements used for these connections are labeled *dbus1*, *dbus2*, and *dbus3*, respectively.

For connecting *dbus* to *alu*, a *qit_vector* type conversion converts the resolved *dbus* type (*wired_qit_vector*) to *qit_vector* for the *alu_a_inp* target. This explicit type conversion is necessary because the base types of *qit_vector* and *wired_qit_vector* are

```
ENTITY memory_address_register_unit IS
    PORT (i12 : IN twelve; o12 : OUT twelve;
            load_page, load_offset, ck : IN qit);
END memory_address_register_unit;
--
ARCHITECTURE behavioral OF memory_address_register_unit IS
BEGIN
    PROCESS (ck)
        VARIABLE internal_state : twelve := zero_12;
    BEGIN
        IF (ck = '0' ) THEN
            IF load_page = '1' THEN
                internal_state (11 DOWNTO 8) := i12 (11 DOWNTO 8);
            END IF;
            IF load_offset = '1' THEN
                internal_state (7 DOWNTO 0) := i12 (7 DOWNTO 0);
            END IF;
            o12 <= internal_state;
        END IF;
    END PROCESS;
END behavioral;
```

FIGURE 9.46
Behavioral description of the Parwan memory address register.

different; this is possible because *qit_vector* and *wired_qit_vector* are closely related types. In the instantiation of *alu*, the *alu_a_inp* signal is associated with the *a_side* of *alu*. The statement labeled *dbus2* connects *dbus* to the *mar_offset_bus*. This guarded block statement uses *dbus_on_mar_offset_bus* in its guard expression and conditionally connects *dbus* to the least significant bits of *mar_bus*. This assignment corresponds to the right hollow triangle shown at the input of *mar_offset_bus* in Figure 9.27. Connection of *dbus* to *databus* is done by the statement labeled *dbus3*, which is also a guarded block. The assignment in this block corresponds to the hollow triangle in Figure 9.27 that connects Parwan to its memory. In the latter two assignments, type conversions were not needed since the types of both sides of the assignments were *wired_qit_vector*. Both these assignments are guarded because their targets are multi-source buses.

In the part of Figure 9.49 that describes register connections, a Parwan register is instantiated and its connections are specified. For example, the instantiation of *ir* (*r2: ir*) is followed by assignments that place its outputs (*ir_out*) on *ir_lines* and *mar_page_bus*. The statement labeled *ir1* connects all eight bits of *ir* outputs to the *ir_lines* outputs of *par_data_path*. The statement labeled *ir2* is a guarded block statement that uses *ir_on_mar_page_bus* in its guard expression. The guarded signal assignment within this block conditionally places the least significant nibble of the output of *ir* on the most significant nibble of *mar_bus* (*mar_page_bus*). In this assignment, the type of *ir_out* signal is converted from *qit_vector* to the type of its target bus by using the *wired_qit_vector* type conversion.

```
┌ENTITY par_data_path IS
│   PORT (databus : INOUT wired_byte BUS := "ZZZZZZZZ";
│            adbus : OUT twelve;
│            clk : IN qit;
│            -- register controls:
│            load_ac, zero_ac,
│            load_ir,
│            increment_pc, load_page_pc, load_offset_pc, reset_pc,
│            load_page_mar, load_offset_mar,
│            load_sr, cm_carry_sr,
│            -- bus connections:
│            pc_on_mar_page_bus, ir_on_mar_page_bus,
│            pc_on_mar_offset_bus, dbus_on_mar_offset_bus,
│            pc_offset_on_dbus, obus_on_dbus, databus_on_dbus,
│            mar_on_adbus,
│            dbus_on_databus,
│            -- logic unit function control inputs:
│            arith_shift_left, arith_shift_right : IN qit;
│            alu_code : IN qit_vector (2 DOWNTO 0);
│            -- outputs to the controller:
│            ir_lines : OUT byte; status : OUT nibble
│            );
└END par_data_path;
```

FIGURE 9.47
Entity declaration of the Parwan data section.

The last part of Figure 9.49 contains the instantiation of the *alu* and *shu* combinational logic units. The port map aspects in these instantiations specify connections of these units according to the structure in Figure 9.27.

9.5.6   Control Section of Parwan

The description of the Parwan control section consists of a series of states each of which keeps its selected control signals active for exactly one clock period. These states are states of a state machine. In the description of this state machine, we use a style similar to the one from the *multiple_state_machine* in Chapter 7 (Section 7.2.2, Figure 7.37). In the example presented in Chapter 7, a single block statement whose guard expression was used to detect the edge of the clock, contained all the blocks for the states of the state machine. With the Parwan controller, however, the clock edge detection is repeated in every state. A hardware implication of this description style or the description style in Chapter 7 is one in which a flip-flop corresponds to each of the states, and a combinatorial logic block at the output of each flip-flop provides the necessary conditions for activating other flip-flops and for issuing control signals for the data section or the memory. Figure 9.50 shows a typical control flip-flop hardware. The logic block in this figure is designated by a bubble.

```
ARCHITECTURE structural OF par_data_path IS
  COMPONENT ac
     PORT (i8: IN byte; o8: OUT byte; load, zero, ck: IN qit);
  END COMPONENT;
  FOR r1: ac USE ENTITY WORK.accumulator_unit (dataflow);
  COMPONENT ir
     PORT (i8: IN byte; o8: OUT byte; load, ck: IN qit);
  END COMPONENT;
  FOR r2: ir USE ENTITY WORK.instruction_register_unit (dataflow);
  COMPONENT pc
     PORT (i12 : IN twelve; o12 : OUT twelve;
             increment, load_page, load_offset, reset, ck : IN qit);
  END COMPONENT;
  FOR r3: pc USE ENTITY WORK.program_counter_unit (behavioral);
  COMPONENT mar
     PORT (i12 : IN twelve; o12 : OUT twelve;
             load_page, load_offset, ck : IN qit);
  END COMPONENT;
  FOR r4: mar USE ENTITY WORK.memory_address_register_unit (behavioral);
  COMPONENT sr
     PORT (in_flags : IN nibble; out_status : OUT nibble;
             load, cm_carry, ck : IN qit );
  END COMPONENT;
  FOR r5 : sr USE ENTITY WORK.status_register_unit (behavioral);
  COMPONENT alu
     PORT (a_side, b_side : IN byte; code : IN qit_vector; in_flags : IN nibble;
             z_out : OUT byte;   out_flags : OUT nibble);
  END COMPONENT;
  FOR l1 : alu USE ENTITY WORK.arithmatic_logic_unit (behavioral);
  COMPONENT shu
     PORT (alu_side : IN byte; arith_shift_left, arith_shift_right : IN qit;
             in_flags : IN nibble; obus_side : OUT byte;   out_flags : OUT nibble);
  END COMPONENT;
  FOR l2 : shu USE ENTITY WORK.shifter_unit (behavioral);
  SIGNAL ac_out, ir_out, alu_out, obus : byte;
  SIGNAL alu_a_inp : byte;
  SIGNAL pc_out, mar_out : twelve;
  SIGNAL dbus : wired_byte BUS;
  SIGNAL alu_flags, shu_flags, sr_out : nibble;
  SIGNAL mar_bus : wired_twelve BUS;
  SIGNAL mar_inp : twelve;
```

FIGURE 9.48
Declarative part of the *par_data_path structural* architecture.

The inputs of logic blocks come from other state flip-flops and from external inputs that influence state transitions in the control section. The outputs of logic blocks are the control signals, some of which become inputs to the data section. State flip-flops issue various control signals by providing active sources for them. If several

```
┌BEGIN
│    ┌──── -- bus connections --
│    │    ┌──dbus1: alu_a_inp <= qit_vector (dbus);
│    │    │ ┌─dbus2: BLOCK (dbus_on_mar_offset_bus = '1')
│    │    │ ├─BEGIN   mar_bus (7 DOWNTO 0) <= GUARDED dbus;
│    │    │ └─END BLOCK dbus2;
│    │    │ ┌─dbus3: BLOCK (dbus_on_databus = '1')
│    │    │ ├─BEGIN   databus <= GUARDED dbus;
│    │    └─└─END BLOCK dbus3;
│    │    ┌─obus1: BLOCK (obus_on_dbus = '1')
│    │    ├─BEGIN   dbus <= GUARDED wired_qit_vector (obus);
│    │    └─END BLOCK obus1;
│    │    ┌─databus1: BLOCK (databus_on_dbus = '1')
│    │    ├─BEGIN   dbus <= GUARDED databus;
│    │    └─END BLOCK databus1;
│    └────mar_bus1: mar_inp <= qit_vector (mar_bus);
│    ┌────- register connections --
│    ┌────r1: ac PORT MAP (obus, ac_out, load_ac, zero_ac, clk);
│    ├───r2: ir PORT MAP (obus, ir_out, load_ir, clk);
│    ├──ir1: ir_lines <= ir_out;
│    ┌─ir2: BLOCK (ir_on_mar_page_bus = '1')
│    ├─BEGIN
│    │
│    │      mar_bus (11 DOWNTO 8) <= GUARDED wired_qit_vector (ir_out (3 DOWNTO 0));
│    └─END BLOCK ir2;
```

FIGURE 9.49

Declarative part of the *par_data_path structural* Architecture. (*continued on following page.*)

control flip-flops issue a control signal, the actual control signal is formed by ORing its various sources together. The *par_data_path* unit uses the result of this OR function as input. Signals used to activate control flip-flops also may have multiple sources; therefore, OR functions also are needed at the inputs of control flip-flops.

Figure 9.51 shows an example for the structure of the control section of the Parwan CPU. As shown in this example, all states are synchronized with the same clock and their outputs contribute to the logic for issuing control signals or for activating other control flip-flops. In this figure, state i is conditionally activated by itself or by state k. State i conditionally activates state j, and state k always becomes active after the clock period during which state j is active. Control signal csx is always issued when state k is active, or when state i is active and certain conditions are held on a, b, and c inputs. Control signal csy becomes active when control is in state j, and certain conditions are held on the d and e inputs.

Figure 9.52 shows the entity declaration of the Parwan control section. Its generic clause contains delay values for memory read and write signals. Its port clause includes outputs to the data section, *ir_lines*, status inputs from the data section, and external memory handshaking and interrupt lines.

The declaration part of the dataflow architecture of *par_control_unit* shown in Figure 9.53 declares a guarded signal for each of the control outputs of the control

```
  r3: pc PORT MAP
      (mar_out, pc_out, increment_pc, load_page_pc, load_offset_pc, reset_pc, clk);
  pc1: BLOCK (pc_on_mar_page_bus = '1')
  BEGIN
      mar_bus (11 DOWNTO 8) <= GUARDED wired_qit_vector (pc_out (11 DOWNTO 8));
  END BLOCK pc1;
  pc2: BLOCK (pc_on_mar_offset_bus = '1')
  BEGIN
      mar_bus (7 DOWNTO 0) <= GUARDED wired_qit_vector (pc_out %(7 DOWNTO 0));
  END BLOCK pc2;
  pc3: BLOCK (pc_offset_on_dbus = '1')
  BEGIN
      dbus <= GUARDED wired_qit_vector (pc_out (7 DOWNTO 0));
  END BLOCK pc3;
  r4: mar PORT MAP (mar_inp, mar_out, load_page_mar, load_offset_mar, clk);
  mar1: BLOCK (mar_on_adbus = '1')
  BEGIN   adbus <= GUARDED mar_out;
  END BLOCK mar1;
  r5: sr PORT MAP (shu_flags, sr_out, load_sr, cm_carry_sr, clk);
  sr1: status <= sr_out;
      -- connection of logical and register structures --
  l1: alu PORT MAP (alu_a_inp, ac_out, alu_code, sr_out, alu_out, alu_flags);
  l2: shu PORT MAP (alu_out, arith_shift_left, arith_shift_right, alu_flags, obus, shu_flags);
END structural;
```

FIGURE 9.49
Statement part of the *par_data_path structural* architecture. (*continued from previous page*)

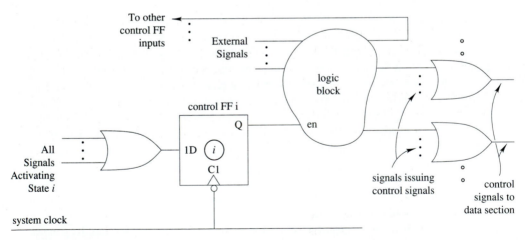

FIGURE 9.50
Typical hardware surrounding a control flip-flop. The logic block in this figure is designated by a bubble.

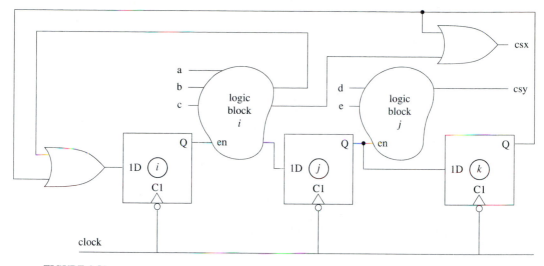

FIGURE 9.51
Example for the structure of Parwan control section.

```
ENTITY par_control_unit IS
   GENERIC (read_delay, write_delay : TIME := 3 NS);
   PORT (clk : IN qit;
            -- register control signals:
            load_ac, zero_ac,
            load_ir,
            increment_pc, load_page_pc, load_offset_pc, reset_pc,
            load_page_mar, load_offset_mar,
            load_sr, cm_carry_sr,
            -- bus connection control signals:
            pc_on_mar_page_bus, ir_on_mar_page_bus,
            pc_on_mar_offset_bus, dbus_on_mar_offset_bus,
            pc_offset_on_dbus, obus_on_dbus, databus_on_dbus,
            mar_on_adbus,
            dbus_on_databus,
            -- logic unit function control outputs:
            arith_shift_left, arith_shift_right : OUT qit;
            alu_code : OUT qit_vector (2 DOWNTO 0);
            -- inputs from the data section:
            ir_lines : IN byte; status : IN nibble;
            -- memory control and other external signals:
            read_mem, write_mem : OUT qit; interrupt : IN qit
         );
END par_control_unit;
```

FIGURE 9.52
Parwan control section entity declaration.

```
ARCHITECTURE dataflow OF par_control_unit IS
   -- oring is implied in the following signals (oi)
   SIGNAL load_ac_oi, zero_ac_oi,
             load_ir_oi,
             increment_pc_oi, load_page_pc_oi, load_offset_pc_oi, reset_pc_oi,
             load_page_mar_oi, load_offset_mar_oi,
             load_sr_oi, cm_carry_sr_oi,
             pc_on_mar_page_bus_oi, ir_on_mar_page_bus_oi,
             pc_on_mar_offset_bus_oi, dbus_on_mar_offset_bus_oi,
             pc_offset_on_dbus_oi, obus_on_dbus_oi, databus_on_dbus_oi,
             mar_on_adbus_oi,
             dbus_on_databus_oi,
             arith_shift_left_oi, arith_shift_right_oi,
             read_mem_oi, write_mem_oi : ored_qit BUS;
   SIGNAL alu_code_oi : ored_qit_vector (2 DOWNTO 0) BUS;
   SIGNAL s : ored_qit_vector (9 DOWNTO 1) REGISTER := "000000001";
```

FIGURE 9.53
Declarative part of the *par_control_unit dataflow* architecture.

section. These signals use the *oring* resolution function in the *basic_utilities* package. The "*_oi*" as the last part of their names identifies them as signals on which oring is implied. The *oring* resolution function ORs multiple drivers on these signals and uses the result for the signal value. Signal *s* of this figure is also a guarded signal with *oring* resolution function. Nine bits of *s* represent the states of the control section, and the *oring* resolution function accounts for the OR gates at the inputs of the state flip-flops.

The statement part of the *dataflow* architecture of *par_control_unit* begins with the assignment of *oring* resolved signals to the actual outputs of the *par_control_unit* shown in Figure 9.54. In fact, this connects the outputs of the implied OR gates to the actual outputs of the control section.

In the remainder of this architecture, guarded block statements for describing the states of the Parwan controller are used. The guard expression of the block statement of state *i* is $s(i)='1'$, where *s* is the resolved signal designated for representation of the states of the controller (see the style used in Section 7.2.2).

Figure 9.55 shows the *s1* block for state 1. In this block, a fetch begins by placing *pc* on *mar* bus, and then initiating the transfer of this data into *mar*. If the interrupt input is active, the *pc* reset input is issued and control returns to state 1. If the CPU is not interrupted, state 2 becomes active on the falling edge of the clock. Also on this edge of the clock, *mar* receives its new value. In coding the data registers and control states, we have made certain that they are all synchronized with the falling edge of the clock.

When in state 2, the *mar* bus has received the new value that was scheduled for it in state 1. State 2 of Parwan, as shown in Figure 9.56, completes the fetch operation by placing *mar* on *adbus* and issuing a *read_mem*. The contents of memory that appear on *databus* must be placed in *ir*. For this purpose, the *databus_on_dbus* control signal is issued, the *a_input* function of *alu* is selected, and the load input of *ir* (*load_ir*) is enabled. On the edge of the clock, control state 3 becomes active and

```
BEGIN
    -- implied or assignments to output signals
    load_ac <= load_ac_oi;
    zero_ac <= zero_ac_oi;
    load_ir <= load_ir_oi;
    increment_pc <= increment_pc_oi;
    load_page_pc <= load_page_pc_oi;
    load_offset_pc <= load_offset_pc_oi;
    reset_pc <= reset_pc_oi;
    load_page_mar <= load_page_mar_oi;
    load_offset_mar <= load_offset_mar_oi;
    load_sr <= load_sr_oi;
    cm_carry_sr <= cm_carry_sr_oi;
    pc_on_mar_page_bus <= pc_on_mar_page_bus_oi;
    ir_on_mar_page_bus <= ir_on_mar_page_bus_oi;
    pc_on_mar_offset_bus <= pc_on_mar_offset_bus_oi;
    dbus_on_mar_offset_bus <= dbus_on_mar_offset_bus_oi;
    pc_offset_on_dbus <= pc_offset_on_dbus_oi;
    obus_on_dbus <= obus_on_dbus_oi;
    databus_on_dbus <= databus_on_dbus_oi;
    mar_on_adbus <= mar_on_adbus_oi;
    dbus_on_databus <= dbus_on_databus_oi;
    arith_shift_left <= arith_shift_left_oi;
    arith_shift_right <= arith_shift_right_oi;
    read_mem <= read_mem_oi;
    write_mem <= write_mem_oi;
    alu_code <= qit_vector (alu_code_oi);
```

FIGURE 9.54
Assigning signals with implied oring to the *par_control_unit* outputs.

ir will have its new value. Also in state 2, the increment function of *pc* is selected so that its value gets incremented on the next falling edge of the clock.

When state 3 becomes active, as shown in Figure 9.57, the newly read instruction is in *ir*. State 3 starts the process of reading the next byte from the memory. At the same time it checks for the number of bytes in the current instruction. If the instruction is a two-byte instruction, the next byte becomes its address and control state 4 is activated to continue the execution of two-byte instructions. On the other hand, if the current instruction is a nonaddress instruction and does not require a second byte, state 3 performs its execution and activates state 2 for fetching the next instruction.

Nonaddress (single-byte) instructions perform operations on the accumulator and flags. For their execution, appropriate *alu* and *shu* functions are selected, and the target register or flag is enabled. For example, for *asr* (arithmetic shift right), the following steps are taken:

1. the *b_input* function of *alu* is selected so that the *alu* output becomes the contents of *ac*,

```
s1: BLOCK (s(1) = '1')
BEGIN -- start of fetch
    -- pc to mar
    pc_on_mar_page_bus_oi <= GUARDED '1';
    pc_on_mar_offset_bus_oi <= GUARDED '1';
    load_page_mar_oi <= GUARDED '1';
    load_offset_mar_oi <= GUARDED '1';
    -- reset pc if interrupt
    reset_pc_oi <= GUARDED '1' WHEN interrupt = '1' ELSE '0';
    -- goto 2 if interrupt is off
    ck: BLOCK ( (clk = '0' AND NOT clk'STABLE) AND GUARD )
    BEGIN
        s(1) <= GUARDED '1' WHEN interrupt = '1' ELSE '0';
        s(2) <= GUARDED '1' WHEN interrupt /= '1' ELSE '0';
    END BLOCK ck;
END BLOCK s1;
```

FIGURE 9.55
State 1: starting a fetch.

```
s2: BLOCK (s(2) = '1')
BEGIN -- fetching continues
    -- read memory into ir
    mar_on_adbus_oi <= GUARDED '1';
    read_mem_oi <= GUARDED '1' AFTER read_delay;
    databus_on_dbus_oi <= GUARDED '1';
    alu_code_oi <= GUARDED ored_qit_vector (a_input);
    load_ir_oi <= GUARDED '1';
    -- increment pc
    increment_pc_oi <= GUARDED '1';
    -- goto 3
    ck: BLOCK ( (clk = '0' AND NOT clk'STABLE) AND GUARD )
    BEGIN
        s(3) <= GUARDED '1';
    END BLOCK ck;
END BLOCK s2;
```

FIGURE 9.56
State 2: completing a fetch.

2. the *arith_shift_right* function of *shu* is selected so that it shifts its inputs (contents of *ac*) one place to the right,

3. the *load_sr* signal (load input of status register) is enabled so that new values of flags, generated by *shu*, are loaded into *sr*, and finally,

4. the load input of *ac* (*load_ac*) is enabled so that this register gets loaded with the output of *shu* (shifted *ac*).

```
s3: BLOCK (s(3) = '1')
BEGIN
    -- pc to mar, for next read
    pc_on_mar_page_bus_oi <= GUARDED '1';
    pc_on_mar_offset_bus_oi <= GUARDED '1';
    load_page_mar_oi <= GUARDED '1';
    load_offset_mar_oi <= GUARDED '1';
    -- goto 4 if not single byte instruction
    ck: BLOCK ( (clk = '0' AND NOT clk'STABLE) AND GUARD )
    BEGIN
        s(4) <= GUARDED
            '1' WHEN ir_lines (7 DOWNTO 4) /= "1110" ELSE '0';
    END BLOCK ck;
    -- perform single byte instructions
    sb: BLOCK ( (ir_lines (7 DOWNTO 4) = "1110") AND GUARD)
    BEGIN
        alu_code_oi <= GUARDED
            ored_qit_vector (b_compl) WHEN ir_lines (1) = '1' ELSE
            ored_qit_vector (b_input);
        arith_shift_left_oi <= GUARDED
            '1' WHEN ir_lines (3 DOWNTO 0) = "1000" ELSE '0';
        arith_shift_right_oi <= GUARDED
            '1' WHEN ir_lines (3 DOWNTO 0) = "1001" ELSE '0';
        load_sr_oi <= GUARDED
            '1' WHEN ( ir_lines (3) = '1' OR ir_lines (1) = '1' ) ELSE '0';
        cm_carry_sr_oi <= GUARDED '1' WHEN ir_lines (2) = '1' ELSE '0';
        load_ac_oi <= GUARDED
            '1' WHEN ( ir_lines (3) = '1' OR ir_lines (1) = '1' OR ir_lines (0)='1' )
                    ELSE '0';
        zero_ac_oi <= GUARDED
            '1' WHEN ( ir_lines (3) = '0' AND ir_lines (0) = '1' ) ELSE '0';
        ck: BLOCK ( (clk = '0' AND NOT clk'STABLE) AND GUARD )
        BEGIN
            s(2) <= GUARDED '1';
        END BLOCK ck;
    END BLOCK sb;
END BLOCK s3;
```

FIGURE 9.57
State 3: preparing for address fetch, execution of single byte instructions.

State 4 becomes active when a full-address or a page-address instruction (instructions requiring two bytes) is being executed. The preparations for reading the address byte (second byte of the instruction) were done in state 3. State 4, shown in Figure 9.58, completes the read operation and makes the newly read byte available at the input of the offset part of *mar*. Because *load_offset_mar* has become active, this byte will be clocked into *mar* on the next falling edge of the clock. If the instruction being executed is a full-address instruction (*lda*, *and*, *add*, *sub*, *jmp*, or *sta*), the page number from *ir* becomes available at the input of the page part of *mar* to be clocked

```
s4: BLOCK (s(4) = '1')
BEGIN -- page from ir, offset from next memory makeup 12-bit address
      -- read memory into mar offset
      mar_on_adbus_oi <= GUARDED '1';
      read_mem_oi <= GUARDED '1' AFTER read_delay;
      databus_on_dbus_oi <= GUARDED '1';
      dbus_on_mar_offset_bus_oi <= GUARDED '1';
      load_offset_mar_oi <= GUARDED '1'; -- completed operand address
      -- page from ir if not branch or jsr
   pg: BLOCK ( (ir_lines (7 DOWNTO 6) /= "11") AND GUARD)
   BEGIN
         ir_on_mar_page_bus_oi <= GUARDED '1';
         load_page_mar_oi <= GUARDED '1';
         -- goto 5 for indirect, 6 for direct
         ck: BLOCK ( (clk = '0' AND NOT clk'STABLE) AND GUARD )
         BEGIN
             s(5) <= GUARDED '1' WHEN ir_lines (4) = '1' ELSE '0'; -- indir
             s(6) <= GUARDED '1' WHEN ir_lines (4) = '0' ELSE '0'; -- direct
         END BLOCK ck;
   END BLOCK pg;
      -- keep page in mar_page if jsr or bra (same-page instructions)
   sp: BLOCK ( (ir_lines (7 DOWNTO 6) = "11") AND GUARD)
   BEGIN
         -- goto 7 for jsr, 9 for bra
   ck: BLOCK ( (clk = '0' AND NOT clk'STABLE) AND GUARD )
         BEGIN
             s(7) <= GUARDED '1' WHEN ir_lines (5) = '0' ELSE '0'; -- jsr
             s(9) <= GUARDED '1' WHEN ir_lines (5) = '1' ELSE '0'; -- bra
         END BLOCK ck;
   END BLOCK sp;
      -- increment pc
      increment_pc_oi <= GUARDED '1';
END BLOCK s4;
```

FIGURE 9.58
State 4: completing address of full address instructions; branching for indirect, direct, *jsr*, and *branch*.

into this register with the next clock. If the instruction being executed is *jsr* or *bra* (page-address instructions), the *mar_page* register retains its current value. This is because these instructions only address within the current page.

State 4 activates states 5 or 6 for handling indirect or direct addressing modes of full-address instructions and it activates states 7 or 9 for *jsr* or *bra* instructions, respectively.

The falling edge of the clock that activates state 5 also loads a full 12-bit address into *mar*. State 5, shown in Figure 9.59, handles the indirect addressing mode. In this state, the memory location pointed to by *mar* is read on the *databus*, and is made available on the input of the *mar_offset* register. Activation of *load_offset_mar* causes *mar* to be loaded with the byte from the memory on the next negative edge of the

```
s5: BLOCK (s(5) = '1')
BEGIN -- indirect addressing
    -- read actual operand from memory into mar offset
    mar_on_adbus_oi <= GUARDED '1';
    read_mem_oi <= GUARDED '1' AFTER read_delay;
    databus_on_dbus_oi <= GUARDED '1';
    dbus_on_mar_offset_bus_oi <= GUARDED '1';
    load_offset_mar_oi <= GUARDED '1';
    -- goto 6
    ck: BLOCK ( (clk = '0' AND NOT clk'STABLE) AND GUARD )
    BEGIN
        s(6) <= GUARDED '1';
    END BLOCK ck;
END BLOCK s5;
```

FIGURE 9.59
State 5: taking care of indirect addressing.

clock. As shown in Figure 9.9, indirect addressing mode only affects the offset part of the address. State 5 activates state 6 which is the same state that was activated by state 4 if direct addressing mode was used.

State 6 becomes active when the instruction being executed is *jmp*, *sta*, *lda*, *and*, *add*, or *sub*. When in this state, *mar* contains the complete operand address. Figure 9.60 shows three nested blocks in the block statement of state 6. These blocks are labeled *jm*, *st*, and *rd*.

The guard expression of the *jm* block is TRUE for the *jmp* instruction. In this case, the *pc* load input, *load_pc*, is enabled to cause the contents of *mar* to be loaded in *pc*. This is followed by activation of state 2 for fetching a new instruction from the memory location pointed to by the new contents of *pc*.

The guard expression of the *st* block becomes active if the opcode of the *sta* instruction is detected on the most significant bits of *ir_lines*. In this case, a write to memory is initiated and contents of *ac* are routed through *alu* to reach the *databus* so that they can be written into the memory.

The third block (*rd*) nested in the block statement of state 6 handles *lda*, *and*, *add*, and *sub*. For these instructions, the actual operand is read from the memory location pointed to by *mar*. When the *databus_on_dbus* control signal is issued, this operand becomes available on the *a_side* of *alu*. (Recall that *dbus* is directly connected to the *a_side* of *alu* in Figure 9.27.) Based on the instruction being executed, a selected signal assignment selects an appropriate function of *alu*. For example, for the *add* instruction, the *a_add_b* function is selected. This causes the adding result of *ac* and data on *a_side* of *alu* to become available on the output of *alu*. This result is loaded in *ac* by issuing the *load_ac* control signal. Activation of *load_sr* in the *rd* block of state 6 updates flags with values that resulted from the *alu* operation. Upon completion of full-address instructions, control branches to state 1 for the next instruction fetch.

State 4 of the Parwan controller caused a memory read operation and targeted the information read from the memory into *mar_offset* register. If the *jsr* instruction

```
s6: BLOCK  (s(6) = '1')
BEGIN
    jm: BLOCK ( (ir_lines (7 DOWNTO 5) = "100") AND GUARD)
    BEGIN
        load_page_pc_oi <= GUARDED '1';
        load_offset_pc_oi <= GUARDED '1';
        -- goto 2
        ck: BLOCK ( (clk = '0' AND NOT clk'STABLE) AND GUARD )
        BEGIN
            s(2) <= GUARDED '1';
        END BLOCK ck;
    END BLOCK jm;
    --
    st: BLOCK ( (ir_lines (7 DOWNTO 5) = "101") AND GUARD)
    BEGIN
        -- mar on adbus, ac on databus, write to memory
        mar_on_adbus_oi <= GUARDED '1';
        alu_code_oi <= GUARDED ored_qit_vector (b_input);
        obus_on_dbus_oi <= GUARDED '1';
        dbus_on_databus_oi <= GUARDED '1';
        write_mem_oi <= GUARDED '1' AFTER write_delay;
        -- goto 1
        ck: BLOCK ( (clk = '0' AND NOT clk'STABLE) AND GUARD )
        BEGIN
            s(1) <= GUARDED '1';
        END BLOCK ck;
    END BLOCK st;
    --
    rd: BLOCK ( (ir_lines (7) = '0') AND GUARD)
    BEGIN
        -- mar on adbus, read memory for operand, perform operation
        mar_on_adbus_oi <= GUARDED '1';
        read_mem_oi <= GUARDED '1' AFTER read_delay;
        databus_on_dbus_oi <= GUARDED '1';
        WITH ir_lines (6 DOWNTO 5) SELECT
            alu_code_oi <= GUARDED
                ored_qit_vector (a_input) WHEN "00",
                ored_qit_vector (a_and_b) WHEN "01",
                ored_qit_vector (a_add_b) WHEN "10",
                ored_qit_vector (a_sub_b) WHEN "11",
                ored_qit_vector (b_input) WHEN OTHERS;
        load_sr_oi <= GUARDED '1';
        load_ac_oi <= GUARDED '1';
        -- goto 1
        ck: BLOCK ( (clk = '0' AND NOT clk'STABLE) AND GUARD )
        BEGIN
            s(1) <= GUARDED '1';
        END BLOCK ck;
    END BLOCK rd;
END BLOCK s6;
```

FIGURE 9.60
State 6: reading the actual operand, and executing *jmp*, *sta*, *lda*, *and*, *add*, and *sub* instructions.

is being executed, the address in the *mar_offset* register becomes the address of the top of subroutine. State 7, shown in Figure 9.61, continues the execution of *jsr*. This state writes the contents of *pc* to the top of the subroutine (pointed by *mar*) and at the same time targets the address of the top of the subroutine (twelve bits of *mar*) for the *pc* register.

Following state 7 on the falling edge of the clock, state 8 of Figure 9.62 becomes active to complete the execution of *jsr*. In this state, *pc* now contains the first location of the subroutine. Since the actual subroutine code begins in the location after the top-of-subroutine, state 8 issues the *increment_pc* signal and activates state 1 for fetching the first instruction of the subroutine.

Control reaches state 9, shown in Figure 9.63, when state 4 is active and a branch instruction is being executed. When state 9 becomes active, the branch address is in the *mar* register. State 9 loads *mar* into *pc* if a match is found between the branch directive (bits 3 to 0), and the status register bits (v, c, z, and n flags). If the branch

```
s7: BLOCK (s(7) = "1")
BEGIN   -- jsr
    -- write pc offset to top of subroutine
    mar_on_adbus_oi <= GUARDED '1';
    pc_offset_on_dbus_oi <= GUARDED '1';
    dbus_on_databus_oi <= GUARDED '1';
    write_mem_oi <= GUARDED '1' AFTER write_delay;
    -- address of subroutine to pc
    load_offset_pc_oi <= GUARDED '1';
    -- goto 8
    ck: BLOCK ( (clk = '0' AND NOT clk'STABLE) AND GUARD )
    BEGIN
        s(8) <= GUARDED '1';
    END BLOCK ck;
END BLOCK s7;
```

FIGURE 9.61
State 7: writing return address of subroutine; making *pc* point to top of subroutine.

```
s8: BLOCK (s(8) = '1')
BEGIN
    -- increment pc
    increment_pc_oi <= GUARDED '1';
    -- goto 1
    ck: BLOCK ( (clk = '0' AND NOT clk'STABLE) AND GUARD )
    BEGIN
        s(1) <= GUARDED '1';
    END BLOCK ck;
END BLOCK s8;
```

FIGURE 9.62
State 8: incrementing *pc* to skip the location reserved for the return address.

```
┌s9: BLOCK  (s(9)  =  '1')
├BEGIN
│     load_offset_pc_oi  <=  GUARDED
│         '1'  WHEN  (status  AND  ir_lines  (3  DOWNTO  0))  /=  "0000"  ELSE  '0';
│     -- goto  1
│     ck: BLOCK  (  (clk  =  '0'  AND  NOT  clk'STABLE)  AND  GUARD  )
│     BEGIN
│         s(1)  <=  GUARDED  '1';
│     END  BLOCK  ck;
└END  BLOCK  s9;
```

FIGURE 9.63
State 9: conditional loading of *pc* for the branch instructions.

condition is not satisfied, *pc* retains its value—this value points to the memory location that follows the branch instruction. In any case, control returns to state 1 for fetching the next instruction.

The last block statement in the *dataflow* architecture of the *par_control_unit* assigns zeros to all state designators (bits of *s*). As described in Chapter 7, this causes a state to be reset after it activates its next state. Figure 9.64 shows this block.

This completes the *dataflow* description of the Parwan controller. The general outline of the circuit corresponding to the descriptions presented above is shown in Figure 9.65. This circuit diagram uses the same notations we employed in Figure 9.50.

9.5.7 Wiring Data and Control Sections

The complete dataflow description of the Parwan processor consists of the *par_data_path* in Section 9.5.5 and the *par_control_unit* in Section 9.5.6. The entity declaration of this CPU is shown in Figure 9.66. This declaration is similar to the one shown in Figure 9.14 for the behavioral description of the Parwan CPU, except that the latter does not use a generic clause.

Figure 9.67 shows the general outline of the *dataflow* architecture of the *par_central_processing_unit*. This description specifies interconnections between the *structural* architecture of the *par_data_path* and the *dataflow* architecture of the *par_control_unit*.

```
┌ck: BLOCK  (  clk  =  '0'  AND  NOT  clk'STABLE  )
├BEGIN
│     s  (9  DOWNTO  1)  <=  GUARDED  "000000000";
└END  BLOCK  ck;
└END  dataflow;
```

FIGURE 9.64
A zero driver is placed on all states, ending the *dataflow* description of the *par_control_unit*.

FIGURE 9.65
General outline of the Parwan controller.

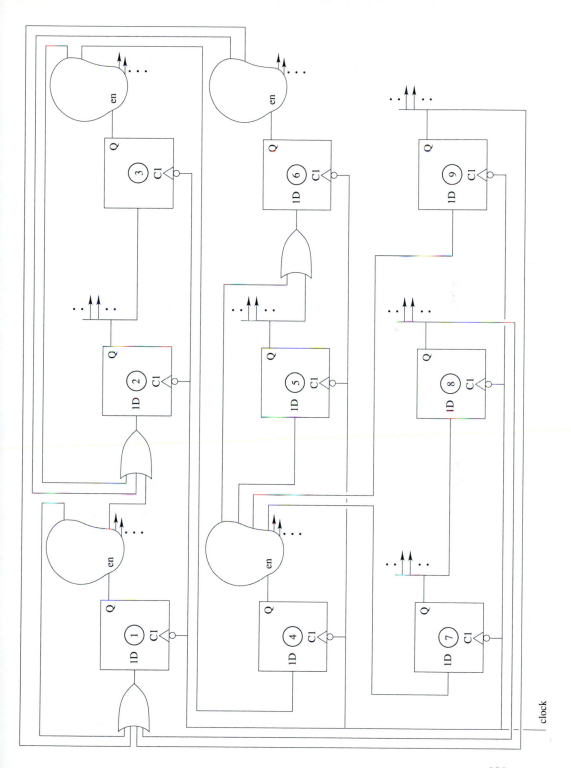

```
ENTITY par_central_processing_unit IS
    PORT (clk : IN qit;
           interrupt : IN qit;
           read_mem, write_mem : OUT qit;
           databus : INOUT wired_byte BUS := "ZZZZZZZZ"; adbus : OUT twelve
           );
END par_central_processing_unit;
```

FIGURE 9.66
Entity declaration of the Parwan CPU for its dataflow description.

The signal names omitted from this figure are the same as those used in Figures 9.47 and 9.52 for the entity declarations of the data section and the control section, respectively.

9.6   A TEST BENCH FOR THE PARWAN CPU

Figure 9.68 shows a simple test bench for the Parwan CPU. This description instantiates the *par_central_processing_unit*, generates waveforms for its interrupt and clock signals, and models a portion of its static RAM. The reason the binding of the *cpu* component is not included in this description is so that configuration declarations can be written to configure it to test the behavioral or the dataflow models of the Parwan CPU. The *mem* process in the *input_output* architecture of the *parwan_tester* includes a 64-byte array that is initialized to several instructions of Parwan. This process waits for *read* or *write* signals to become '1' in order to perform the corresponding memory operations. To read a byte, it uses the integer equivalent of *address* to index the memory and places the byte extracted from *memory* on the *data* bus. This data stays valid until *read* becomes '0', at which time the *mem* process drives data lines with 'Z'. When *write* becomes active, after writing data to memory, the process waits for removal of *write* before checking for another read or write request.

   Figure 9.69 shows the configuration declarations for binding the *cpu* instance of the *par_central_processing_unit* in the test bench of Figure 9.68 to the *behavioral* or *dataflow* descriptions of the Parwan CPU. Therefore, we can use the same architecture for testing both versions of the *par_central_processing_unit*.

   The simulation of *behavioral* and *dataflow* configurations in Figure 9.69 indicate that the two descriptions of the Parwan processor are functionally equivalent. The timing of events, however, in these descriptions is different. This is because the clocking information was not available during the development of the behavioral description. The exact clocking and sequence of events became known only when we designed the bussing and register structure of this machine. We based our dataflow description on this bussing structure (see Figure 9.27); this is the reason for clock level accuracy of the dataflow description.

   The simulation run for the execution of the test program in Figure 9.68 took 0.7 seconds for the behavioral model, and 4.4 seconds for the dataflow model of the Parwan CPU. Clearly, the price we are paying for accurate simulation results is CPU cycles.

```
ARCHITECTURE dataflow OF par_central_processing_unit IS
   COMPONENT par_data_path
   PORT (databus : INOUT wired_byte;   adbus : OUT twelve;
           clk : IN qit;
           load_ac, zero_ac,
             .  .  .
           alu_code : IN qit_vector (2 DOWNTO 0);
           ir_lines : OUT byte; status : OUT nibble
           );
   END COMPONENT;
   FOR data: par_data_path USE ENTITY WORK.par_data_path (structural);
   COMPONENT par_control_unit
   PORT (clk : IN qit;
           load_ac, zero_ac,
             .  .  .
           alu_code : OUT qit_vector (2 DOWNTO 0);
           ir_lines : IN byte; status : IN nibble;
           read_mem, write_mem : OUT qit; interrupt : IN qit
           );
   END COMPONENT;
   FOR ctrl: par_control_unit USE ENTITY WORK.par_control_unit (dataflow);
   SIGNAL load_ac, zero_ac,
             .  .  .
   SIGNAL alu_code : qit_vector (2 DOWNTO 0);
   SIGNAL ir_lines : byte;
   SIGNAL status : nibble;
BEGIN
   data: par_data_path PORT MAP
           (databus, adbus,
            clk,
            load_ac, zero_ac,
             .  .  .
            alu_code,
            ir_lines, status
            );
   ctrl: par_control_unit PORT MAP
           (clk,
            load_ac, zero_ac,
             .  .  .
            alu_code,
            ir_lines, status,
            read_mem, write_mem, interrupt
            );
END dataflow;
```

FIGURE 9.67
The general outline of *dataflow* architecture of the Parwan CPU.

```
ARCHITECTURE input_output OF parwan_tester IS
    COMPONENT parwan PORT (clk : IN qit;   interrupt : IN qit;
        read_mem, write_mem : OUT qit;
        databus : INOUT wired_byte; adbus : OUT twelve );
    END COMPONENT;
    SIGNAL clock, interrupt, read, write : qit;
    SIGNAL data : wired_byte := "ZZZZZZZZ";
    SIGNAL address : twelve;
    TYPE byte_memory IS ARRAY ( INTEGER RANGE <> ) OF byte;
BEGIN
    int : interrupt <= '1', '0' AFTER 4500 NS;
    clk : clock <= NOT clock AFTER 1 US WHEN NOW <= 140 US ELSE clock;
    cpu : parwan PORT MAP (clock, interrupt, read, write, data, address);
    mem : PROCESS
        VARIABLE memory : byte_memory ( 0 TO 63 ) :=
            ("00000000", "00011000", "10100000", "00011001", --lda 24, sta 25
             "00100000", "00011010", "01000000", "00011011", --and 26, add 27
             "11100010", "11101001", "01100000", "00011100", --cac, asr, sub 28
             "00010000", "00011101", "11000000", "00100100", --lda i 29, jsr 36
             "11101000", "11100000", "10000000", "00100000", --asl, nop, jmp 32
             "00000000", "00000000", "00000000", "00000000",
             "00001100", "00011111", "00000000", "00000000", --(24, 25, 26, 27)
             "00001100", "00011111", "00000000", "01011010", --(28, 29, 30, 31)
             "10000000", "00010010", "00000000", "00000000", --jmp 18
             "00000000", "11100010", "10010000", "00100100", --   , cma, jmp i 36
             "00000000", "00000000", "00000000", "00000000",
             "00000000", "00000000", "00000000", "00000000",
             "00000000", "00000000", "00000000", "00000000",
             "00000000", "00000000", "00000000", "00000000",
             "00000000", "00000000", "00000000", "00000000",
             "00000000", "00000000", "00000000", "00000000" );
        VARIABLE ia : INTEGER;
    BEGIN
        WAIT ON read, write;
        qit2int (address, ia);
        IF read = '1' THEN
            IF ia >= 64 THEN  data <= "ZZZZZZZZ";
            ELSE  data <= wired_byte ( memory (ia) );
            END IF;
            WAIT UNTIL read = '0';
            data <= "ZZZZZZZZ";
        ELSIF write = '1' THEN
            IF ia < 64 THEN   memory (ia) := byte ( data );
            END IF;
            WAIT UNTIL write = '0';
        END IF;
    END PROCESS mem;
END input_output;
```

FIGURE 9.68
A simple test bench for Parwan behavioral and dataflow descriptions.

```
⎡CONFIGURATION behavior OF parwan_tester IS
⎢   FOR input_output
⎢      FOR cpu : parwan
⎢         USE ENTITY behavioral.par_central_processing_unit(behavioral);
⎢      END FOR;
⎢   END FOR;
⎣END behavior;
```
(a)

```
⎡CONFIGURATION dataflow OF parwan_tester IS
⎢   FOR input_output
⎢      FOR cpu : parwan
⎢         USE ENTITY par_dataflow.par_central_processing_unit(dataflow);
⎢      END FOR;
⎢   END FOR;
⎣END dataflow;
```
(b)

FIGURE 9.69
Configuring *input_output* architecture of the Parwan tester (a) for testing *behavioral* architecture of the *par_central_processing_unit*, (b) for testing *dataflow* architecture of *par_central_processing_unit*.

9.7 SUMMARY

This chapter showed how VHDL can be used to describe a system at the behavioral level before the system is even designed, and at the dataflow level after major design decisions have been made. The behavioral description aids designers as they verify their understanding of the problem, while the dataflow description can be used to verify the bussing and register structure of the design. A design carried to the stage where a dataflow model can be generated is only a few simple steps away from complete hardware realization. For completing the design of Parwan, flip-flop and gate interconnections should replace the component descriptions in the Parwan dataflow model.

Descriptions in this chapter cover the major language issues discussed in the earlier chapters. A complete understanding of these descriptions requires good comprehension of the VHDL syntax and semantics. Readers who understand all the descriptions in this chapter to the point where they can develop similar models can consider themselves proficient in the VHDL hardware description language.

REFERENCES

1. Hill, F. J., and G. R. Peterson, "Digital Systems: Hardware Organization and Design," 3rd ed., John Wiley and Sons, New York, 1987.
2. Armstrong, J. R., "Chip-Level Modeling with VHDL," Prentice-Hall Inc., Englewood Cliffs, N.J., 1988.

PROBLEMS

9.1. Make a list of eight simple instructions you think would be useful and possible to add to Parwan.

9.2. In Parwan assembly code, write a program to move a block of data that is stored in the memory. The data begins at location 4:00 and ends at 4:63, and is to be moved to page 5 starting at 5:64.

9.3. A block of data in the Parwan memory begins at location 1:00 and ends at 1:63. Write a program in Parwan assembly language to find the largest positive number in these locations.

9.4. Show the VHDL description of the Mark-1 machine whose ISPS description appeared in Figure 1.3 of Chapter 1.

9.5. Write a procedure for reading Parwan memory from an external file. Assume address and data in this file are in hexadecimal number representation and are arranged as shown here:

> page:offset data

Name this procedure *read_memory* and use this subprogram declaration:

> PROCEDURE read_memory (addr : IN qit_vector; data : OUT qit_vector;
> found : OUT BOOLEAN; file_name : IN STRING);

The *read_memory* procedure searches an entire memory file for an address that matches its *addr* argument. If the address is found, it returns the *qit* equivalent of the data appearing on the same line of the file as the address. If the address is not found, the *found* parameter is returned as FALSE. File name is used as the parameter so that the file declaration can take place each time the procedure is called.

9.6. Write a procedure for writing Parwan memory to an external file such that the address is passed to this procedure as a *qit_vector* of size 12, and the data as a *qit_vector* of size 8. Each time the procedure is called, one line containing address and data should be appended to the end of the file. This information is written to the file in hexadecimal using the format shown here:

> page:offset data

Name this procedure *write_memory* and use this subprogram declaration:

> PROCEDURE write_memory (addr : IN qit_vector; data : IN qit_vector;
> VARIABLE memory_file : OUT TEXT);

The *memory_file* parameter in this procedure should be associated with a file object which is declared outside the procedure.

9.7. Rewrite the Parwan test bench such that the memory read and write are done from and to external files instead of to a declared array as they are shown in Figure 9.68. For this purpose, use the procedures developed in Problems 9.5 and 9.6. When a read from the memory is to be done, a call should be made to the *read_memory* procedure and the data read by the procedure should be placed on the *databus*. When a memory write is to be done, a call to *write_memory* should append the address and data to the end of a memory write file. Use this test bench to verify correctness of the changes that you will be making to Parwan in the problems that follow.

9.8. Modify the behavioral description of the Parwan controller such that the *jsr* instruction can use indirect addressing.

9.9. Suggest a set of instructions for a more complete interrupt handling than what is presently available in Parwan.

9.10. Parwan can be modified to use only three bits for distinguishing between various non-address instructions. We can, therefore, reserve bit 3 of the instruction register as an opcode bit for extending Parwan instructions. In addition, two more non-address instructions can be added to the Parwan instructions. Modify the behavioral description of Parwan such that non-address instructions use 11100xxx opcode. For xxx use 000, 001, 010, 011, 100, and 101 for *nop*, *cla*, *cma*, *cmc*, *asl*, and *asr*, respectively.

9.11. Use the method suggested in Problem 9.10 to add an instruction for immediate loading of the accumulator. This instruction can use one of the extra opcodes that become available by modifying opcodes of non-address instructions. For *ldi* (load accumulator immediate), you may use the 11101000 opcode. The second byte of an *ldi* contains the byte that is to be loaded into the memory. Modify the behavioral description of Parwan for the execution of this instruction.

9.12. Add a stack pointer to the register and bussing structure of Parwan for the implementation of a software stack. Restrict the stack to the last page of the memory. Use the method of opcode expansion suggested in Problem 9.10 to make room for a new instruction, and use 11101001 for an *lds* instruction that loads the stack pointer with the data in the next instruction byte. Show all bus connections, registers, and necessary control signals.

9.13. Use the method suggested in Problem 9.10, and the stack pointer of Problem 9.12 to add two new non-address instructions, *push* and *pop*. Use 11100110 for *push* and 11100111 for *pop*. Modify the behavioral description of Parwan for the execution of these instructions.

9.14. Use the stack implementation in Problem 9.12 to modify the *jsr* instruction such that it pushes the return address onto the top of the stack. Add a new *rts* instruction that causes a return from the subroutine. For this instruction, use the opcode expansion method suggested in Problem 9.10, and use 11101010 for its opcode. Modify the behavioral description of Parwan for the execution of these instructions.

9.15. Modify the dataflow description of Parwan for implementing *jsr* as specified in Problem 9.8.

9.16. Show the dataflow implementation of the opcode extension scheme suggested in Problem 9.10. Show all required bus connections and modify the controller of Parwan.

9.17. Modify the dataflow description of Parwan for the implementation of the *ldi* instruction as specified in Problem 9.11. Show all required bus connections and modify the Parwan controller.

9.18. Modify the Parwan dataflow description for the implementation of *lds*, *push* and *pop* instructions (see Problem 9.12 and Problem 9.13). Show all required bus connections, write a description for the stack pointer (*sp*), and insert this unit in the data path description of Parwan. Also, modify the Parwan controller so that it properly executes these instructions.

9.19. Modify the Parwan dataflow description to implement a version of *jsr* that uses the stack in Problems 9.12 (also see Problem 9.14). Show all required bus connections and modify the Parwan controller to properly execute this instruction.

9.20. Use the stack in Problem 9.12 to implement a better interrupt handling for Parwan. The new system should have an *int* input which becomes '1' when interrupt is requested. The CPU identifies an interrupting device by reading the address of its interrupt service routine from location 0:00 of the memory. To service an interrupt, the CPU jumps to predefined memory locations for each of the interrupt sources. Assume an external priority logic determines the device with highest priority and generates its service routine address. Your solution to this problem should also include implementation of a *return_from_interrupt* instruction.

APPENDIX
A

BASIC
UTILITIES
PACKAGE

The code for the *basic_utilities* package shown in this appendix appears here in its final form as it was developed and explained in the book. All the types, procedures, and functions presented in the chapters of this book have been added to this package as we proceeded through the book. Thus, the code in this appendix presents the *basic_utilities* package as it now stands with all the code for the examples and tools that were presented in the book. Here is the package:

```
PACKAGE basic_utilities IS
    TYPE qit IS ('0', '1', 'Z', 'X');
    TYPE qit_2d IS ARRAY (qit, qit) OF qit;
    TYPE qit_1d IS ARRAY (qit) OF qit;
    TYPE qit_vector IS ARRAY (NATURAL RANGE <>) OF qit;
    SUBTYPE tit IS qit RANGE '0' TO 'Z';
    TYPE tit_vector IS ARRAY (NATURAL RANGE <>) OF tit;
    TYPE integer_vector IS ARRAY (NATURAL RANGE <>) OF INTEGER;
    TYPE logic_data IS FILE OF CHARACTER;
    TYPE capacitance IS RANGE 0 TO 1E16
    UNITS
        ffr;   -- Femto Farads (base unit)
        pfr = 1000 ffr;
        nfr = 1000 pfr;
        ufr = 1000 nfr;
        mfr = 1000 ufr;
        far = 1000 mfr;
        kfr = 1000 far;
    END UNITS;
    TYPE resistance IS RANGE 0 TO 1E16
    UNITS
        l_o;   -- Milli-Ohms (base unit)
        ohms = 1000 l_o;
```

316

```
    k_o  =  1000 ohms;
    m_o  =  1000 k_o;
    g_o  =  1000 m_o;
END  UNITS;

    FUNCTION fgl (w, x, gl : BIT) RETURN BIT;
    FUNCTION feq (w, x, eq : BIT) RETURN BIT;
    PROCEDURE bin2int (bin : IN BIT_VECTOR; int : OUT INTEGER);
    PROCEDURE int2bin (int : IN INTEGER;  bin : OUT BIT_VECTOR);
    FUNCTION inc (x : BIT_VECTOR) RETURN BIT_VECTOR;
    PROCEDURE qit2int (qin : IN qit_vector; int : OUT INTEGER);
    PROCEDURE int2qit (int : IN INTEGER;  qin : OUT qit_vector);
    FUNCTION bit2qit_vector (bin : BIT_VECTOR) RETURN qit_vector;
    FUNCTION qit2bit_vector (qin : qit_vector) RETURN BIT_VECTOR;
    FUNCTION inc (x : qit_vector) RETURN qit_vector;
    PROCEDURE apply_data (
       SIGNAL target : OUT BIT_VECTOR;
       CONSTANT values : IN integer_vector;  CONSTANT period : IN TIME);

    PROCEDURE assign_bits (
       SIGNAL s : OUT BIT; file_name : IN STRING; period : IN TIME);
    PROCEDURE assign_bits (
       SIGNAL s : OUT qit; file_name : IN STRING; period : IN TIME);
    FUNCTION "AND" (a, b : qit) RETURN qit;
    FUNCTION "OR" (a, b : qit) RETURN qit;
    FUNCTION "NOT" (a : qit) RETURN qit;
    FUNCTION wire (a, b : qit) RETURN qit;
    FUNCTION "*" (a : resistance; b : capacitance) RETURN TIME;
    --
    FUNCTION oring ( drivers : qit_vector) RETURN qit;
    SUBTYPE ored_qit IS oring qit;
    TYPE ored_qit_vector IS ARRAY (NATURAL RANGE <>) OF ored_qit;
    --
    FUNCTION anding ( drivers : qit_vector) RETURN qit;
    SUBTYPE anded_qit IS anding qit;
    TYPE anded_qit_vector IS ARRAY (NATURAL RANGE <>) OF anded_qit;
    --
    FUNCTION wiring ( drivers : qit_vector) RETURN qit;
    SUBTYPE wired_qit IS wiring qit;
    TYPE wired_qit_vector IS ARRAY (NATURAL RANGE <>) OF wired_qit;
    --
    FUNCTION oring ( drivers : BIT_VECTOR) RETURN BIT;
    SUBTYPE ored_bit IS oring BIT;
    TYPE ored_bit_vector IS ARRAY (NATURAL RANGE <>) OF ored_bit;
    --
    FUNCTION anding ( drivers : BIT_VECTOR) RETURN BIT;
    SUBTYPE anded_bit IS anding bit;
    TYPE anded_bit_vector IS ARRAY (NATURAL RANGE <>) OF anded_bit;
END  basic_utilities;

PACKAGE BODY basic_utilities IS
  FUNCTION "AND" (a, b : qit) RETURN qit IS
    CONSTANT qit_and_table : qit_2d := (
                                        ('0','0','0','0'),
                                        ('0','1','1','X'),
                                        ('0','1','1','X'),
                                        ('0','X','X','X'));
  BEGIN
    RETURN qit_and_table (a, b);
```

```vhdl
END "AND";

FUNCTION "OR" (a, b : qit) RETURN qit IS
   CONSTANT qit_or_table : qit_2d := (
                                ('0','1','1','X'),
                                ('1','1','1','1'),
                                ('1','1','1','1'),
                                ('X','1','1','X'));
BEGIN
   RETURN qit_or_table (a, b);
END "OR";

FUNCTION "NOT" (a : qit) RETURN qit IS
   CONSTANT qit_not_table : qit_1d := ('1','0','0','X');
BEGIN
   RETURN qit_not_table (a);
END "NOT";

FUNCTION wire (a, b : qit) RETURN qit IS
   CONSTANT qit_wire_table : qit_2d := (
                                ('0','X','0','X'),
                                ('X','1','1','X'),
                                ('0','1','Z','X'),
                                ('X','X','X','X'));
BEGIN
   RETURN qit_wire_table (a, b);
END wire;

FUNCTION "*" (a : resistance; b : capacitance) RETURN TIME IS
BEGIN
   RETURN   ( ( a / 1 l_o) * ( b / 1 ffr ) * 1 FS ) / 1000;
END "*";

FUNCTION fgl (w, x, gl : BIT) RETURN BIT IS
BEGIN
   RETURN  (w AND gl) OR (NOT x  AND  gl) OR (w  AND  NOT x);
END fgl;

FUNCTION feq (w, x, eq : BIT) RETURN BIT IS
BEGIN
   RETURN  (w AND x AND eq) OR (NOT w  AND  NOT x  AND  eq);
END feq;

PROCEDURE bin2int (bin : IN BIT_VECTOR; int : OUT INTEGER) IS
   VARIABLE result: INTEGER;
BEGIN
   result := 0;
   FOR i IN bin'RANGE LOOP
     IF bin(i) = '1' THEN
         result := result + 2**i;
     END IF;
   END LOOP;
   int := result;
END bin2int;

PROCEDURE int2bin (int : IN INTEGER;  bin : OUT BIT_VECTOR) IS
   VARIABLE tmp : INTEGER;
BEGIN
   tmp := int;
```

```
      FOR i IN 0 TO (bin'LENGTH - 1) LOOP
        IF (tmp MOD 2  =  1) THEN
           bin (i) := '1';
         ELSE bin (i) := '0';
         END IF;
         tmp := tmp / 2;
      END LOOP;
  END int2bin;

  FUNCTION bit2qit_vector (bin : BIT_VECTOR) RETURN qit_vector IS
     VARIABLE q : qit_vector (bin'RANGE);
  BEGIN
     FOR i IN bin'RANGE LOOP
        IF bin(i) = '1' THEN q(i) := '1'
        ELSE
           q(i) := '0';
        END IF;
     END LOOP;
     RETURN q;
  END bit2qit_vector;

  FUNCTION qit2bit_vector (qin : qit_vector) RETURN BIT_VECTOR IS
     VARIABLE b : BIT_VECTOR (qin'RANGE);
  BEGIN
     FOR i IN qin'RANGE LOOP
        IF qin(i) = '1' THEN b(i) := '1'
        ELSE
           b(i) := '0';
        END IF;
     END LOOP;
     RETURN b;
  END qit2bit_vector;

  FUNCTION inc (x : BIT_VECTOR) RETURN BIT_VECTOR IS
     VARIABLE i : INTEGER;
     VARIABLE t : BIT_VECTOR (x'RANGE);
  BEGIN
     bin2int (x, i);
     i := i + 1; IF i >= 2**x'LENGTH THEN i := 0; END IF;
     int2bin (i, t);
     RETURN t;
  END inc;

  PROCEDURE qit2int (qin : IN qit_vector; int : OUT INTEGER) IS
     VARIABLE result: INTEGER;
  BEGIN
     result := 0;
     FOR i IN 0 TO (qin'LENGTH - 1) LOOP
        IF qin(i) = '1' THEN
           result := result + 2**i;
        END IF;
     END LOOP;
     int := result;
  END qit2int;

  PROCEDURE int2qit (int : IN INTEGER;  qin : OUT qit_vector) IS
     VARIABLE tmp : INTEGER;
  BEGIN
     tmp := int;
```

```vhdl
      FOR i IN 0 TO (qin'LENGTH - 1) LOOP
        IF (tmp MOD 2  =  1) THEN
          qin (i) := '1';
        ELSE qin (i) := '0';
        END IF;
        tmp := tmp / 2;
      END LOOP;
    END int2qit;

    FUNCTION inc (x : qit_vector) RETURN qit_vector IS
      VARIABLE i : INTEGER;
      VARIABLE t : qit_vector (x'RANGE);
    BEGIN
      qit2int (x, i);
      i := i + 1; IF i >= 2**x'LENGTH THEN i := 0; END IF;
      int2qit (i, t);
      RETURN t;
    END inc;

    PROCEDURE apply_data (
      SIGNAL target : OUT BIT_VECTOR;
      CONSTANT values : IN integer_vector; CONSTANT period : IN TIME)
    IS
      VARIABLE buf : BIT_VECTOR (target'RANGE);
    BEGIN
      FOR i IN values'RANGE LOOP
        int2bin (values(i), buf);
        target <= TRANSPORT buf AFTER i * period;
      END LOOP;
    END apply_data;

    PROCEDURE assign_bits (
      SIGNAL s : OUT BIT; file_name : IN STRING; period : IN TIME)
    IS
      VARIABLE char : CHARACTER;
      VARIABLE current : TIME := 0 NS;
      FILE input_value_file : logic_data IS IN file_name;
    BEGIN
      WHILE NOT ENDFILE (input_value_file) LOOP
        READ (input_value_file, char);
        IF char = '0' OR char = '1' THEN
          current := current + period;
          IF char = '0' THEN
            s <= TRANSPORT '0' AFTER current;
          ELSIF char = '1' THEN
            s <= TRANSPORT '1' AFTER current;
          END IF;
        END IF;
      END LOOP;
    END assign_bits;

    PROCEDURE assign_bits (
      SIGNAL s : OUT qit; file_name : IN STRING; period : IN TIME)
    IS
      VARIABLE char : CHARACTER;
      VARIABLE current : TIME := 0 NS;
      FILE input_value_file : logic_data IS IN file_name;
    BEGIN
      WHILE NOT ENDFILE (input_value_file) LOOP
```

```
        READ (input_value_file, char);
        current := current + period;
        CASE char IS
          WHEN '0' => s <= TRANSPORT '0' AFTER current;
          WHEN '1' => s <= TRANSPORT '1' AFTER current;
          WHEN 'Z' | 'z' => s <= TRANSPORT 'Z' AFTER current;
          WHEN 'X' | 'x' => s <= TRANSPORT 'X' AFTER current;
          WHEN OTHERS => current := current - period;
        END CASE;
      END LOOP;
END assign_bits;

FUNCTION oring ( drivers : qit_vector) RETURN qit IS
    VARIABLE accumulate : qit := '0';
BEGIN
    FOR i IN drivers'RANGE LOOP
      accumulate := accumulate OR drivers(i);
    END LOOP;
    RETURN accumulate;
END oring;

FUNCTION anding ( drivers : qit_vector) RETURN qit IS
    VARIABLE accumulate : qit := '1';
BEGIN
    FOR i IN drivers'RANGE LOOP
      accumulate := accumulate AND drivers(i);
    END LOOP;
    RETURN accumulate;
END anding;

FUNCTION wiring ( drivers : qit_vector) RETURN qit IS
    VARIABLE accumulate : qit := 'Z';
BEGIN
    FOR i IN drivers'RANGE LOOP
      accumulate := wire (accumulate, drivers(i));
    END LOOP;
    RETURN accumulate;
END wiring;

FUNCTION oring ( drivers : BIT_VECTOR) RETURN BIT IS
    VARIABLE accumulate : BIT := '0';
BEGIN
    FOR i IN drivers'RANGE LOOP
      accumulate := accumulate OR drivers(i);
    END LOOP;
    RETURN accumulate;
END oring;

FUNCTION anding ( drivers : BIT_VECTOR) RETURN BIT IS
    VARIABLE accumulate : BIT := '1';
BEGIN
    FOR i IN drivers'RANGE LOOP
      accumulate := accumulate AND drivers(i);
    END LOOP;
    RETURN accumulate;
END anding;

END basic_utilities;
```

B

SIMULATION ENVIRONMENTS

In this appendix, sample session runs for four VHDL simulation systems are presented. The purpose of this presentation is to provide a quick reference for the users of these software packages and, also to illustrate the general features of VHDL simulation environments. For all four packages, the same example is used; this example illustrates only the main features of a simulation system. Interactive use of the system, setting breakpoints, formatting outputs, using the VHDL tool in a CAD design environment, stepping through the simulation, debugging the code, and many other advanced features are not discussed here.

The following type fonts help the readability of run session dialogues:

Operating system and simulation software prompts are shown by: `system prompt.`

User commands are shown by: **user command.**

Responses from the host machine and run results are shown by: *host response.*

Response from the VHDL simulation system is shown by: vhdl response.

We use the following font for comments: our comments.

B.1   A SESSION OF THE VDS VHDL ENVIRONMENT

This section presents a sample session for simulating a small example using the VHDL Development System (VDS) of Cadence Design Systems.[1] The simulation was performed on a SUN-4 machine. For this simulation, you need these files: FILE: and2.vhd; – Input file name.

```
ENTITY and2 IS
    PORT (x1, x2: IN BIT; z: OUT BIT);
END and2;
ARCHITECTURE run_demo OF and2 IS
BEGIN
    z <= x1 AND x2 AFTER 5 NS;
END run_demo;
```

FILE: test.vhd; – A simple test bench.

```
ENTITY tester IS END tester;
ARCHITECTURE io OF tester IS
    COMPONENT and2 PORT (x1, x2 : IN BIT; z : OUT BIT);
    END COMPONENT;
    FOR ALL : and2 USE ENTITY WORK.and2(run_demo);
    SIGNAL a, b, c : BIT;
BEGIN
    c1 : and2 PORT MAP (a, b, c);
    a <= '0', '1' AFTER 100 NS, '0' AFTER 200 NS, '1' AFTER 300 NS;
    b <= '0', '1' AFTER 150 NS, '0' AFTER 250 NS, '1' AFTER 350 NS;
END io;
```

FILE: test.rcl; – Report control file.

```
SIMULATION_REPORT test IS
BEGIN
    REMOVE_PAGE_ID;
    SELECT_SIGNAL : a, b, c;
    SAMPLE_SIGNALS BY_EVENT IN NS USING '.';
END test;
```

Session Run Follows:

```
nu>
nu>    ls
and2.vhd   test.rcl   test.vhd
nu>
nu>
```

We will assume that environmental variables have already been set.

---

[1]Cadence Design Systems; 555 River Oaks Parkway; San Jose, CA 95134, Tel: 408-943-1284

```
nu>
nu>
```

Originally the WORK library of the *VDS* system is empty.

```
nu>   vds dir
Standard VHDL 1076 Support Environment Version 3.1 - 1 April 1991
Copyright (C) 1991 Cadence Design Systems, All rights reserved.

VHDVDS-I-NO_UNITS - No units found in <<navabi>>.
nu>   vhdl and2.vhd
Standard VHDL 1076 Support Environment Version 3.1 - 1 April 1991
Copyright (C) 1991 Cadence Design Systems,  All rights reserved.

nu>
nu>
```

AND2 Entity and Architectures are compiled into the WORK library. The *dir* command shows contents of this library.

```
nu>   vds dir
Standard VHDL 1076 Support Environment Version 3.1 - 1 April 1991
Copyright (C) 1991 Cadence Design Systems,  All rights reserved.
Library <<navabi>>

AND2                        Entity         22:22:00 03-APR-1991
AND2(RUN_DEMO)              *Architecture   22:22:04 03-APR-1991

nu>
nu>
```

For analyzing the TOP unit the -top option has to be specified with the *vhdl* command.

```
nu>
nu>   vhdl -top test.vhd
Standard VHDL 1076 Support Environment Version 3.1 - 1 April 1991
Copyright (C) 1991 Cadence Design Systems,  All rights reserved.

nu>
nu>   vds dir
Standard VHDL 1076 Support Environment Version 3.1 - 1 April 1991
Copyright (C) 1991 Cadence Design Systems,  All rights reserved.
Library <<navabi>>

AND2                        Entity         22:22:00 03-APR-1991
AND2(RUN_DEMO)              *Architecture   22:22:04 03-APR-1991
TESTER                      Entity         22:23:06 03-APR-1991
TESTER(IO)                  *Architecture   22:23:10 03-APR-1991
nu>
nu>
```

The top unit has to be built before simulation. Use the *build* command for this purpose.

```
nu>
nu>   build -repl 'tester(io)'
```

Standard VHDL 1076 Support Environment Version 3.1 - 1 April 1991
Copyright (C) 1991 Cadence Design Systems, All rights reserved.

nu>
nu>

Successful execution of the *build* program generates a Kernel.

nu> **vds dir**
Standard VHDL 1076 Support Environment Version 3.1 - 1 April 1991
Copyright (C) 1991 Cadence Design Systems, All rights reserved.
Library <<navabi>>

AND2	Entity	22:22:00 03-APR-1991
AND2(RUN_DEMO)	*Architecture	22:22:04 03-APR-1991
IO	Kernel	22:24:03 03-APR-1991
TESTER	Entity	22:23:06 03-APR-1991
TESTER(IO)	*Architecture	22:23:10 03-APR-1991

nu>
nu>

The Kernel can now be simulated using the *sim* command.

nu> **sim io**
Standard VHDL 1076 Support Environment Version 3.1 - 1 April 1991
Copyright (C) 1991 Cadence Design Systems, All rights reserved.

VHDSIM-N-SIGTRAN Signal Tracing turned on
VHDSIM-N-QUIESCE Quiescent state reached with no response after 355 ns

nu>
nu>

Simulation generates a run file from which a report can be generated. Report generation is done by the *rg* command.

nu> **rg io 'test.rcl'**
Standard VHDL 1076 Support Environment Version 3.1 - 1 April 1991
Copyright (C) 1991 Cadence Design Systems, All rights reserved.

nu>
nu>

The *io.rpt* file is created in the present directory.

nu> **ls**
and2.vhd   io.rpt   test.rcl   test.vhd
nu>
nu> **cat io.rpt**

Vhdl Simulation Report

Kernel Library Name: <<navabi>>IO
Kernel Creation Date: APR-03-1991

Kernel Creation Time: 22:24:22
Run Identifer: 1
Run Date: APR-03-1991
Run Time: 22:24:22

Report Control Language File: test.rcl
Report Output File : io.rpt

Max Time: 9223372036854775807
Max Delta: 2147483646

Report Control Language :

```
SIMULATION_REPORT test IS
BEGIN
   REMOVE_PAGE_ID;
     SELECT_SIGNAL : a, b, c;
      SAMPLE_SIGNALS BY_EVENT IN NS USING '.';
END test;
```

Report Format Information :

Time is in NS relative to the start of simulation
Time period for report is from 0 NS to End of Simulation
Signal values are reported by event   ('.' indicates no event)

TIME	\-SIGNAL NAMES\-		
(NS)	A	B	C
0	'0'	'0'	'0'
100	'1'	...	...
150	...	'1'	...
155	...	...	'1'
200	'0'	...	...
205	...	...	'0'
250	...	'0'	...
300	'1'	...	...
350	...	'1'	...
355	...	...	'1'

```
nu>
nu>
```

Simulation of the two-input AND gate is completed.

```
nu>
nu>
```

B.2   A SESSION OF THE V-SYSTEM/WINDOWS VHDL ENVIRONMENT

This section presents a sample session for simulating a small example using the VHDL simulation environment of Model Technology Incorporated.[2] The V-System/Windows

---

[2]Model Technology Inc.; 15455 NW Greenbrier Pkwy, Ste 210; Beaverton, OR 97006; Tel: 503-690-6838

requires an Intel 80286, 386 or 486 based Personal Computer. The simulation run shown here was performed on Microsoft Windows running on a 286-based PC. Files used in this run are shown here:

FILE: and2.vhd; – Input file name.

```
ENTITY and2 IS
    PORT (x1, x2: IN BIT; z: OUT BIT);
END and2;
ARCHITECTURE run_demo OF and2 IS
BEGIN
    z <= x1 AND x2 AFTER 5 NS;
END run_demo;
```

FILE: test.vhd; – A simple test bench.

```
ENTITY tester IS END tester;
ARCHITECTURE io OF tester IS
    COMPONENT and2 PORT (x1, x2 : IN BIT; z : OUT BIT);
    END COMPONENT;
    FOR ALL : and2 USE ENTITY WORK.and2(run_demo);
    SIGNAL a, b, c : BIT;
BEGIN
    c1 : and2 PORT MAP (a, b, c);
    a <= '0', '1' AFTER 100 NS, '0' AFTER 200 NS, '1' AFTER 300 NS;
    b <= '0', '1' AFTER 150 NS, '0' AFTER 250 NS, '1' AFTER 350 NS;
END io;
```

Session Run Follows:

After invoking V-System from the Windows environment, a window with the "Front" prompt appears.

```
Front>
Front>
```

Initially, the WORK library is empty. The *vdir* command shows the entries in this library.

```
Front>    vdir
Front>
Front>
```

Compile *and2.vhd* into the library. For this purpose, either type in the command, or use dialogue boxes from the windows.

```
Front>    vcom and2.vhd
# -- Loading package standard
# -- Compiling entity and2
# -- Compiling architecture run_demo of and2
Front>
Front>
```

The new design has been added to the library. Use *vdir* to list items in the WORK library.

```
Front>    vdir
# ENTITY and2
Front>
Front>
```

Compile *test.vhd* into the WORK library.

```
Front>    vcom test.vhd
# -- Loading package standard
# -- Compiling entity tester
# -- Compiling architecture io of tester
# -- Loading entity and2
Front>
Front>
```

The new design has been added to the library.

```
Front>    vdir
# ENTITY and2
# ENTITY tester
Front>
Front>
```

Start the simulation by issuing the *vsim* command at the prompt.

```
Front>    vsim
```

In the "Simulation Parameter" window specify *test* for *primary*, and *io* for *secondary*. When done, the "Vsim" window opens, and the following appears:

```
Vsim>
# Loading C:\VHDL\STD.standard
# Loading WORK.tester[io]
# Loading WORK.and2[run_demo]
Vsim>
Vsim>
```

At the prompt, list the signals to be observed.

```
Vsim>    list a b c
```

A "List" window opens with the initial values of the *a*, *b* and *c* signals. To start the simulation, use the *run* command at the Vsim prompt in the "Vsim" window. Use 1000 for the maximum time.

```
Vsim>    run 1000
```

In the "List" window values of signals appear. Simulation stops at 355 nanoseconds.

```
ns  a b c
 0  0 0 0
100  1 0 0
150  1 1 0
155  1 1 1
200  0 1 1
205  0 1 0
250  0 0 0
300  1 0 0
350  1 1 0
355  1 1 1
```

Simulation of the two-input AND gate is completed. Exit from open windows.

```
Sim>    exit
Front>   exit
```

B.3   A SESSION IN THE VLK VHDL ENVIRONMENT

This section presents a sample session for simulating a small example using the VLK VHDL simulation environment of Open Solutions Incorporated.[3] The simulation was performed on a SUN-4 compatible machine. For this simulation the following files are needed:

FILE: and2.vhd; – Input file name.

```
ENTITY and2 IS
   PORT (x1, x2: IN BIT; z: OUT BIT);
END and2;
ARCHITECTURE run_demo OF and2 IS
BEGIN
   z <= x1 AND x2 AFTER 5 NS;
END run_demo;
```

FILE: test.vhd; – A simple test bench.

```
ENTITY tester IS END tester;
ARCHITECTURE io OF tester IS
   COMPONENT and2 PORT (x1, x2 : IN BIT; z : OUT BIT);
   END COMPONENT;
   FOR ALL : and2 USE ENTITY WORK.and2(run_demo);
   SIGNAL a, b, c : BIT;
```

---

[3]Open Solutions, Inc.; 15245 Shady Grove Road, Suite 310; Rockville, MD 20850; Tel: 301-963-5200

```
BEGIN
  c1 : and2 PORT MAP (a, b, c);
  a <= '0', '1' AFTER 100 NS, '0' AFTER 200 NS, '1' AFTER 300 NS;
  b <= '0', '1' AFTER 150 NS, '0' AFTER 250 NS, '1' AFTER 350 NS;
END io;
```

Session Run Follows:

```
nu>
nu>    ls
and2.vhd    test.vhd
nu>
nu>
```

Use the *setwork* command to create the working library in your current directory.

```
nu>    setwork
Setting WORK to dls_navabi
Setting dls_navabi to /u1/navabi/vhdl_vlk/user
nu>
```

Compile *and2.vhd* into the WORK library.

```
nu>    compile and2.vhd
......
```

The following units have been compiled:

```
and2
and2-run_demo
nu>
```

New files for the ENTITY and ARCHITECTURE of *and2* have been added to the present subdirectory.

```
nu>    ls
and2.vhd          and2.vhdlview      and2-run_demo.vhdlview
test.vhd
nu>
```

Compile the test bench contained in the *test.vhd* file.

```
nu>    compile test.vhd
......
```

The following units have been compiled:

```
tester
tester-io

nu>
```

New files have been added to the present subdirectory.

```
nu>    ls
and2.vhd              and2.vhdlview          and2-run_demo.vhdlview
test.vhd              tester-io.vhdlview
nu>
```

Build the simulation model using the *build* command.

```
nu>    build tester
Building complete.
To execute the simulation model, type 'simulate tester'
nu>
```

A simulation file is added to the working subdirectory.

```
nu>    ls
and2.vhd            and2.vhdlview        and2-run_demo.vhdlview
test.vhd            tester.sim*          tester-io.vhdlview
nu>
```

The circuit can now be simulated. Use the *simulate* command.

```
nu>    simulate tester
%KER-I-Elab,  Elaborating.
%KER-I-Init,  Initializing.
%KER-I-Simul,  Simulating.
%KER-I-TimeHi, Simulation terminating; time reached Time'High.
%KER-I-Complete, Simulation Complete.
nu>
nu>
```

A trace file has been added to the present working directory.

```
nu>    ls
and2.vhd            and2.vhdlview        and2-run_demo.vhdlview
test.vhd            tester.sim*          tester-io.vhdlview
tester.trace
nu>
```

Use the *format* program to create a file listing signals in the trace file.

```
nu>    format tester -preview
nu>
```

A control file has been created.

```
nu>    ls
and2.vhd            and2.vhdlview        and2-run_demo.vhdlview
test.vhd            tester.sim*          tester-io.vhdlview
tester.trace        tester.control
nu>
nu>
```

The control file contains a list of signals, and can be edited if necessary to remove or add signals.

```
nu>    cat tester.control
DISPLAY 1 # /tester(io).a
DISPLAY 2 # /tester(io).b
DISPLAY 3 # /tester(io).c
nu>
nu>
```

Use the *format* program to generate the wave file listing values of signals in the control file.

```
nu>    format tester
%FMT-I-Create, Creating formatted wave file: tester.wave.
%FMT-I-Width, 3 signal(s) formatted, requiring 27 columns.
nu>
nu>
```

The waveform file lists events and transactions on signals.

```
nu>    cat tester.wave
Formatted Simulation Output
Signal          Signal
Number          Path Name
----------------------------
          1    : /tester(io).a
          2    : /tester(io).b
          3    : /tester(io).c
T(fs) + Delta       1    2    3
----------     --   ---  ---  ---
          0+ 0:   '0' '0' '0'
          0+ 1: *'0'*'0' '0'
   5000000+ 0:   '0' '0'*'0'
 100000000+ 0: *'1' '0' '0'
 105000000+ 0:   '1' '0'*'0'
 150000000+ 0:   '1'*'1' '0'
 155000000+ 0:   '1' '1'*'1'
 200000000+ 0: *'0' '1' '1'
 205000000+ 0:   '0' '1'*'0'
 250000000+ 0:   '0'*'0' '0'
 255000000+ 0:   '0' '0'*'0'
 300000000+ 0: *'1' '0' '0'
 305000000+ 0:   '1' '0'*'0'
 350000000+ 0:   '1'*'1' '0'
 355000000+ 0:   '1' '1'*'1'
nu>
nu>
```

Simulation of the two-input AND gate is completed.

```
nu>
nu>
```

B.4 A SESSION OF THE VHDL XL SYSTEM

This section presents a sample session for simulating a small example using the VHDL XL System of Cadence Design Systems.[4] The simulation was performed on a SUN-4 machine. For this simulation the following files are needed:

```
FILE: and2.vhd; -- Input file name.
ENTITY and2 IS
    PORT (x1, x2: IN BIT; z: OUT BIT);
END and2;
ARCHITECTURE run_demo OF and2 IS
BEGIN
    z <= x1 AND x2 AFTER 5 NS;
END run_demo;
```

FILE: test.vhd; – A simple test bench.

```
ENTITY tester IS END tester;
ARCHITECTURE io OF tester IS
    COMPONENT and2 PORT (x1, x2 : IN BIT; z : OUT BIT);
    END COMPONENT;
    FOR ALL : and2 USE ENTITY WORK.and2(run_demo);
    SIGNAL a, b, c : BIT;
BEGIN
    c1 : and2 PORT MAP (a, b, c);
    a <= '0', '1' AFTER 100 NS, '0' AFTER 200 NS, '1' AFTER 300 NS;
    b <= '0', '1' AFTER 150 NS, '0' AFTER 250 NS, '1' AFTER 350 NS;
END io;
```

Session Run Follows:

Invoke the VHDL shell

```
unix>    vsh
VHDL-XL 1.1      Mar 26, 1992   14:42:18
    * Copyright Cadence Design Systems, Inc. 1990, 1991.      *
    *       All Rights Reserved.          Licensed Software.   *
    * Confidential and proprietary information which is the    *
    *       property of Cadence Design Systems, Inc.           *
```

Create directory to use as work library.

```
vhdl-xl[1]   mkdir sample
```

Define logical WORK as *sample* directory

```
vhdl-xl[2]    define_library WORK sample
```

Analyze the contents of file and2.vhd

---

[4]Cadence Design Systems; 555 River Oaks Parkway; San Jose, CA 95134; Tel: 408-943-1284

```
vhdl-xl[3]    analyze and2.vhd
VHDL-XL 1.1      Mar 26, 1992   14:42:42
    * Copyright Cadence Design Systems, Inc. 1990, 1991.    *
    *       All Rights Reserved.          Licensed Software.    *
    * Confidential and proprietary information which is the    *
    *        property of Cadence Design Systems, Inc.    *
Analyzing file "/home/sample/and2.vhd"
    entity declaration:          And2
    architecture body:             Run_Demo
Analysis of 9 lines is complete.  No errors were detected.
CPU time = 0.0 secs for analysis + 0.2 secs for compilation
End of VHDL-XL 1.1      Mar 26, 1992   14:42:43
```

List the contents of the work library

```
vhdl-xl[4]    list_units work
And2                entity_declaration
And2.Run_Demo   architecture_body
```

Analyze the contents of file tester.vhd

```
vhdl-xl[5]    analyze tester.vhd
VHDL-XL 1.1      Mar 26, 1992   14:42:56
    * Copyright Cadence Design Systems, Inc. 1990, 1991.    *
    *       All Rights Reserved.          Licensed Software.    *
    * Confidential and proprietary information which is the    *
    *        property of Cadence Design Systems, Inc.    *
Analyzing file "/home/sample/tester.vhd"
    entity declaration:          Tester
    architecture body:             Io
Analysis of 17 lines is complete.  No errors were detected.
CPU time = 0.1 secs for analysis + 0.2 secs for compilation
End of VHDL-XL 1.1      Mar 26, 1992   14:42:56
```

List contents of WORK library

```
vhdl-xl[6]    list_units WORK
And2                entity_declaration
And2.Run_Demo   architecture_body
Tester              entity_declaration
Tester.Io           architecture_body
```

Invoke simulation

```
vhdl-xl[7]    simulate -d WORK.tester.io
VHDL-XL 1.1      Mar 26, 1992   14:43:14
    * Copyright Cadence Design Systems, Inc. 1990, 1991.    *
    *       All Rights Reserved.          Licensed Software.    *
    * Confidential and proprietary information which is the    *
    *        property of Cadence Design Systems, Inc.    *

Elaborating  ...
Simulating  ...
```

Current File is /home/sample/tester.vhd

Specify signals to monitor

```
debug[1]    monitor a,b,c
```

Continue simulation until completion

```
debug[2]    continue
                    0 ns  A = '0'   B = '0'   C = '0'
                  100 ns  A = '1'   B = '0'   C = '0'
                  150 ns  A = '1'   B = '1'   C = '0'
                  155 ns  A = '1'   B = '1'   C = '1'
                  200 ns  A = '0'   B = '1'   C = '1'
                  205 ns  A = '0'   B = '1'   C = '0'
                  250 ns  A = '0'   B = '0'   C = '0'
                  300 ns  A = '1'   B = '0'   C = '0'
                  350 ns  A = '1'   B = '1'   C = '0'
                  355 ns  A = '1'   B = '1'   C = '1'
88 simulation events 14 simulation cycles
CPU time: 0 secs in elaboration + 0 secs in simulation
Data structure takes 58308 bytes of memory
End of VHDL-XL 1.1     Mar 26, 1992   14:43:22
```

Exit VHDL shell

```
vhdl-xl[8]    exit
End of VHDL-XL 1.1     Mar 26, 1992   14:43:25
```

APPENDIX
C

STANDARD MSI 74LS PACKAGES

Several 7400 standard packages are presented in this appendix. The delays used are simplified and are based on the typical values listed in the TTL Logic data book.

C.1 74LS85 4-BIT MAGNITUDE COMPARATOR

```
ENTITY ls85_comparator IS
   GENERIC (prop_delay : TIME := 11 NS);
   PORT (a, b : IN qit_vector (3 DOWNTO 0);  gt, eq, lt : IN qit;
         a_gt_b, a_eq_b, a_lt_b : OUT qit);
END ls85_comparator;
ARCHITECTURE behavioral OF ls85_comparator IS
BEGIN
   PROCESS (a, b, gt, eq, lt)
      VARIABLE ai, bi : INTEGER;
   BEGIN
      qit2int (a, ai);
      qit2int (b, bi);
      IF ai > bi THEN
         a_gt_b <= '1' AFTER prop_delay;
         a_eq_b <= '0' AFTER prop_delay;
         a_lt_b <= '0' AFTER prop_delay;
      ELSIF ai < bi THEN
         a_gt_b <= '0' AFTER prop_delay;
         a_eq_b <= '0' AFTER prop_delay;
         a_lt_b <= '1' AFTER prop_delay;
      ELSIF ai = bi THEN
         a_gt_b <= gt AFTER prop_delay;
         a_eq_b <= eq AFTER prop_delay;
         a_lt_b <= lt AFTER prop_delay;
      END IF;
   END PROCESS;
END behavioral;
```

C.2   74LS157 QUADRUPLE 2-LINE TO 1-LINE MULTIPLEXER

```
ENTITY ls157 IS
   GENERIC (prop_delay : TIME := 18 NS;
   PORT (g_bar, s : IN qit;
            a4, b4 : IN qit_vector(3 DOWNTO 0);
            y4 : OUT qit_vector(3 DOWNTO 0));
END ls157;
ARCHITECTURE dataflow OF ls157 IS
BEGIN
   PROCESS (a4, b4, g_bar, s)
   BEGIN
      IF g_bar = '0' THEN
         IF s = '0' THEN
            y4 <= a4 AFTER prop_delay;
         ELSE
            y4 <= b4 AFTER prop_delay;
         END IF;
      ELSE
         y4 <= "0000";
      END IF;
   END PROCESS;
END dataflow;
```

C.3   74LS163 SYNCHRONOUS 4-BIT COUNTER

```
ENTITY ls163_counter IS
   GENERIC (prop_delay : TIME := 18 NS);
   PORT (clk, clr_bar, ld_bar, enp, ent : IN qit;
            abcd : IN qit_vector (3 DOWNTO 0);
            q_abcd : OUT qit_vector (3 DOWNTO 0); rco : OUT qit);
END ls163_counter;
ARCHITECTURE behavioral OF ls163_counter IS
BEGIN
   counting : PROCESS (clk)
      VARIABLE internal_count : qit_vector (3 DOWNTO 0) := "0000";
   BEGIN
      IF (clk = '1') THEN
         IF (clr_bar = '0') THEN
            internal_count := "0000";
         ELSIF (ld_bar = '0') THEN
            internal_count := abcd;
         ELSIF (enp = '1' AND ent = '1') THEN
            internal_count := inc (internal_count);
            IF (internal_count = "1111") THEN
               rco <= '1' AFTER prop_delay;
            ELSE
               rco <= '0';
            END IF;
         END IF;
         q_abcd <= internal_count AFTER prop_delay;
      END IF;
   END PROCESS counting;
END behavioral;
```

C.4   74LS283 4-BIT BINARY FULL ADDER

```
ENTITY ls283 IS
    GENERIC (prop_delay : TIME := 14 NS; prop_delay1 : TIME := 16 NS);
    PORT (c0 : IN qit; c4 : OUT qit;
              a4, b4 : IN qit_vector (3 DOWNTO 0);
              s4 : OUT qit_vetor (3 DOWNTO 0));
END ls283;
LIBRARY tutorial;
USE tutorial.t_utilities.ALL;
ARCHITECTURE behavioral OF ls283 IS
BEGIN
    adder : PROCESS (a4,b4,c0)
        VARIABLE atemp,btemp,ytemp : INTEGER := 0;
        VARIABLE stemp : qit_vector(3 DOWNTO 0) := "0000";
    BEGIN
        qit_to_int (a4,atemp);
        qit_to_int (b4,btemp);
        IF (c0 = '1') THEN
              ytemp := atemp + btemp + 1;
        ELSE
              ytemp := atemp + btemp;
        ENDIF;
        IF ytemp > 15 THEN
              c4 <= '1' AFTER prop_delay;
        ELSE
              c4 <= '0' AFTER prop_delay;
        END IF;
        int_to_qit (ytemp,stemp);
        s4 <= stemp AFTER prop_delay1;
    END PROCESS adder;
END behavioral;
```

C.5   74LS373 OCTAL D-TYPE TRANSPARENT LATCHES

```
ENTITY ls373_register IS
    GENERIC (prop_delay : TIME := 15 NS);
    PORT (clk, oc_bar : IN qit; d8 : IN qit_vector (7 DOWNTO 0);
              q8 : OUT qit_vector (7 DOWNTO 0));
END ls373_register;
ARCHITECTURE dataflow OF ls373_register IS
    SIGNAL state qit_vector (7 DOWNTO 0);
BEGIN
    reg: BLOCK ( clk = '1' )
    BEGIN
        state <= GUARDED d8 AFTER prop_delay;
    END BLOCK reg;
    q8 <= state WHEN oc_bar = '0' ELSE "ZZZZZZZZ";
END dataflow;
```

C.6   74LS377 OCTAL D-TYPE FLIP-FLOPS

```
ENTITY ls377_register IS
    GENERIC (prop_delay : TIME := 17 NS);
    PORT (clk, g_bar : IN qit; d8 : IN qit_vector (7 DOWNTO 0);
              q8 : OUT qit_vector (7 DOWNTO 0));
END ls377_register;
```

```
ARCHITECTURE dataflow OF ls377_register IS
   SIGNAL GUARD : BOOLEAN;
BEGIN
   GUARD <= NOT clk'STABLE AND clk = '1' AND (g_bar = '0');
   q8 <= GUARDED d8 AFTER prop_delay;
END dataflow;
```

C.7   74LS299 UNIVERSAL SHIFT-REGISTER

```
ENTITY LS299 IS
   GENERIC (prop_delay : TIME := 27 NS);
   PORT (clk, clr_bar, lin, rin : IN qit;
         s, g_bar : IN qit_vector (1 DOWNTO 0);
         qq : OUT qit_vector (7 DOWNTO 0);
END LS299;
ARCHITECTURE behavioral OF LS299 IS
   SIGNAL iq : qit_vector (7 DOWNTO 0);
BEGIN
   clocking : PROCESS (clk,clr_bar)
   BEGIN
      IF clr_bar = '1' THEN
         iq <= "00000000";
         ELSE IF (clk'EVENT AND clk = '1') THEN
            CASE s IS
               WHEN "01" =>
                  iq <= rin & iq (7 DOWNTO 1);
               WHEN "10" =>
                  iq <= iq (6) & iq (5 DOWNTO 0) & lin;
               WHEN "01" =>
                  iq <= qq;
               WHEN OTHERS => NULL;
            END CASE;
         END IF;
      END IF;
   END PROCESS clocking;
   tri_state: PROCESS (iq, g_bar)
   BEGIN
      IF g_bar = "00" THEN
         IF s /= "11" THEN
            qq <= iq;
         ELSE
            qq <= "ZZZZZZZZ";
         END IF;
      ELSE
         qq <= "ZZZZZZZZ";
      END IF;
   END PROCESS tri_state;
   qa <= iq(7);
   qh <= iq(0);
END dataflow;
```

C.8   74LS541 TRANCEIVER

```
ENTITY ls541 IS
   GENERIC (prop_delay : TIME := 10 NS);
   PORT (g_bar : IN qit_vector (1 DOWNTO 0);
         a8 : IN qit_vector (7 DOWNTO 0);
         y8 : OUT qit_vector (7 DOWNTO 0));
END ls541;
```

```
ARCHITECTURE dataflow OF ls541 IS
BEGIN
  y8 <= a8 AFTER prop_delay WHEN g_bar = "00" ELSE
  "ZZZZZZZZ";
END dataflow;
```

This appendix shows complete descriptions for the entities relating to the Parwan CPU that we only presented as code fragments in Chapter 9. Section D.1 contains the complete behavioral description of Parwan. This description was presented in Figures 9.15 to 9.26. The complete dataflow description of Parwan Controller presented in Figures 9.52 to 9.64 is shown here in Section D.2.

D.1 PARWAN BEHAVIORAL DESCRIPTION

```
LIBRARY cmos;
USE cmos.basic_utilities.ALL;
LIBRARY par_library;
USE par_library.par_utilities.ALL;
USE par_library.par_parameters.ALL;
--
ENTITY par_central_processing_unit IS
    GENERIC (read_high_time, read_low_time,
             write_high_time, write_low_time : TIME := 2 US;
             cycle_time : TIME := 4 US; run_time : TIME := 140 US);
    PORT (clk : IN qit;
          interrupt : IN qit;
          read_mem, write_mem : OUT qit;
          databus : INOUT wired_byte BUS := "ZZZZZZZZ"; adbus : OUT twelve
         );
END par_central_processing_unit;
--
```

```
ARCHITECTURE behavioral OF par_central_processing_unit IS
BEGIN
    PROCESS
        VARIABLE pc : twelve;
        VARIABLE ac, byte1, byte2 : byte;
        VARIABLE v, c, z, n : qit;
        VARIABLE temp : qit_vector (9 DOWNTO 0);
    BEGIN
        IF NOW > run_time THEN WAIT; END IF;
        IF interrupt = '1' THEN
            pc := zero_12;
            WAIT FOR cycle_time;
        ELSE    -- no interrupt
            adbus <= pc;
            read_mem <= '1';   WAIT FOR read_high_time;
            byte1 := byte (databus);
            read_mem <= '0';   WAIT FOR read_low_time;
            pc := inc (pc);
            IF byte1 (7 DOWNTO 4) = single_byte_instructions THEN
                CASE byte1 (3 DOWNTO 0) IS
                    WHEN cla =>
                        ac := zero_8;
                    WHEN cma =>
                        ac := NOT ac;
                        IF ac = zero_8 THEN z := '1'; END IF;
                        n := ac (7);
                    WHEN cmc =>
                        c := NOT c;
                    WHEN asl =>
                        c := ac (7);
                        ac := ac (6 DOWNTO 0) & '0';
                        n := ac (7);
                        IF c /= n THEN v := '1'; END IF;
                    WHEN asr =>
                        ac := ac (7) & ac (7 DOWNTO 1);
                        IF ac = zero_8 THEN z := '1'; END IF;
                        n := ac (7);
                    WHEN OTHERS => NULL;
                END CASE;
            ELSE    -- two-byte instructions
                adbus <= pc;
                read_mem <= '1';   WAIT FOR read_high_time;
                byte2 := byte (databus);
                read_mem <= '0';   WAIT FOR read_low_time;
                pc := inc (pc);
                IF byte1 (7 DOWNTO 5) = jsr THEN
                    databus <= wired_byte (pc (7 DOWNTO 0) );
                    adbus (7 DOWNTO 0) <= byte2;
                    write_mem <= '1';   WAIT FOR write_high_time;
                    write_mem <= '0';   WAIT FOR write_low_time;
                    databus <= "ZZZZZZZZ";
                    pc (7 DOWNTO 0) := inc (byte2);
                ELSIF byte1 (7 DOWNTO 4) = bra THEN
                    IF
                        ( byte1 (3) = '1' AND v = '1' ) OR
                        ( byte1 (2) = '1' AND c = '1' ) OR
                        ( byte1 (1) = '1' AND z = '1' ) OR
                        ( byte1 (0) = '1' AND n = '1' )
                    THEN
```

```
                pc (7 DOWNTO 0) := byte2;
              END IF;
          ELSE -- all other two-byte instructions
              IF byte1 (4) = indirect THEN
                  adbus (11 DOWNTO 8) <= byte1 (3 DOWNTO 0);
                  adbus (7 DOWNTO 0) <= byte2;
                  read_mem <= '1';   WAIT FOR read_high_time;
                  byte2 := byte (databus);
                  read_mem <= '0';   WAIT FOR read_low_time;
              END IF; -- ends indirect
              IF byte1 (7 DOWNTO 5) = jmp THEN
                  pc := byte1 (3 DOWNTO 0) & byte2;
              ELSIF byte1 (7 DOWNTO 5) = sta THEN
                  adbus <= byte1 (3 DOWNTO 0) & byte2;
                  databus <= wired_byte (ac);
                  write_mem <= '1';   WAIT FOR write_high_time;
                  write_mem <= '0';   WAIT FOR write_low_time;
                  databus <= "ZZZZZZZZ";
              ELSE -- read operand for lda, and, add, sub
                  adbus (11 DOWNTO 8) <= byte1 (3 DOWNTO 0);
                  adbus (7 DOWNTO 0) <= byte2;
                  read_mem <= '1';   WAIT FOR read_high_time;
                  CASE byte1 (7 DOWNTO 5) IS
                    WHEN lda =>
                       ac := byte (databus);
                    WHEN ann =>
                       ac := ac AND byte (databus);
                    WHEN add =>
                       temp := add_cv (ac, byte (databus), c);
                       ac := temp (7 DOWNTO 0);
                       c := temp (8);
                       v := temp (9);
                    WHEN sbb =>
                       temp := sub_cv (ac, byte (databus), c);
                       ac := temp (7 DOWNTO 0);
                       c := temp (8);
                       v := temp (9);
                    WHEN OTHERS => NULL;
                  END CASE;
                  IF ac = zero_8 THEN z := '1'; END IF;
                  n := ac (7);
                  read_mem <= '0';   WAIT FOR read_low_time;
              END IF; -- jmp / sta / lda, and, add, sub
          END IF; -- jsr / bra / other double-byte instructions
      END IF; -- single-byte / double-byte
  END IF; -- interrupt / otherwise
  END PROCESS;
END behavioral;
```

D.2   CONTROLLER OF PARWAN DATAFLOW DESCRIPTION

```
LIBRARY cmos;
USE cmos.basic_utilities.ALL;
LIBRARY par_library;
USE par_library.par_utilities.ALL;
USE WORK.alu_operations.ALL;
```

```
--
ENTITY par_control_unit IS
   GENERIC (read_delay, write_delay : TIME := 3 NS);
   PORT (clk : IN qit;
           -- register control signals:
           load_ac, zero_ac,
           load_ir,
           increment_pc, load_page_pc, load_offset_pc, reset_pc,
           load_page_mar, load_offset_mar,
           load_sr, cm_carry_sr,
           -- bus connection control signals:
           pc_on_mar_page_bus, ir_on_mar_page_bus,
           pc_on_mar_offset_bus, dbus_on_mar_offset_bus,
           pc_offset_on_dbus, obus_on_dbus, databus_on_dbus,
           mar_on_adbus,
           dbus_on_databus,
           -- logic unit function control outputs:
           arith_shift_left, arith_shift_right : OUT qit;
           alu_code : OUT qit_vector (2 DOWNTO 0);
           -- inputs from the data section:
           ir_lines : IN byte; status : IN nibble;
           -- memory control and other external signals:
           read_mem, write_mem : OUT qit; interrupt : IN qit
         );
END par_control_unit;
--


ARCHITECTURE dataflow OF par_control_unit IS
   -- oring is implied in the following signals (oi)
     SIGNAL load_ac_oi, zero_ac_oi,
            load_ir_oi,
            increment_pc_oi, load_page_pc_oi, load_offset_pc_oi, reset_pc_oi,
            load_page_mar_oi, load_offset_mar_oi,
            load_sr_oi, cm_carry_sr_oi,
            pc_on_mar_page_bus_oi, ir_on_mar_page_bus_oi,
            pc_on_mar_offset_bus_oi, dbus_on_mar_offset_bus_oi,
            pc_offset_on_dbus_oi, obus_on_dbus_oi, databus_on_dbus_oi,
            mar_on_adbus_oi,
            dbus_on_databus_oi,
            arith_shift_left_oi, arith_shift_right_oi,
            read_mem_oi, write_mem_oi : ored_qit BUS;
     SIGNAL alu_code_oi : ored_qit_vector (2 DOWNTO 0) BUS;
     SIGNAL s : ored_qit_vector (9 DOWNTO 1) REGISTER := "000000001";
BEGIN
   -- implied or assignments to output signals
     load_ac <= load_ac_oi;
     zero_ac <= zero_ac_oi;
     load_ir <= load_ir_oi;
     increment_pc <= increment_pc_oi;
     load_page_pc <= load_page_pc_oi;
     load_offset_pc <= load_offset_pc_oi;
     reset_pc <= reset_pc_oi;
     load_page_mar <= load_page_mar_oi;
     load_offset_mar <= load_offset_mar_oi;
     load_sr <= load_sr_oi;
     cm_carry_sr <= cm_carry_sr_oi;
     pc_on_mar_page_bus <= pc_on_mar_page_bus_oi;
     ir_on_mar_page_bus <= ir_on_mar_page_bus_oi;
     pc_on_mar_offset_bus <= pc_on_mar_offset_bus_oi;
```

```
  dbus_on_mar_offset_bus <= dbus_on_mar_offset_bus_oi;
  pc_offset_on_dbus <= pc_offset_on_dbus_oi;
  obus_on_dbus <= obus_on_dbus_oi;
  databus_on_dbus <= databus_on_dbus_oi;
  mar_on_adbus <= mar_on_adbus_oi;
  dbus_on_databus <= dbus_on_databus_oi;
  arith_shift_left <= arith_shift_left_oi;
  arith_shift_right <= arith_shift_right_oi;
  read_mem <= read_mem_oi;
  write_mem <= write_mem_oi;
  alu_code <= qit_vector (alu_code_oi);
------------
s1: BLOCK (s(1) = '1')
BEGIN -- start of fetch
   -- pc to mar
   pc_on_mar_page_bus_oi <= GUARDED '1';
   pc_on_mar_offset_bus_oi <= GUARDED '1';
   load_page_mar_oi <= GUARDED '1';
   load_offset_mar_oi <= GUARDED '1';
   -- reset pc if interrupt
   reset_pc_oi <= GUARDED '1' WHEN interrupt = '1' ELSE '0';
   -- goto 2 if interrupt is off
   ck: BLOCK ( (clk = '0' AND NOT clk'STABLE) AND GUARD )
   BEGIN
      s(1) <= GUARDED '1' WHEN interrupt = '1' ELSE '0';
      s(2) <= GUARDED '1' WHEN interrupt /= '1' ELSE '0';
   END BLOCK ck;
END BLOCK s1;
-------------
s2: BLOCK (s(2) = '1')
BEGIN -- fetching continues
   -- read memory into ir
   mar_on_adbus_oi <= GUARDED '1';
   read_mem_oi <= GUARDED '1' AFTER read_delay;
   databus_on_dbus_oi <= GUARDED '1';
   alu_code_oi <= GUARDED ored_qit_vector (a_input);
   load_ir_oi <= GUARDED '1';
   -- increment pc
   increment_pc_oi <= GUARDED '1';
   -- goto 3
   ck: BLOCK ( (clk = '0' AND NOT clk'STABLE) AND GUARD )
   BEGIN
      s(3) <= GUARDED '1';
   END BLOCK ck;
END BLOCK s2;
-------------
s3: BLOCK (s(3) = '1')
BEGIN
   -- pc to mar, for next read
   pc_on_mar_page_bus_oi <= GUARDED '1';
   pc_on_mar_offset_bus_oi <= GUARDED '1';
   load_page_mar_oi <= GUARDED '1';
   load_offset_mar_oi <= GUARDED '1';
   -- goto 4 if not single byte instruction
   ck: BLOCK ( (clk = '0' AND NOT clk'STABLE) AND GUARD )
   BEGIN
      s(4) <= GUARDED '1' WHEN ir_lines (7 DOWNTO 4) /= "1110" ELSE '0';
   END BLOCK ck;
   -- perform single byte instructions
```

```
sb: BLOCK ( (ir_lines (7 DOWNTO 4) = "1110") AND GUARD)
BEGIN
    alu_code_oi <= GUARDED
        ored_qit_vector (b_compl) WHEN ir_lines (1) = '1' ELSE
        ored_qit_vector (b_input);
    arith_shift_left_oi <= GUARDED
        '1' WHEN ir_lines (3 DOWNTO 0) = "1000" ELSE '0';
    arith_shift_right_oi <= GUARDED
        '1' WHEN ir_lines (3 DOWNTO 0) = "1001" ELSE '0';
    load_sr_oi <= GUARDED
        '1' WHEN ( ir_lines (3) = '1' OR ir_lines (1) = '1' ) ELSE '0';
    cm_carry_sr_oi <= GUARDED '1' WHEN ir_lines (2) = '1' ELSE '0';
    load_ac_oi <= GUARDED
        '1' WHEN ( ir_lines (3) = '1' OR ir_lines (1) = '1' OR ir_lines (0)='1' ) ELSE '0';
    zero_ac_oi <= GUARDED
        '1' WHEN ( ir_lines (3) = '0' AND ir_lines (0) = '1' ) ELSE '0';
    ck: BLOCK ( (clk = '0' AND NOT clk'STABLE) AND GUARD )
    BEGIN
        s(2) <= GUARDED '1';
    END BLOCK ck;
END BLOCK sb;
END BLOCK s3;
-------------
s4: BLOCK (s(4) = '1')
BEGIN -- page from ir, and offset from next memory makeup 12-bit address
    -- read memory into mar offset
    mar_on_adbus_oi <= GUARDED '1';
    read_mem_oi <= GUARDED '1' AFTER read_delay;
    databus_on_dbus_oi <= GUARDED '1';
    dbus_on_mar_offset_bus_oi <= GUARDED '1';
    load_offset_mar_oi <= GUARDED
            '1'; -- completed operand (dir/indir) address
    -- page from ir if not branch or jsr
    pg: BLOCK ( (ir_lines (7 DOWNTO 6) /= "11") AND GUARD)
    BEGIN
        ir_on_mar_page_bus_oi <= GUARDED '1';
        load_page_mar_oi <= GUARDED '1';
        -- goto 5 for indirect, 6 for direct
        ck: BLOCK ( (clk = '0' AND NOT clk'STABLE) AND GUARD )
        BEGIN
            s(5) <= GUARDED '1' WHEN ir_lines (4) = '1' ELSE '0'; -- indir
            s(6) <= GUARDED '1' WHEN ir_lines (4) = '0' ELSE '0'; -- direct
        END BLOCK ck;
    END BLOCK pg;
    -- keep page in mar_page if jsr or bra (same-page instructions)
    sp: BLOCK ( (ir_lines (7 DOWNTO 6) = "11") AND GUARD)
    BEGIN
        -- goto 7 for jsr, 9 for bra
        ck: BLOCK ( (clk = '0' AND NOT clk'STABLE) AND GUARD )
        BEGIN
            s(7) <= GUARDED '1' WHEN ir_lines (5) = '0' ELSE '0'; -- jsr
            s(9) <= GUARDED '1' WHEN ir_lines (5) = '1' ELSE '0'; -- bra
        END BLOCK ck;
    END BLOCK sp;
        -- increment pc
    increment_pc_oi <= GUARDED '1';
END BLOCK s4;
-------------
s5: BLOCK (s(5) = '1')
```

```
BEGIN -- indirect addressing
   -- read actual operand from memory into mar offset
   mar_on_adbus_oi <= GUARDED '1';
   read_mem_oi <= GUARDED '1' AFTER read_delay;
   databus_on_dbus_oi <= GUARDED '1';
   dbus_on_mar_offset_bus_oi <= GUARDED '1';
   load_offset_mar_oi <= GUARDED '1';
   -- goto 6
   ck: BLOCK ( (clk = '0' AND NOT clk'STABLE) AND GUARD )
   BEGIN
      s(6) <= GUARDED '1';
   END BLOCK ck;
END BLOCK s5;
-------------
s6: BLOCK (s(6) = '1')
BEGIN
   jm: BLOCK ( (ir_lines (7 DOWNTO 5) = "100") AND GUARD)
   BEGIN
      load_page_pc_oi <= GUARDED '1';
      load_offset_pc_oi <= GUARDED '1';
      -- goto 2
      ck: BLOCK ( (clk = '0' AND NOT clk'STABLE) AND GUARD )
      BEGIN
         s(2) <= GUARDED '1';
      END BLOCK ck;
   END BLOCK jm;

   --
   st: BLOCK ( (ir_lines (7 DOWNTO 5) = "101") AND GUARD)
   BEGIN
      -- mar on adbus, ac on databus, write to memory
      mar_on_adbus_oi <= GUARDED '1';
      alu_code_oi <= GUARDED ored_qit_vector (b_input);
      obus_on_dbus_oi <= GUARDED '1';
      dbus_on_databus_oi <= GUARDED '1';
      write_mem_oi <= GUARDED '1' AFTER write_delay;
      -- goto 1
      ck: BLOCK ( (clk = '0' AND NOT clk'STABLE) AND GUARD )
      BEGIN
         s(1) <= GUARDED '1';
      END BLOCK ck;
   END BLOCK st;

   --
   rd: BLOCK ( (ir_lines (7) = '0') AND GUARD)
   BEGIN
      -- mar on adbus, read memory for operand, perform operation
      mar_on_adbus_oi <= GUARDED '1';
      read_mem_oi <= GUARDED '1' AFTER read_delay;
      databus_on_dbus_oi <= GUARDED '1';
      WITH ir_lines (6 DOWNTO 5) SELECT
         alu_code_oi <= GUARDED
            ored_qit_vector (a_input) WHEN "00",
            ored_qit_vector (a_and_b) WHEN "01",
            ored_qit_vector (a_add_b) WHEN "10",
            ored_qit_vector (a_sub_b) WHEN "11",
            ored_qit_vector (b_input) WHEN OTHERS;
      load_sr_oi <= GUARDED '1';
      load_ac_oi <= GUARDED '1';
      -- goto 1
      ck: BLOCK ( (clk = '0' AND NOT clk'STABLE) AND GUARD )
```

```
            BEGIN
                s(1) <= GUARDED '1';
            END BLOCK ck;
        END BLOCK rd;
    END BLOCK s6;
    ---------------
    s7: BLOCK (s(7) = '1')
    BEGIN    -- jsr
        -- write pc offset to top of subroutine
        mar_on_adbus_oi <= GUARDED '1';
        pc_offset_on_dbus_oi <= GUARDED '1';
        dbus_on_databus_oi <= GUARDED '1';
        write_mem_oi <= GUARDED '1' AFTER write_delay;
        -- address of subroutine to pc
        load_offset_pc_oi <= GUARDED '1';
        -- goto 8
        ck: BLOCK ( ((clk = '0' AND NOT clk'STABLE) AND GUARD )
        BEGIN
            s(8) <= GUARDED '1';
        END BLOCK ck;
    END BLOCK s7;
    -------------
    s8: BLOCK (s(8) = '1')
    BEGIN
        -- increment pc
        increment_pc_oi <= GUARDED '1';
        -- goto 1
        ck: BLOCK ( ((clk = '0' AND NOT clk'STABLE) AND GUARD )
        BEGIN
            s(1) <= GUARDED '1';
        END BLOCK ck;
    END BLOCK s8;
    -------------
    s9: BLOCK (s(9) = '1')
    BEGIN
        load_offset_pc_oi <= GUARDED
            '1' WHEN (status AND ir_lines (3 DOWNTO 0)) /= "0000" ELSE '0';
        -- goto 1
        ck: BLOCK ( ((clk = '0' AND NOT clk'STABLE) AND GUARD )
        BEGIN
            s(1) <= GUARDED '1';
        END BLOCK ck;
    END BLOCK s9;
    ---------------
    ck: BLOCK ( clk = '0' AND NOT clk'STABLE )
    BEGIN
        s (9 DOWNTO 1) <= GUARDED "000000000";
    END BLOCK ck;
END dataflow;
```

APPENDIX
E

VHDL LANGUAGE GRAMMAR

This appendix contains the formal grammar of the standard 1076-1987 VHDL language in BNF format.[1] In this format, productions are on the left hand side of an equivalence, two colons and an equal sign are used for equivalence, vertical bars for oring, square brackets for optional parts, and curly brackets for parts that zero or more of them may be used.

As in the chapters of this book, we have used uppercase letters for the language reserved words. The language productions are ordered alphabetically with page numbers corresponding to pages in the book where an example production is presented.

abstract_literal ::=   decimal_literal | based_literal   [27]

access_type_definition ::=   ACCESS subtype_indication   [365]

actual_designator ::=   [32]

---

[1] The information contained herein in Helvetica is copyrighted information of the IEEE, extracted from IEEE Std 1076-1987, IEEE Standard VHDL Reference Manual copyright ©1987 by the Institute of Electrical and Electronics Engineers, Inc. This information was written within the context of IEEE Std 1076-1987 and the IEEE takes no responsibility for or liability resulting from the reader's misinterpretation of said information resulting from the placement and context. Information is reproduced with the permission of the IEEE.

```
expression
| signal_name
| variable_name
| OPEN
```

actual_parameter_part ::=   parameter_association_list   [92]

actual_part ::=   [92]
    actual_designator
    | function_name (actual_designator)

adding_operator ::= + | - | &   [38]

aggregate ::=   [158]
    (element_association { , element_association })

alias_declaration ::=   [158]
    ALIAS identifier : subtype_indication IS name ;

allocator ::=   [---]
    NEW subtype_indication
    | NEW qualified_expression

architecture_body ::=   [32]
    ARCHITECTURE identifier OF entity_name IS
      architecture_declarative_part
    BEGIN
      architecture_statement_part
    END [architecture_simple_name] ;

architecture_declarative_part ::=   [52]
    { block_declarative_item }

architecture_statement_part ::=   [52]
    { concurrent_statement }

array_type_definition ::=   [140]
    unconstrained_array_definition | constrained_array_definition

assertion_statement ::=   [228]
    ASSERT condition
      [REPORT expression]
      [SEVERITY expression] ;

association_element ::=   [106]
    [formal_part =>] actual_part

association_list ::=   [106]
    association_element { , association_element }

attribute_declaration ::=   [165]
    ATTRIBUTE identifier : type_mark ;

attribute_designator ::=   attribute_simple_name   [166]

attribute_name ::=   [166]
    prefix ' attribute_designator [(static_expression)]
```
```

attribute_specification ::=   [166]
  ATTRIBUTE attribute_designator OF entity_specification IS expression ;

base ::= integer   [123]

base_specifier ::=   B | O | X   [123]

base_unit_declaration ::=   identifier ;   [123]

based_integer ::=   [123]
  extended_digit { [underline] extended_digit }

based_literal ::=   [123]
  base ├ based_integer [. based_integer] ┤ [exponent]

basic_character ::=   [123]
  basic_graphic_character | format_effector

basic_graphic_character ::=   [123]
  upper_case_letter | digit | special_character| space_character

binding_indication ::=   [82]
  entity_aspect
  [generic_map_aspect]
  [port_map_aspect]

bit_string_literal ::=   base_specifier " bit_value "   [75]

bit_value ::=   extended_digit { [underline] extended_digit }   [75]

block_configuration ::=   [112]
  FOR block_specification
   { use_clause }
   { configuration_item }
  END FOR ;

block_declarative_item ::=   [52]
  subprogram_declaration
  | subprogram_body
  | type_declaration
  | subtype_declaration
  | constant_declaration
  | signal_declaration
  | file_declaration
  | alias_declaration
  | component_declaration
  | attribute_declaration
  | attribute_specification
  | configuration_specification
  | disconnection_specification
  | use_clause

block_declarative_part ::=   [52]
  { block_declarative_item }

block_header ::=   [---]
  [generic_clause
  [generic_map_aspect ;]]
  [port_clause

```
    [ port_map_aspect  ;  ]  ]
block_specification  ::=                                                    [113]
  architecture_name
  | block_statement_label
  | generate_statement_label  [  (  index_specification  )  ]

block_statement  ::=                                                        [181]
  block_label  :
    BLOCK  [  (  guard_expression  )  ]
      block_header
      block_declarative_part
    BEGIN
      block_statement_part
    END  BLOCK  [  block_label  ]  ;

block_statement_part  ::=                                                   [182]
  {  concurrent_statement  }

case_statement  ::=                                                         [155]
  CASE  expression  IS
    case_statement_alternative
    {  case_statement_alternative  }
  END  CASE  ;

case_statement_alternative  ::=                                             [155]
  WHEN  choices  =>
    sequence_of_statements

character_literal  ::=  '  graphic_character  '                             [132]

choice  ::=                                                                 [155]
  simple_expression
  | discrete_range
  | element_simple_name
  | OTHERS

choices  ::=    choice  {  |  choice  }                                     [155]

component_configuration  ::=                                                [112]
  FOR  component_specification
    [  USE  binding_indication  ;  ]
    [  block_configuration  ]
  END  FOR  ;

component_declaration  ::=                                                  [65]
  COMPONENT  identifier
    [  local_generic_clause  ]
    [  local_port_clause  ]
  END  COMPONENT  ;

component_instantiation_statement  ::=                                      [105]
  instantiation_label  :
    component_name
      [  generic_map_aspect  ]
      [  port_map_aspect  ]  ;

component_specification  ::=                                                [65]
  instantiation_list  :  component_name
```

composite_type_definition ::=   [158]
  array_type_definition
  | record_type_definition

concurrent_assertion_statement ::=   [230]
  [label :] assertion_statement

concurrent_procedure_call ::=   [243]
  [label :] procedure_call_statement

concurrent_signal_assignment_statement ::=   [37]
        [label :] conditional_signal_assignment
  | [label :] selected_signal_assignment

concurrent_statement ::=   [72]
  block_statement
  | process_statement
  | concurrent_procedure_call
  | concurrent_assertion_statement
  | concurrent_signal_assignment_statement
  | component_instantiation_statement
  | generate_statement

condition ::=   boolean_expression   [134]

condition_clause ::=   UNTIL condition   [234]

conditional_signal_assignment ::=   [133]
  target   <= options conditional_waveforms ;

conditional_waveforms ::=   [134]
  { waveform WHEN condition ELSE }
  waveform

configuration_declaration ::=   [111]
  CONFIGURATION identifier OF entity_name IS
    configuration_declarative_part
    block_configuration
  END [configuration_simple_name] ;

configuration_declarative_item ::=   [113]
  use_clause
  | attribute_specification

configuration_declarative_part ::=   [113]
  { configuration_declarative_item }

configuration_item ::=   [113]
  block_configuration
  | component_configuration

configuration_specification ::=   [66]
  FOR component_specification USE binding_indication ;

constant_declaration ::=   [136]
  CONSTANT identifier_list : subtype_indication [:= expression] ;

constrained_array_definition ::=   [140]
  ARRAY index_constraint OF element_subtype_indication

```
constraint ::=                                                          [140]
  range_constraint
  | index_constraint

context_clause ::=  { context_item }                                    [127]

context_item ::=                                                        [127]
  library_clause
  | use_clause

decimal_literal ::= integer [ . integer ] [ exponent ]                  [137]

declaration ::=                                                         [148]
  type_declaration
  | subtype_declaration
  | object_declaration
  | file_declaration
  | interface_declaration
  | alias_declaration
  | attribute_declaration
  | component_declaration
  | entity_declaration
  | configuration_declaration
  | subprogram_declaration
  | package_declaration

design_file ::= design_unit { design_unit }                             [127]

design_unit ::= context_clause library_unit                             [127]

designator ::= identifier  |  operator_symbol                           [93]

direction ::= TO | DOWNTO                                               [140]

disconnection_specification ::=                                         [196]
  DISCONNECT guarded_signal_specification AFTER time_expression ;

discrete_range ::= discrete_subtype_indication | range                  [140]

element_association ::=                                                 [158]
  [ choices => ] expression

element_declaration ::=                                                 [65]
  identifier_list : element_subtype_definition ;

element_subtype_definition ::= subtype_indication                       [140]

entity_aspect ::=                                                       [82]
      ENTITY entity_name [ ( architecture_identifier) ]
  | CONFIGURATION configuration_name
  | OPEN

entity_class ::=                                                        [166]
  ENTITY | ARCHITECTURE  | CONFIGURATION
  | PROCEDURE  | FUNCTION  | PACKAGE
  | TYPE  | SUBTYPE | CONSTANT
  | SIGNAL  | VARIABLE | COMPONENT
  | LABEL
```

entity_declaration ::=   [30]
  ENTITY identifier IS
    entity_header
    entity_declarative_part
  [BEGIN
    entity_statement_part]
  END [entity_simple_name] ;

entity_declarative_item ::=   [205]
  subprogram_declaration
  | subprogram_body
  | type_declaration
  | subtype_declaration
  | constant_declaration
  | signal_declaration
  | file_declaration
  | alias_declaration
  | attribute_declaration
  | attribute_specification
  | disconnection_specification
  | use_clause

entity_declarative_part ::=   [205]
  { entity_declarative_item }

entity_designator ::=   simple_name | operator_symbol   [166]

entity_header ::=   [58]
  [formal_generic_clause]
  [formal_port_clause]

entity_name_list ::=   [167]
  entity_designator { , entity_designator }
  | OTHERS
  | ALL

entity_specification ::=   [166]
  entity_name_list : entity_class

entity_statement ::=   [253]
  concurrent_assertion_statement
  | passive_concurrent_procedure_call
  | passive_process_statement

entity_statement_part ::=   [253]
  { entity_statement }

enumeration_literal ::= identifier | character_literal   [133]

enumeration_type_definition ::=   [133]
  (enumeration_literal { , enumeration_literal })

exit_statement ::=   [227]
  EXIT [loop_label] [WHEN condition] ;

exponent ::= E [+] integer | E - integer   [137]

expression ::=   [37]

```
| relation { AND relation }
| relation { OR relation }
| relation { XOR relation }
| relation [ NAND relation ]
| relation [ NOR relation ]
```

extended_digit ::= digit | letter   [123]

factor ::=   [38]
  primary [** primary]
  | ABS primary
  | NOT primary

file_declaration ::=   [147]
FILE identifier : subtype_indication IS [mode] file_logical_name ;

file_logical_name ::=   string_expression   [147]

file_type_definition ::=   [147]
  FILE OF type_mark

floating_type_definition   :=   range_constraint   [365]

formal_designator ::=   [106]
  generic_name
  | port_name
  | parameter_name

formal_parameter_list ::=   parameter_interface_list   [93]

formal_part ::=   [106]
  formal_designator
  | function_name (formal_designator)

full_type_declaration ::=   [133]
  TYPE identifier IS type_definition ;

function_call ::=   [89]
  function_name [(actual_parameter_part)]

generate_statement ::=   [71]
  generate_label :
    generation_scheme GENERATE
      { concurrent_statement }
    END GENERATE [generate_label] ;

generation_scheme ::=   [72]
  FOR generate_parameter_specification
  | IF condition

generic_clause ::=   [102]
  GENERIC (generic_list) ;

generic_list ::= generic_interface_list   [102]

generic_map_aspect ::=   [106]
  GENERIC MAP (generic_association_list)

graphic_character ::=   [365]

basic_graphic_character | lower_case_letter | other_special_character

guarded_signal_specification ::=   [194]
  guarded_signal_list : type_mark

identifier ::=   [30]
  letter { [underline] letter_or_digit }

identifier_list ::= identifier { , identifier }   [52]

if_statement ::=   [95]
  IF condition THEN
    sequence_of_statements
  { ELSIF condition THEN
    sequence_of_statements }
  [ELSE
    sequence_of_statements]
  END IF ;

incomplete_type_declaration ::=   TYPE identifier ;   [---]

index_constraint ::= (discrete_range { , discrete_range })   [141]

index_specification   ::=   [142]
  discrete_range
  | static_expression

index_subtype_definition ::= type_mark RANGE <>   [143]

indexed_name ::=   prefix (expression { , expression })   [141]

instantiation_list ::=   [82]
  instantiation_label { , instantiation_label }
  | OTHERS
  | ALL

integer ::= digit { [underline] digit }   [365]

integer_type_definition ::= range_constraint   [365]

interface_constant_declaration ::=   [99]
  [CONSTANT] identifier_list : [IN] subtype_indication [:= static_expression]

interface_declaration ::=   [99]
  interface_constant_declaration
  | interface_signal_declaration
  | interface_variable_declaration

interface_element ::=   interface_declaration   [99]

interface_list ::=   [99]
  interface_element { ; interface_element }

interface_signal_declaration ::=   [100]
  [SIGNAL] identifier_list : [mode] subtype_indication [BUS] [:=
  static_expression]

interface_variable_declaration ::=   [100]
  [VARIABLE] identifier_list : [mode] subtype_indication [:= static_expression]

```
iteration_scheme ::=                                              [94]
  WHILE condition
  | FOR loop_parameter_specification

label ::= identifier                                              [67]

letter ::= upper_case_letter | lower_case_letter                 [365]

letter_or_digit ::= letter | digit                               [365]

library_clause ::=   LIBRARY logical_name_list ;                 [126]

library_unit ::=                                                 [126]
  primary_unit
  | secondary_unit

literal ::=                                                      [365]
  numeric_literal
  | enumeration_literal
  | string_literal
  | bit_string_literal
  | NULL

logical_name ::= identifier                                      [126]

logical_name_list ::= logical_name { , logical_name }            [126]

logical_operator ::=   AND | OR | NAND | NOR | XOR               [38]

loop_statement ::=                                               [94]
  [ loop_label : ]
    [ iteration_scheme ] LOOP
      sequence_of_statements
    END LOOP [ loop_label ] ;

miscellaneous_operator ::=   ** | ABS | NOT                      [38]

mode ::=   IN | OUT | INOUT | BUFFER | LINKAGE                   [59]

multiplying_operator ::=   * | / | MOD | REM                     [38]

name ::=                                                         [158]
  simple_name
  | operator_symbol
  | selected_name
  | indexed_name
  | slice_name
  | attribute_name

next_statement ::=                                               [227]
  NEXT [ loop_label ] [ WHEN condition ] ;

null_statement ::= NULL ;                                        [239]

numeric_literal ::=                                              [365]
  abstract_literal
  | physical_literal

object_declaration ::=                                           [39]
```

```
  constant_declaration
| signal_declaration
| variable_declaration
```

operator_symbol ::=   string_literal   [38]

options ::=   [GUARDED] [TRANSPORT]   [181]

package_body ::=   [100]
 PACKAGE BODY package_simple_name IS
   package_body_declarative_part
 END [package_simple_name] ;

package_body_declarative_item ::=   [100]
 subprogram_declaration
| subprogram_body
| type_declaration
| subtype_declaration
| constant_declaration
| file_declaration
| alias_declaration
| use_clause

package_body_declarative_part ::=   [100]
 { package_body_declarative_item }

package_declaration ::=   [97]
 PACKAGE identifier IS
   package_declarative_part
 END [package_simple_name] ;

package_declarative_item ::=   [99]
 subprogram_declaration
| type_declaration
| subtype_declaration
| constant_declaration
| signal_declaration
| file_declaration
| alias_declaration
| component_declaration
| attribute_declaration
| attribute_specification
| disconnection_specification
| use_clause

package_declarative_part ::=   [99]
 { package_declarative_item }

parameter_specification ::=   [94]
 identifier IN discrete_range

physical_literal ::= [abstract_literal] unit_name   [138]

physical_type_definition ::=   [138]
 range_constraint
   UNITS
     base_unit_declaration
     { secondary_unit_declaration }
   END UNITS
```
```

```
port_clause  ::=                                                          [58]
  PORT  (  port_list  )  ;


port_list  ::=  port_interface_list                                       [59]


port_map_aspect  ::=                                                      [75]
  PORT  MAP  (  port_association_list  )


prefix  ::=                                                               [65]
  name
  |  function_call


primary  ::=                                                             [65]
  name
  |  literal
  |  aggregate
  |  function_call
  |  qualified_expression
  |  type_conversion
  |  allocator
  |  (  expression  )


primary_unit  ::=                                                        [58]
  entity_declaration
  |  configuration_declaration
  |  package_declaration


procedure_call_statement  ::=                                            [148]
  procedure_name  [  (  actual_parameter_part  )  ]  ;


process_declarative_item  ::=                                            [227]
  subprogram_declaration
  |  subprogram_body
  |  type_declaration
  |  subtype_declaration
  |  constant_declaration
  |  variable_declaration
  |  file_declaration
  |  alias_declaration
  |  attribute_declaration
  |  attribute_specification
  |  use_clause


process_declarative_part  ::=                                           [227]
  {  process_declarative_item  }


process_statement  ::=                                                  [227]
  [  process_label  :  ]
    process  [  (  sensitivity_list  )  ]
      process_declarative_part
    BEGIN
      process_statement_part
    END  process  [  process_label  ]  ;


process_statement_part  ::=                                            [227]
  {  sequential_statement  }


qualified_expression  ::=                                              [---]
  type_mark  '  (  expression  )
```

```
               |  type_mark  '  aggregate

range  ::=                                                             [140]
  range_attribute_name
  |  simple_expression  direction  simple_expression

range_constraint  ::=    RANGE  range                                  [138]

record_type_definition  ::=                                            [158]
  RECORD
    element_declaration
    {  element_declaration  }
  END  RECORD

relation  ::=                                                          [250]
  simple_expression  [  relational_operator  simple_expression  ]

relational_operator  ::=    =   |   /=   |   <   |   <=   |   >   |   >=   [250]

return_statement  ::=                                                  [151]
  RETURN  [  expression  ]  ;

scalar_type_definition  ::=                                            [132]
  enumeration_type_definition    |  integer_type_definition
  |  floating_type_definition        |  physical_type_definition

secondary_unit  ::=                                                    [52]
  architecture_body
  |  package_body

secondary_unit_declaration  ::=    identifier  =  physical_literal  ;  [138]

selected_name  ::=    prefix  .  suffix                                [65]

selected_signal_assignment  ::=                                        [178]
  WITH  expression  SELECT
    target  <=  options  selected_waveforms  ;

selected_waveforms  ::=                                                [178]
  {  waveform  WHEN  choices  ,  }
  waveform  WHEN  choices

sensitivity_clause  ::=    ON  sensitivity_list                        [235]

sensitivity_list  ::=    signal_name  {  ,  signal_name  }             [227]

sequence_of_statements  ::=                                            [94]
  {  sequential_statement  }

sequential_statement  ::=                                              [227]
  wait_statement
  |  assertion_statement
  |  signal_assignment_statement
  |  variable_assignment_statement
  |  procedure_call_statement
  |  if_statement
  |  case_statement
  |  loop_statement
  |  next_statement
```

```
    | exit_statement
    | return_statement
    | null_statement
```

sign ::= + | -   [38]

signal_assignment_statement ::=   [41]
    target <= [TRANSPORT] waveform ;

signal_declaration ::=   [66]
    signal identifier_list : subtype_indication [signal_kind] [:= expression] ;

signal_kind ::= REGISTER | BUS   [194]

signal_list ::=   [197]
    signal_name { , signal_name }
    | OTHERS
    | ALL

simple_expression ::=   [102]
    [sign] term { adding_operator term }

simple_name ::= identifier   [27]

slice_name ::= prefix (discrete_range)   [141]

string_literal ::= " { graphic_character } "   [246]

subprogram_body ::=   [93]
    subprogram_specification IS
      subprogram_declarative_part
    BEGIN
      subprogram_statement_part
    END [designator] ;

subprogram_declaration ::=   [93]
    subprogram_specification ;

subprogram_declarative_item ::=   [93]
    subprogram_declaration
    | subprogram_body
    | type_declaration
    | subtype_declaration
    | constant_declaration
    | variable_declaration
    | file_declaration
    | alias_declaration
    | attribute_declaration
    | attribute_specification
    | use_clause

subprogram_declarative_part ::=   [93]
    { subprogram_declarative_item }

subprogram_specification ::=   [93]
    PROCEDURE designator [(formal_parameter_list)]
    | FUNCTION   designator [(formal_parameter_list)]   RETURN type_mark

subprogram_statement_part ::=   [93]
```
```

```
{ sequential_statement }
```

subtype_declaration ::=   [157]
  SUBTYPE identifier IS subtype_indication ;

subtype_indication ::=   [140]
  [resolution_function_name] type_mark [constraint]

suffix ::=   [127]
  simple_name
  | character_literal
  | operator_symbol
  | ALL

target ::=   [41]
  name
  | aggregate

term ::=   [72]
  factor { multiplying_operator factor }

timeout_clause ::=   FOR time_expression   [234]

type_conversion ::=   type_mark (expression)   [274]

type_declaration ::=   [133]
  full_type_declaration
  | incomplete_type_declaration

type_definition ::=   [132]
  scalar_type_definition
  | composite_type_definition
  | access_type_definition
  | file_type_definition

type_mark ::=   [157]
  type_name
  | subtype_name

unconstrained_array_definition ::=   [144]
  ARRAY (index_subtype_definition { , index_subtype_definition })
    OF element_subtype_indication

use_clause ::=   [98]
  USE selected_name { , selected_name } ;

variable_assignment_statement ::=   [95]
  target := expression ;

variable_declaration ::=   [95]
  VARIABLE identifier_list : subtype_indication [:= expression] ;

wait_statement ::=   [231]
  WAIT [sensitivity_clause] [condition_clause] [timeout_clause] ;

waveform ::=   [178]
  waveform_element { , waveform_element }

waveform_element ::=   [178]
  value_expression [AFTER time_expression]
  | NULL [AFTER time_expression]

APPENDIX
F

VHDL
STANDARD
PACKAGES

This appendix presents standard VHDL packages. Section F.1 presents the STAN-DARD package and Section F.2 presents the TEXTIO package. In all the descriptions in this book, we assume that all types and functions in the STANDARD package are visible and that you must explicitly declare the TEXTIO package when you need it.

In this appendix, we have deviated from our convention of using uppercase letters for VHDL keywords and standards, and use uppercase letters only for VHDL keywords. This is done to make the entities defined by the package more apparent.

F.1 THE STANDARD PACKAGE

The STANDARD package defines primitive types, subtypes and functions and it resides in the STD library:

```
--  Package STANDARD as defined in Chapter 14, Section 2 of the IEEE Standard
--  VHDL Language Reference Manual (IEEE Std. 1076-1987).
--
PACKAGE standard IS
 TYPE boolean IS (false,true);
 TYPE bit IS ('0', '1');
 TYPE character IS (
   nul, soh, stx, etx, eot, enq, ack, bel,
   bs,  ht,  lf,  vt,  ff,  cr,  so,  si,
   dle, dc1, dc2, dc3, dc4, nak, syn, etb,
```

```
    can, em,  sub, esc, fsp, gsp, rsp, usp,
    ' ', '!', '"', '#', '$', '⊕', '&', ''',
    '(', ')', '*', '+', ',', '-', '.', '/',
    '0', '1', '2', '3', '4', '5', '6', '7',
    '8', '9', ':', ';', '<', '=', '>', '?',
    '@', 'A', 'B', 'C', 'D', 'E', 'F', 'G',
    'H', 'I', 'J', 'K', 'L', 'M', 'N', 'O',
    'P', 'Q', 'R', 'S', 'T', 'U', 'V', 'W',
    'X', 'Y', 'Z', '[', ' \ ', ']', '^ ', '_',
    ''', 'a', 'b', 'c', 'd', 'e', 'f', 'g',
    'h', 'i', 'j', 'k', 'l', 'm', 'n', 'o',
    'p', 'q', 'r', 's', 't', 'u', 'v', 'w',
    'x', 'y', 'z', '{', '|', '}', ' ', del);
TYPE severity_level IS (note, warning, error, failure);
TYPE integer IS RANGE -2147483648 TO 2147483647;
TYPE real IS RANGE -1.0E38 TO 1.0E38;
TYPE time IS RANGE -2147483647 TO 2147483647
  UNITS
    fs;
    ps = 1000 fs;
    ns = 1000 ps;
    us = 1000 ns;
    ms = 1000 us;
    sec = 1000 ms;
    min = 60 sec;
    hr = 60 min;
  END UNITS;
FUNCTION now RETURN time;
SUBTYPE natural IS integer RANGE 0 TO integer'HIGH;
SUBTYPE positive IS integer RANGE 1 TO integer'HIGH;
TYPE string IS ARRAY (positive RANGE <>) OF character;
TYPE bit_vector IS ARRAY (natural RANGE <>) OF bit;
END standard;
```

F.2 TEXTIO PACKAGE

The TEXTIO package defines types, procedures, and functions for standard text I/O from ASCII files and it resides in the STD library:

```
--  Package TEXTIO as defined in Chapter 14, Section 3 of the IEEE Standard
--  VHDL Language Reference Manual (IEEE Std. 1076-1987).
--
PACKAGE textio IS
    TYPE line IS ACCESS string;
    TYPE text IS FILE OF string;
    TYPE side IS (right, left);
    SUBTYPE width IS natural;

    FILE input : text IS IN "std_input";
    FILE output : text IS OUT "std_output";

    PROCEDURE readline (VARIABLE f:IN text; l: INOUT line);

    PROCEDURE read (l: INOUT line; value: OUT bit; good : OUT boolean);
    PROCEDURE read (l: INOUT line; value: OUT bit);

    PROCEDURE read (l: INOUT line; value: OUT bit_vector; good : OUT boolean);
```

```
PROCEDURE read (l: INOUT line; value: OUT bit_vector);

PROCEDURE read (l: INOUT line; value: OUT boolean; good : OUT boolean);
PROCEDURE read (l: INOUT line; value: OUT boolean);

PROCEDURE read (l: INOUT line; value: OUT character; good : OUT boolean);
PROCEDURE read (l: INOUT line; value: OUT character);

PROCEDURE read (l: INOUT line; value: OUT integer; good : OUT boolean);
PROCEDURE read (l: INOUT line; value: OUT integer);

PROCEDURE read (l: INOUT line; value: OUT real; good : OUT boolean);
PROCEDURE read (l: INOUT line; value: OUT real);

PROCEDURE read (l: INOUT line; value: OUT string; good : OUT boolean);
PROCEDURE read (l: INOUT line; value: OUT string);

PROCEDURE read (l: INOUT line; value: OUT time; good : OUT boolean);
PROCEDURE read (l: INOUT line; value: OUT time);

PROCEDURE writeline (f: OUT TEXT; L : INOUT line);

PROCEDURE write (l: INOUT line; value : IN bit;
                      justified: IN side := right; field: IN width := 0);

PROCEDURE write (l: INOUT line; value : IN bit_vector;
                      justified: IN side := right; field: IN width := 0);

PROCEDURE write (l: INOUT line; value : IN boolean;
                      justified: IN side := right; field: IN width := 0);

PROCEDURE write (l: INOUT line; value : IN character;
                      justified: IN side := right; field: IN width := 0);

PROCEDURE write (l: INOUT line; value : IN integer;
                      justified: IN side := right; field: IN width := 0);

PROCEDURE write (l: INOUT line; value : IN real;
                      justified: IN side := right;
                      field: IN width := 0; digits: IN natural := 0);

PROCEDURE write (l: INOUT line; value : IN string;
                      justified: IN side := right; field: IN width := 0);

PROCEDURE write (l: INOUT line; value : IN time;
                      justified: IN side := right;
                      field: IN width := 0; unit: IN time := ns);

--  FUNCTION endfile (VARIABLE f: IN text) RETURN BOOLEAN;
--  This function is implicitly defined when a file type is declared.

END textio;
```

concurrent execution, 20
concurrent procedure call, 243
concurrent signal assignment, 39, 210
concurrent statement, 72, 73, 92, 134, 181, 184, 220, 225
conditional signal assignment, 133, 134, 164, 180, 182, 184, 235
conditional waveform, 134
conditional waveforms, 134
configuration, 65, 110, 116, 121, 166, 252
configuration declaration, 87, 110–114, 121, 252, 310
configuration specification, 60, 65, 66, 77, 79, 82, 110, 112, 113, 121, 252
configurations, 22
CONLAN, 16, 17
constant, 39, 166, 220
constant array, 143
constant declaration, 136, 138, 149
constant table, 149
constant value expression, 137
continuous waveform, 245
control flip-flop, 297
control section, 280, 282, 296, 297, 300
control signal, 279, 280, 282, 292, 295–297
control unit, 200
controller, 23, 151, 279, 280, 300, 305, 308
counter, 209, 248
CPU structure, 259
current state, 235
customizing, 87

dash, 52
data path, 2, 219, 259, 279
data path design, 24
data section, 280, 282, 291–293, 296
data selection, 174
databus, 276, 304
dataflow, 12, 13, 24, 34, 208, 209, 260, 267, 269, 272, 277, 280, 282, 286, 297, 310
dataflow level, 34, 200
debugging, 322
declarative part, 31, 32, 64, 148, 166, 220, 224
decoder, 180
default class, 92
default generic value, 106
default value, 106, 110
delay, 22
delta, 40, 183
delta delay, 44, 46, 224
delta duration, 161
DeMorgan's theorem, 61
Department of Defense, 16

descending range, 140, 144
design, 3
Design Automation, 3
design configuration, 88
design entity, 22
design entry, 3
design environment, 322
design library, 22, 67
design management, 3
design manufacturing, 16
design parametrization, 88
direct addressing, 305
DISCONNECT, 197
disconnected, 181, 186, 195
disconnection, 195, 196, 197
disconnection delay, 196
disconnection specification, 196, 197
discrete range, 141, 142
discrete range specification, 142
distance, 137
documentation, 3, 15, 16, 18
DoD, 16, 18, 19, 21, 22
driver, 43, 46, 47, 49, 189, 192, 195, 196
driving value, 202, 241

edge detection, 22, 162
edge trigger, 230, 248
elaboration, 43
element declaration, 157
ENDFILE, 240
ENDFILE operation, 147
English, 15
ENTITY, 26
entity, 82, 166
entity class, 166, 167
entity declaration, 22, 57–59, 63, 230, 231
entity statement part, 231
enumerate, 21
enumeration, 132
enumeration element, 132, 135, 154, 157, 201
enumeration literal, 233
enumeration type, 132, 135, 140, 148, 154, 157, 158, 161, 201
enumeration type definition, 132
ERROR, 228
event, 43–46, 77, 161, 183, 195, 199
event driven simulation, 8, 9, 10
exit statement, 226, 227
explicit GUARD signal, 249
explicit type conversion, 137, 157, 293
exponential, 137
expression, 136
external file, 156, 240, 247